Robert and John Pitcairn

Titans of Rail, Oil and Glass

WILLIAM R. HUBER

Forewords by David Bear *and* Bruce Henderson

McFarland & Company, Inc., Publishers
Jefferson, North Carolina

ISBN (print) 978-1-4766-9691-1
ISBN (ebook) 978-1-4766-5508-6

LIBRARY OF CONGRESS CATALOGING DATA ARE AVAILABLE

© 2025 William R. Huber. All rights reserved

No part of this book may be reproduced or transmitted in any form or by any means, electronic or mechanical, including photocopying or recording, or by any information storage and retrieval system, without permission in writing from the publisher.

Front cover images (top to bottom): Robert Pitcairn (from "Notable Men of Pittsburgh and Vicinity" by Percy Frazier Smith, 1901); John Pitcairn (courtesy of Academy of the New Church Archives Photo Collection); Baldwin Locomotive Works Philadelphia (BLW), Pennsylvania Railroad (PRR) 6707 (ETH-Bibliothek Zürich, Bildarchiv / Fotograf: Unbekannt / Ans_05373-1997 / Public Domain Mark).

Back cover image: Bryn Athyn campus with cathedral in foreground, Glencairn at rear left, and Cairnwood at rear right (courtesy of Bryn Athyn Historic District Archives at Glencairn Museum).

Printed in the United States of America

McFarland & Company, Inc., Publishers
Box 611, Jefferson, North Carolina 28640
www.mcfarlandpub.com

*To Angie,
for her wisdom and patience*

"Genius, that power which dazzles mortal eyes,
Is oft but perseverance in disguise.
Continuous effort of itself implies,
In spite of countless falls, the power to rise."
—Henry Austin, "Perseverance Conquers All" (March 1911)

Table of Contents

Acknowledgments   ix
Foreword by David Bear   1
Foreword by Bruce Henderson   3
Preface   5
Introduction   7

1. Finding a Home   9
2. Welcome to America   16
3. Dots and Dashes   22
4. Emanuel Swedenborg   27
5. The Pennsylvania Railroad   36
6. Railroads and the Civil War   44
7. John: Railroads, Oil and Church   52
8. Robert: Family, Railroads and Church   60
9. Travels with John   67
10. Blood on the Tracks—Part 1   79
11. Blood on the Tracks—Part 2   87
12. Marriage and Divorce   99
13. Glass and Gas   107
14. Antediluvian Johnstown   118
15. South Fork Fishing & Hunting Club   124
16. The Johnstown Flood—Part 1   133
17. The Johnstown Flood—Part 2   144
18. Unintended Consequences   158
19. Into the Country—Bryn Athyn   169
20. Life Goes On   176
21. Pitcairns After John   184

Epilogue and Retrospection	196
Appendix I: Pitcairn Family Trees	201
Appendix II: Visiting Bryn Athyn	206
Chapter Notes	209
Bibliography	219
Index	229

Acknowledgments

Writing a book is not a solitary task. Many people and organizations provided input, and I have been blessed in having subject matter experts volunteer their knowledge and suggestions. At the substantial risk of missing some who helped, I will name the most significant contributors.

Neil Coleman, author of the outstanding book *Johnstown's Flood of 1889*, spent an entire day showing us the site of the infamous Johnstown Flood. Moreover, his review of my Johnstown chapters provided insights that clarified the events that precipitated and followed the flood.

Neil also arranged for Doug Bosley, chief of interpretation and visitor services at the Allegheny Portage Railroad National Historic Site, National Park Service, to give us an extensive tour of the still-standing clubhouse of the South Fork Fishing & Hunting Club. Doug's deep knowledge and willingness to share it mark him as a true professional.

Another of Neil Coleman's contributions was to connect me with Richard Burkert, former president of the Johnstown Area Heritage Association. Richard is *the* historian of Johnstown and gave me several leads to arcane but fascinating information about Andrew Carnegie, Thomas Carnegie, Robert Pitcairn, and Henry Clay Frick. Richard also reviewed the Johnstown chapters.

Only sparse documentation exists for the eldest Pitcairn brother, Robert. But Tim Engleman of the Shadyside Presbyterian Church graciously shared his research and reviewed my chapters on Robert.

Librarians rarely receive the credit they deserve, so I want to thank Lee Ann Draud at Detre Library of the Senator John Heinz History Center in Pittsburgh for her help in tracking down the Bennett letters discussed in Chapters 2 and 3.

With his seemingly endless fount of knowledge, David T. Bear reviewed the manuscript, made numerous corrections and improvements, and generously agreed to write a foreword.

Bryn Athyn was an unexpected delight, primarily because of the exceptional guides through the buildings and grounds. Lisa Parker-Adams and Carol Henderson provided a warm welcome and fascinating insights into the lives and accomplishments of John Pitcairn and his family. Lisa, along with Carol's husband, Bruce Henderson, reviewed relevant chapters and added critical information and encouragement. Bruce also wrote a foreword for the book emphasizing the portions related to John Pitcairn. Archivist Gregory Jackson of the Bryn Athyn Historic Landmark

District located and granted permission to publish several images credited to the Bryn Athyn Historic District Archives at Glencairn Museum.

My other reviewers—Patricia Hite, Virgil Koning, the late Bill Reed, and my wife, Angie—provided suggestions to make the complex story readable. I truly appreciate their efforts and patience.

As anyone who has published a book knows, a knowledgeable editor is essential to success. Layla Milholen of McFarland has been that editor for me. Her advice, skill, and patience made this book possible.

Foreword
by David Bear

I was honored when Bill Huber asked me to write a foreword for *Robert and John Pitcairn: Titans of Rail, Oil and Glass*.

Bill and I met several years ago when he contacted me regarding his biography of the inventor/industrialist George Westinghouse.

While not a historian, I am a writer, former newspaper editor, and public radio producer who, for four decades, has lived near what was Solitude, Westinghouse's Pittsburgh estate and creative center. I learned much about Westinghouse in recent years by spearheading local efforts to refurbish the Pittsburgh park that bears his name. So I was happy to offer Bill what help I could in the book that became *George Westinghouse: Powering the World*.

Reading that manuscript, I was quickly impressed by Bill's ability to weave a tale that is both engaging and informative, discursive yet detailed. He identifies and follows seemingly disparate threads, then combines them into unique and insightful narratives.

He writes with the perspective of a trained engineer, the attention to detail of an investigative reporter, and the sense of wonder of a naturally curious storyteller. As a result, his biography of George Westinghouse is the most accessible and informative recounting of that remarkable life that has ever been written.

In this book, Bill follows the remarkable lives of two of the Pitcairn brothers, Robert (b. 1836) and John (b. 1841), who were born in a mill town in central Scotland and brought to the U.S. as children when their parents immigrated to Allegheny City, Pennsylvania.

Bill tweezes out the woolen yarn of their stories and weaves it into an engaging tartan of a tale that also traces the evolution of American industry and transportation.

The story follows forest trails first hacked over the Allegheny Mountains by British fusiliers, canals excavated along rivers and valleys, and the early railroads that rendered those canals obsolete.

Bill weaves a broad cloth as he explores and elucidates the development of related technologies: the telegraph; the early oil industry; the iron forges and the steel furnaces; and the coal mines, coke ovens, and natural gas wells that fueled their endless fires. He also provides a historical perspective on diverse issues, from the

Great Railroad Strike of 1877 to the 1889 Johnstown Flood and its apocalyptic aftermath. Reflecting the diverse interests of the Pitcairn brothers, Bill also traces the creation, growth, and evolution of a new U.S. industry: plate glass production.

Nor does Bill focus solely on the leading roles the Pitcairn brothers played in shaping America's industrialization. He also examines the converse—the role of industrialization in shaping them as men.

Also examined are the spiritual precepts and guides the two Pitcairns followed, from John Calvin to Emanuel Swedenborg, and their impact on the birth and evolution of American philanthropy.

Overall, it is a wonderfully enjoyable, comprehensive, and informative exploration of a transformative era in American history and an appreciation of the parts Robert and John Pitcairn played in that saga.

In short, you have made an excellent choice in buying this book. Enjoy the journey.

David Bear, president of the Westinghouse Legacy and initial organizer of the Westinghouse Park 2nd Century Coalition, spent his professional career as a writer. Bear produced and hosted public radio series, including A Century of Heroes *for the Carnegie Hero Fund and* Dinosaurs and More *for the Carnegie Museum of Natural History.*

Foreword
by Bruce Henderson

Like many of America's titans of industry—Carnegie, Rockefeller, Frick—the Pitcairn brothers had humble roots. John Pitcairn started from nothing, and wealth was never an end in itself. He was just 14 when he arrived in America from Scotland with his family and began seeking his fortune. But it was his faith that guided his life, not power and acquisition. In many ways he was the conscience of his peers.

I am honored to contribute this foreword to Bill Huber's impressive book and very much share in his appreciation for the legacy of John Pitcairn.

In addition to building his fortune and reputation with the Pennsylvania Railroad and Pittsburgh Plate Glass, John was a driving force in establishing the New Church (formally the General Church of the New Jerusalem) in America. The religion is based on what is believed to be direct revelation from God through the prominent Swedish scientist and theologian Emanuel Swedenborg (1688–1772). He never tried to start a church on his own, seeing his role simply as "a servant of the Lord." But readers did launch churches, first in England, then in America, which now have spread throughout the world.

This book is Bill Huber's quest to find what drove John Pitcairn's life and separated him from his peers. It's amazing that it all began at age 14 as a railroad telegrapher. That he quickly rose though management positions in railroads, pioneered in the emerging oil industry, and led Pittsburgh Plate Glass to dominate its field demonstrates what a gifted business leader he was. But he was driven as well by securing the future of his faith.

That faith was the essence of the man. While others were consumed with empire building, he quietly stood apart as a man of principle and conscience. He not only had a resolute faith but lived it, every day. He viewed everything—in business and in private life—through the prism of his beliefs. This is why he was first a leader in his church, second a leader in industry.

He led the establishment of Bryn Athyn, just north of Philadelphia, which became the international center of the church—and the center of his life. He was the visionary for the distinctive Bryn Athyn Cathedral, completed by his son, Raymond, who also built the magnificent home, Glencairn, nearby.

While John was securing his empire—and his fortune—he was projecting a vision for his church. This included long tours in Europe and the Holy Land with family and friends, which always included talks with church leaders. But he also devoted a keen eye to acquiring an impressive collection of religious art and artifacts, which have turned Glencairn into a renowned museum of religious art and history. His business success helped to fuel the establishment of the church and the Academy of the New Church in Bryn Athyn—and sustains them still through generous endowments.

John didn't marry until his 40s, after a long courtship of the love of his life, Gertrude Starkey. She bore him six children before dying tragically in her 40s. John was crushed but remained devoted to her. He never remarried and looked forward to being reunited with her in heaven, after his own death at age 75.

Having moved from Pittsburgh to Philadelphia, John began leading railroad excursions of church followers to an idyllic spot north of the city for picnics and pleasure. As he acquired land in the area, a community of homes quickly sprouted in what became Bryn Athyn. It eventually included an elementary school, the Academy Secondary Schools and College, the cathedral, and Cairnwood, the beautiful French provincial estate of John and Gertrude.

John would no doubt be humbled but pleased that the cathedral, Cairnwood, Glencairn, and Cairncrest—home of his youngest son, Harold—are now part of an official National Historic District. All but Cairncrest—now offices for the General Church—are open for public tours. Photos of each are included in this book.

It is all quite a monument to the life, dreams, and faith of John Pitcairn.

Bruce Henderson had a 40-year career in journalism. He served for 12 years as director of development and communications for the General Church and the Academy of the New Church. He now edits New Church Life—*the international publication of the church—out of Harold Pitcairn's office in Cairncrest. He has written three books on Swedenborgian teachings.*

Preface

As I near completion of one of my books, I start asking myself who will be the focus of my next one. The ideal subject for a biography should be famous but not too well known. They should be attractive to potential readers but not so attractive that other writers have already told their stories.

While writing my biography of George Westinghouse, I often encountered Robert Pitcairn. He was one of the first to recognize Westinghouse's genius and the utility of his revolutionary air brake for stopping trains. Robert Pitcairn was a founder and board member of Westinghouse Air Brake Company, a lifelong friend of Westinghouse, and a top executive of the Pennsylvania Railroad.

Initial research on Robert Pitcairn revealed that his brother, John Pitcairn, cofounded Pittsburgh Plate Glass Company as well as a religious community near Philadelphia. My book idea expanded to become the story of the Pitcairn brothers.

Then I found links between the Pitcairn brothers and the Carnegie brothers, Andrew and Thomas. All were born within eight years and 50 miles of each other in Scotland and immigrated to Allegheny City, near Pittsburgh, in the 1840s. All four became friends as teenagers, and Andrew led the way to the telegraph company and then the Pennsylvania Railroad.

The fact that I grew up in and around Pittsburgh, including a time when I had a Pitcairn, Pennsylvania, mailing address, added to the allure. Finally, in my late teen years, I lived in Johnstown, Pennsylvania, a location indelibly linked to the Pennsylvania Railroad and Robert Pitcairn.

Robert and John Pitcairn: Titans of Rail, Oil and Glass had to be my next book.

Introduction

The Pitcairn brothers were born in Johnstone, Renfrewshire, Scotland—Robert on May 6, 1836, and John on January 10, 1841. They came to the United States with their parents and siblings in 1846 and settled in an immigrant community across the Allegheny River from smoke-polluted Pittsburgh. The brothers followed the early lead of their friend, Andrew Carnegie, working first for the nascent telegraph company and then for the Pennsylvania Railroad (PRR).

Robert continued to emulate Carnegie and eventually replaced him in 1865 as superintendent of the Pittsburgh Division of the PRR. For many years, starting in 1881, the PRR was the largest corporation in the world.[1] In 1902, Robert Pitcairn was named assistant to the president of the PRR.

John Pitcairn led a more diverse professional life, moving from railroads to oil exploration and processing to glass manufacturing.

Robert and John Pitcairn were not only witnesses to history but also participants in it. During the Civil War, they played crucial roles with the Pennsylvania Railroad in transporting troops and supplies for the Union Army.

John personally accompanied Abraham Lincoln on a large portion of his tense journey from Harrisburg, Pennsylvania, to Philadelphia and then to Washington, D.C., for his inauguration as president. He subsequently managed the return of Lincoln's body through Pennsylvania on its trip for burial in Springfield, Illinois.

Robert was literally in the middle of the violence during the bloody but mostly forgotten 1877 railroad strike in Pittsburgh, in which over 60 people were killed.

In 1889, he was superintendent of the Pittsburgh Division of the PRR during the calamitous Johnstown Flood. Robert rode the first train that attempted to reach Johnstown. When it was stopped by rising water, he aided in the rescue of survivors and recovery of corpses from the surging Conemaugh River. After the flood, he supervised the rapid rebuilding of devastated track, bridges, and rolling stock.

In 1897, Robert and his wife entertained President William McKinley and his wife, Ida, at their Cairncarque home in Pittsburgh.

In 1883, John cofounded and later led the Pittsburgh Plate Glass Company as it grew to dominate the U.S. glass industry. He then applied much of his fortune to create the Swedenborg-focused religious community of Bryn Athyn north of Philadelphia.

Robert was also dedicated to serving God through his church, Shadyside Presbyterian in Pittsburgh.

These immigrant Scotsmen combined intelligence, perseverance, and timing to become titans of industry in the late 19th and early 20th centuries.

1

Finding a Home

"A simple way to take measure of a country is to look at how many want in....
And how many want out."

—Tony Blair

An Ocean Voyage

John Pitcairn's voyage across the Atlantic Ocean must have been full of uncertainty. Of course, we don't know his thoughts, but he must have pondered if this trip was the right decision for him and his young family. Was it fair to his daughter, Janet, to take her so far from her birthplace? Were job prospects here any better than the place he had left?

But it was too late to change his mind. The coast of Great Britain dominated the skyline, and soon the Pitcairn family would be back in Scotland.

John and his family were returning to the ancestral home of the Pitcairns. On June 3, 1250, King Alexander III of Scotland had granted land to John de Pitcarne, making him the First Lord of Innernethy.[1]

Eighteen generations and 552 years after John de Pitcarne received his grant, on November 11, 1802, John Pitcairn was born at Johnstone, Renfrewshire, Scotland.[2] John was the youngest of three sons born to Alexander Pitcairn and Janet (Currie) Pitcairn.*

Appendix I provides family trees for various members of the Pitcairn family.

John married his first wife, Janet Munro, in Kilbarchan, Renfrewshire, Scotland, on August 8, 1824.[3] The couple welcomed a daughter, Helen, on June 12, 1825. Helen Pitcairn later married Robert B. Rush and moved to Salem, Brown County, Ohio, where she died on March 1, 1874, at age 48.[4] Sadly, Janet Munro Pitcairn died in 1827.[5]

---

* There are famous Pitcairn family members in history, in particular British Marine Major John Pitcairn, who led his troops in the Revolutionary War battles of Lexington and Concord in 1775. John's son, Robert Pitcairn, then 15 years old, was aboard the HMS *Swallow* in 1767 when he was the first to see an unknown island in the Pacific Ocean. The ship's captain named it Pitcairn's Island in the boy's honor. Although a relationship between that Pitcairn family and the one of interest in this book is likely, it has never been verified. Twenty-two years later, on April 28, 1789, Fletcher Christian and several crewmates on the ship HMS *Bounty* mutinied against Captain William Bligh, and most settled on Pitcairn Island.

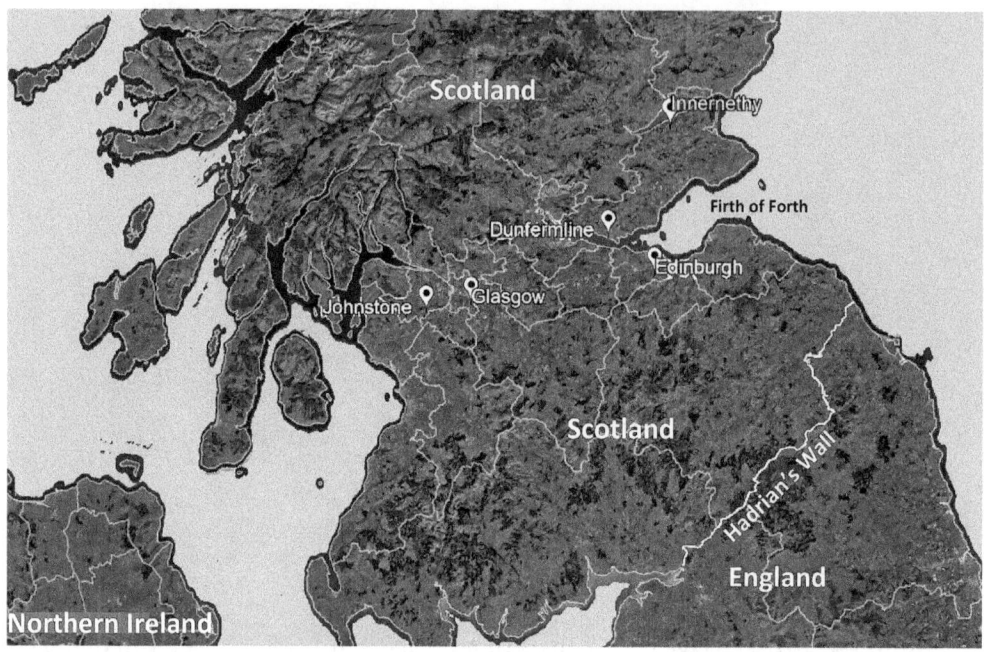

Important locations in Scotland (Google Earth; 12/13/2015).

After Janet's death, John Pitcairn married again, this time to Agnes McEwan, on December 20, 1828. The couple had a daughter, Catherine, born in Johnstone on October 25, 1829.

John Pitcairn was a skilled mechanic and ran a machine shop in Johnstone. However, misplaced trust in his unscrupulous partner led to the failure of the business. After John paid off his creditors, he, Agnes, and their daughter Catherine emigrated to the United States aboard the ship *Floyd*, arriving in New York on May 3, 1830.[6] They settled first in Brooklyn, New York, and then in Paterson, New Jersey, where their second daughter, Janet, was born on October 22, 1831.

Return to Scotland

But business success in the United States eluded John, so now the family was back in Johnstone, Scotland. Over the next 14 years, four more children were born to the couple, bringing their family to three girls and three boys.[7]

Children of John Pitcairn and Agnes McEwan

Name	Sex	Birth Date and Location	Death Date and Location (Age)
Catherine	F	October 25, 1829 Johnstone, Renfrewshire, Scotland	August 16, 1892 Christian Co., Illinois (62)
Janet	F	October 22, 1831 Paterson, Passaic Co., New Jersey	June 2, 1922 Pittsburgh, Allegheny Co., PA (90)
Robert	M	May 6, 1836 Johnstone, Renfrewshire, Scotland	July 25, 1909 Pittsburgh, Allegheny Co., PA (73)

Name	Sex	Birth Date and Location	Death Date and Location (Age)
Margaret	F	May 18, 1838 Johnstone, Renfrewshire, Scotland	November 27, 1904 Bryn Athyn, Montgomery Co., PA (66)
John Jr.	M	January 10, 1841 Johnstone, Renfrewshire, Scotland	July 22, 1916 Bryn Athyn, Montgomery Co., PA (75)
Hugh	M	August 16, 1845 Johnstone, Renfrewshire, Scotland	July 19, 1911 Hamburg, Germany (65)

However, business conditions in the U.S. and Great Britain collapsed during the Panic of 1837. The Panic started in the spring of 1837 and lasted until the mid–1840s. While starting abruptly, the causes of the Panic extended back several years. A simplified view identifies two executive actions as triggers:

- In 1832, President Andrew Jackson vetoed the rechartering of the Bank of the United States and redistributed federal funds held there to smaller state banks across the country. The resulting power vacuum led to a lack of standardization and reduction of oversight of banking practices. As a result, some banks printed their own paper currency and made loans in excess of their gold and silver reserves.
- In 1836, Jackson issued an executive order mandating that federal land could be purchased only with gold or silver. When people attempted to redeem their paper currency for specie (gold or silver coin), the banks could not meet the demand and closed.

Hundreds of banks failed, the currency lost value or even became worthless, prices soared, and farmers and business owners suffered severe losses.[8]

Back to the United States

By 1846, the economy in the U.S. had recovered, and John Pitcairn's two older brothers, Robert and Alexander, encouraged him to bring his family there once again.

The family agreed to another try in the U.S. and departed from Liverpool, England, with 66 other passengers aboard the ship *Venice* in mid–August 1846. The *Venice* weighed 558 tons and was captained by R.H. Dunlevy. One passenger died en route, but the rest arrived safely at Philadelphia on October 1, 1846.[9]

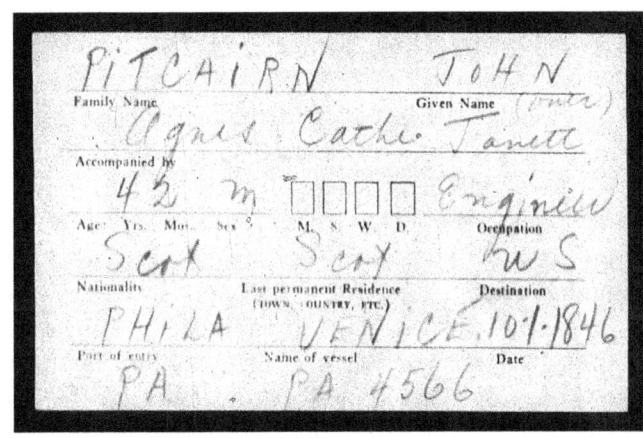

Passenger destination card for the John Pitcairn Sr. family (familysearch.org).

Crossing Pennsylvania

The Pitcairns' final destination was Allegheny City, just west of Pittsburgh, where John's brothers had settled with their families. There is no definitive record of how the family traveled to Pittsburgh, but they likely took the Pennsylvania Main Line Canal.

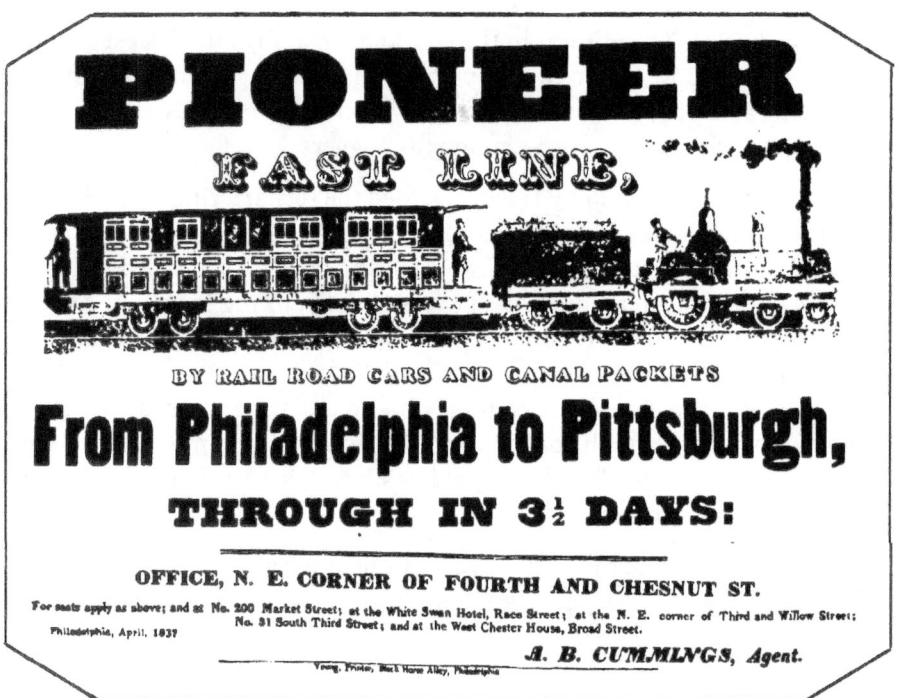

Advertisement for railroad and canal travel from Philadelphia to Pittsburgh (*Philadelphia Inquirer*, April 18, 1837).

Pennsylvania Main Line Canal

The state of New York had completed the Erie Canal across upstate New York from Albany to Buffalo on Lake Erie in 1825. To compete for the lucrative trade with the American West, on February 25, 1826, Pennsylvania governor John Andrew Shulze signed "An act to provide for the commencement of a canal to be constructed at the expense of the State." The ceremonial first spadeful of dirt was turned in Harrisburg on July 4, 1826, with actual construction to commence at each end.[10]

Building the Main Line Canal turned out to be a massive and expensive undertaking, eventually costing over $12.1 million.[11] While the 364-mile-long Erie Canal used 83 locks to overcome elevation changes,[12] the Main Line Canal would require 174 locks plus a 37-mile railroad over the Allegheny Mountains. Opened on April 15, 1834, the Main Line Canal cut the travel time from Philadelphia to Pittsburgh from 23 days to just four.

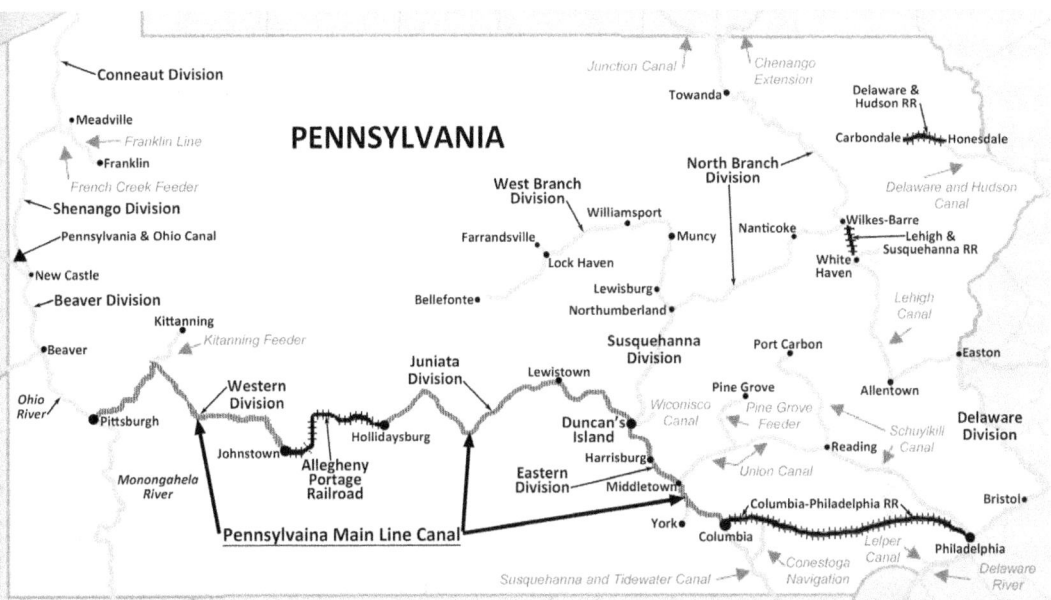

Historic canals of Pennsylvania in the 19th century, with the Pennsylvania Main Line Canal highlighted. Not all canals existed simultaneously (Wikimedia Commons).

Starting from the east, the so-called "canal" combined:

- An 82-mile railroad from Philadelphia to Columbia, Pennsylvania;
- The 45-mile Eastern Division Canal, with 17 locks, from Columbia northwest along the Susquehanna River to Duncan's Island near Duncannon;
- The 127-mile Juniata Division Canal, with 91 locks, from Duncan's Island to Hollidaysburg;
- From Hollidaysburg, the unique 37-mile Allegheny Portage Railroad carried canal boats on railroad flatcars up five inclined planes and down five more. The total lift going west was 1,398 feet to a peak of 2,354 feet above sea level. From there, the cars descended 1,178 feet to the canal basin at Johnstown. Stationary steam-driven engines at the top of each inclined plane pulled hemp ropes (changed to John Roebling's steel wire ropes in 1844[13]) to provide the motive power to raise and lower the railroad cars;
- The 104-mile Western Division Canal linked the canal basin at Johnstown via a path along the Conemaugh, Kiskiminetas, and Allegheny Rivers to Pittsburgh. The Western Division included 66 locks, 16 aqueducts, 10 river dams, and two tunnels.[14]

Pennsylvania Main Line Canal Statistics

	Western Division	Allegheny Portage RR	Juniata Division	Eastern Division	Columbia-Philadelphia RR	Total
Length	104 miles	37 miles	127 miles	45 miles	82 miles	395 miles
Locks	66		91	17		174
Tunnels	2	1				3

	Western Division	Allegheny Portage RR	Juniata Division	Eastern Division	Columbia-Philadelphia RR	Total
Inclined Planes		10			2	12
Year Opened	1831	1834	1832	1833	1834	

Two sections of a packet boat being pulled up an inclined plane on the Allegheny Portage Railroad near Hollidaysburg (author's collection).

The Pitcairn family traveled through two tunnels along the route of the canal. One, called the Staple Bend Tunnel, was 901 feet long and was the first railroad tunnel built in America. It had rails so that the flat cars carrying canal boats on the Allegheny Portage Railroad could be drawn through by horses.

Further west, at the village of Tunnelton, the canal passed through the Bow Ridge Tunnel and then directly onto an aqueduct that carried it over the Conemaugh River.

A third tunnel provided a canal boat route between the Allegheny and Monongahela

West entrance to Staple Bend Tunnel (photograph by the author).

Rivers in Pittsburgh but was rarely used.

In March 1842, four years before the Pitcairns arrived, Charles Dickens traveled across America from Boston as far west as St. Louis. Dickens described travel by canal boat on the Pennsylvania Main Line Canal:

> The exquisite beauty of the opening day, when light came gleaming off from everything; the lazy motion of the boat, when one lay idly on the deck, looking through, rather than at, the deep blue sky; the gliding on at night, so noiselessly, past frowning hills, sullen with dark trees, and sometimes angry in one red burning spot high up where unseen men lay crouching round a fire; the shining out of the bright stars, undisturbed by noise of wheels or steam or any sound than the liquid rippling of the water as the boat went on—all these were pure delights.[15]

Dickens was not so sanguine about the sleeping arrangements.

> (About) ten o'clock or thereabout, he found suspended on either side of the cabin, three long tiers of hanging book-shelves designed apparently for volumes of the small octavo size. Looking with attention at these contrivances (wondering to find such literary preparations in such a place) I descried on each shelf a sort of microscopic sheet and blanket; then I began dimly to comprehend that the passengers were the library, and that they were to be arranged edgewise on these shelves till morning.[16]

Dickens found travel on the Allegheny Portage Railroad even more thrilling.

> Occasionally the rails are laid upon the extreme verge of the giddy precipice and looking down from the carriage window, the traveler gazes sheer down without a stone or scrap of fence between into the mountain depths below.[17]

The Pennsylvania Main Line Canal, especially the Allegheny Portage Railroad, was an engineering marvel. The journey would have fascinated the engineer in John Pitcairn, Sr., and especially his 10-year-old son, Robert.

In mid–October 1846, four days after departing from Philadelphia, John and Agnes Pitcairn and their six children arrived in Allegheny City, debarking at the canal basin near present-day PNC Park.[18] They must have been optimistic about being in a place where jobs were plentiful, but anxious about the challenges of a new environment plagued by pollution and populated by ethnic gangs.

Sign at the site of Bow Ridge Tunnel and Aqueduct, Tunnelton, Pennsylvania (photograph by the author).

Sign text: This site is unique because of the presence of an aqueduct and tunnel so close together. This unusual structure was required by the canal engineer, Alonzo Livermore, to move canal boats from one side of Bow Ridge to the other. Westbound boats emerged from the tunnel and immediately passed onto the aqueduct that spanned the Conemaugh River. The only remains of the aqueduct are the foundations of the piers that once supported the aqueduct.

2

Welcome to America

> "Allegheny City on the other side of the river, looks somewhat cleaner, but the whole region is filled with smoke and dust from the great number of furnaces always in blast, the factories and the steamboats, all of which use bituminous coal."
> —Thomas U. Walter (1856)

Allegheny City

In October 1846, the Pitcairns settled in Allegheny City, north and west of Pittsburgh. The area was initially platted in 1788, with lots being sold to the public or given to Revolutionary War veterans as payment for their service. German immigrants settled there, later joined by Croats and other ethnic groups. Allegheny became a borough in 1828.

The opening of the Pennsylvania Main Line Canal in 1834 brought goods and people to Allegheny, and its population had increased to 10,000 people in 1840. By 1890, after annexing nearby settlements and municipalities, it had grown to 125,000, and by 1899, Allegheny City was the third-largest city in Pennsylvania, behind only Philadelphia and Pittsburgh.

Pittsburgh had sought to annex Allegheny City for years, but the residents of Allegheny City opposed the merger. Then, in 1906, Pennsylvania changed the law so that the combined vote of residents of the two cities would determine the outcome. On June 12, 1906, the citizens of Allegheny City voted 2:1 against a merger, but the far more numerous Pittsburghers overwhelmingly favored it. Allegheny City residents filed a lawsuit challenging the result, but on December 9, 1907, the U.S. Supreme Court affirmed the annexation. Allegheny City mayor Charles F. Kirschler walked across an Allegheny River bridge to ceremonially surrender control of city government to Pittsburgh mayor George W. Guthrie.[1] Allegheny City became Pittsburgh's North Side.

The Pitcairns lived in the Slabtown section of Allegheny City, an area favored by newly arrived immigrants. Living conditions were deplorable. The air was black with smoke from coal-burning factories and houses. Municipal water arrived in Allegheny City in 1848, but there were no gas lines, and therefore no street lighting

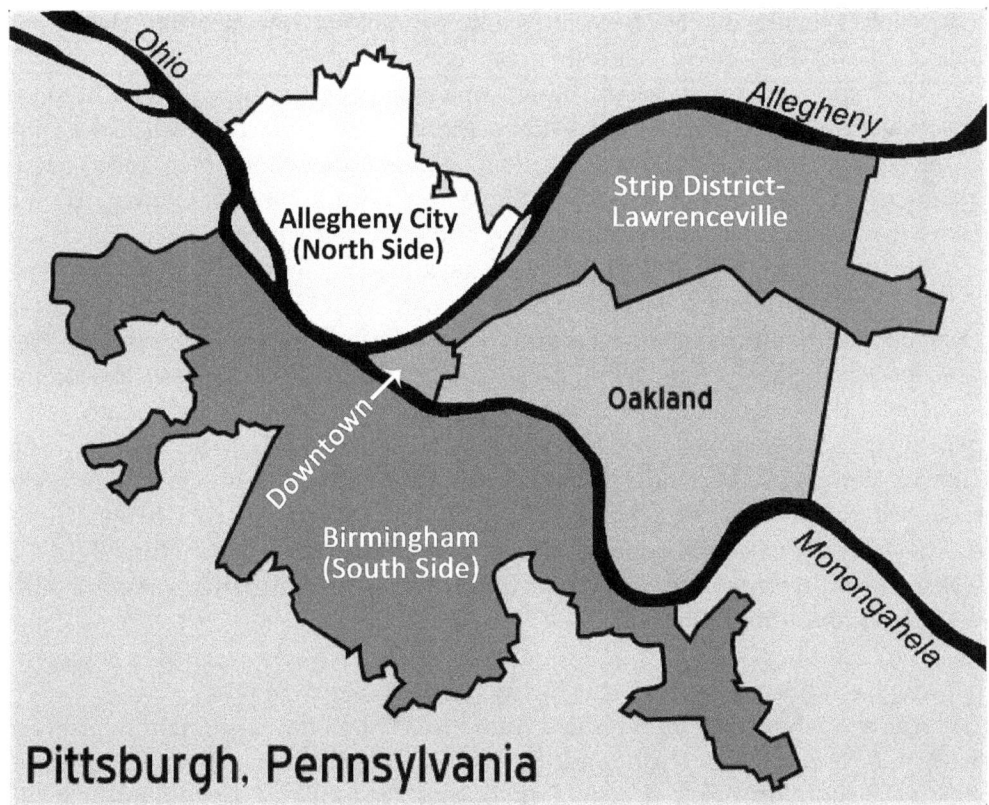

Simplified map of Pittsburgh including Allegheny City (Wikimedia Commons).

until 1853. There were no underground sewers or sanitation systems of any kind, and dogs, rats, and hogs roamed free. Frequent floods filled the streets with stormwater, garbage, and sewage. Cholera epidemics struck in 1849, 1850, 1854, and 1855.[2] But, unlike their former home in Scotland, jobs were plentiful.

Another Scottish Family Arrives

In September 1848, another Scottish immigrant family arrived in Allegheny City.

The father, William "Will" Carnegie, saw his skill at weaving devalued by changing tastes and the march of technology. In Dunfermline, Scotland, Will had built a prosperous business weaving delicate damask cloth on four hand-powered looms, one that he operated and three others run by apprentices. Demand for the fabric was strong, especially from the American market, where fine damask tablecloths and napkins denoted elegance and refinement. While the production of more coarse materials such as cotton and wool moved from hand-operated to power looms, the delicacy of the fabric and designs protected, at least temporarily, the damask weavers.[3]

However, the Panic of 1837 devastated the U.S. economy, and the demand for luxury items such as damask tablecloths disappeared. By September 1837, thousands of Scottish weavers were suddenly unemployed.

The transition from successful businessman to idleness devastated Will. At 33, he was rudderless and, as his neighbor, William Macgregor, described him, "a decent chap … but no hard worker…. He was regular in his habits, a gude churchman, and as moral a gentleman as one could wish—but he didna love to work. Would idle away his time even when he had a web (cloth). Was reading and such, much given to foolishness."[4]

Fortunately for Will, he had married a hard-driving, fiery redhead named Margaret "Mag" Morrison on December 19, 1834. With Will's loom silent, it fell to Mag to support the family by repairing shoes, cooking potted meat, and selling vegetables from local farmers. More and more, she also made the critical decisions for the family.

Given the sad state of the economy, it is not surprising that Mag Carnegie's twin sisters and their husbands (Anne and Andrew Aitken; Catherine "Kitty" and Thomas Hogan) had emigrated to the United States in the summer of 1840. Margaret hoped to follow them but was dissuaded by their reports of unsettled conditions in Allegheny City, Pennsylvania, where they lived. The "unsettled conditions" in the U.S. were the direct result of the Panic of 1837. At that time, America was not a shining beacon for immigrants.

Will and Mag Carnegie had a son, Andrew, born November 25, 1835. A daughter, Anne, was born in January 1838 but was sickly and died in 1841.

Andrew, whom his mother called Andra, started school at age eight, typical for Scottish boys at the time. He attended the low-cost Rolland School on Priory Lane, which was more factory than school. It consisted of a single large room where the headmaster, Robert Martin, taught all of the approximately 185 students. Rows of benches, called "forms," were arrayed on the floor below Martin's raised platform. Each form had an older student, called a monitor or a dictator, who acted as a teacher's aide for his row of students. Martin provided words or simple arithmetic sums to the monitors, and they would repeat them to their charges. The students were to write down the dictated information on slates and then recite it in unison when prompted to do so. The entire instructional method consisted of memorization and recitation. Young Andra excelled at both, and his classmates viewed him as a teacher's pet. His exemption from catechism lessons bolstered that opinion. All other students had to recite from the 107 questions and answers in the Shorter Catechism of the Scottish Presbyterian Church,[5] but Andrew's father arranged for his exemption.

Andrew Carnegie was not liked by everyone. The local women thought him rude and selfish. Every morning before school, Andrew had to fetch water from the town well for the household. The women established the order of drawing water by placing their pails in line the previous evening. To avoid being late for school, Andrew ignored the preset priority and pushed his way to the front of the line. He later said, "I would not be put down even by these venerable old dames. I earned the reputation of being an awfu' laddie. In this way I probably developed the strain of argumentativeness, or perhaps combativeness, which has always remained with me."[6]

Mag and Will had often discussed leaving for the U.S. as her sisters had done in 1840. But reports of life in the new country were far from rosy. Wages for those few who could find work were high, but so were prices. However, that gloomy outlook changed in 1846. Both sisters and their husbands had decided that the U.S. was a better place to be than Scotland.

Another change in Will and Mag's family reopened the issue of leaving Scotland. On October 2, 1844, Mag gave birth to Thomas, a brother for Andrew and a fourth person to feed on their meager income.

Will Carnegie had never seriously considered leaving his home. He knew no other place or skill and viewed himself, at 43, as too old to learn. But Margaret faced reality. She had given up on Will because he had given up on himself. But the boys, Andrew and Thomas, had their lives ahead of them, not in their decaying hometown but in promising Pennsylvania.

Margaret decided the family would emigrate to the United States and held a public auction to sell everything, including Will's remaining and obsolete loom. George Lauder, Mag's brother-in-law, opposed the move but helped anyway. He arranged their passage on a 380-ton former whaling vessel, the *Wiscasset*, departing Glasgow in early July 1848. Just one year before, the *Wiscasset* had been hauling whale oil and whalebone for a Sag Harbor, New York, whaling firm.[7]

Even after selling all their possessions, the Carnegies were short of the money they needed for their passage. Only a 20-pound donation from Mag's girlhood friend, Ailie Ferguson Henderson, allowed them to cover expenses.

Just getting to Glasgow would take the family further from home than any of them had ever been. On arrival, they were herded onto the *Wiscasset*, where they found small bunks in crowded quarters below deck. The *Wiscasset* carried 144 passengers in steerage and nine in cabins. The ship's manifest listed William as a 40-year-old weaver (he was 44), Margaret as 34 (she was 38), Andrew as 15 (he was 12), and Thomas as four (he would be four on October 2).[8]

The adults dreaded the endless days at sea; the children anticipated a great adventure.

The voyage from Glasgow to New York City aboard the *Wiscasset* took 42 days, and young Andrew enjoyed each one. He suffered not at all from seasickness, smiled easily, and chatted freely with children and adults alike. He became a mascot and helper to the sailors and shared their Sunday meals.[9]

It is unlikely that any of the other passengers on board enjoyed the passage. The accommodations in steerage were notoriously crowded, dark, and unsanitary, with no privacy. Food was scarce and mostly spoiled, and the water was warm and polluted.

No one died during the voyage, but one male baby, Robert Logan Anderson, was born on July 5, 1848.[10] Robert would later reside in Osceola, Stark County, Illinois, and have eight children with his wife, Maggie (Forbes) Anderson.[11]

A New World

The *Wiscasset* arrived in New York harbor on August 14, 1848, along with four other ships laden with passengers from overseas. On that day, 842 immigrants arrived in New York.[12]

The New York arrivals were a small part of a massive migration to the United States.[13] In 1850, the first year for which such statistics are available, over 2.2 million immigrants came to the United States.[14] That influx was just under 10 percent of the U.S. population of 23.2 million.

Unlike most immigrants around them, Will and Margaret spoke, read, and wrote English and had contacts in the U.S. who could help them get settled. They knew where they were going, Allegheny City, but not precisely how to get there. Relatives there would furnish a place to live until they could find their own lodgings.

The immediate issue was how to travel to Allegheny City, specifically whether to go southwest to Philadelphia or north to Albany. If they went to Philadelphia, they could cross Pennsylvania, as John Pitcairn, Sr., and his family had done, on the Pennsylvania Main Line Canal. But as they were in New York City, they were advised to take the Erie Canal from Albany across New York state to Lake Erie and then board a sequence of other watercraft to get to the Pittsburgh area. It was bad advice.

The family sailed up the Hudson River to Albany, across upstate New York to Buffalo via the Erie Canal, from Buffalo to Cleveland on a Lake Erie steamboat, then on three more canals to Akron, Ohio, and New Castle and Beaver, Pennsylvania. Finally, after an uncomfortable night fighting hordes of mosquitos, they boarded an Ohio River steamer for the short trip upriver to Allegheny City.[15]

Will, Mag, Andrew, and Tom Carnegie had traveled almost 800 miles to get from New York City to Allegheny City, twice as far as John Pitcairn and his family on their journey from Philadelphia.

Mag's sisters, Annie Aitken and Kitty Hogan, and sister-in-law Maria Morris met the new arrivals at the boat landing in Pittsburgh. Also present to welcome the bewildered immigrants was James Bennett, an English immigrant who had founded the American pottery industry in East Liverpool, Ohio. Seeking larger markets, Bennett and Brothers relocated to Pittsburgh in 1844. They built a new pottery at Washington Street between Franklin and Harmony Streets in East Birmingham (now known as the South Side), across the Monongahela River from Pittsburgh. Bennett and Brothers also opened a wholesale and retail outlet on Wood Street in Pittsburgh.[16]

While living in East Liverpool, James Bennett met William and Maria Morris. William was Mag's brother and had shortened his surname from Morrison to Morris.[17] When William and Maria learned their relatives were coming to the U.S., they contacted James Bennett and asked if he would help establish the immigrants. James readily agreed and met the family at the wharf in Pittsburgh along with Mag's sisters and sister-in-law. Bennett, who is my great-great-grandfather, would play a key role in launching Andrew Carnegie's career.

After family embraces and introductions to James Bennett, the family completed their journey to 336 Rebecca Street (later Reedsdale Street) in Allegheny City. That property held two houses owned by the sisters and Kitty's husband, Thomas Hogan (Annie's husband, Andrew Aitken, had died in 1841). The new family was invited to live rent-free in the upstairs rooms of a cottage at the rear of the property until they could find their own lodgings. Thomas Hogan's older brother, Andrew, was a weaver and occupied the ground floor of the cottage.*

Thus did Andrew Carnegie, his parents, and his brother join the Pitcairn family in Allegheny City in September 1848. The Pitcairn boys, Robert (12), John (7), and Hugh (3), became close friends with Andrew (12) and Thomas (4) Carnegie.

---

* These houses were demolished in the late 1960s during the construction of Three Rivers Stadium.

3

Dots and Dashes

"[It would not be long] ere the whole surface of this country would be channeled for those nerves which are to diffuse, with the speed of thought, a knowledge of all that is occurring throughout the land, making, in fact, one neighborhood of the whole country."
—Samuel F.B. Morse

Until the 1830s, there were two alternatives for communicating across long distances. The first required a messenger to travel physically from the sender to the receiver. The limited speed of the messenger, even when riding on horseback, was a severe drawback. The second relied on smoke signals, drumbeats, or semaphores and was subject to weather and distance limitations. Such communication also lacked security and privacy.

The long-sought solution to the problem of reliable, fast, long-distance communication emerged from work done in the 1830s by two groups of inventors: Sir William Cooke and Sir Charles Wheatstone in England, and Samuel Finley Breese Morse, Leonard Gale, and Alfred Vail in the U.S.

Morse's system was simplicity itself, consisting of an electric battery, a switch (called an operator's key) to control the battery's connection to a wire, and a wire stretching from the sender to the receiver many miles away. A sensor (called a sounder) at the receiving end responded to the presence or absence of electricity on the incoming wire. Morse and Vail developed a code relating a series of "dots" (short bursts of electricity) and "dashes" (bursts of electricity three times longer than dots) to the letters of the alphabet and numbers. For example, the letter "S" is represented by three sequential dots (•••). The letter "O" is three successive dashes (---). Morse code, sent over telegraph lines, enabled virtually instant communication between distant locations.

In 1843, the U.S. Congress provided $30,000 to demonstrate the telegraph. As a result, Morse and Vail built a system of poles and wires between Washington, D.C., and Baltimore, Maryland. Over that primitive link, on May 24, 1844, Morse sent Vail the historic first message: "What hath God wrought!" In 1845, the telegraph wires were extended to link Philadelphia to Baltimore.[1]

The telegraph arrived in Pittsburgh in 1846, when Henry O'Reilly completed a telegraph line from Philadelphia. O'Reilly was a visionary promoter with more ideas than money. Along with inventor Samuel Morse and former U.S. Postmaster General Amos Kendall, he received an ambiguous contract in June 1845 to establish a telegraph line from the East Coast to the Great Lakes. Starting in September 1845, O'Reilly's men installed chestnut poles spaced about 300 feet apart to support thin copper wires to carry the signals. In late December 1846, Henry O'Reilly completed a telegraph line between Philadelphia and Pittsburgh. The first telegraph message arrived in Pittsburgh on December 29, and the delay of three days to receive news from Philadelphia became three seconds.[2]

Andrew Carnegie Gets a Job

To help meet family expenses, Andrew Carnegie worked at menial jobs starting in 1849, when he was 13 years old. First, he ran through the Blackstock Cotton Mill exchanging empty thread bobbins for full ones. Then he moved to the bobbin factory, where he dunked new bobbins in oil before they were sent to the cotton mills. But these were mindless jobs requiring no skill. At 14, Andy was ready for meaningful work.[3]

Then, as now, finding a job often depends as much on whom you know as it does on what you know. From their arrival in Pittsburgh in late 1848, the Carnegies knew an influential Pittsburgh resident, James Bennett. Letters written in 1905, over 50 years later, reveal the impact of James Bennett on Andrew Carnegie's early career and therefore that of the Pitcairn brothers.

The letters now reside in the Detre Library and Archives in the Senator John Heinz History Center in Pittsburgh.

The first of the letters was written on April 28, 1905, from aboard the HMS *Baltic* en route to Europe. William T. Gillinder wrote to his grandfather, Edwin Bennett (James's younger brother):

H.M.S. Baltic

Dear Grandpa,

For all the motion there is on this ship one could almost imagine himself on one of those Tolchester* boats.

Aunt Bertha will tell you about the boat and the send-off the folks gave us.

Yesterday in conversation with Mr. Carnegie (then 69 years old) I asked him if he ever knew a Mr. James Bennett. "Know him—why it was through him that I got my first position."

Well, he was interested, asked me what relation James Bennett was to me—asked about his brothers and when I told him you were living in Baltimore, he asked me for your address and said the next time he went to Baltimore he would call on you.

My question seemed to take him back many years and he grew reminiscent—very interesting too. He said that several weeks ago his sister had come across a box of old letters which she sent him to go over—among them he found a letter from James Bennett to him telling him what a grand, good woman his [Carnegie's] mother was and how they appreciated her services in their trouble—it appears that Mrs. Carnegie went to help out at the home of James Bennett when Mrs. B. was sick. He said that the letter was such a beautiful tribute to the worth and goodness of his mother—that he had put it amongst his heirlooms and it was one of his most cherished possessions.

We must have talked for nearly an hour, much to the wonderment of Sallie and my other traveling companions.

---

* The Tolchester Marina was and is located on the Eastern shore of the Chesapeake Bay.

Mr. Carnegie is an unusually small man—about the size of Mr. Thomas Mellon. Has blue eyes and whether it was the subject or not I found him a most unassuming conversationalist—wears a yellow flannel shirt and has a huge rough overcoat with a hood—he is quite spry in his movements and has a good grip—for when he parted he shook hands and said how glad he was that I had given him the chance of talking about his early days—I rather think he will write to you before long.

We are well so far and enjoying every minute of the trip.

With love to all and lots for yourself.

Affectionately,

Your Grandson

Wm. T. Gillinder

Two days later, Carnegie himself wrote to Edwin Bennett:

H.M.S. Baltic

Mid-Ocean

My Dear Mr. Bennett,

I have met your grandson on board who told me of you & of your wondering if I was the Carnegie whom your brother James in Pittsburgh knew. Yes indeed I am he & no other.

When at my sister's [Lucy Carnegie, widow of Andrew's brother, Thomas, and Andrew's sister-in-law] in Florida [Cumberland Island, Georgia] recently she gave me a package of old letters to look over & among these I found one from your brother telling me he could never thank my mother sufficiently for the good she had done Mrs. Bennett in her illness. She wished my mother to come & stay with her a while & this she did until Mrs. Bennett was out of danger. In this letter he also said he would help me if I ever had a chance to make a beginning as an investor. I put the letter away with a few others too precious to destroy. The tribute to my mother was sweet indeed, but all who knew that heroine were impressed.

I hear you are eighty-seven & still hearty & possessed of your faculties & the beloved patriarch of your grand-children. Blessed man you are—wish I could wish you another eighty-seven or a million years here. I see no reason for transplanting us but as we have nothing to do but bow to the inevitable our part is to meet it like men.

With every good wish for you & yours.

Sincerely yours,

Andrew Carnegie

Based on these two letters, James Bennett must have provided a strong positive reference for young Andrew Carnegie. As a result, in 1850, when 14-year-old Andrew heard of a possible job at the rapidly growing telegraph company, he was "wild with delight."[4] Mag agreed to the proposition, especially given the increase in salary to $2.50 per week. Only Will disagreed. He was concerned about the welfare of his undersized son traveling throughout the unfamiliar and dangerous city. However, Will withdrew his objection after Andrew's former employer agreed to hire him back to his job at the bobbin factory if the messenger job did not work out.

The final hurdle required Andrew to interview with Mr. Brooks at the telegraph office at Third and Wood Streets in Pittsburgh. Andrew and Will walked the one mile from Allegheny City across the river on the wooden St. Clair Street Bridge.* The interview was successful, and Andrew started immediately.

---

* The current bridge at the same location is the Sixth Street Bridge, renamed the Roberto Clemente Bridge in 1998.

The first requirement for delivering telegrams is to know the destination. Andrew resolved to memorize the businesses in order on every street he encountered. As he learned more and more streets, he recited in his mind each firm on those streets. The next important detail was learning to identify by sight each business owner who was to receive telegrams. If he had a telegram intended for one of these people and saw him or her on the street, he could deliver the message in person, thus saving time both for himself and the person receiving the telegram. Of course, the recipient was pleased to be recognized by Andrew and gained a positive image of the boy.

Andrew Carnegie learned even more lasting lessons from his time with O'Reilly Telegraph. The telegrams he delivered revealed details of business transactions: negotiations on price, who ordered what and for how much, credit arrangements, business alliances, and who succeeded and who failed. These lessons would serve him well in his future business dealings.

As the cities of Pittsburgh and Allegheny City grew, so did the volume of telegrams and the need for messengers. The first boy added after Andrew was 14-year-old David McCargo, who was, like Andrew, a Scotsman's son. Born the same year as Andrew, but in Pittsburgh, David and Andrew became close friends.

Soon another messenger was required, and Mr. Brooks asked Andrew for a recommendation. Andrew immediately suggested his chum and fellow Scotsman, 13-year-old Robert Pitcairn. Thus, Andy, Davy, and Bob were the three Scotsmen who delivered all the telegrams for the renamed Eastern Telegraph Line in Pittsburgh.[5]

Because they delivered telegrams, Andy, Davy, Bob, and a fourth recruit, Harry Oliver, were often allowed inside the Pittsburgh Theater to view the spectacular live plays. According to Andrew, "[They] all fell under the fascination of the footlights, and every opportunity to attend the theater was eagerly embraced." A bit later, Carnegie attended a performance of *Macbeth* and was enthralled with the magic captured by Shakespeare's words.[6]

After about one year as a messenger, the office manager, Colonel John P. Glass, began to assign Andy to watch after the affairs of the office when Glass was absent for brief periods. In that role, Andy would accept messages from customers and assign the other messengers to deliver telegrams that came in over the wires. Glass had political ambitions* and meetings began to demand more of his time, so young Carnegie became proficient at running the affairs of the telegraph office.

Messenger Boy to Operator

In addition to delivering telegrams, the messengers were responsible for sweeping the operating room each morning before the telegraph operators arrived. Being left alone with the telegraph keys provided an opportunity to practice sending messages to each other.

---

*Colonel John Glass was elected to the Pennsylvania House of Representatives in 1864 and became Speaker of the House on January 1, 1867.

One morning, before any operators had arrived, an urgent message started coming in from Philadelphia. The operator on the other end asked if anyone in the room could accept the transmission, and Andrew replied that he would try if the operator on the other end would send slowly. Andy received the message and awaited the arrival of his supervisor with some trepidation. Would he be praised or condemned for taking such responsibility? The boss was pleased but warned Carnegie to be careful to avoid mistakes when taking important messages. From then on, Andrew often filled in when an operator took a break or was otherwise absent.

Standard practice was to record incoming telegraph messages on a paper tape, which the operator then read to a copyist, who wrote the contents for later delivery. An experienced operator could learn to understand the letters in the message by sound, thus bypassing the paper tape. One of the Pittsburgh operators acquired that skill and encouraged Carnegie to try it. Andrew quickly caught on. When substituting for an absent operator while still using the paper tape procedure, the copyist assigned to work with Andrew refused to copy for a mere messenger. So Andrew turned off the paper tape, picked up the copy pad and pencil, and wrote the message directly from the sound of the dots and dashes. The copyist was amazed and quickly took back his pad and pencil lest he be made obsolete by such a skilled operator.

Soon after Andrew's demonstration, Joseph Taylor, the Greenburg operator, requested a two-week absence and asked Carnegie's boss, David Brooks, if he could send a substitute. Brooks asked Andrew if he thought he was up to the challenge, and he quickly said yes. Andrew was 17 years old.[7]

4

Emanuel Swedenborg

"There is no death, only a transition from one state of consciousness to another."

—Emanuel Swedenborg

Religion played a significant role in the lives of several members of the Carnegie and Pitcairn families. An early influence for both families was the teaching of Emanuel Swedenborg, a Swedish scientist, philosopher, theologian, and true polymath.

Swedenborg was born in Stockholm, Sweden, on January 29, 1688. His father, Jesper, was a Lutheran pastor and professor at the University of Uppsala. His mother, Sara, died when he was eight, but her sweet nature influenced Emanuel throughout his life. The family name was Swedberg until Jesper became Bishop of Skara in 1719. At that time, Queen Ulrika Eleonora of Sweden ennobled the family, and their surname became Swedenborg. Jesper also served as a chaplain to the Swedish royal family, giving him access to the highest social and political circles.[1]

Emanuel Swedenborg entered the University of Uppsala at the age of 11 in 1699. His instruction was mainly in Latin, but he also learned Greek, Hebrew, English, French, Dutch, and Italian.

He completed his formal studies in 1709 at age 21. For the next five years, he traveled abroad, stopping first in England, where he met Sir Isaac Newton and Edmund Halley and studied geology, botany, and zoology.

Upon returning to Sweden, he focused on scientific and technical studies and published books on chemistry, physics, and algebra. In 1734 he published, in Latin,* a three-volume book titled *Opera Philosophica et Mineralia* (*Philosophical and Metallurgical Works*). Swedenborg then moved to human anatomy, publishing a two-volume treatise called *Oeconomia Regni Animalis* (*Dynamics of the Soul's Domain*) in 1740 and 1741. The first volume dealt with the heart and blood, and the second with the brain, nervous system, and soul. In the latter volume, Swedenborg searched for a connection between the spiritual and physical worlds (correspondences). Between 1720 and 1745, Swedenborg wrote 20 books on civil, scientific, and philosophical subjects. He also practiced manual skills, including watchmaking, bookbinding, cabinet making, engraving, and lens grinding. In addition, he made models of a glider airplane and a submarine, the latter long before anyone

---

* Swedenborg wrote in Latin because it was the most universal language at that time.

else had considered the possibility. Several observers have placed Emanuel Swedenborg in the company of historical geniuses like Leonardo da Vinci and Galileo Galilei.[2]

Swedenborg was also devoted to public service. At age 28, he was appointed by King Charles XII as extraordinary assessor on the Royal Board of Mines. In this position, he was responsible for supervising and developing mining, then one of Sweden's most important industries. Swedenborg served in that position for 31 years, inspecting mines for safety and preparing detailed reports on the quantity and quality of ore being mined. He also arbitrated labor disputes, suggested improvements, and collected taxes on mining properties.

As a noble, he served for 50 years in the House of Nobles, where he prepared pamphlets on the economy, tax structure, foreign policy, and the development of natural resources. In addition, Emanuel edited the first scientific journal published in Sweden. As a result of his excellent performance, King Charles asked him to serve as an engineering advisor to the Crown. In that position, he supervised the construction of a dry dock, a canal, and a transport system for moving large warships over land.

Swedenborg's work was all based on the assumption that the prime reality, the source of everything, is divine force. He rejected a purely material explanation for the universe.[3]

At age 56, in 1744, Swedenborg had gone as far as he could in developing a scientific explanation for the mysteries of human existence. He felt dissatisfied that his work had not resulted in a clear answer. But then his life took a new and strange turn.

Starting in 1744, Swedenborg experienced a spiritual crisis. First, he had intense dreams and visions that gave him a sense of spiritual unworthiness, a feeling that he must purify himself of sin. Then, starting in 1745 and for the remaining 27 years of his life, the visions occurred during the day when Swedenborg was fully awake. He recorded in his diary that he was in contact with the spiritual world and the afterlife and began to write about the meaning of the Bible based on the knowledge gained from his visions.[4] Swedenborg came to believe that God had called him to transmit a new revelation to the world.

He wrote of his interactions in the spirit world:

> Of the Lord's Divine Mercy it has been granted me now for several years to be constantly and uninterruptedly in company with spirits and angels, hearing them speak and in turn speaking with them. In this way it has been given me to hear and see wonderful things in the other life which have never before come to the knowledge of any man nor into his idea.... I have been instructed in regard to the different kinds of spirits, the state of souls after death, hell, or the lamentable state of the unfaithful, heaven, or the blessed state of the faithful, and especially in regard to the doctrine of faith which is acknowledged in the universal heaven.[5]

He insisted that he was taught by the Lord alone through angels but not by the knowledge of angels.

During the balance of his life, Swedenborg wrote prodigiously, always in Latin. However, he did not start writing about his experiences in the spirit world until three years after the visits began. Among his better-known publications are:

- *Arcana Coelestia*, or *Heavenly Mysteries* or *Secrets of Heaven*, eight volumes initially published from 1749 to 1756, interpreting Genesis and Exodus verse by verse;
- *De Coelo et ejus Mirabilibus et de Inferno*, or *On Heaven and Its Wonders and On Hell*, published in 1758;
- *Apocalypsis Explicata*, or *Apocalypse Explained*, the first volume published in 1766; four volumes published posthumously in 1785, containing his commentaries on the Book of Revelation; and
- *Vera Christiana Religio*, or *True Christian Religion*, written when he was 83 and published in 1771.[6]

Until 1759, Swedenborg lived a normal but secluded life. He never married, but otherwise his friends noticed nothing unusual about his activities or behavior. But in July 1759, he attended a party with 15 other guests at a friend's home in Gothenburg, 250 miles from Stockholm. Emanuel suddenly became highly disturbed and retreated to the garden. Upon returning, he told the group that a severe fire had broken out in Stockholm, not far from his home. Fearing that his manuscripts might be burned, he remained greatly concerned for several hours. Finally, he cried out, "Thank God! The fire is extinguished at the third door from my house." The next day, Swedenborg provided details of the fire, including how it had been extinguished.

Two days after the fire, a messenger arrived from Stockholm with more information that verified Swedenborg's vision.[7]

At least two other instances of Swedenborg's specific communication with the spirit world, one in 1760 and one in 1761, are documented. In the first case, the widow of the Dutch ambassador in Stockholm requested his help in finding a receipt for a payment made by her late husband. In the second, Swedish Queen Louisa Ulrika sought information from her brother, who had died in 1759. In both cases, Swedenborg learned from his spirit correspondents the desired details, much to the amazement of the women who had asked for his assistance.[8]

During one of his visits to the spirit world, Swedenborg learned that John Wesley, the

Emanuel Swedenborg at age 75, holding a copy of *Apocalypse Revealed* **(Wikimedia Commons).**

founder of Methodism, desired to talk with him, so he wrote to Wesley to propose a meeting. Upon receiving the letter, Wesley was amazed because he did wish to meet Swedenborg but had told no one of his desire.

Wesley was about to embark on a six-month revivalist tour, so he suggested a meeting date after the trip. Swedenborg replied that the proposed date would be too late because he would die on March 29, 1772. That date was precisely when Swedenborg died.[9]

A friend later wrote, "Someone might think that Swedenborg was eccentric and whimsical, but the very reverse was the case. He was very easy and pleasant in company, talked on every subject that came up, accommodating himself to the ideas of the company, and never speaking of his own views unless he was asked about them."[10]

Although Swedenborg was never a preacher, Swedenborgian societies based on his writings appeared in the 1780s. The first Swedenborgian New Jerusalem Church congregation was founded in London around 1789, and four branches of that church survive today, with about 7,000 U.S. members and 60,000 worldwide.[11,12]

Overview of Swedenborg's Doctrine

Swedenborg published 14,000 pages and left another 28,000 in manuscript form,[13] so attempting to summarize his doctrine in a few paragraphs is bound to ignore critical aspects.

Jonathan Rose, in the video *Who was Swedenborg?*, provides a brief overview of Swedenborg's theology and writings and says, "Swedenborg's work gives unique perspectives on the nature of God, the spiritual world, the Bible, the human mind, and the path to salvation."[14]

Regarding the Christian church, Swedenborg wrote, "The falsities of the dogmas of the faith of the present Church must first be exposed and rejected before the truths of the dogmas of the New Church are revealed and received."[15]

Regarding the Trinity, he taught that there is a divine Trinity of Father, Son, and Holy Ghost, but that "this Trinity consisteth not of three distinct persons, but is united as body, soul, and operation in man, in the one person of the Lord Jesus Christ, who therefore is the God of Heaven, and alone to be worshipped; being Creator from eternity, Redeemer in time, and Regenerator to eternity."[16]

The Swedenborg Foundation lists the following doctrinal aspects of his teaching:

God: Unipersonal (existing as one person); modalistic (one person revealed as three forms) and apparent pantheistic tendencies (God is in all things);
Jesus: Jehovah (the Father) incarnate as man;
Holy Spirit: An "operation" proceeding from God;
Salvation: By faith and works;
Man: The "symbol" of God;
Satan: The personification of evil;

The Fall: Symbolic;

The Bible: Contains the Word of the Lord but is authoritative only when interpreted by Swedenborg;

Spiritual World and Scripture: Every portion of the spiritual world, every part of physical creation including man, and every word of Scripture allegedly contains degrees of *arcana coelestia*, or heavenly secrets, which only the true mystic or spiritually enlightened can understand;

Death: Continuation of life on earth in the spirit world, its quality being dictated by man's spiritual condition at death;

Heaven and Hell: Temporal places or states of mind.[17]

Another way to understand Swedenborg's beliefs is to compare them to evangelical Christianity.[18]

Swedenborg "New Church"	Evangelical Christianity
Non-trinitarian	Believe in the Trinity
One person—not three	One God in three persons
Virgin birth accepted	Virgin birth accepted
Jesus obtained a new divine humanity	Jesus's humanity was like other humans
God is ontologically human	God is not human except in the incarnation
Believers and infants baptized by sprinkling	Age and methods vary
Re-baptism of Christians	Most do not re-baptize
Lord's Supper with unleavened bread and wine	Lord's Supper with unleavened bread and wine or grape juice
29 OT and 5 NT books are inspired word of God	All OT and NT books are inspired word of God
Some view Swedenborg's writings as inspired word of God	Reject Swedenborg's writings
Three levels of meaning to Scripture; literal meaning might not be true	Bible is inerrant; it should be contextually interpreted
Denies original sin	Original sin—sin nature from Adam
Live well, believe rightly, and you will be saved	Salvation does not come from doing good things
Everyone who lives a good life can have a place in Heaven	Jesus Christ's death and resurrection for our sins is the only way to Heaven
Rejects one-time salvation experience	Salvation is a "born again" experience
We play an active role in our salvation	Salvation is by God's Grace
Humans become angels at death	Angels are a different type of being than humans
Reject the penal aspect of the atonement	Jesus's blood was payment for our sins
Christ came because of the power of hell	Christ came to save us from our sins by His death and resurrection
People in hell have a decent life	Hell is a place of torment and suffering
Eternal marriage	No marriage in heaven
Some New Church groups ordain gay and lesbian ministers	Homosexuality is sinful

Swedenborgian Doctrine in America

The religious writings and doctrine of Emanuel Swedenborg reached the U.S. in the person of James Glen in 1784. Glen was born in Glasgow, Scotland, in about 1750 and attended Glasgow University in 1766 but never graduated. Instead, he traveled to Demerara, Guiana (now Guyana), off the northeast coast of South America in the early 1770s, and created a prosperous plantation there.

Glen sailed back to London in 1783. En route, the ship captain loaned him *On Heaven and Its Wonders and On Hell* by Emanuel Swedenborg. Glen read the book and later declared it "to be the happiest day of his life, which thus brought to his view the glories of the heavenly state, and the stupendous realities of the eternal world."[19]

In London, Glen saw an announcement of a public meeting of those interested in Swedenborg's doctrine. He attended with ten others on December 15, 1783, and they agreed to obtain copies of all of Swedenborg's published works. The group met again in January 1784 and formed the Theosophical Society, which was dedicated to translating, printing, and distributing Swedenborg's writings.[20]

In June 1784, Glen packed a box full of Swedenborg books and departed for Philadelphia. There, at Bell's Auction House on Third Street, he discussed Swedenborgian philosophy with a "very small audience." An aspiring Philadelphia lawyer, John Young, was one of the attendees at that lecture and soon became an enthusiastic supporter.* Young solicited Benjamin Franklin and Robert Morris, among others, to support publishing Swedenborg's *True Christian Religion*.[21]

James Glen visited other parts of Pennsylvania, as well as Virginia and Kentucky, before returning to his Demerara plantation. At all stops, he presented his enthusiasm for Swedenborg and established small worship groups. Having brought Swedenborgian principles to the United States, Glen retired to Demerara and died in 1814 at age 64.

Some small groups dissipated, but a few thrived, especially in Baltimore, Boston, and several Pennsylvania cities including Philadelphia, Harrisburg, Greensburg, and Bedford. New Jerusalem Societies built dedicated structures in Baltimore, Boston, and Philadelphia. John Hargrove, a former Methodist Episcopal preacher from Baltimore, adopted the Swedenborgian doctrine and presented it in Washington, D.C., to President Thomas Jefferson and Congress on December 26, 1802. He preached again in 1804 to both houses of Congress.[22]

Other prominent followers of Swedenborg included Ralph Waldo Emerson, Henry David Thoreau, Benjamin Franklin, and Helen Keller. Emerson called him "a colossal soul who lies vast abroad on his times, uncomprehended by them.... He is not to be measured by whole colleges of ordinary scholars."[23] Helen Keller said he was "an eye among the blind, an ear among the deaf, a voice crying in the wilderness" and said he was "one of the noblest champions Christianity has ever known."[24]

One of the Boston believers in the teachings of Swedenborg was a young man

---

* Young moved west to Greensburg, Pennsylvania, in 1789 to open a law office. He practiced there until 1806 when Governor McKean appointed him as president judge of the Tenth Judicial District of Pennsylvania (including Somerset, Cambria, Indiana, Armstrong, and Westmoreland Counties). Young served in that position until his retirement in late 1837.

named John Chapman. He was eccentric—small, wiry, restless, with long, dark hair, a patchy, unshaven beard, and black eyes that were said to sparkle with a peculiar brightness. He went barefoot, even in snow and ice. Chapman first surfaced in the Allegheny Valley of western Pennsylvania in 1798 and then moved west through Ohio with a horse cart loaded with apple seeds to grow orchards. John Chapman became better known as Johnny Appleseed.[25]

He traveled the midwest, from Pennsylvania to Michigan, selling or giving away apple seeds along with portions of or complete Swedenborg books. Judge John Young of Greensburg provided the book copies for Chapman to distribute.[26] If invited to stay the night, Johnny would gratefully accept and offer "NEWS RIGHT FRESH FROM HEAVEN." One woman recalls the scene: "We can hear him read now, just as he did that summer day, when we were busy upstairs quilting. His was a strange eloquence at times, and he was undoubtedly a man of genius."[27]

Historical marker in Franklin, Pennsylvania, commemorating Johnny Appleseed (photograph by and courtesy of Mike Wintermantel)

John "Johnny Appleseed" Chapman died peacefully on March 18, 1845, at age 70, after devoting 47 years to distributing apple seeds and Swedenborgian wisdom.

Swedenborgians in Pittsburgh

James Glen, John Young, John Chapman, and others spread the doctrine, and an active Swedenborgian New Church Society grew in the Pittsburgh area.

Annie Aitken, Mag Carnegie's sister and Andrew's aunt, was among the first to follow Swedenborg's teaching, and she passed on her knowledge to her twin sister, Kitty Hogan. Kitty encouraged her husband, Thomas, to attend services at the fledgling Swedenborgian New Jerusalem Church. Will Carnegie had rejected the severe restrictions of the Presbyterian Church while in Scotland. But, finding no branch of the Erskine Secessionist Church of Scotland in the U.S., he also attended the New Jerusalem Church. Mag had no interest in Swedenborg, his philosophy, or any organized religion, but allowed Will to take Andrew.

Annie Aitken was also the source of information about Swedenborg for the Pitcairn family. Recall that John Pitcairn, Sr., had two older brothers, Alexander and Robert, who had preceded John and his family to America. Alexander Pitcairn emigrated in about 1830 and settled in Pittsburgh, where he was a weaver. He had become disenchanted with the Presbyterian Church, and around 1847 he discussed his concerns with a fellow Scotsman, Thomas Hogan. Thomas invited Alexander to his home to meet his wife, Catherine. As mentioned earlier, Catherine received her Swedenborg doctrines from her sister, Annie Aitken. After a brief discussion with Alexander Pitcairn, Catherine handed him a copy of Swedenborg's *True Christian Religion*.

Alexander Pitcairn recognized the truth of Swedenborg's writing and spread the news of his enlightenment to his two brothers, Robert and John, Sr. All five of Alexander's sons became associated with the New Jerusalem Church, as did eight of Robert's 11 children. In about 1849, the entire family of John Pitcairn, Sr., his wife Agnes, and their six children were baptized by New Jerusalem Church pastor David Powell.[28]

Especially for young John Pitcairn, Jr., who was then just eight years old, that ceremony marked the start of a lifetime of devotion and service to the New Jerusalem Church.

By the end of 1849, the New Jerusalem Church in Pittsburgh had about 50 adult members. Annie Aitken, Andrew Carnegie's aunt, taught Sunday school to 20 children, including Robert and John Pitcairn and Andrew Carnegie.[29] Robert, John, and Andrew sang in the Sunday school choir of the New Jerusalem Church.[30]

William Henry Benade

A man who would later significantly impact John Pitcairn, Jr., and the New Jerusalem Church came from a strict Moravian background. William Henry Benade was born October 3, 1816, in Lititz, Pennsylvania, the third son of Andrew and Maria Henry Benade.[31] Andrew Benade was a Moravian pastor, first at his birthplace of Kleinwelka, Saxony, Prussia, and later at Nazareth, Bethlehem, and Lititz, Pennsylvania.

When William was six, his father was elevated to bishop, and the family moved to Salem, North Carolina. William started school in Salem and studied German, English, grammar, geography, literature, history, art, and music. Through literature, the students learned morality. Music, both vocal and instrumental, was an essential part of the curriculum.

After several years at Salem, the Benade family returned to Lititz, where William entered the John Beck Academy. In addition to standard school subjects, Beck taught evening classes with demonstrations and analysis of physical objects such as an air pump, electrical equipment, natural history charts with specimens of rare fish and animals, and a telescope for astronomy. At Beck's school, William Benade learned practices and techniques that would carry over to what would become the Academy of the New Church.

In 1828, when William was 12, he moved to Nazareth Hall in Nazareth, Pennsylvania, the secondary school that most Moravian pastors' sons attended. After completing his studies in two years, William's father asked him what occupation he wished to pursue. William quickly responded, "The ministry." His father, Andrew, accepted that answer but encouraged William to study theology from sources beyond the Moravian doctrines, reflecting Andrew's growing skepticism of conventional Moravian beliefs.[32]

William finished his theological education at Nazareth Hall in 1835 and taught there until 1838. He received high marks for his teaching ability and knowledge of classical literature, but his doubts about Moravian doctrine and practice grew.

On August 29, 1841, Bishop Andrew Benade ordained his son, William Henry Benade, as a deacon of the Moravian church. During his initial assignments, William learned of Emanuel Swedenborg and started studying Swedenborg's book, *The New Christian Religion*.

By the time William was scheduled to assume the pulpit of the Moravian church in Philadelphia on June 24, 1844, he was conflicted. He later wrote that "there came to me, almost at once, the conviction that these Writings [of Swedenborg] are the Second Coming of the Lord Himself." At age 27, about to take responsibility for a Moravian church whose doctrines he seriously doubted, what should he do? He decided to salt his sermons with some of the truths he had learned from Swedenborg's writings but without attribution to the author.

Benade continued the subtle indoctrination of his congregation for several months. Finally, he believed the new ideas were gaining acceptance, so on October 27, 1844, he revealed the source of his possibly heretical views. The reception was not warm.

Three days after William's sermon, Bishop Andrew Benade, William's father and president of the Provincial Helpers' Conference of the Moravian Church, received a strongly worded letter of complaint from 13 members of William's congregation. As a result, William Benade was censured and resigned from the Moravian church.

On his next visit home, William found his father studying Swedenborg's writings. Both Andrew and his wife were moving away from Moravian beliefs and toward Swedenborg's teachings. For his part, by early 1845, William Benade was ready to be baptized into the New Church.[33]

5

The Pennsylvania Railroad

> *"Every child should be taught that useful work is worship and that intelligent labor is the highest form of prayer."*
> —Robert G. Ingersoll

It was 1852, and 17-year-old Andrew Carnegie had agreed to fill in for Joseph Taylor, the telegraph operator at Greensburg. It was Andy's first solo trip outside of the Pittsburgh area, his first stay in a public house (hotel), and his first restaurant meal. He was thrilled by all of it.

After successfully completing his two-week assignment in Greensburg, Andy returned to the Pittsburgh office with an enhanced reputation. When another operator was needed, Mr. Brooks, Andy's boss, recommended him to the general superintendent, James D. Reid. Reid heartily approved, and Andy became an assistant operator at a salary of $25 per month. In addition, he made an extra dollar per week by copying press dispatches for distribution to various news outlets.

Andy was enthusiastic about his new assignment. One of his frequent customers was Thomas A. Scott, who had been named third assistant superintendent in charge of the Western Division of the Pennsylvania Railroad on December 15, 1852.[1] Scott often communicated with his boss, Altoona-based general superintendent Herman J. Lombaert. One day, Scott's assistant brought a message to send and said that Scott asked him whether he thought Carnegie might be available to become his clerk and telegraph operator. The assistant told Scott, "That is impossible. He is now an operator." On hearing this, Carnegie said, "Not so fast. He can have me. I want to get out of a mere office life. Please go and tell him so." On February 1, 1853, Andrew Carnegie became Thomas Scott's clerk and operator, earning $35 per month.[2]

Scott had started with the fledgling Pennsylvania Railroad in 1850 as a station agent in Duncansville, Pennsylvania, eight miles south of Altoona. The rapid expansion of railroads in general, and the PRR in particular, provided opportunities for capable employees such as Scott, and he moved quickly up the company ladder. He became general superintendent of the Mountain District of Altoona, headquartered in Duncansville, in 1852. Later in 1852, he was promoted to general agent of PRR's Pittsburgh office and then to third assistant superintendent. That was when he hired Andrew Carnegie.[3]

Origins of the Pennsylvania Railroad

The canals and Allegheny Portage Railroad comprising the Pennsylvania Main Line Canal suffered several significant limitations. They froze in the winter, flooded in spring, and dried up in the summer. Passengers and freight had to be transferred from water transport to rail cars to cross the mountains. The unreliability of the complex system of steam engines and inclined planes begged for an all-rail solution.

In 1846, a new organization called the Pennsylvania Railroad Company (PRR) filed for a charter with the Commonwealth of Pennsylvania to build a railroad between Harrisburg and Pittsburgh. Such a line would eliminate the canals and Allegheny Portage Railroad, allowing a train to travel by rail unimpeded across the state. The state approved the application on February 25, 1847. Later that year, the PRR hired J. Edgar Thomson as its chief engineer.

Born February 10, 1808, in Springfield Township, Delaware County, Pennsylvania, John Edgar Thomson received little formal education. Instead, he learned by working with his father, a civil engineer, to construct the Chesapeake and Delaware Canal. At 19, he worked on a survey crew establishing the route of the Philadelphia and Columbia Railroad. He later worked for the Camden and Amboy Railroad, becoming head of the engineering division in 1830 at age 22. Two years later, the new Georgia Railroad hired Thomson as chief engineer. He determined the route of the tracks, negotiated and managed construction contracts, and operated sections as they were completed. By 1845, he had completed the railroad from Augusta to present-day Atlanta. At 173 miles, it was the longest railroad in the world at that time. He became nationally known for his railroad expertise, and the PRR hired him in 1847.[4]

The work of creating an all-rail route across Pennsylvania can be divided into two projects: first, eliminate the water-borne (canal) segments of the Pennsylvania Main Line Canal; second, replace the Allegheny Portage Railroad with regular train rails (no more inclined planes served by stationary steam engines).

Eliminating the Canal Segments

Replacing the canal segments required selecting a path suitable for train rails. Edgar Thomson inspected the many potential routes to determine their feasibility. In the east, he settled on a route along river valleys from Harrisburg to Altoona (then called Robinson's Summit) at the eastern base of the Allegheny Mountains. In the west, he built rail lines, generally tracing the canal route between Johnstown and Pittsburgh.

Bypass the Allegheny Portage Railroad

In 1851, in a vain attempt to compete with the upstart PRR, the state commenced work on the New Portage Railroad on a path that would bypass the inclined planes.

While the state continued to waste money on its doomed New Portage Railroad venture, the PRR chipped away at the route of the Allegheny Portage Railroad. On April 1, 1852, the PRR opened a six-mile section from Johnstown east to the Conemaugh Viaduct near Mineral Point. This rail connection bypassed the westernmost inclined plane (Plane No. 1) and the Staple Bend Tunnel of the Allegheny Portage Railroad.[5]

Thomson realized that developing a train route over the mountains from Altoona would take time and money. Until that link could be established, he built a six-mile rail line from Altoona to Hollidaysburg, thus connecting the rail lines east of Altoona to those of the Allegheny Portage Railroad. With the completion of these lines in 1852, the PRR could claim to have a rail connection from Philadelphia to Pittsburgh, but that route included multiple railroad companies and the Allegheny Portage Railroad. The first train from Philadelphia via the hybrid rail connection arrived in Pittsburgh on the evening of December 10, 1852. J. Edgar Thomson, by then president of the PRR, arrived on that first train and "gave personal supervision to the arrangements being made for the accommodation of the traffic."[6]

In parallel with eliminating the canal portions, Thomson and his principal assistant, Herman Haupt, surveyed potential routes across the mountains from Altoona. Their objective was to eliminate the need for the Allegheny Portage Railroad.

Horseshoe Curve aerial photograph. The eastbound tracks go to Altoona, Harrisburg, and Philadelphia. The westbound tracks go to Gallitzin, Johnstown, and Pittsburgh. In the middle of the curve is Kittanning Point Reservoir, the first of a series of three dams constructed between 1881 and 1929 to supply drinking water to the city of Altoona (Seamless Data Warehouse, United States Geological Survey).

Thomson and Haupt developed a creative and unprecedented solution, the now world-famous 220-degree Horseshoe Curve west of Altoona. Using the natural contour of the mountains, the maximum grade* on the curve was held to just 1.87 percent, well within the capability of steam engines at the time.

Construction on the Horseshoe Curve started in 1850.

On February 15, 1854, the Horseshoe Curve was completed and opened for service.[7]

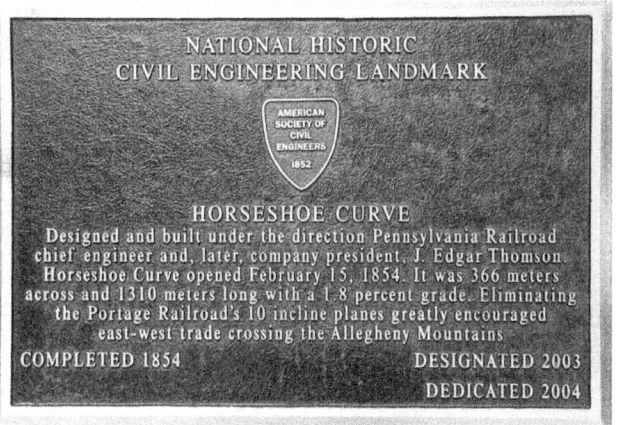

Horseshoe Curve plaque (photograph by the author).

East portal of two of the tunnels at Gallitzin, with the Allegheny Tunnel on the left, opened in 1854 and enlarged to two tracks in 1995. The Gallitzin Tunnel (HAER no. PA-516), on the right, was opened in 1904 and closed in 1995 (Historic American Buildings Survey; National Park Service).

---

*Railroad grade is the amount of vertical rise per 100 feet of track, expressed as a percentage. For example, if the track rose one foot in 100 feet of horizontal distance, the grade would be 1 percent.

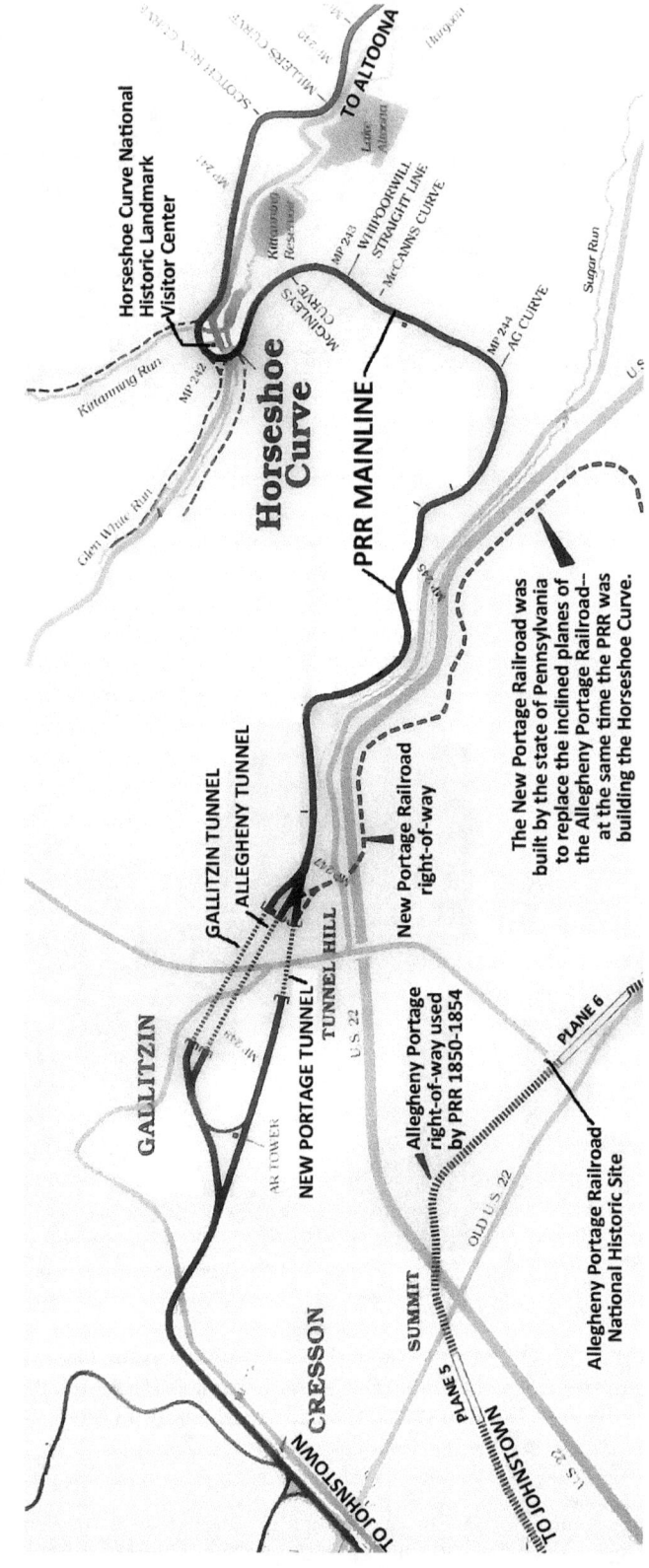

Map showing Cresson to the west, the three tunnels at Gallitzin in the center, and the Horseshoe Curve to the east (photograph at the Horseshoe Curve Visitors Center by the author).

A 3,612-foot-long tunnel (originally named the Summit Tunnel, now called the Allegheny Tunnel) at Gallitzin, Pennsylvania, about six miles west of the Horseshoe Curve, also opened in 1854. The Horseshoe Curve and the Summit Tunnel completed the 363-mile all-rail route across from Philadelphia to Pittsburgh.[8]

Confusingly, the route of the state of Pennsylvania's New Portage Railroad also included a tunnel at Gallitzin, separate but parallel to the Allegheny Tunnel built by the PRR for its mainline. The state's tunnel, opened in 1855, is south of the other two tunnels.[9]

Beginning a Lifelong Relationship

Once Andrew Carnegie found his footing with the PRR, he saw where his friend from the telegraph office, Robert Pitcairn, could fit in and obtained an interview for him. In July 1853, 17-year-old Robert was hired and began as a telegraph operator and assistant ticket agent at Mountain House near Hollidaysburg at the east end of the Allegheny Portage Railroad.[10] Robert and his family had first traveled past this point on their way to Allegheny City just seven years earlier.

When the PRR completed its rail line over the mountains in 1854, there was no more need for the ingenious but unreliable Allegheny Portage Railroad. So Robert Pitcairn transferred to the Altoona office, where he worked as a telegraph operator for General Superintendent Herman Lombaert.

The General Office was a university of railroading where Pitcairn learned all aspects of operating the complex organization. Edgar Thomson and Herman Lombaert established separate but interrelated transportation, engineering, comptroller, and commercial departments. Lombaert emphasized discipline, order, and regularity but also focused on passenger safety and comfort. For example, he added the saloon car, water coolers, heaters, and lights for passenger convenience. On Lombaert's watch, Woodruff sleeping cars were added, first to the Harrisburg-Pittsburgh route and then to the Philadelphia-to-Pittsburgh trains. The lessons Herman Lombaert taught about how to run a railroad stayed with Robert Pitcairn throughout his career.[11]

Pitcairn displayed integrity, discipline, and judgment in all his professional actions. While retiring and quiet, he earned the esteem and friendship of his managers and coworkers. His intelligence, self-confidence, tenacity, and ability to focus despite surrounding distractions made him a perfect fit for the chaos of operating multiple trains and their associated crews.

The Brothers Pitcairn

At the beginning of 1855, when Robert was not yet 19, he was promoted to chief clerk of the general superintendent's office. He invited his brother, John Pitcairn, Jr., to join him as an office boy in Altoona. On his 14th birthday, January 10, 1855, John left Pittsburgh for Altoona carrying two books his mother had given him—a Bible and Emanuel Swedenborg's *True Christian Religion*.

Herman Lombaert, the general superintendent, and Enoch Lewis, the superintendent of the PRR Middle Division, looked after young John Pitcairn as he ran errands for them during his long days from 7:30 a.m. to 9:00 p.m. Both men invited John into their homes and suggested readings to extend his limited education. John saw Lombaert as "a man always on duty" and tried to follow his example. He viewed Enoch Lewis and his wife as "highly cultured and refined...; their frequent invitations to visit at their house were a great source of pleasure and profit.... Mrs. Lewis guided my reading by suggesting appropriate books and opening her library to me."[12]

In his spare time, John read his religious books along with works by Shakespeare and other British writers, including Sir Walter Scott and Lord Byron. John would continue self-study throughout his life, eventually learning Hebrew, Greek, Latin, French, and German. Through the Lewises, John met the Justice family of Philadelphia. He later wrote, "The delightful week I spent in 1857 with the Justice family in Philadelphia, at their invitation, and their kind reception, form a very pleasant memory connected with sightseeing around the interesting city, with its memorial halls, museums, and art galleries."[13]

His time at the PRR shaped John Pitcairn's character. In looking back, he said,

> I have always regarded my experience and training in the railroad service as of utmost importance in the development of character. The railroad service at that time resembled the military service more than any other occupation. Prompt and absolute obedience, so necessary in the development of the youth, made a basis for the wise government of the man when he was called upon to exercise authority. The principle involved is that the child and the youth should not do his own will, but the will of his parent, or guardian, and the adult should not do his own will, but the will of the Lord, as expressed in His Commandments and the principles of Truth and Justice.[14]

Like his brother Robert and Andrew Carnegie before him, John learned telegraphy while working at the PRR, a vital skill in the railroad industry.

While Robert Pitcairn was working as chief clerk in General Superintendent Lombaert's PRR office in Altoona, he met Elizabeth Erb Rigg. On July 26, 1856, the couple married. Robert was 20 years old, and Elizabeth was just 15. Their first child, Agnes Laurene, was born on June 21, 1857, and another daughter, Lillian, followed on December 19, 1858.[15]

Robert remained as chief clerk until 1858, when he was transferred to Fort Wayne, Indiana, to supervise the construction of the Pittsburgh, Fort Wayne, and Chicago Railroad (PFW&CRR).

Soon after Robert arrived in Fort Wayne, he wrote to his brother, John, saying, "I have been thinking about you going to college & think if you can afford it you better go but for goodness sake hurry up. Remember every moment now is lost for this is the chance to gain your reputation."[16]

John finished his formal education in Allegheny City at the end of 1859, then joined Robert in Fort Wayne where, at 18 years old, he became assistant superintendent and train dispatcher of the PFW&CRR.

1860 was a momentous year for the Pitcairn brothers. On August 1, 1860, Robert Pitcairn, age 24, left Fort Wayne to become superintendent of the PRR Middle Division, the position that had been held by his friend and mentor, Enoch Lewis. The Middle

Division extended from Mifflin, 40 miles northwest of Harrisburg, to Conemaugh, east of Johnstown, and included the Horseshoe Curve and Gallitzin Tunnels.[17]

At the same time, John Pitcairn, age 19, moved from Fort Wayne to Philadelphia, where he became secretary to George C. Franciscus, superintendent of the Philadelphia Division of the PRR. The Philadelphia Division extended west 100 miles to Harrisburg and south toward Baltimore, and traffic was heavy in both directions. When his boss was away, John had to keep all the trains moving without accidents or undue delay.

In Philadelphia, John met several people associated with the Swedenborgian New Church. The Reverend William Benade would be John's pastor, friend, and spiritual guide for most of his life. Dr. Rudolph Tafel was a New Church scholar and would be John's traveling companion on many trips. Dr. George Starkey was a homeopathic physician and father of Gertrude Starkey, who would later become John Pitcairn's wife.[18]

Expanding the PRR

The state's New Portage Railroad opened on July 1, 1855, replacing the original Allegheny Portage Railroad.[19] However, with the opening of the all-rail line of the PRR on February 15, 1854, the New Portage Railroad was obsolete before it was completed.

With no further need for the Pennsylvania Main Line Canal, the state of Pennsylvania sold it to the Pennsylvania Railroad on August 1, 1857. The price was $7.5 million, to be paid in PRR 5 percent bonds in installments until July 31, 1894.

Included in the purchase were the main line canals on each side of the Allegheny Mountains, the New Portage Railroad, the double-track Columbia-Philadelphia Railroad, and all real estate, locomotives, and cars connected with the property.[20]

The Johnstown-to-Pittsburgh canals were abandoned in 1865. In 1867, the PRR formed the Pennsylvania Canal Company and transferred its remaining canal properties to that organization. Those canals were used to haul freight until about 1875, when the business declined. Virtually all Pennsylvania's canals ceased to operate by 1901.[21]

The PRR shut down the New Portage Railroad in October 1857. But in the 1890s, the railroad tunnel at Gallitzin, called the New Portage Tunnel, was expanded to two tracks and reopened for eastbound traffic.[22]

The Columbia-Philadelphia Railroad, initially surveyed by J. Edgar Thomson, became part of the mainline of the PRR.

Among the real estate parcels included in the sale of the Pennsylvania Main Line Canal were the Eastern and Western Canal Reservoirs, located at Hollidaysburg and South Fork, Pennsylvania, respectively. These reservoirs had supplied water to the canals in dry seasons. The Western Canal Reservoir, better known as Lake Conemaugh, would be the dominant factor in the Johnstown Flood of 1889.

J. Edgar Thomson continued as president of the PRR until his death on May 27, 1874. During his tenure, the PRR became the largest business enterprise in the world and a model for effective management. Its tracks spanned from Boston in the east to St. Louis in the west, and from Cincinnati and Washington, D.C., in the south to the Great Lakes in the north.[23]

6

Railroads and the Civil War

> "Throughout the war while the Federal Government took control of the railroads and established the United States Military Railroads, the Confederacy left control in the hands of private companies up until February 1865 by which time it was too late to make a difference."
> —George A. McLean, Jr.

A Pivotal Year

At the beginning of 1861, J. Edgar Thomson was president of the Pennsylvania Railroad, and Thomas Scott was vice president.

Andrew Carnegie, age 25, was superintendent of the Pittsburgh Division of the Pennsylvania Railroad, and his brother, Tom, age 16, was his secretary.

Robert Pitcairn, age 24, and his brother John, age 19, were also working for the PRR, Robert in Altoona and John in Philadelphia.

By the end of 1861, the American Civil War had changed everything.

Abraham Lincoln Elected President

On November 6, 1860, Abraham Lincoln was elected the 16th president of the United States. But the states were far from united. Lincoln won in 16 northern free states as well as California and Oregon. However, he carried just two of the 996 counties in the southern slave states.[1]

The southern states would not accept Lincoln as their president. On December 20, 1860, South Carolina seceded from the United States. Mississippi, Florida, Alabama, Georgia, Louisiana, and Texas followed suit in January and February 1861.

Lincoln's aide, John Nicolay, reported, "His mail was infested with brutal and vulgar menace, and warnings of all sorts came to him from zealous or nervous friends."[2]

To get from his Springfield, Illinois, home to Washington, D.C., for his planned March 4, 1861, inauguration, Lincoln would travel by rail. He publicized his route and timing so the public could see their new president. All went well for the first part of the trip. Lincoln arrived at the Continental Hotel (later the site of the Benjamin Franklin Hotel and now a ballroom and 412-unit luxury apartment building) in Philadelphia on February 21. Detective Allan Pinkerton and Samuel Felton, president of the Philadelphia, Wilmington, and Baltimore Railroad (PW&BRR), had learned from separate sources of a plot to assassinate Lincoln. Felton's spy had warned of a "deep-laid conspiracy to capture Washington, destroy all the avenues leading to it from the North, East, and West, and thus prevent the inauguration of Mr. Lincoln in the Capitol of the country."[3]

For his trip from Philadelphia to Washington, Lincoln would have to pass through Baltimore, a town split by violent forces opposed to and in favor of slavery. In those early days of railroading, multiple rail companies serving a single city often established separate terminals with no connecting railroad tracks. That was the case in Baltimore. Lincoln initially planned to travel from Philadelphia to Baltimore's Calvert Street Station on a PW&BRR train. From there, the train cars would be separately hauled by horse teams to the Baltimore and Ohio Railroad's Camden Station, where the train would be reassembled behind a B&O engine to complete the journey to Washington. Pinkerton and Felton were sure that any attack would occur while horses pulled Lincoln's train car through Baltimore.

Pinkerton developed an elaborate plan to fool the plotters, complete with decoy carriages, false identities, and disguises. He would move Lincoln through Baltimore ahead of the published schedule.

But before departing for Washington, Lincoln had committed to raising the American flag over Independence Hall in Philadelphia and then going to Harrisburg to address the Pennsylvania Legislature there.

John Pitcairn, Jr., assistant to the superintendent of the Philadelphia Division of the PRR, accompanied Lincoln on his journey and gave a first-person report.

> We left for Harrisburg by a special train of two cars, in which were Mr. Lincoln and quite a number of prominent politicians. [After the ceremonies in Harrisburg], Towards dusk a closed carriage was taken to a public road crossing about a mile east of Harrisburg, where I was waiting with a locomotive and an ordinary passenger car. [The] carriage drove up, out of which stepped Mr. Franciscus [Pitcairn's boss], Enoch Lewis, the Division Superintendent of the PRR, Mr. Lincoln, and his intimate friend, Col. Ward M. Lamon, all of whom entered the car. I called the flagman, and we started for Philadelphia. The car was not lighted except by a lantern which I carried.
>
> The next stop was at Downington to take water, where all the gentlemen, excepting Mr. Lincoln, stepped out for a sandwich and a cup of coffee. I asked Mr. Lincoln if I could bring him anything, and he requested me to bring him a cup of tea and a roll.
>
> [Pitcairn's story continues:] We then proceeded to West Philadelphia—where Allan Pinkerton was waiting with a carriage into which Mr. Lincoln, Col. Lamon and Mr. Pinkerton stepped, and were driven to Broad and Pine Street Station. Mr. Lincoln occupied a section of a Woodruff Sleeping Car, arriving incognito in Washington early the following morning, greatly to the relief of the few persons who were in the secret, as well as to the public at large.[4]

Lincoln passed through Baltimore in his sleeping car at 3:00 a.m., at a different time, on a different train, and arriving at a different station than expected. The plotters were foiled, at least this time. On March 4, 1861, Abraham Lincoln was inaugurated as the 16th president of the United States.[5]

From left: Allan Pinkerton, President Abraham Lincoln, and Major General John Alexander McClernand at Antietam, Maryland, during the Civil War, 1862 (Library of Congress).

Beginning of the Civil War

Just 39 days later, at 4:30 a.m. on April 12, 1861, Confederate General Pierre Gustav Toutant Beauregard commenced bombarding Fort Sumter in the harbor of Charleston, South Carolina. That dramatic action changed years of talk and opinions into decisions and actions and triggered the American Civil War. After 34 hours of shelling, Major Robert Anderson surrendered Fort Sumter. Virginia, Arkansas, Tennessee, and North Carolina joined the seceding states. West Virginia separated from Virginia in 1863 and became a Union state.

Importance of Railroads

No other means of transportation could match the carrying capacity, speed, reliability, and cost of railroads. Compared to steamships, trains could carry almost

50 times as much freight and reach far more locations because their routes were more direct and not limited to rivers.

In addition to its advantages in human, natural, and industrial resources, the North had over 21,000 miles of rail tracks, while the South barely exceeded 9,000 miles.

Moreover, the North had a single railroad gauge, while the South had two different and incompatible ones. Gauge is the distance between tracks, with "standard gauge" being 4 feet, 8½ inches and "broad gauge" being 5 feet. Most Virginia and North Carolina railroads were standard gauge, while most other southern states used broad-gauge rails. Also, when two or more railroads served a city, as we saw earlier in Baltimore, they usually had their own terminals, which might be separated by many miles. For example, the Confederate capital of Richmond was served by six railroads, but not one interchanged with another, so moving supplies by rail required removing them from one set of railcars, transporting them by wagon, and reloading them onto the next set of cars.[6]

Union General William Tecumseh Sherman wrote in his 1875 memoirs about the vital role of the railroads in his Atlanta campaign:

> Our trains from Nashville forward were operated under military rules, and ran about ten miles an hour in gangs of four trains of ten cars each. Four such groups of trains daily made one hundred and sixty cars, of ten tons each, carrying sixteen hundred tons, which exceeded the absolute necessity of the army, and allowed for the accidents that were common and inevitable. But, as I have recorded, that single stem of railroad, four hundred and seventy-three miles long, supplied an army of one hundred thousand men and thirty-five thousand animals for the period of one hundred and ninety-six days, viz., from May 1 to November 12, 1864. To have delivered regularly that amount of food and forage by ordinary wagons would have required thirty-six thousand eight hundred wagons of six mules each, allowing each wagon to have hauled two tons twenty miles each day, a simple impossibility in roads such as then existed in that region of country. Therefore, I reiterate that the Atlanta campaign was an impossibility without these railroads; and only then, because we had the men and means to maintain and defend them, in addition to what were necessary to overcome the enemy.[7]

The Pennsylvania Railroad During the Civil War

The Union government and the Pennsylvania Railroad immediately took steps to ensure safe and efficient transportation. Newly inaugurated President Lincoln called for 75,000 volunteers to augment the 16,000-man Union Army. Troops from the northern states started moving, primarily by railroad, to answer the call.

On April 17, 1861, U.S. Secretary of War Simon Cameron asked J. Edgar Thomson, president of the PRR, to personally manage the transportation of troops and munitions bound for Washington, D.C., via the PRR. On the same day, Pennsylvania governor Andrew Curtin summoned Tom Scott, vice president of the PRR, to Harrisburg to establish a military telegraph in the governor's office. Curtin placed Scott in charge of all railroads and troop movements in the state.

Controlling possession of and transporting arms and ammunition was a priority for both Union and Confederate forces. On April 17, 1861, a Virginia (Confederate) militia unit left Richmond with the objective of seizing the federal arsenal at Harpers Ferry, then in Virginia.

Eighteen months earlier, on October 16, 1859, abolitionist John Brown had unsuccessfully attempted the same feat. Brown's band of 22 men was thwarted by a company of U.S. Marines led by Colonel Robert E. Lee. Brown was convicted of treason and murder and hanged on December 2, 1859.

The Virginia militiamen were also unsuccessful in capturing the arsenal. The federal garrison stationed there set fire to the arsenal before fleeing, so the Virginia troops were able to occupy Harpers Ferry but captured no armaments.

Arms and ammunition were also critical for the Union forces. The primary storage location for weapons and ammunition in the Middle Atlantic region was the Allegheny U.S. Arsenal between 39th and 40th Streets in the Strip District of Pittsburgh.

On April 20, 1862, on orders from Major Fitz John Porter, Scott telegraphed Andrew Carnegie to send arms and armaments from the arsenal, along with volunteer troops, to Harrisburg. Carnegie arranged for the requested arms shipment and transportation to Harrisburg for 1,100 volunteers from Ohio.[8]

On September 17, 1862, just five months after the arms and armaments left the arsenal, a massive explosion likely caused by a spark from a horse's iron horseshoe rocked Allegheny Arsenal. Three thunderous explosions subsequently destroyed the laboratory, where women, girls, and boys produced 128,000 rifle cartridges daily. In Pittsburgh's deadliest industrial accident and the Civil War's worst civilian disaster, 78 people died.[9]

Trouble at Baltimore

Maryland was a critical state, as it controlled access to the Union capital at Washington, D.C. But the state's population was split, with strong sympathizers on both the Union and Confederate sides. Baltimore in particular became a battleground, with troop movement to Washington stopped by southern partisans who established blockades, ripped up tracks, and burned bridges along the route from Baltimore to Annapolis Junction.

The chaos around Baltimore necessitated an alternate route from the north to Washington. J. Edgar Thomson proposed a rail route from Philadelphia southwest to Perryville, Maryland; then by steamship down the Chesapeake Bay to Annapolis; then by existing railroad lines to Annapolis Junction and finally to Washington. Secretary of War Simon Cameron adopted that plan and on April 27, 1861, placed PRR vice president Tom Scott in charge of railroads between Annapolis and Washington. One of Scott's first actions was to send for four young PRR telegraphers who formed the nucleus of the Army's Telegraph Corps.

Scott also sent for Andrew Carnegie, who joined him at the end of April. Carnegie and his crew repaired the line from Annapolis to Annapolis Junction and ensured it was suitable for heavy trains.[10]

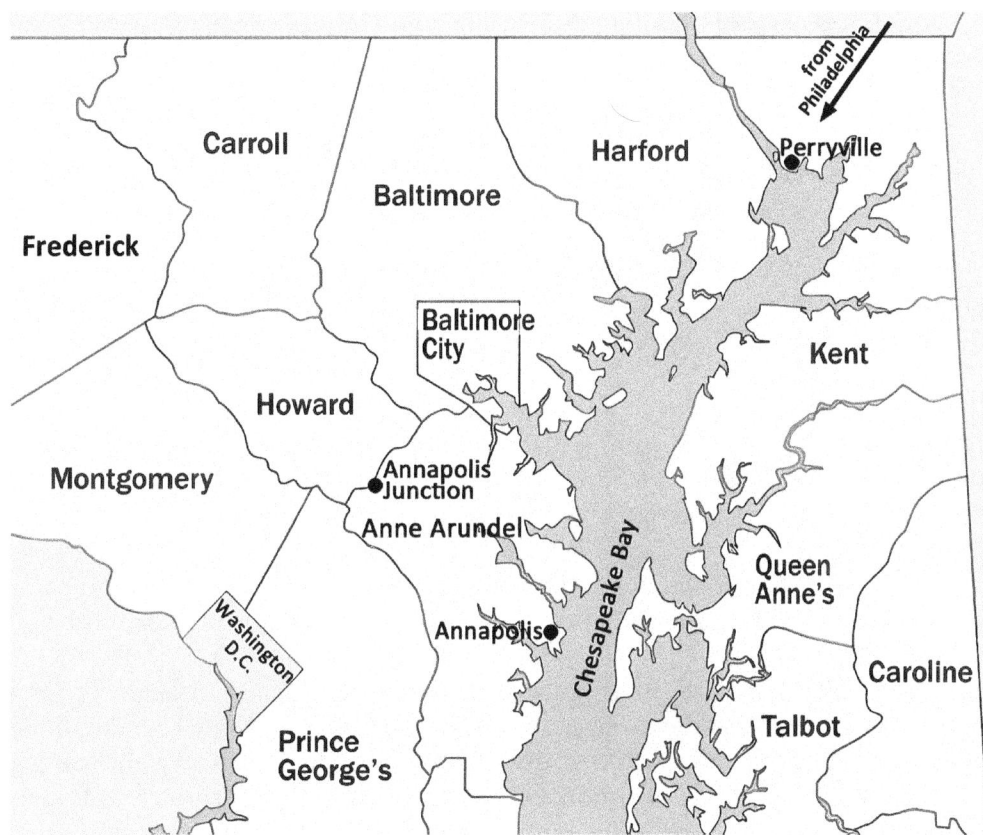

The alternate route to Washington from Philadelphia, avoiding Baltimore, was via Perryville, Baltimore City, Annapolis Junction, Annapolis, and Washington, D.C. (created by author).

Scott Becomes a Soldier

To give him military standing, Simon Cameron appointed Tom Scott as colonel in the District of Columbia Volunteers on May 3, 1861.

On May 4, the Maryland Senate effectively ended the state's secessionist movement by rejecting a bill creating a bogus Committee of Public Safety. On May 7, the Baltimore & Ohio Railroad resumed regular train service between Baltimore and Washington. On May 16, service expanded to four daily round trips, with two connecting to Philadelphia and New York trains.

On May 23, Secretary Cameron gave Tom Scott control of all U.S. military railroads and telegraphs. Scott placed Andrew Carnegie in charge of two Maryland railroad lines, one from Washington to Relay, Maryland, and one from Annapolis to Annapolis Junction.[11]

On August 1, 1861, Cameron named Thomas Scott assistant secretary of war in charge of the Transportation Department. Scott appointed Andrew Carnegie as his assistant in Washington, D.C. In *Lincoln in the Telegraph Office*, David Homer Bates recalls,

When Carnegie reached Washington his first task was to establish a ferry to Alexandria and to extend the Baltimore and Ohio Railroad track from the old depot in Washington, along Maryland Avenue to and across the Potomac, so that locomotives and cars might be crossed for use in Virginia. Long Bridge, over the Potomac, had to be rebuilt, and I recall the fact that under the direction of Carnegie and R.F. Morley the railroad between Washington and Alexandria was completed in the remarkably short period of seven days. All hands, from Carnegie down, worked day and night to accomplish the task.[12]

In late August 1861, Carnegie requested to end his military assignments. Scott approved the request, and Carnegie returned to the PRR Western Division in Pittsburgh.[13]

On September 25, 1861, the PRR board of directors granted Tom Scott an indefinite leave of absence so he could continue in his government post. But in January 1862, President Lincoln replaced Secretary of War Simon Cameron with Edwin M. Stanton. Stanton took office on January 20 and, opposite to Cameron, favored the B&O Railroad over the PRR. Under Stanton, Tom Scott was gradually marginalized.

On May 10, 1862, Scott notified Stanton that he would resign as assistant secretary of war effective June 1, but he retained his military status until he retired on October 22, 1863.[14]

While still in office, Scott assigned Robert and John Pitcairn to Chambersburg to manage the trains on the Cumberland Valley Railroad (CVRR), which the Union government had taken over. Robert dispatched trains during the day and John at night. Tens of thousands of Union soldiers traveled from Harrisburg to Hagerstown via the CVRR. The Pitcairn brothers remained at their critical posts for several months. After the CVRR assignment, the Pitcairns returned to their regular PRR posts, John as assistant to the superintendent of the Philadelphia Division of the PRR under George Franciscus and Robert as superintendent of the PRR Middle Division.[15]

Death of a President

The Civil War ended on April 9, 1865. Less than one week later, on April 15, John Wilkes Booth assassinated President Abraham Lincoln at Ford's Theatre. The train carrying Lincoln's body, along with that of his son, Willie, who had died of typhoid fever in 1862, left Washington, D.C., on April 21, 1865. At each stop, Lincoln's casket was taken off the train and placed on a horse-drawn hearse that carried it to a public building for viewing. In Philadelphia, Lincoln's body lay in state in the east wing of Independence Hall.[16]

As the dispatcher for the Philadelphia Division of the PRR, John Pitcairn would have routed Lincoln's train through eastern Pennsylvania. The 20-year-old John Pitcairn had helped carry Lincoln to his inauguration in 1861; now, at age 24, he helped convey Lincoln's body to his Springfield, Illinois, funeral in 1865.

More Responsibility

On April 1, 1865, Andrew Carnegie resigned as superintendent of the Pittsburgh Division of the Pennsylvania Railroad. On that same day, Robert Pitcairn was named successor to his friend in that prestigious and challenging position.

John Pitcairn was also given more responsibility. In mid-1866, he was promoted to assistant superintendent of the Middle Division of the PRR, with headquarters in Harrisburg. In the Pennsylvania capital, John learned the intricacies of state government and found time to attend cultural presentations in Harrisburg, Pittsburgh, Philadelphia, and New York City. Moreover, with an open train ticket, he could visit all of these cities at a moment's notice.

John especially enjoyed Philadelphia, where he renewed his friendships with the Swedenborgian believers, including Dr. George R. Starkey and Dr. Rudolph Leonhard Tafel, an eminent Swedenborgian scholar. He also met Rudolph's younger brother, Louis Hermann Tafel, a producer of homeopathic medicines.

7

John: Railroads, Oil and Church

> *"I do not think that there is any other quality so essential to success of any kind as the quality of perseverance.*
> *It overcomes almost everything, even nature."*
> —John D. Rockefeller

After the Civil War, Andrew and Thomas Carnegie moved from the Pennsylvania Railroad to concentrate their attention on the iron and steel industry. At the same time, the Pitcairn brothers, Robert and John, retained their focus on railroads.

On April 1, 1865, Robert replaced Andrew Carnegie as superintendent of the Pittsburgh Division of the Pennsylvania Railroad.

On April 10, 1866, John was named assistant superintendent of the Middle Division of the Pennsylvania Railroad with his office in Harrisburg. After a year in that position, John was promoted to Superintendent of the Middle Division of the Philadelphia and Erie Railroad (P&E RR), a branch of the PRR with headquarters at Renovo in north-central Pennsylvania.[1]

John Pitcairn's new assignment proved to be a challenge. The Middle Division of the P&E RR extended from Lock Haven, near the center of Pennsylvania, northwest through Warren, where the Western Division continued to the port of Erie on Lake Erie. Much of the route was mountainous and sparsely populated, making it both scenic and challenging to maintain. Tracks alongside creeks at the bottom of narrow mountain valleys were prone to flooding and washouts. In addition, weak previous management left John with serious personnel issues that threatened to culminate in a strike. Once advertised as "the resort town in the mountains,"[2] Renovo was not at all like Harrisburg, Pittsburgh, or Philadelphia, where John had enjoyed unlimited cultural activities. Instead, it was a small town with a peak population of 5,000, almost all of whom depended on the railroad for their livelihoods.

But with the enthusiasm characteristic of a 26-year-old, John Pitcairn got to work. To familiarize himself with the terrain, he walked the entire length of the Middle Division, 145 miles, across bridges, through tunnels, and past a multitude of small towns and villages on the route. He repeated this journey twice each year, looking for potential trouble spots and devising workarounds. John also met and talked with the conductors and brakemen as he rode in the coaches; in the engines, he listened to the engineers and firemen. When he encountered problems, with either the physical plant or the personnel, he took action. For example, he fired a dispatcher for stealing a barrel of flour, and in October 1867, one engineer was let go for immorality and two more for "fast and reckless running."[3]

A minor fire on a train entering Renovo impacted John's future. Two cars carrying oil from the booming oil region in nearby Venango County caught fire when their axle bearings overheated (a condition commonly called a "hotbox"). As tank cars were not yet in use, the oil was probably carried in wooden tubs or barrels. The resulting fire lit up Renovo but did little damage. However, it did make John Pitcairn aware of the riches starting to flow from the western Pennsylvania wells.

John was frugal but recognized a potentially profitable investment when he saw one. From his close association with railroads, he realized that coal was a commodity in continuous demand. West of Renovo was the German Catholic town of St. Mary's, home of the St. Mary's Coal Company. Pitcairn initially bought 800 shares of the company and later 2,000 more.

The New Jerusalem Church

In 1849, when John Pitcairn was just eight years old and living in Allegheny City, he had been baptized as a member of the New Jerusalem Church. The New Church, as it was often called, followed the principles extensively documented by Emanuel Swedenborg. Since his baptism, John had continued to delve into Swedenborg's writings.

John's quest for knowledge was aided when a pastor of the New Church, William Benade, arrived in Pittsburgh in 1864 and established a church on the second floor of a building at Wood and Sixth Streets. John Pitcairn and William Benade would become close friends and dominant figures in the growth of the New Church in the U.S. and abroad.

John Pitcairn Promotes the New Church

In July 1868, John took his first extended break from work to visit Canada and New England before attending the General Convention of the New Jerusalem Church in Portland, Maine. While near Ottawa, he visited his mother's sisters, his Aunts Mary and Sallie McEwan. After noting their advanced ages and spartan living conditions, John wrote to them, saying, "I have been thinking considerably of you, and [conclude] that you are not as comfortably off as you might be. You both are getting too advanced in years to do much work, and I propose to make you an allowance of $100 each to be sent twice a year on the first of January and the first of July."[4] The aunts gratefully accepted John's offer.

At the New Jerusalem General Convention, John arranged for Dr. N.C. Burnham, a New Church minister, to come to Renovo to deliver three lectures on New Church theology. On March 3–5, 1869, Dr. Burnham presented his sermons at the

Ladies' Waiting Room of the Renovo railroad station, the finest meeting hall in town. At least two Renovo families joined the New Church as a result.

Another Railroad

John Pitcairn's transformation of the Middle Division of the Philadelphia and Erie Railroad did not go unnoticed. In May 1869, President Edward F. Gay of the nearby Oil Creek and Allegheny River Railroad offered John the position of general manager of that railroad at a salary of $3,600 per year. After consulting with his older brother, Robert, John accepted the offer, even though it was 10 percent below what he had requested.[5]

Upon John's return to Renovo at 5:00 a.m. on July 3, he was surprised and delighted to find 200 employees of the P&E RR gathered in the Ladies' Waiting Room of the railroad station to send him off in style. After speeches and ceremonies, John was presented with a gold watch and chain, which he proudly wore for the rest of his life.

In typical fashion, John invited all to dine with him the following evening. About 50 came to eat, hear speeches, sing, and laugh at "recitations by J. Pitcairn, Jr." The celebration closed with the great Scottish song, *Auld Lang Syne*.[6]

The Oil Creek and Allegheny River Railroad, usually referred to as the Oil Creek, resulted from the merger of three small railroads on January 2, 1868. Its main line consisted of 17 miles of super-broad-gauge rails (six feet wide instead of the "standard" gauge of 4 feet, 8½ inches) between Corry and Titusville, Pennsylvania. The tracks were laid in a tremendous hurry, through an unbroken forest. Excavations and heavy earthworks were things not to be thought

Gold watch presented to John Pitcairn upon his retirement as superintendent of the Middle Division of the Philadelphia and Erie RR. Mr. W.R. Forsyth, chief clerk of the railroad, offered this dedication: "During your residence amongst us, your official intercourse with the employees has been no less so from the firm, quiet, gentlemanly and unostentatious manner of its performance; and while the former has brought its merited promotion, the latter has no less won the esteem of those with whom you have had to deal" (photo by the author; courtesy of Cairnwood Estate).

of. With but trifling exceptions, the track is laid on the surface of the ground, and follows its inequities. When a ravine was struck, the line made a detour around its head, if possible, rather than cross it on bridge, trestle or embankment. If an obstinate stump resisted the muscle of the shovel brigade and the ingenuity of the gang-master, it was suffered to stand still in its sulkiness, and the track was laid around it. Such up-hill, down-hill, twisting and turning have rarely been seen in railroad engineering. But the road pays, and that is the main point.[7]

Railroad historian James B. Stevenson described the success of the Oil Creek road: "During its first 14 months, the Oil Creek carried nearly a half-million filled barrels of oil, ... 22,227 tons of merchandise and almost 60,000 passengers." "The elated directors of the Oil Creek declared their first annual dividend—a whopping 25 percent."[8]

The Oil Creek was still growing when John Pitcairn took over, and it added 50 miles of track in 1869 to serve the burgeoning oil extraction industry. Stevenson reported, "Oil derricks lined the hills every foot of the way down the valley to the Miller Farm, about 3½ miles south of Titusville."[9]

While in Pittsburgh to attend church on a Sunday in August 1869, John, probably at the suggestion of his brother, Robert, examined the recent invention of young George Westinghouse, the air brake. Westinghouse had just launched his Westinghouse Air Brake Company to manufacture the system that would become standard on all trains in the coming years and fundamentally transform transportation worldwide. John Pitcairn wrote in his journal that he "can speak for its perfect success."[10] However, there is no record of whether he installed air brakes on his railroad.

The oil boom was so important that the president of the United States, Ulysses S. Grant, came to northwestern Pennsylvania to inspect the source of the excitement. On

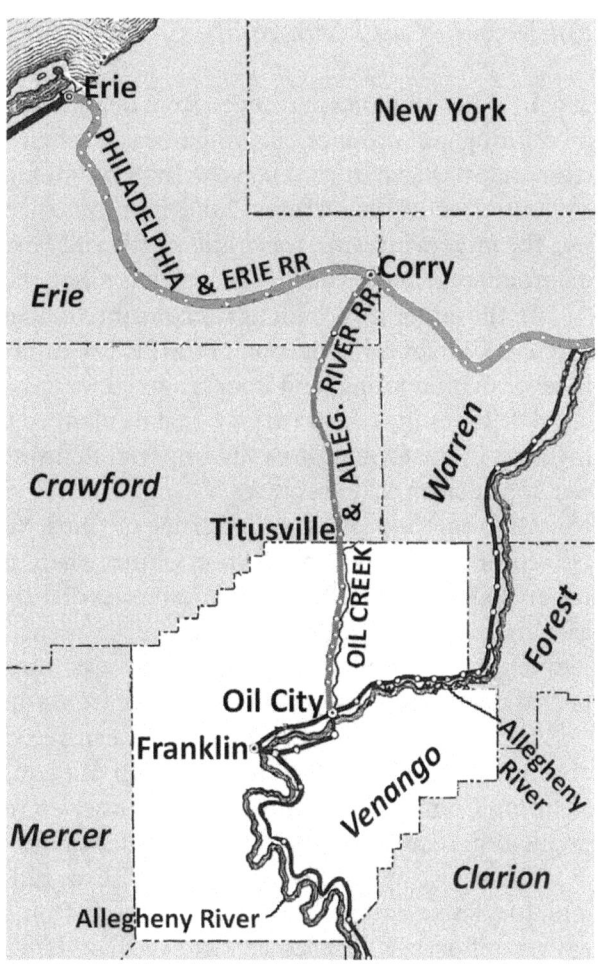

Route of the Oil Creek & Allegheny River RR, from Oil City, Pennsylvania, in the south to Corry, on the Philadelphia & Erie RR, in the north (1871 map adapted by the author).

September 14, 1871, John Pitcairn met Grant's coach at Corry, where John's Oil Creek RR met the Philadelphia and Erie RR. Grant, his family, and his entourage joined Pitcairn on a special train bound for Oil City. The train stopped to greet crowds in Titusville, Petroleum Center, Columbia, Rouseville, and Oil City. Unlike his predecessor, Abraham Lincoln, Grant was no orator; he gave the same speech at every stop.

> Fellow citizens—I feel very grateful to you for this kind reception. This is my first visit to the Oil Regions. I am aware that this section of the country furnished its full share of men and means for the suppression of the rebellion, and your efforts in the discovery and production of petroleum aided materially in supplying the sinews of war, as a medium of exchange, taking the place of cotton. You are aware that this is a much longer speech than I usually make. I again return you my thanks.[11]

Oil Refining and Monopolies

In 1870, John Pitcairn moved from being a railroad employee to a partner in two oil refining and production companies. The first, of which John was president and treasurer, was a venture called the Imperial Refining Company located in Oil City. The initial facility could refine 2,000 barrels of oil per day. The second, in which John was the largest investor, was Vandergrift and Forman Company, which focused on oil production and owned 90 oil well lots along the Allegheny River.

In the fall of 1871, John again consulted Robert, who was superintendent of the Western (Pittsburgh) Division of the PRR. John wanted to exit the railroad business in favor of oil refining, and Robert agreed with that decision. John informed the Oil Creek RR president, Edward Gay, that he planned to leave the railroad. Gay, who was involved in the formation of the Imperial Refining Company, confided that he, too, was considering other ventures.

Oil from the ground, called crude oil, must be refined to create useful products. Oil refining dates back to 512 AD in China, where refined crude oil was used for heating and lubricants. More modern refineries distill crude oil into petroleum naphtha, gasoline, diesel fuel, asphalt, heating oil, kerosene, liquefied petroleum, and jet fuel.[12] Refineries are enormous, capital-intensive ventures, and crude oil is typically transported to refineries a significant distance from where it comes out of the ground.

In John Pitcairn's day, a few refineries existed in the midwest (principally around Cleveland) and in the oil region of Pennsylvania (such as John's Imperial Refining Company). However, most refineries were clustered around the eastern population centers of New York and Philadelphia.

Transporting oil was big business. Three railroads shared in hauling crude oil and, to a lesser extent, refined oil products from the Pennsylvania oil fields to the eastern refineries: Tom Scott's PRR; William H. Vanderbilt's New York Central; and Jay Gould's Erie Railroad. In addition, smaller feeder railroads, such as John Pitcairn's Oil Creek, carried crude oil from the wells to those three trunk railroads.

With hundreds of wells shipping oil over multiple feeder railroads, then onto the three trunk railroads, and finally to about 80 competing refineries, the situation was chaotic. To bring order to the confusion, in late 1871, John D. Rockefeller of the Standard Oil Company and Tom Scott of the PRR proposed that the leading refiners combine to control the oil trade. The combine, confusingly called the South Improvement Company (SIC), would feed oil on a quota basis to the three trunk railroads. The PRR would receive and ship 45 percent of the oil, while the New York Central and Erie Railroads would each handle 27.5 percent. In turn, the railroads would provide rebates to reduce the cost of shipping. Refiners not in the combine would receive no such rebates and would be forced to pay kickbacks or drawbacks to the refiners in the combine.

For example, SIC-member refiners would pay $1.50 to ship one barrel of crude oil from the oil region in Pennsylvania to refiners in New York City. Non-SIC refiners would pay $2.56 to ship a barrel, and $1.06 of that amount would return to the SIC treasury to be divided among SIC refiners. No refiner not part of the South Improvement Company could survive under those conditions.[13] Furthermore, SIC would limit oil production, as refining capacity of 40,000 barrels per day far exceeded the market demand of 16,000 barrels.

By today's standards and laws, the South Improvement Company was illegally restraining trade. While possibly "legal" in 1871, it certainly violated free and open competition as practiced in the United States. To avoid adverse public reaction, all members were sworn to secrecy. Participants were required to sign a pledge of confidentiality:

> I, (name), do faithfully promise upon my honour and faith as a gentleman that I will keep secret all transactions which I may have with the corporation known as the South Improvement Company; that, should I fail to complete any bargains with the said company, all the preliminary conversations shall be kept strictly private; and, finally, that I will not disclose the price for which I dispose of my product, or any other facts which may in any way bring to light the internal workings or organization of the company. All this I do freely promise. Witnessed by _____ Signed _____.[14]

But with so many people participating, the plans of the SIC were bound to leak, and they did.[15]

John Pitcairn was conflicted. As the PRR was part owner of the Oil Creek RR and Tom Scott of the PRR was one of the founders of the South Improvement Company, Pitcairn might be expected to support the SIC. Furthermore, as president of the Imperial Refining Company, John could have joined the SIC as a refiner and profited from the power of the organization. But his ties were to the people of the oil region. If the SIC had its way, the small refiners of the area would be forced into bankruptcy, and the oil producers would have to ship their oil according to quotas set by the SIC. John's emotional ties to the region won out over pure business considerations. So he refused to join the SIC and resolved to fight to kill it.

The Pennsylvania oil fields drilled 100 new wells per month at an average cost of $6,000 each. Existing wells produced six million barrels of oil per year, much of which was sent worldwide, making oil the fourth-ranked export of the country. That production supported a population of 30,000 people.

On February 20, 1872, news that an outside organization, the South Improvement Company, was attempting to control the refining and transportation of oil from the producers in the Venango County region of Pennsylvania broke into the open.

In her iconic *History of the Standard Oil Company*, Ida Tarbell wrote, "a big hand reached out from nobody knew where, to steal their conquest and throttle their future. The suddenness and the blackness of the assault on their business stirred to the bottom their manhood and their sense of fair play, and the whole region arose in a revolt which is scarcely paralleled in the commercial history of the United States."[16]

A meeting of oil producers and area citizens held at Tidioute, Pennsylvania, on February 26, 1872, produced the following resolution:

> *Resolved*, that we producers and citizens of this section are fully determined to devote our entire energies and means from now on to defeat the machinations of the "South Improvement Co." and that we will leave no stone unturned and exhaust all our resources to that end, and that we pick up the gage of battle, thrown down by this gigantic monopoly, and we will fight it out on that line if it takes all summer.[17]

At another mass meeting in Oil City on March 1, John Pitcairn made an extraordinary offer. With the concurrence of President Edward Gay, John offered to sell the Oil Creek and Allegheny River Railroad to the oil producers and refiners for less than it would cost them to build a new railroad. Such a purchase would give the oilmen control of their transportation and blunt the impact of the South Improvement Company.

The General Committee that had been organized to fight the South Improvement Company adopted the following actions:

- No new oil wells; stop those in progress;
- Withhold oil from the market for 60 days;
- Ship no oil on railroads associated with the South Improvement Company; and
- Refine oil region oil locally, not in Cleveland or New York.[18]

Of course, withholding oil from the market and refusing to ship via South Improvement railroads was costly for the oil producers but also put enormous pressure on the railroads and refiners of the SIC. One report said that employment at Rockefeller's Standard Oil Company dropped from 1,200 to just 70 because of the oil producers' boycott.[19]

On March 11, 1872, a petition bearing the names of 5,000 oil producers, refiners, and shippers was sent to the Pennsylvania Legislature in Harrisburg, calling for passage of a free pipe bill promoting the construction of oil pipelines to compete with the trunk railroads.

Throughout March, John Pitcairn participated in a flurry of public mass meetings and private conferences with Tom Scott and Alexander Cassatt of the PRR, William H. Vanderbilt of the New York Central, and General George B. McClellan of the Erie Railroad. Finally, on March 28, the railroads realized that the grand plan to monopolize oil transportation was doomed to failure and canceled their contracts with the South Improvement Company. On April 2, the Pennsylvania Legislature repealed the charter for the SIC and approved the construction of a pipeline to carry oil from the oil regions to remote refineries. After its tumultuous 29-day life, the South Improvement Company was dead.

The King Is Dead! Long Live the King!

The stated aim of the South Improvement Company was to substitute order for the chaos that existed in the production, transportation, and refining of oil. However, with the SIC gone, the chaos remained. To address that issue, an existing confederation, the National Refiners' Association, would emerge in April 1872 with a more comprehensive charter. The NRA board would buy crude oil, allot each refinery a quota, and negotiate with the railroads for uniform rates.

Who better to run the National Refiners' Association than consummate oil tycoon and businessman John D. Rockefeller? The head of the Standard Oil Company now had his nose under the tent of the Pennsylvania oil producers and refiners.

Meanwhile, John Pitcairn realized his desire to move from railroading to oil refining. In a series of transactions starting on July 29, 1872, the Oil Creek and Allegheny River RR became the Allegheny River RR on September 4. John was no longer an employee but was now a partner in the Imperial Refining Company and the oil production firm of Vandergrift & Forman. In November, the latter company started building oil and natural gas pipelines, including the first gas pipeline into Pittsburgh.

As Pitcairn's interests moved from oil refining to his New Jerusalem Church, he decided to sell Imperial Refining. The obvious candidate to buy was the Standard Oil Company, so John broached the subject with John D. Rockefeller on January 9, 1873. Rockefeller was interested, but only at his lowball price. It took another year for Rockefeller to come around, but on January 22, 1874, John and his partner, Jacob Vandergrift, sold the refinery to Standard Oil at cost, $236,418.[20]

John Pitcairn, just turned 33 and still unmarried, was ready for domestic and international travel, increased involvement in his New Jerusalem Church, and new business opportunities.

8

Robert: Family, Railroads and Church

> *"If you want to be respected by others, the great thing is to respect yourself.*
> *Only by that, only by self-respect will you compel others to respect you."*
>
> —Fyodor Dostoevsky

Robert Pitcairn had two passions in life—his family (wife Elizabeth and their two young daughters, Agnes and Lillian) and his Pennsylvania Railroad. But in August 1866, he would add a third.

The Pitcairns and many neighboring families attended a Sunday school that had been established in Shadyside, east of Pittsburgh, on April 29, 1860. By 1863, the meetings had expanded to include Bible study and home-based prayer. But the community had grown too large to meet in members' homes. A dedicated building was needed.

On August 10, 1866, 12 men, including Robert Pitcairn, met at the home of David Aiken, Jr., to plan a new church. By the end of the meeting, they had pledged $4,550 to purchase land and erect a building for Presbyterian worship, including a "Sabbath School and a select weekday school."[1] By the end of August, pledges had doubled, a charter and constitution had been drafted, and a 1.5-acre lot had been purchased from Thomas Aiken for $3,000. On September 1, the nascent church applied to the Allegheny County Court of Common Pleas for a charter, and on September 12, a petition for the organization of a church was sent to the Presbytery of Ohio.

Without waiting for formal approvals, construction of the building that would be the first Shadyside Presbyterian Church began on August 27, 1866. Thomas Aiken was the architect. The Court granted the requested charter on September 29, 1866.

The first church building was at the corner of Amberson Avenue and Westminster Streets in Shadyside.

The Pitcairn mansion, Cairncarque, was just two blocks away on Ellsworth Avenue. *Cairn* is a Scottish word meaning a mound of rough stones, and *carque* in Scottish means conversation or gossip.

While waiting for the church building to be completed, Robert Pitcairn arranged for the congregation to use the Pennsylvania Railroad station in Shadyside for their Sunday evening worship services. They attended their home churches for

First Shadyside Presbyterian Church, circa 1890 (permission of Shadyside Presbyterian Church).

Sunday morning services. The railroad station served as a church meeting hall from September 9, 1866, until July 7, 1867. The meetings there were described as "regularly sustained, largely attended and productive of much good."[2] Music was an integral part of services, even at the railroad station. Robert was appointed choir leader.

Finally, on July 8, 1867, the church building was completed, and a large group of supporters met to consecrate the facility, which had pews to accommodate 375 people.

On March 19, 1868, Robert and Elizabeth Pitcairn welcomed a third daughter,

Cairncarque, residence of Robert Pitcairn family, Ellsworth and Amberson Avenues, Shadyside, Pittsburgh, Pennsylvania (Palmer's Pictorial Pittsburgh and Prominent Pittsburghers, 1905).

Susan Blanche Pitcairn, to their family. It had been almost ten years since the birth of their previous child, so household routines had to be adjusted for the infant.

Perhaps the additional responsibilities of having a young child caused Robert to tender his resignation as choir leader exactly one year after his appointment, on July 7, 1868. But two days later, the minutes of the Session (the ruling body of Shadyside Presbyterian Church) record: "The resignation of Mr. R. Pitcairn as leader of the choir was received—and after due consideration it was resolved not to accept it, but that he be continued leader of the choir, with authority to employ an organist subject to the approval of the Session."[3]

Six months later, at the Session meeting of January 28, 1869, Robert's resignation was accepted, with the following commendation, "Resolved that in accepting the resignation of Mr. Pitcairn as leader of the choir, we hereby express to him our appreciation of his services, in having so faithfully discharged the duties of the position assigned to him in the midst of constant and serious discouragements."[4]

Leaving the choir director post in no way signaled dissatisfaction with Shadyside Presbyterian Church. On the contrary, the Pitcairns would continue to worship there for the rest of their lives.

Continued growth in the congregation led to the construction of a second church building, which was completed in 1875. As we will see in Chapter 18, Robert became a fixture in the church's leadership.

The Shadyside Presbyterian Church of Robert Pitcairn is just 2.4 miles from the current Pittsburgh New Church that teaches the Swedenborgian theology of John Pitcairn.

Robert Pitcairn, the Man

The clearest view of Robert Pitcairn emerges in a letter he wrote to his brother, Hugh Pitcairn, on February 1, 1866. Hugh, age 20, had just been appointed superintendent of the Susquehanna Division of the Northern Central Railroad.

> Dear Hugh,
> ...I rejoice very much at your appointment and trust in my heart that you will succeed....
> "There is a tide in the affairs of men which if taken at the flood leads on to fortune and fame...." How can you take advantage of the flood? By bearing your honor meekly. Not appearing to feel your position, but still show you have confidence in your ability. Putting on no airs, but still being decided and dignified, always remembering that your youth is against you. By keeping a close mouth and not showing your ignorance. A Pitcairn can't blow, can't talk well and his only chance is in keeping quiet. By having no confidants unless it is your brother, John. By putting nothing on paper that you can't say verbally unless it is a train order. Always be careful what you write, remembering that it may appear against you when least expected. Be careful, weighing all your actions, doing nothing rash, being sure to get all the facts before you decide a question. Having no temper. You will always make a fool of yourself unless you control your temper. Having no feelings, but calmly and dispassionately weighing everything and acting earnestly and for the best interest of the company without regard to yourself.... Talking very little with the employees, but still being pleasant to them.
> Always examine your messages, reading them often and seeing if a misconstruction can be taken therefrom, trying every message to make it more pointed, more clear, and more safe. An accident would kill you. A mistake that the men or operators would discover would make them lose confidence in you, which would hurt you much.... Take no risks. In case of doubt take the safe course. The above is the amount of my fifteen years of railroad experience; it might be of benefit to you to read them morning, noon and night.
> With much love I am your affectionate brother,
> Robert[5]

Hugh Pitcairn

Hugh Pitcairn, the youngest of the Pitcairn siblings, was born in Scotland on August 16, 1845. Following the lead of his brothers Robert and John, he began his career in the railroad industry. Immediately after starting as superintendent of the Susquehanna Division of the Northern Central Railway, Hugh married Susan Frances "Fannie" Sherfy on February 7, 1866. They had two boys, but Fannie died on November 30, 1874.

Between 1868 and 1875, Hugh held superintendent positions with the Lehigh and Susquehanna Railroad (two years), the Evansville, Henderson and Nashville Railroad (two years), and the Pittsburgh, Cincinnati, and St. Louis Railroad (three years).

In 1875, his diverse interests led him to purchase a half interest in the *Altoona Tribune*, a Pennsylvania daily newspaper. In the same year, he undertook the study of medicine at Hahnemann Medical College in Philadelphia.

On June 7, 1876, while studying at Hahnemann, Hugh Pitcairn married Anna Monroe "Annie" Sherfy, the sister of his first wife. Hugh and Annie had five children:

four boys followed by a lone girl. After finishing at Hahnemann, Hugh moved to the Universities of Berlin and Vienna for two years of postgraduate study. He and his family then returned to Pennsylvania, where he practiced medicine in Harrisburg until 1897.

On July 28, 1897, President William McKinley appointed Hugh as consul at Hamburg, Germany. President Theodore Roosevelt promoted him to the post of consul general to Hamburg on January 5, 1903, the first person to serve in that position.

In November 1908, Hugh resigned from his diplomatic post to return to medical practice and his duties as majority owner of the *Altoona Tribune*. He died in Hamburg, Germany, on July 19, 1914, and is buried at Fairview Cemetery in Altoona.[6]

Working on the Railroad

Robert Pitcairn had replaced Andrew Carnegie as superintendent of the Pittsburgh Division of the Pennsylvania Railroad on April 1, 1865, and the Civil War ended eight days later. Building and operating railroads had become a national obsession, and Pitcairn, just 29, was in the middle of the action.

The superintendent of the Pittsburgh Division was the most critical operating position in the company. Pittsburgh was the gateway for all traffic to and from the west. The area's rivers and hilly terrain, coupled with a multitude of competing customers, including Carnegie's steel plants, added challenges unmatched anywhere on the line.

William Bender Wilson, the noted historian who wrote *History of the Pennsylvania Railroad Company*, said of Robert Pitcairn,

> [H]e was a man above the ordinary and was able to solve (the challenges) and make of the division a powerful agency in the development of the commonwealth. [H]e started out on the principle that while the executive officer should hold a firm grasp on the reins of power he should administer the affairs of the division in the spirit of co-operation and co-ordination. One of his earliest moves was permanently instituting a meeting with his staff for conference, to be held weekly.... In these meetings he listened to reports and suggestions, heard criticisms and advised, instructed and directed. This conference was practically a school of the railroad that advised the superintendent, broadened the staff and established a standard of excellence.[7]

Robert Pitcairn had grown up in the railroad business, and he recognized a technical advancement when he saw one, so when he heard about a new way of stopping trains called an air brake, Pitcairn visited the inventor, George Westinghouse.

Pitcairn listened to Westinghouse's well-rehearsed sales pitch and said, "If I can get my people interested, I believe there is enough in the invention to be worth a fair trial."[8] Pitcairn returned soon after, this time with Superintendent Edwin Williams of the Altoona Division and Alexander Cassatt, assistant superintendent of motive power for the PRR. The railroad men agreed to provide the track, train, engineer, and crew for an air brake trial free of charge if Westinghouse would manufacture and install all of the braking equipment. The Pennsylvania Railroad was on its way to becoming the world's largest railroad, transportation company, and corporation, so convincing the "Pennsy" to convert to his air brakes would have been a monumental victory for Westinghouse. But George and his partner, Ralph Baggaley, lacked the money to build the necessary equipment.

A few months later, Westinghouse finally demonstrated his air brake system on the Panhandle Railroad from Pittsburgh to Steubenville, Ohio. Westinghouse equipped a train consisting of an engine, a tender, and four cars with his new system. On a fateful day in April 1869, the train's last car was occupied by officers of the Panhandle Company, railroad men from other lines, and guests. Westinghouse provided final instructions to the train's engineer, Daniel Tate, and wished him luck as he left the cab. As soon as Westinghouse had boarded the last car, the train started to move.

The tracks from the Panhandle Station in Pittsburgh entered a tunnel, one-sixth of a mile long, through Grant Hill, emerging at Fourth Avenue, a regular stop to pick up passengers. After two more road crossings, the tracks crossed the Monongahela River and then hit open country on the way to Steubenville. As there was to be no stop at Fourth Avenue or anywhere else en route, Tate accelerated the train to about 30 miles per hour.

Just as the train emerged from the tunnel, Tate saw a horse-drawn wagon crossing the tracks at Second Avenue. Simultaneously, the wagon driver heard and saw the approaching train just two blocks away. In a panic, the driver lashed his horses, and they reacted by lunging forward. The sudden movement dislodged the loose crosswise plank the driver was using for a seat, and he plunged to the ground across one of the rails.

Meanwhile, Tate instinctively grabbed the brake valve and twisted, just as Westinghouse had instructed him. Pressurized air coursed from the air reservoir through the hoses and to the brake cylinders on each car. The sudden increased pressure jammed the brake shoes against the wheels and, with a loud metal-on-metal screech, brought the train to an abrupt stop, just four feet from the fallen wagon driver.

Other than being frightened, the wagon driver was unharmed. Tate rushed to the rear of the train to check on his riders, including at least three levels of his bosses. All the passengers were bruised and sore from the sudden stop, some having been thrown the length of the car. But all were elated that the wagon driver was safe, and they were now convinced that the Westinghouse air brake was a rousing success.[9]

Just three months after this initial success, 22-year-old George Westinghouse filed a charter under Pennsylvania law for the Westinghouse Air Brake Company. The initial capitalization was set at $500,000. In addition to Westinghouse, the board of directors included Ralph Baggaley, Robert Pitcairn, W.W. Card, Alexander J. Cassatt, Edwin H. Williams, and G.D. Whitcomb. Pitcairn and Westinghouse became close friends and business partners.

In early 1870, the Westinghouse Air Brake Company began operations in leased space at Liberty Avenue and 25th Street in Pittsburgh. A March 1, 1871, letter from George Westinghouse to a customer lists Robert Pitcairn as treasurer of the company and Ralph Baggaley (spelled Bagaley) as secretary.*

---

* The letter is at the Detre Library and Archives in the Senator John Heinz History Center in Pittsburgh.

PRR management recognized Robert Pitcairn's capabilities and, on February 14, 1874, added "General Agent" to his "Superintendent" title. As general agent, he interacted with the company's commercial interests (customers) and all transportation lines connecting with the railroad.[10]

1874 brought another joy to the Robert Pitcairn family. On October 2, Elizabeth delivered their fourth child and first son, Robert Pitcairn, Jr.

R.P.

Robert Pitcairn wrote hundreds of letters, memos, and notes each week and soon abbreviated his signature to "R.P." His employees became comfortable greeting him as R.P. As the Pennsylvania Railroad was a dominant employer in the Pittsburgh region, he soon became R.P. to everyone. Thus, it was a term of both familiarity and respect.

Robert Pitcairn, superintendent and general agent of the Pennsylvania Railroad ("Notable Men of Pittsburgh and Vicinity" by Percy Frazier Smith, 1901).

9

Travels with John

"Don't tell me how educated you are, tell me how much you have traveled."

—Mohammed

The New Church Grows

Walter Cameron Childs and his business partner, Franklin "Frank" Ballou, were searching for a more rational and meaningful religious belief. Probably guided by John Pitcairn, Childs and Ballou found and read the two-volume treatise *True Christian Religion* by Emanuel Swedenborg. Intrigued by the writings, they contacted the Rev. William Benade, John's friend and a New Jerusalem Church minister practicing in Pittsburgh. Benade discipled Childs and Ballou and brought them into the New Church in 1870.

With the additions of John Pitcairn, Walter Childs, Franklin Ballou, and many others, Benade's New Church required a larger meeting place, so in 1873 the congregation built and dedicated a new building at Isabella and Sandusky Streets in Allegheny City, the present site of the Andy Warhol Museum. The property and structure cost $20,000. The following year, Andrew Carnegie donated his first church organ to the church. Unfortunately, the one-story building was too small for the organ, so it had to be enlarged.[1]

Today, the Swedenborgian church in Pittsburgh, called the Pittsburgh New Church, is at 299 Le Roi Road in the Point Breeze community of the city's East End.

European Tour

In early 1874, John Pitcairn sold his Imperial Refining Company to John D. Rockefeller's Standard Oil Company. In return, John and his partner, Jacob Vandergrift, each received about $53,000 in cash and 500 shares of Standard Oil stock. By 1875, the stock would be worth $285 per share, so John was well off. At 33, he was ready to see the world.[2]

On May 16, 1874, John Pitcairn and Walter Childs boarded the French steamship

Periere en route to Brest, France. With a shared faith, the cheerful and energetic Walter Childs was a perfect traveling companion for John. In preparation for the trip, John arranged for lessons in French and German for Walter and himself.

After landing in France on May 26, 1874, John and Walter toured the coast and then the wine country before arriving in Paris in mid–June. During the week of August 10, they attended the Paris conference of the New Jerusalem Church, where they encountered the Rev. Rudolph Leonhard Tafel, a New Church minister. Back in 1866, when John was working for the Pennsylvania Railroad, he had met and become friends with the Reverend Tafel in Philadelphia.

When the conference concluded, the Reverend Tafel and his wife joined John and Walter on a tour of Switzerland, Germany, and Italy. In Zurich, St. Gallen (Switzerland), and Stuttgart, the Reverend Tafel conducted services for local New Church adherents and their guests.

After the Tafels returned to London in October, Pitcairn and Childs continued their sightseeing and visits with New Church members. In Italy, John was especially impressed by Venice and a nighttime gondola ride there. Ten years later, he would share that experience with his new wife, Gertrude, on their honeymoon.

During their meetings with New Church members, a recurring discussion was how Swedenborgian beliefs should be encouraged. Their experiences, supported by the opinion of the Reverend Benade, convinced them that the Christian world would not readily accept the doctrines of the New Church. Therefore, they came to believe that the New Church could grow best by educating and indoctrinating the children of its own members in Swedenborg's teachings.

After returning to France in November, John was called home to discuss a threatened lawsuit connected to his former Imperial Refining Company. He sailed on December 9 and arrived in New York on December 21. After spending Christmas in Pittsburgh with the Reverend Benade and Franklin Ballou, John went to Oil City. There, he discovered a mistake in the Imperial Refining books and resolved it to everyone's satisfaction.

In January 1875, John Pitcairn returned to Europe to resume his vacation with Walter Childs. After stays in France, England, Scotland, and Ireland, Pitcairn and Childs sailed home, arriving in New York on May 31, 1875.[3]

Scouting the West

With the transcontinental railroad's completion in 1869, many eastern entrepreneurs began to explore opportunities in the western U.S. One of John Pitcairn's business partners, Hascal L. Taylor of Fredonia, New York, offered to pay John's expenses if he would travel west and evaluate business prospects there. Pitcairn agreed, and with his friend and fellow New Church member, Frank Ballou, left Pittsburgh by train on January 17, 1876.

After a stop in Chicago, they crossed the Mississippi River on the Government Bridge at Rock Island, Illinois, and proceeded to Omaha. They passed through the

Wyoming Territory (Wyoming would not become a state until 1890), Utah, and Nevada. Their train became snowbound in the Humboldt Mountains of northwestern Nevada. John recorded the ordeal in his diary:

> Four locomotives labored in vain to extricate us, and there we remained for over 40 hours with scarcely anything to eat. Fourteen locomotives and a gang of Chinamen finally succeeded in getting us out, and we proceeded on our way, rejoicing.[4]

The weary travelers decided to bypass their original destination, Carson City, Nevada, because of reports of heavy snow there. They continued west through the Sacramento Valley to Oakland and finally San Francisco. They arrived at the sumptuous Palace Hotel on January 27, 1876. The Palace, commissioned by famed San Francisco banker William Chapman Ralston, had opened just four months earlier, on October 2, 1875.

Tragically, on August 26, 1875, Ralston's Bank of California failed before the $5 million, 755-room Palace Hotel project was completed. The next day, Ralston drowned while swimming in San Francisco Bay.[5]

About three years after John Pitcairn's visit, in October 1878, Andrew Carnegie stayed at the Palace Hotel while on his round-the-world tour and commented:

> A palace truly! Where shall we find its equal? Windsor Hotel, good-bye! You must yield the palm to your great Western rival, as far as structure goes, though in all other respects you may keep the foremost place. There is no other hotel building in the world equal to this. The court of the Grand at Paris is poor compared to that of the Palace. Its general effect at night, when brilliantly lighted, is superb; its furniture, rooms and appointments are all fine, but then it tells you all over it was built to "whip all creation," and the millions of its lucky owner enabled him to triumph.[6]

Accompanied by a police escort, Pitcairn and Ballou toured Chinatown, where the residents were celebrating Chinese New Year. In addition to the public areas teeming with performers and noise, they visited tenements filled from cellar to roof with Chinese people living in dark and dirty rooms. After seeing a brothel and an opium den, they emerged from the darkness to sample a superb meal at a Chinese restaurant.

On Sunday, January 30, 1876, the young men attended a New Jerusalem Church and met with the pastor, the Rev. John Worcester, to discuss New Church doctrine. Then they rode the eight miles west to the Pacific Ocean by carriage for lunch, which they had at Adolph Sutro's Cliff House while watching sea lions frolic on Seal Rocks.[7]

The following day, John and Frank boarded a steamship bound for San Diego. They marveled at massive schools of fish, a whale, and "oil springs" from underwater petroleum deposits. From San Diego, they drove south to the monument marking the Mexico–U.S. boundary placed in 1848 at the end of the Mexican–American War.

On the way back north, the adventurers stopped at the booming town of Los Angeles, which had a population of 15,000. Vineyards and orchards of orange trees covered the open land, and John calculated that one grove of 2,500 trees would yield a gross income of $5,000 per year.

After returning to San Francisco and again hearing the Reverend Worcester

Seal Rocks and the Cliff House from Lands End, circa 1868 (Amon Carter Museum of American Art).

preach at the New Church, the easterners headed to their original destination, Carson City, Nevada. They arrived by train at 4:00 a.m. on February 24.

As the mining of precious metal was of particular interest to the trip's sponsor, Hascal Taylor, Pitcairn and Ballou spent a week exploring the silver mines in the area, dubbed the Comstock Lode. They donned miners' suits and descended 1,500 feet to the lowest drift of the Consolidated Virginia Mine, home of the Big Bonanza. Discovered in 1873, it was the richest strike in the 14-year history of the Comstock Lode. Thanks mainly to the Big Bonanza, 1876, the year of John and Frank's visit, saw the peak ore production from the Comstock, $38 million.[8]

The visitors found "the mines exceedingly well-ventilated, timbers whitewashed, and well-lighted with candles."[9] They clearly had visited a showcase mine, as workers in many mines on the Comstock faced temperatures so high that they could work just 15 minutes before taking 30-minute breaks to cool off with ice and ice water. Prussian immigrant Adolph Sutro worked almost nine years to provide a tunnel (completed in 1878) at the base of the mines to drain the hot water and provide a path for cool air to enter and ventilate the Comstock mines.[10]

Pitcairn and Ballou returned to San Francisco, where John had arranged to receive a one-month course in metallurgy and ore assaying from Professor Henry Garber Hanks. Hanks would later become the first state mineralogist of California. They learned how to perform accurate assays of various minerals such as gold, silver, copper, and mercury and found their ore samples from the Big Bonanza to be worth $413 per ton in gold and $405 in silver.

April and May of 1876 were again devoted to touring. The pair first traveled northeast of San Francisco to visit hot springs, geysers, and a petrified forest of giant redwood trees. Then they ventured south of San Jose to see a massive cinnabar (also called quicksilver or mercury) mine that had yielded 23,000 tons of mercury.

They headed further north on April 22, sailing up the Pacific coast to the mouth of the Columbia River between Oregon and the Washington Territory. John and

Frank viewed Mt. Hood and Mt. Rainier as well as the major towns in the area—Portland, The Dalles, Kalama, Olympia, and as far north as Victoria, British Columbia. But they were most impressed by the enormity of the Columbia River and the size of the salmon harvest there. John noted that over one million cans of salmon were shipped from Portland in 1875.

From Portland, the intrepid pair headed south by train to Roseburg, Oregon, and then 175 miles by tortuous stagecoach to Redding, California. Finally, another train returned them to San Francisco on May 11, 1876.

Just four days later, John and Frank again boarded a stagecoach, this time headed for Angel's Camp to view a gold mining operation. Angel's Camp was about ten miles south of San Andreas, the county seat of Calaveras County, and one of the earliest important gold mining centers in California.

Calaveras County was made famous by Mark Twain's 1865 short story, "The Celebrated Jumping Frog of Calaveras County." However, they saw not frogs but Sequoiadendron giganteum (giant sequoia), many over 30 feet in diameter. John called them "certainly the greatest wonder of the vegetable kingdom."[11]

They then continued on horseback to explore Yosemite Valley, where they "lunched at Glacier Point, after which we redescended and continued past El Capitan and Cathedral Rocks to Bridal Veil Falls ... [made] doubly beautiful by a brilliant rainbow, excelling in splendor anything I have witnessed."[12]

After an eventful four-and-a-half-month excursion to the western U.S., John Pitcairn and Frank Ballou boarded their train east on May 24, 1876. After a brief stop in Chicago, they arrived in Pittsburgh at 2:00 a.m. on June 2.[13]

Academy of the New Church

During the previous two years, discussions among the Rev. William Benade, Walter Childs, Frank Ballou, and John Pitcairn concluded that the New Church would not grow by recruiting members of other Christian denominations. Instead, desired growth would occur by educating and thus retaining children from families already in the New Church. To initiate that effort, the men published a series of pamphlets called *Words for the New Church*, which they circulated to the governing bodies of the New Church in the U.S. and England. The response was mixed at best.

Undaunted, supporters of the internal education approach met in New York in 1875 while attending the General Convention of the New Church. There, they created the Academy of the New Church and unanimously elected the Rev. William Benade as president. Church-sponsored schools were not new to the New Church, but the Academy would provide instruction based on the specific teachings of Swedenborg's theological works, and that emphasis was new.

On June 19, 1876, soon after John Pitcairn and Frank Ballou returned from their trip to the western U.S., President Benade provided a formal statement of purpose for the Academy. A meeting was held in Philadelphia, and following a holy ceremony, the 12 Academy founders who were present signed the document. Upon the official founding of the Academy, three ministers started teaching nine young theology students in their homes. Dr. N.C. Burnham taught in Lancaster, Pennsylvania; the Rev. Louis Hermann Tafel (younger brother of the Rev. Rudolph Leonhard Tafel) in Philadelphia; and the Rev. William Benade in Pittsburgh. The divinely inspired and authoritative writings of Emanuel Swedenborg formed the basis of the curriculum. All learning was to be obtained in the light of those documents. Books of the Bible listed in his writings as being fully inspired could also be used for instruction. But those books were to be interpreted based on Swedenborg's teaching, which exposed their hidden and deeper meanings and apparent contradictions.

Travels Abroad

With the Academy of the New Church established, the Reverend Benade (now called Bishop Benade) wanted to visit Egypt to look for secrets of the Ancient Church, which according to Swedenborg once flourished there. He also wished to tour the Holy Land and Greece.

John Pitcairn, always ready to visit new places, decided to accompany Benade and pay for their journey. Included in the entourage were six others, including John's older sister, Margaret Pitcairn, and two of his nieces, 16-year-old Agnes and 14-year-old Helen.

On Sunday, June 30, 1877, Pitcairn, Benade, and their traveling companions boarded the White Star Line's ship *Germaine* headed for Europe. Also onboard and among those entitled to the elite dining and lounge areas was William Rockefeller, brother of John D.

After eight smooth days at sea, the *Germaine* docked at Queenstown (now named Cobh), County Cork, Ireland. The *Titanic* would sail from this same port on her ill-fated voyage in 1912.

The Benade-Pitcairn party toured Ireland, stopping at the Blarney Castle near Cork on July 11. John Pitcairn recorded a legend related to kissing the Blarney Stone:

> There is a stone there
> That whoever kisses,
> Oh! he never misses
> To grow eloquent.
> 'Tis he may clamber
> To a lady's chamber
> Or become a member
> Of Parliament.
> A clever spouter
> He'll sure turn out, or
> An out-and-outer
> To be let alone!
> Don't hope to hinder him
> Or to bewilder him.
> Sure he's a pilgrim
> From the Blarney stone.[14]

Blarney Castle; the Blarney Stone is at the top of the rectangular building (photograph by the author).

The travelers moved on to London on July 28. Wherever they were on Sundays, they attended services led by either Bishop Benade or a pastor from a local New Church. In London, the local pastor was John's friend and traveling companion, Dr. Rudolph L. Tafel.

The annual General Conference of the New Church in England began on August 13, 1877, in Birmingham, with Benade, Pitcairn, and the Pitcairn ladies in attendance. John Pitcairn urged the delegates to read the first issue of *Words for the New Church*, saying that it was considered the most important work of the New Church by many American members.

The Academy Advances

Even with Bishop Benade and John Pitcairn traveling in Europe, the Academy continued to prosper. The first school building of the Academy of the New Church opened on Monday, September 3, 1877.[15] The Theological School operated from Philadelphia's Cherry Street Church and School, established earlier by the Reverend Benade. The initial nine students were taught by four clergymen, augmented by two homeopathic physicians who instructed in anatomy, zoology, and botany. While several teachers had other jobs that provided income, at least three clergymen worked full-time at the school and required financial support. John Pitcairn recognized that need and willingly provided it during his lifetime and by endowments after his death. On November 3, 1877, the Philadelphia courts granted a charter to the Academy, permitting it to operate as an authorized institution of higher learning and providing the right to grant degrees.

Travel Interrupted

Benade and Pitcairn's plans to continue to Egypt were delayed by the Tenth Russo-Turkish War (April 24, 1877, to March 3, 1878), so they settled in Paris for the duration, learned French, and visited with New Church members.

Finally, on January 4, 1878, hostilities subsided enough to allow the travelers to proceed. Once in Cairo, they did the usual tourist activities, visiting the Giza pyramids, the Sphinx, and the Egyptian Museum. But of course, they wanted a deeper experience, so John hired Lewis Mansour, a dragoman (combination guide, interpreter, and tour director), a boat (the dahabeah *Sylvia*),* the captain, a cabin servant, a "first-class" cook, and ten hands to man the boat.

The contract also included all stores, provisions, lights, and laundry sufficient for "a trip up the Nile to the first or second cataract and back."[16] (The Aswan High Dam, which opened on July 21, 1970, was built at the first cataract of the Nile. A cataract in this context is a steep rapids in a river. The second cataract was in Nubia and is now submerged under Lake Nassar, created by the Aswan Dam.)

Benade and Pitcairn's Nile River voyage cost 360 British pounds, or about $68,000 in 2024 American dollars.

The destination of primary interest to Bishop Benade on this Nile adventure was Tell el-Amarna, the site of the ruins and tombs of the city of Akhenaten. The city was built about 1348 BC by Pharaoh Amenhotep IV, under whose brief rule Egypt became monotheistic, worshiping only the sun god, Aton. Amenhotep IV's wife was Nefertiti.[17] However, the Egyptian guidebook warned against visiting Tell el-Amarna because of troublesome Bedouins nearby.

Benade could not leave the boat because of severe lower back pain. Undaunted, Pitcairn, Mansour the dragoman, and two crewmen started the 4.5-mile trek to the ruins. After about a mile, two large Bedouins, one carrying an 18-inch dagger, joined them. Mansour and one of the Bedouins engaged in an intense conversation in Arabic. When Pitcairn asked the substance of their talk, Mansour's reply was not reassuring. The Bedouin had suggested killing and robbing Pitcairn. Mansour advised John to keep his revolver at the ready. Mansour then warned the Bedouins that they would be shot if they threatened the party and were placed under arrest. After tying the hands of the Bedouins together behind their backs, the group proceeded to Tell el-Amarna, keeping the Bedouins in front of them. At the ruins, John entered and, in the light of a candle, drew pictures of the inscriptions he found on the walls.

---

* A dahabeah is shallow-bottomed, barge-like vessel with two or more sails that has been used primarily as a passenger boat on the Nile River for thousands of years.

As the motley party returned to the dahabeah, a group of screaming men and women approached them. Keeping the crowd at bay with their guns, Mansour ordered them to bring their sheikh. Soon the sheikh arrived and sat in the center of a 40-foot circle of Bedouin tribesmen. Mansour presented the case against the two troublesome Bedouins, and the crewmen from the dahabeah affirmed his accusations. The sheikh immediately passed judgment—fifty lashes or three months in prison for the chief culprit. The offending Bedouin chose the lashes, which were administered by one of the tribesmen.

Pitcairn, Benade, and the rest of their party continued their journey with no further trauma. Their 78-day voyage reached the second cataract of the Nile at the edge of Sudan and the Nubian Desert before returning downriver to Cairo.[18]

The Holy Land

Upon leaving Cairo on April 10, 1878, Benade and Pitcairn sailed north to the Mediterranean Sea. After stopping at Port Said at the entrance to the Suez Canal, they landed in Jaffa, an ancient port in the oldest part of Tel Aviv. There they procured camping equipment, five mules to carry it, and five horses to carry them and their servants. Suitably provisioned, they rode southeast over 40 miles to Jerusalem, arriving there on April 17. John's diary reported,

> The soil of Canaan is, if anything, less holy than that of other parts of the earth, having been defiled, for thousands of years, by the worst of all nations, and now largely desert, sterile and useless. It was indeed hard to believe that this devastated region with its thriftless and poverty-stricken inhabitants was once a "land flowing with milk and honey."[19]

The men viewed the holy places in and around Jerusalem, including the Church of the Holy Sepulcher, the Pool of Siloam, the reputed tomb of Moses (now the site of the Golden Dome on the Temple Mount), the Garden of Gethsemane, and the Western (Wailing) Wall of the Temple Mount.

They also visited the leper hospital, which contained between 30 and 40 patients. John reported, "[Leprosy is] not now regarded as contagious but hereditary, the only means of exterminating it being to forbid patients to marry."[20]

Touring Palestine was far different before the establishment of Israel in 1947 than it is now. Then, ungoverned tribes of Bedouins and Druses might attack without provocation, which was why John carried a revolver and shotgun for defense. Despite the danger, Benade and Pitcairn pushed on to visit the Church of the Nativity in Bethlehem, the Dead Sea, Jericho, the Church of the Annunciation in Nazareth, and Tiberias on the shore of the Sea of Galilee. Amazingly, they accomplished all their travel on horseback and camped in a tent at night.

From Palestine, Benade and Pitcairn visited Damascus and Beirut before sailing northwest to Greece. On the way, they passed the Island of Patmos, where John the Apostle lived in exile while writing Revelation, the last book in the Bible. Finally, the travelers arrived in Piraeus, the port for the city of Athens, in mid–May 1878. They visited the tourist attractions in Athens, including Socrates's tomb, but John recorded no diary entry regarding the Parthenon and other buildings on the

John Pitcairn (standing at left) and William Benade (seated at right) at their camp outside the walls of Jerusalem (courtesy of Glencairn Museum. Image Library).

Acropolis. John did, however, rise early one morning to climb the Lycabettus, the highest hill in Athens at 907 feet. From the top, he would have had a spectacular view of the Acropolis and Athens below.

The Pitcairn party left Greece by ship and arrived at Marseilles on the south coast of France five days after leaving Athens. From there, they traveled by train to Paris and stayed for three weeks until June 22, when John received a telegram calling him back to the United States. John's ship landed in New York on July 3, and he left by train for the Pennsylvania Oil Region. But John had been recalled not for oil but because of dissension regarding the Academy.[21]

New Church Divisions

Has there ever been a church movement that has not encountered differences among its members, ranging from fundamental doctrine to style of music to misbehavior by its leaders? The New Church did not escape division, with disagreement focused on the degree of adherence to Swedenborg's writings. The Academy followed Swedenborg rigorously, while the governing convention accepted some and neglected other teachings.

To gain new members, followers of the convention attempted to evangelize members of the "Old Church," that is, the established denominations. Of particular concern were Swedenborg's writings on sexual mores in his volume titled *Conjugal Love*. In that 700-plus-page treatise, Swedenborg taught that earthly marriages in which the husband and wife were genuinely and totally devoted to each other would continue in heaven.

The problem came in applying those teachings in the real world. A modern commentary on *Conjugal Love* observes,

The true idea—that marriage is essentially meant as a progressive union of two souls and minds—is today absent from the world's serious thought. In the Christian World no true idea of conjugal love and of marriage prevails. The old Christian Church is in spiritual adultery; and there is no true marriage of good and truth in it.[22]

To avoid problems with the Old Church members they were seeking to convert, the followers of the convention ignored some of Swedenborg's writings, especially *Conjugal Love*.

Because the Academy believed in indoctrinating the children of current members to gain adherents, the teachings in *Conjugal Love* were of less concern.

Back to Europe

With the division within the New Church unresolved, Pitcairn returned to Europe, leaving New York on October 5, 1878, and arriving in Liverpool on October 15.

In corresponding with Benade, who had returned to Italy while John was in the

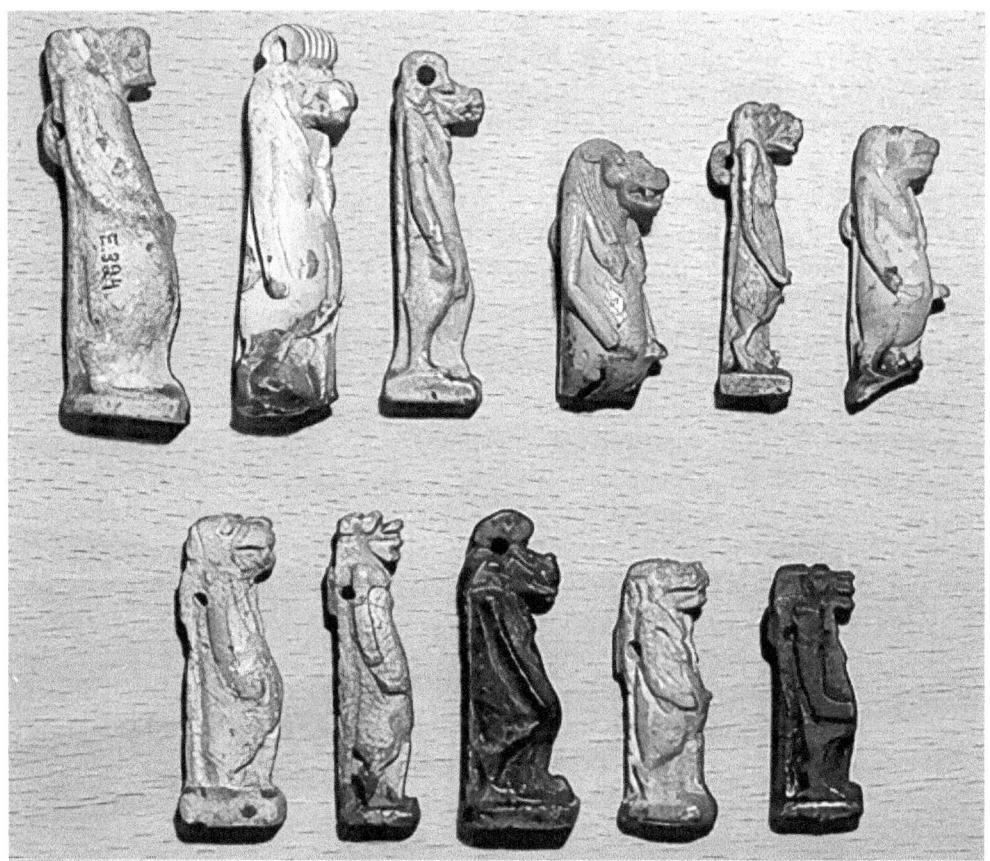

Egyptian amulets from the Lanzone Collection—image published in *Glencairn Museum News*, No. 8, 2015 (courtesy of C. Edward Gyllenhaal). © Glencairn Museum).

U.S., John learned of the Lanzone Collection of Egyptian antiquities. The exhibition was housed in Turin and contained 1,300 Egyptian amulets and other items.

Upon seeing the collection, Benade conceived a plan to create a museum for the Academy of the New Church, with the Lanzone Collection as its initial holding. John Pitcairn approved the idea and agreed to purchase the artifacts for the New Church for 300 British pounds (~$50,000 in 2021).[23]

John, ever vigilant for oil enterprises, visited the Galicia area of southern Poland to evaluate the oil industry there. Unable to negotiate a favorable deal, he returned to Paris. While waiting for his ship to New York to depart, he attended several plays and a Sunday New Church service. Finally, on May 9, he boarded the steamship *Amerique* at Le Havre and arrived in New York on May 19, 1879.

Oil Pipelines and the New Church

John Pitcairn had two overriding interests—the oil business and the New Church. He would soon have to make a choice.

The latest development in oil was pipelines, which would augment and, in some areas, replace railroads as the more efficient method of transporting oil, both crude and refined. On November 13, 1878, John's business associates had formed the Tidewater Pipe Line Company to build a 109-mile, six-inch-diameter pipeline over the Allegheny Mountains from Coryville in the oil region to Williamsport, Pennsylvania. From there, the oil would be shipped by rail to Chester, Pennsylvania, and other refineries in the east. If successful, it would be the first long-distance oil pipeline in the world. Such a pipeline was a direct challenge to the railroad empire of John D. Rockefeller and his Standard Oil Company. Pitcairn owned stock in Tidewater but was not an active participant.

Tidewater hired General Herman Haupt to manage the project. Haupt had previously worked with J. Edgar Thomson to build the Horseshoe Curve for the Pennsylvania Railroad. On February 22, 1879, in the middle of winter, construction started with 18-foot sections of wrought iron pipe laid on top of the ground. The pipeline crossed rugged mountains, streams, and rivers on its path to Williamsport. Ninety days later, the pipeline was completed. On May 28, 1879, the pump at Coryville was fired up, and 250 barrels of oil per hour started flowing through the pipe. One week later, on June 4, oil started arriving at Williamsport.[24]

Officials of the Tidewater Pipe Line Company gathered in Coryville to celebrate the momentous occasion. But John Pitcairn was not among them. He had elected instead to attend the General Convention of the New Church in New York City. The oil business took second place to the New Church in John Pitcairn's mind and heart.

10

Blood on the Tracks—Part 1

"We draw our strength from the very despair in which we have been forced to live.
 We shall endure."

—Cesar Chavez

The Great Railroad Strike of 1877 caused six times as many deaths in Pittsburgh than the far more infamous 1892 Homestead Strike, but it is much less widely known. Robert Pitcairn was superintendent of the Pittsburgh Division of the Pennsylvania Railroad at the time of the strike and played a prominent role in every aspect.

Granger Laws

In the late 1860s and early 1870s, four midwestern states (Minnesota, Iowa, Wisconsin, and Illinois) passed so-called Granger Laws. Promoted by a group of farmers known as the National Grange, the Granger Laws aimed to regulate rapidly rising railroad fare prices and fees for grain elevator crop storage. Railroads and grain elevator operators opposed the state laws, and the dispute ended in the U.S. Supreme Court with the *Munn v. Illinois* case that was decided in March 1877. The Court upheld the Illinois law and reasoned that a state has a legitimate police power to regulate private enterprises that may adversely impact the public interest. The Court ruled that a state might act "even though in so doing it may indirectly operate upon commerce outside its jurisdiction." The Court later upheld state efforts to regulate railroad rates.[1]

The *Munn* decision impacted the autonomy of the railroads in setting rates and was the first step toward the passage of the Interstate Commerce Act of 1887. That law limited railroads to rates that were "reasonable and just," forbade rebates to high-volume users, and made it illegal to charge higher rates for shorter hauls. The act also created the Interstate Commerce Commission to hear evidence and render decisions on individual cases.[2]

Facing declining revenues because of state regulation of rates, the major eastern railroads agreed to stop their rate wars. The heads of the railroads—John W. Garrett of the B&O, William H. Vanderbilt of the New York Central, Hugh J. Jewett of the Erie, and Tom Scott of the PRR—met to adjust shipping rates for their mutual benefit. They also discussed the need for wage reductions and how to combat ensuing strikes. It is believed, but not documented, that the four leaders agreed to "strike insurance"—when one railroad cut workers' wages and suffered a strike, the other three would handle its lost traffic. When that strike was over, the next railroad would cut wages, with the same guarantee of support from the others.[3]

The Panic of 1873

Called the "Great Depression" until the financial collapse of 1929 set a new standard, the Panic of 1873 started with a stock market crash in Europe. Soon, the Panic spread to the U.S., exacerbated by massive speculative investments in railroads, property losses in the Great Chicago Fire (1871) and Great Boston Fire (1872), and the Coinage Act of 1873, which demonetized silver in the U.S.

On September 18, 1873, the banking firm of Jay Cooke & Company declared bankruptcy, triggering a cascade of bank and insurance company failures. The New York Stock Exchange closed for ten days, and factories began to lay off workers.

By the end of the year, 89 of the country's 364 railroads had failed. New railroad construction fell dramatically, from 7,500 miles of track in 1872 to just 1,600 miles in 1875. Between 1873 and 1875, 18,000 businesses declared bankruptcy. In a vicious downward spiral, lower demand for products and services led to employers reducing output and cutting wages and jobs. By 1876, the overall unemployment rate shot up to 14 percent.[4]

Job Loss to Technology

Another factor specifically affected employment in the railroad industry. In one of the first instances of technology adversely impacting jobs, George Westinghouse's invention and installation of the railroad air brake meant that far fewer brakemen were required to operate trains. Instead of several brakemen per train manually applying brakes to each railroad car sequentially, the train engineer controlled the application of all brakes simultaneously from the locomotive cab. Westinghouse and Robert Pitcairn were close friends, and Pitcairn served on the Board of Directors of the Westinghouse Air Brake Company from its inception in 1869.[5]

All these factors—the Granger Laws, the lasting effects of the Panic of 1873, and air brake technology displacing workers—combined to reduce the demand for railroad workers and cut their wages.

Politics

The elections of 1876 further divided the country along economic lines. The Republican Party faced strong headwinds during President U.S. Grant's second term (March 1873 to March 1877). Although Grant had little control over the causes, the

Panic of 1873 occurred on his watch, and his monetary policies aggravated the situation. In addition, a string of scandals linked to Grant's friends and appointees plagued the administration. The most infamous was the Crédit Mobilier Scandal, which implicated eight Republican U.S. senators and representatives as well as Grant's vice president, Schuyler Colfax.

For the 1876 election, the Republicans chose Rutherford B. Hayes to be their presidential candidate: a war hero, a champion of Black suffrage, a man with a strong reputation for integrity, and the incumbent governor of Ohio, a crucial swing state.

The Democratic presidential candidate was Samuel Jones Tilden, a strong reformer who helped break up the infamous Tweed Ring in New York City, a strong political organizer, and the incumbent governor of New York, another vital state.

The election of 1876 was the closest, most hostile, and most controversial in the history of the United States up to that time. The turnout of eligible voters was 82 percent, a level never achieved before or since. For the first time, all voters cast their ballots on the same day, November 7, 1876. Early returns showed Tilden in the lead, but the next morning revealed that Hayes had unexpectedly carried California, Oregon, and Nevada. Still undecided were Florida, Louisiana, and South Carolina.

Tilden had won the popular vote by 250,000 votes but was one vote shy of the electoral vote majority. If Hayes could win all the disputed states (Florida, Louisiana, and South Carolina), he would win by one electoral vote.

Republican-controlled canvassing boards in the disputed states, citing voter intimidation and possibly influenced by bribery, invalidated enough Democratic votes to make Hayes victorious in those states. But the fight was not over. Electors met in state capitals to cast their electoral votes for president on December 6, 1876. Two sets of electors, Republican and Democratic, showed up in the disputed states to cast their votes. All of the electors' votes were then forwarded to Washington, D.C., for counting by the presiding officer of the Senate, Republican Thomas W. Ferry, in the presence of both houses of Congress. But which votes should Ferry count?

In a rare show of bipartisanship, Congress wrote and passed the Electoral Commission Act in January 1877. Under that act, a commission consisting of five senators (three Republicans and two Democrats), five representatives (two Republicans and three Democrats), and five Supreme Court justices (two Republicans, two Democrats, and one independent, Justice David Davis) would decide which electoral votes to count. What could possibly go wrong?

What went wrong was a misguided effort to tilt the outcome by Tilden's nephew, Colonel William T. Pelton. In the middle of January 1877, the Illinois legislature began voting for the state's U.S. senator. At that time, and until the ratification of the 17th Amendment to the Constitution in 1913, state legislatures chose U.S. senators. Democrats and Republicans balanced each other, thus giving power to five independent members. Pelton proposed to the Democrats and independents that his uncle, Justice David Davis, would be a suitable candidate. Pelton believed that if Democratic legislators elected Davis, he would favor Tilden in the Electoral Commission. Pelton's scheme backfired when Davis resigned from the Electoral Commission and was elected to be the U.S. senator from Illinois.

Davis's replacement on the Electoral Commission was Justice Joseph P.

Bradley, a Republican. The commission awarded the disputed states to Hayes by a party-line vote, giving him 185 electoral votes to 184 for Samuel Tilden. Democrats, knowing that defeat was imminent, turned to delay. Filibusters, motions for recess, and finally a shouting match on the floor of Congress delayed action until March 3, the day before the next president was to be inaugurated. Eventually, the electoral vote was certified, and Rutherford B. Hayes became the 19th U.S. president on March 4, 1877.[6]

There is a back story to how the Democrats agreed to end their filibuster, which could have delayed the naming of the president to beyond Inauguration Day and precipitated a constitutional crisis. Representatives of Tilden and Hayes met in utmost secrecy in the Wormley Hotel at the end of February 1877 to negotiate a compromise. The terms of the unwritten deal can be summarized as follows:

1. Remove all remaining U.S. military forces from the former Confederate states. At the time, U.S. troops remained only in Louisiana, South Carolina, and Florida, but the compromise completed their withdrawal from the region.
2. Appoint at least one southern Democrat to Hayes's cabinet. (David M. Key of Tennessee was appointed as postmaster general.)
3. Construct another transcontinental railroad using the route of the Texas and Pacific in the south. (This had been part of the "Scott Plan," proposed by Thomas A. Scott of the Pennsylvania Railroad; he had initiated negotiations resulting in the final compromise.)
4. Pass legislation to help industrialize the South and restore its economy following the Civil War and Reconstruction.
5. Allow southern states to deal with Black people without northern interference.

In exchange, Democrats would accept Republican Hayes as president by not employing the filibuster during the joint session of Congress needed to confirm the election.[7]

A statement by Tilden oddly foreshadowed the 2020 presidential election. When Tilden returned from a European trip in October 1877, the failed Democratic nominee credited his loss to "a great fraud, which the American people have not condoned and never will condone—never, never, never."[8]

Oil as a Weapon—Wage Cuts and Workweek Reductions

From 1872, when John D. Rockefeller became head of the National Refiners' Association, he set about consolidating the oil and pipeline industries under the control of his Standard Oil Company. Tom Scott of the Pennsylvania Railroad sought to compete with Rockefeller by building new pipelines from the Pennsylvania oilfields to seaboard refineries and cutting transportation rates for oil refiners. But Scott seemed to forget that two-thirds of the substantial amount of oil the PRR shipped came from Standard Oil.

Rockefeller hated competition and threatened to shift his oil shipments from the PRR to the New York Central and Erie Railroads. However, Scott remained intransigent, so Rockefeller shipped no more oil to his Pittsburgh refineries (via the PRR) and instead upped production at his Cleveland refineries. Also, Standard Oil undercut Scott's refinery prices everywhere they competed. The loss of oil shipments from Standard Oil severely damaged the finances of the PRR.[9]

In May 1877, the Pennsylvania Railroad cut wages of all employees by 10 percent. They made another 10 percent cut in June. On July 13, the Baltimore & Ohio Railroad cut the wages of all employees earning more than $1 a day by 10 percent. This reduction followed a similar cut in the fall of 1876. The B&O also cut the workweek to just two or three days. At about the same time, B&O announced a 10 percent dividend for its investors.

The Strikes Begin in Martinsburg, West Virginia

On July 14, 1877, 40 disgruntled B&O locomotive firemen walked off their jobs in Martinsburg, West Virginia, stranding a train full of cattle. By the end of the day, blockades by workers prevented the movement of freight trains near Baltimore and in West Virginia. However, passenger and mail trains were not stopped. Thus started the first of the nation's many railroad strikes.[10]

Railroad workers from Baltimore, as well as points west, converged on Martinsburg. By July 16, all train traffic was forced to a standstill as politicians, police, local military leaders, and railroad officials tried to resolve the stalemate. But reason had given way to emotion, and attempts to address the mob were met with derision and ridicule. The mayor of Martinsburg, A.P. Shutt, ordered his policemen to arrest the ringleaders, but that proved impossible.

Captain Thomas Sharp, B&O's master of transportation, arrived to assess the situation and sent a full report to company headquarters in Baltimore. Officials there telegraphed Maryland governor Henry M. Matthews, who immediately ordered Colonel C.J. Faulkner to mobilize the Berkeley Light Infantry at Martinsburg.

The infantry members responded promptly but with mixed emotions, as many were also railroaders. They sympathized with the strikers, as did many in the community. The following day, an engineer and fireman, surrounded by Faulkner's troops, moved an engine from the roundhouse, connected it to a waiting cattle train, and slowly proceeded from a siding to the mainline. But strikers had reversed the switch. When one of the troops, Private John Poisal, attempted to correct the switch, striker William Vandergriff injured him with a bullet from a small handgun. Poisal and another soldier fired back, inflicting wounds that resulted in Vandergriff's death on July 28. No further violence ensued, and the engine was returned to the roundhouse.[11]

Colonel Faulkner reported to the governor that he lacked the resources to control the situation. Governor Matthews responded by dispatching the Wheeling (West Virginia) Light Infantry to assist. The two sides remained in a standoff until John W. Garrett, president of the B&O, pleaded with Matthews for action.

The governor telegraphed the recently inaugurated President Rutherford B. Hayes, explaining the impasse and his steps to resolve it. Hayes sent Brevet Major

General W.H. French, Colonel of the Fourth U.S. Artillery, to Martinsburg along with 200 men. French's first action was to issue a handbill informing everyone in the area that traffic on the B&O must no longer be interfered with and that anyone who impeded the movement of U.S. troops did so at their own peril. The strike ended, and peace returned to Martinsburg.[12]

Trouble Moves to Maryland

The problems did not end at Martinsburg; they simply moved farther up the tracks. B&O management next expected trouble at Cumberland, Maryland, about 45 miles west of Martinsburg, so they asked Governor John Lee Carroll for help. Having learned from Martinsburg that local militia was ineffective against their neighbors, on July 20, 1877, Carroll ordered Brigadier General James R. Herbert to lead two regiments of the Maryland National Guard by train from Baltimore.

The first unit, the Guard's Fifth Regiment, headed from their armory to Baltimore's Camden Station, 1.6 miles south, around 7:00 p.m. Local factory workers on their way home initially cheered the soldiers. But when the Guard neared Camden Station, an excited crowd of several hundred men who had learned of the Guards' mission jeered and cursed the soldiers. The rear companies of the Guard were attacked with stones, bricks, clubs, and revolvers. The soldiers were forced to break ranks and run to the depot.

The ten-car train that was to carry the soldiers to Cumberland, pulled by Engine 380, was in place along the platform. But the rioters had other ideas. They attacked the engine with stones and pistols, resulting in damage so severe that the engine had to be removed from service. With police help, the soldiers defended Camden Station and awaited the arrival of the Sixth Regiment.[13]

At about 8:15 p.m., several companies of the Sixth Regiment prepared to depart on the 1.2-mile march from their armory, but now the protesting mob had grown to 2,500 angry men mixed with women and children. Company I of the Sixth Regiment, with 40 men led by Colonel Peters, descended the steps inside the armory and emerged through the doors. The violence was uncontrolled. Besieged by rocks, bricks, and bullets, a few of the soldiers fired their rifles over the heads of the mob. When the warning shots had no effect, and despite orders not to fire, several troops aimed lower and hit some protesters. The angry mob fell back but quickly reassembled. Bullets from soldiers' muskets and rioters' pistols, rocks, clubs, and shouts filled the air.

Seeing the chaos below, some soldiers remaining in the armory fired on the crowd from their elevated position on the second floor. One bullet hit a 32-year-old demonstrator, Thomas V. Byrne, who died instantly. Of course, his death further infuriated the mob, which launched an avalanche of rocks and bricks on the building.

Company F, and then Company B, followed behind. Their reception was no less violent, nor was their response. Soldiers and rioters lay wounded, bleeding, and dying in the streets.

After a horrific half-hour battle, the remnants of the Sixth Regiment, 53 of the 74 who had left the armory, arrived at Camden Station.

Camden Station was no sanctuary. The mob vandalized railroad cars and equipment, drove a locomotive off the tracks, and ignited wooden freight cars in the train yard. The rioters succeeded in setting the depot on fire, and for a while, the soldiers and others inside feared that they would be incinerated if they remained or slaughtered if they fled. The Baltimore Fire Department responded but was kept away from the building by the mob. Relief came in the form of the city police, who drove back the protesters, allowing the firemen to extinguish the blaze.

Governor Carroll telegraphed President Hayes for federal help. Hayes sent 500

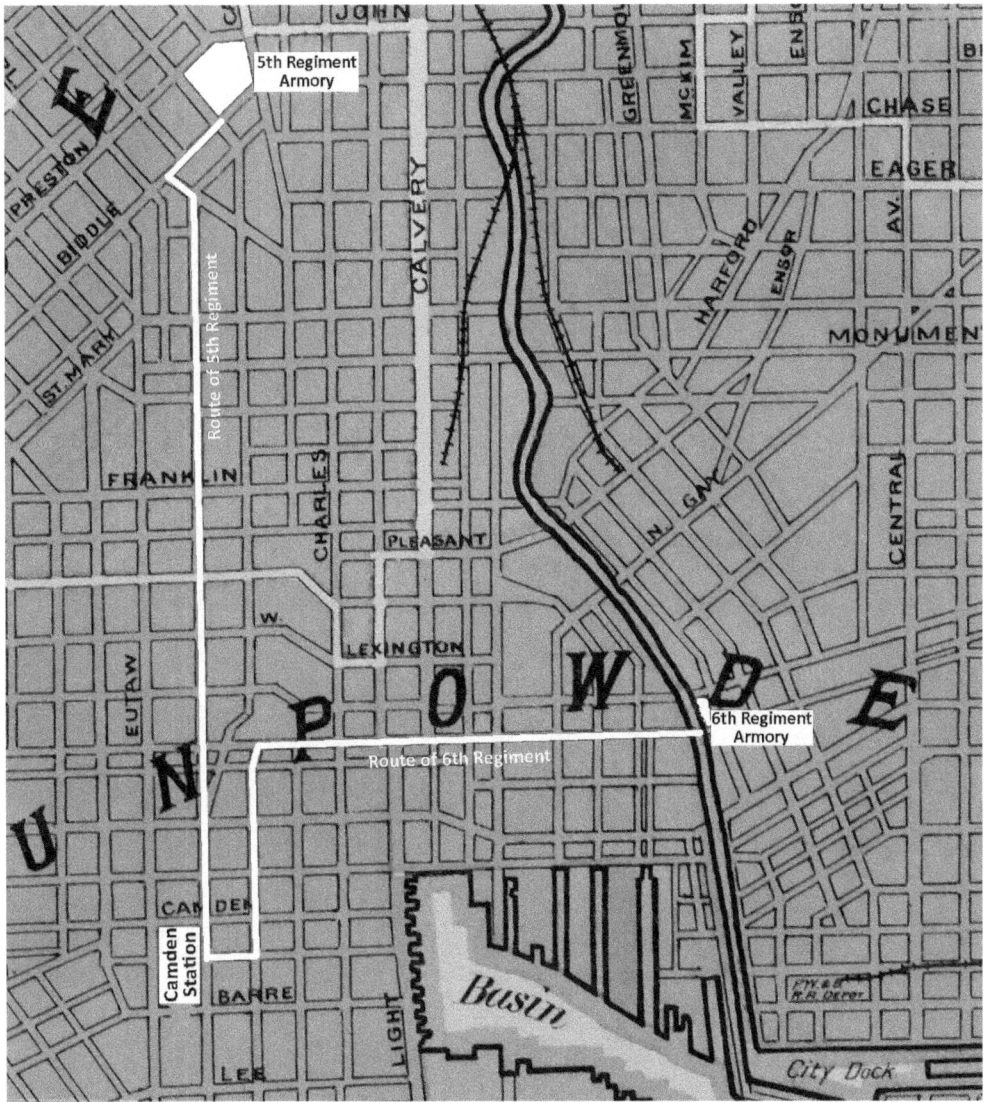

Routes of the Maryland National Guard regiments to Camden Station in Baltimore during the 1877 Railroad Riots (adapted from Sanborn Fire Insurance Map of 1890).

U.S. Marines from Norfolk and four infantry companies from Fort Monroe, all of which arrived after the crisis had passed.

A count of casualties on July 21 revealed nine killed and 25 wounded. Three of the wounded were not expected to survive. After all the bloodshed, peace was restored.[14]

11

Blood on the Tracks—Part 2

"Remember that you are fighting more than your own fight.
You are fighting for the entire working class and you must stand together."
—William Dudley "Big Bill" Haywood

Contagious Violence Hits Pittsburgh

July 21, 1877, was not a peaceful day in Pittsburgh, but rather one of conflict and death.

The PRR was ripe for turbulence. Robert Pitcairn had recently announced that all eastbound freight trains would be "double-headers." The size of an ordinary freight train was 17 cars, but double-headers could contain up to 36 cars pulled by two engines. Doubling up saved the railroad money by requiring one train crew to do the work of two. Pitcairn later testified that it was not unusual to run double-headers from Pittsburgh east to Derry (Derry is 45 miles east of Pittsburgh), but that the new directive expanded the use of double-headers to all eastbound trains.[1] For every two trains converted from single-headers to one double-header, one conductor, one flagman, and two brakemen were no longer needed.[2]

At 8:00 a.m. on Thursday, July 19, the order was posted to "shape up a double-header." Flagman Gus Harris refused. Other workers followed Harris's example. When trainmaster David Garrett asked another flagman, Andrew Hice, to form up the double-header, Hice replied, "It's a question of bread or blood, and we're going to resist. If I go to the penitentiary I can get bread and water, and that's about all I can get now." Within an hour, incoming and outgoing trains were halted, and an angry crowd had gathered in the Pittsburgh train yard.[3]

Work stoppages and train blockades were one thing in Martinsburg, West Virginia, and Cumberland, Maryland. They were of far greater importance in Pittsburgh, a major rail hub and the leading industrial city in the U.S. With its iron furnaces, steel mills, and oil refineries, a rail strike in Pittsburgh would have an immediate and devastating impact on the entire nation. PRR president Tom Scott and Pittsburgh Division superintendent Robert Pitcairn demanded military protection for railroad property. Pennsylvania governor John F. Hartranft was unavailable because of a trip to Wyoming, so Scott appealed directly to President Hayes. Hayes, who because of the Wormley Hotel agreement owed his position as president to Scott, ordered the strikers to disperse within 24 hours.

Unlike other service disruptions that were unorganized and spontaneous, the Pittsburgh work stoppage was led by the Trainmen's Union, which had been organized in early June. Its unlikely leader was 25-year-old Robert Ammons, a railroad brakeman. Ammons called a membership meeting for July 19 at Pittsburgh's Phoenix Hall. There, the men reiterated their opposition to double-headers and made other demands, which they presented to the PRR in a meeting with Robert Pitcairn the next day, as follows:

> Brotherhood of Locomotive Engineers,
> Pittsburgh Division, No. 50,
> Pittsburgh, Pa., July 20, 1877.

To the Superintendent Western Division, Pennsylvania Railroad:

First. We, the undersigned committee appointed by the employees of the western division of the Pennsylvania Railroad Company, do hereby demand from the said company, through the proper officers of said company, the wages as per department of engineers, firemen, conductors, brakemen, and flagmen as received prior to June 1, 1877,

Second. That each and every employee that has been dismissed for taking part or parts in said strikes to be restored to their respective positions.

Third. That the classification of each of said department be abolished now and forever hereafter.

Fourth. That engineers and conductors receive the wages as received by said engineers and conductors of the highest class prior to June 1, 1877.

Fifth. That the running of double trains be abolished, excepting coal trains.

Sixth. That each and every engine, whether road or shifting, shall have its own fireman. Respectfully submitted to you for immediate consideration.

> J. S. McCauley,
> D. H. Newhard,
> John Shana,
> G. Harris,
> J. P. Kessler,
> Committee.[4]

Pitcairn told the men he could not possibly send their demands to Tom Scott.[5]

Two actions boosted the strength of the Trainmen's Union. A mill worker attending the July 19 meeting pledged the support of his fellow workers, and the prestigious Brotherhood of Locomotive Engineers joined the Trainmen's Union in their fight.

A committee appointed by the Pennsylvania General Assembly to investigate the railroad disruptions of 1877 issued its report on May 23, 1878. Robert Pitcairn offered key testimony to the committee. When asked by the committee "whether there were any differences of opinion or disagreements between the Pennsylvania Railroad Company and the employees prior to the 20th of July last," Pitcairn replied,

> Yes. There was a good deal of friction and complaint. Committees called upon me, and committees from the different divisions of the road visited Mr. Scott, the president, and had conferences with him on the subject. They complained because of the [wage] reduction. He

explained that the cause of it was the condition of the country, and that as soon as business would become brighter, that then the company would entertain their petitions and would act fairly with them, when the committee, as they informed me, as Colonel Scott and others informed me, professed their satisfaction, and said there would be no trouble, but that they would work harmoniously.[6]

As in Martinsburg, initial efforts to resolve the issues proved ineffective. First, on July 20, police were called to keep order. But because of recent layoffs, just eight policemen were available. Next, a local militia unit was mobilized to reinforce the police, but was composed mostly of laborers sympathetic to the problems of their fellow workers. They soon laid down their weapons and mingled with the strikers.

After seeing the futility of relying on the local militia, city officials, at the urging of Robert Pitcairn, called on Governor Hartranft for help. The governor ordered the First Division of the Pennsylvania National Guard from Philadelphia to send 600 troops. Then, as now, there was no love lost between Pittsburgh and Philadelphia residents. At 3:00 a.m. on July 21, under General Robert Morton Brinton's command, the guardsmen departed from Philadelphia on two trains, bringing artillery and two Gatling guns. As the trains passed through Harrisburg, Altoona, and other towns, local workers expressed their displeasure by lobbing rocks, bricks, and coal at the trains, breaking many windows.

When the soldiers reached Pittsburgh, they were greeted by jeers and airborne missiles as the trains proceeded west through town. When they arrived at the Union Depot around 4:00 p.m., the troops ate a hearty dinner while their leaders met with local officials and railroad officers.

After feasting, the troops marched out in formation back east toward 28th Street, where the rail yards merged onto the mainline tracks. About 500 feet from their goal, they stopped to allow officials to address the assembled crowd.

Gathered between the troops and the crowd were Allegheny County sheriff R.C. Fife; Major General Albert Pearson of the Allegheny County militia; General Brinton of the Philadelphia Guard unit; and two PRR officials, Vice President Alexander Cassatt and Western Division superintendent Robert Pitcairn. Pitcairn later testified that he "saw quite a number of (ex-PRR) men who had been discharged for cause as well as suspended on account of the reduction (because of using double-headers)."[7]

Sheriff Fife stepped forward and attempted to talk to the mob, but their jeers and catcalls rendered him inaudible. Fife and Cassatt left in disgust to return to the Union Depot, leaving the military men to deal with the rioters as they saw fit.[8] Robert Pitcairn was unable to retreat and remained to witness the bloodshed that followed.[9]

The guards faced a hostile crowd of 2,000 strikers and sympathizers at the tracks and another 10,000 on the nearby hill. After being cursed and pelted with all manner of projectiles, including pistol bullets, the guardsmen, with fixed bayonets, advanced on the crowd. When that had no effect, several guardsmen fired into the air. That only energized the crowd, so the soldiers aimed lower with their muskets, firing directly at the mob with disastrous results. Twenty were killed, including an 18-year-old local militiaman, one woman, and three children.

Robert Pitcairn later provided the investigating committee with an eyewitness account of the violence at 28th Street. He testified:

By Senator Yutzy:

Q. *Were not shots fired from the crowd before the firing commenced?*
A. Yes; two shots were fired. I was near to the men.

Q. *Fired at the military?*
A. Yes; and stones came around and clouded the horizon.

Q. *Before there was any firing by the military?*
A. Yes, sir.

Q. *Was any command given to fire?*
A. No; all the officers I saw were begging the men not to fire.

By Senator Yutzy:

Q. *When the soldiers went up they did not attempt to injure the crowd? Were any of the soldiers hit and wounded at that time, before the firing—before they attempted to fire?*
A. I saw two or three wounded right around me.

Q. *Before that firing began?*
A. Yes, sir.

Q. *In other words, they attempted to do it without using force. Just by pressing back the crowd?*
A. Yes, sir.

By Mr. Lindsey:

Q. *Will you describe the crowd? Who composed it?*
A. The crowd immediately around Twenty-eighth street, on the track, were workingmen—mill men. The other men, from their appearance on the hillside, were citizens. A great many people that I knew.

By Mr. Lindsey:

Q. *How long did the militia stand fire from the mob? Stand those stones and clubs before they fired?*
A. Then the company moved up and got in the crowd, and there was a man in the crowd hollered shoot, and two pistol shots and a great many stones followed, and then the soldiers commenced firing, and then there was shooting just that quick.

Q. *Was any order given for the soldiers to shoot?*
A. No.

By Senator Yutzy:

Q. *Was it a scattering fire, or did it appear to be a volley?*
A. It was in every way and in every direction.

By Mr. Dewees:

Q. When those shots were fired, you were among the military?
  A. I was among the military, in the hollow square.

By Mr. Lindsey:

Q. Proceed with the military movements?
  A. They dispersed the crowd by the firing, and as soon as I got out, I went down to my office, at Twenty-sixth street. Then General Pearson and General Brinton were discussing what to do next, and whether Twenty-eighth street was a proper position for them to take, or to go up the hill or to come into the shops.[10]

The furious strike supporters forced the soldiers to retreat to the PRR Roundhouse two blocks southwest at 26th Street and Liberty Avenue. The crowd laid siege to the roundhouse, pelting it with stones, bricks, and bullets. But the roundhouse was like a fortress, with double walls, the outer one of iron. The mob also blocked attempts to deliver food and water to the troops inside. Still unable to force the guardsmen out, the protesters devised another plan.

The roundhouse was slightly lower than the surrounding land, so the railroad tracks rose as they left the roundhouse. The mob took advantage of the terrain by igniting freight cars carrying oil, coal, and high-proof whiskey. Then, starting at midnight, they sent the flaming cars careening down the tracks to the roundhouse below.

By 5:00 a.m. on July 22, General Brinton and his troops were forced to evacuate the burning roundhouse. With no cover, they used rifles and the two Gatling guns to shoot their way out. They first headed northwest away from the crowd, then avoided most of the protesters by fleeing northeast on Penn Avenue. But they drew fire from windows overlooking the street, snipers at intersections, and even a police station. Their objective was the Allegheny U.S. Arsenal, between 39th and 40th Streets, where General Brinton expected to find refuge.[11] That same arsenal had supplied guns and ammunition to Union forces at the start of the Civil War in 1861.

But Major A.R. Buffington, Commander of the Arsenal, refused entry to Brinton and his exhausted troops. Buffington had earlier denied arms, ammunition, and his six-pounder cannon to the rioters. He was now faced with a ragtag group of soldiers he did not recognize, led by a shabby-looking officer whose insignia designating his rank had been torn off.

General Brinton begged for food and water, or at least shelter. He said he knew nothing about the city, and everybody was against him and his men. Buffington would have none of it. He did accept and treat the wounded militiamen but pointed Brinton and the rest of his Guard Division toward the nearby Allegheny River bridge. They marched on to Sharpsburg and eventually ended at the Allegheny City Poor Farm, where they received food and drink and were allowed to sleep on the surrounding grounds.[12]

Other rioters adopted the idea of fire to get their revenge and torched every PRR property in sight. One by one, railroad cars were set ablaze and sent among both

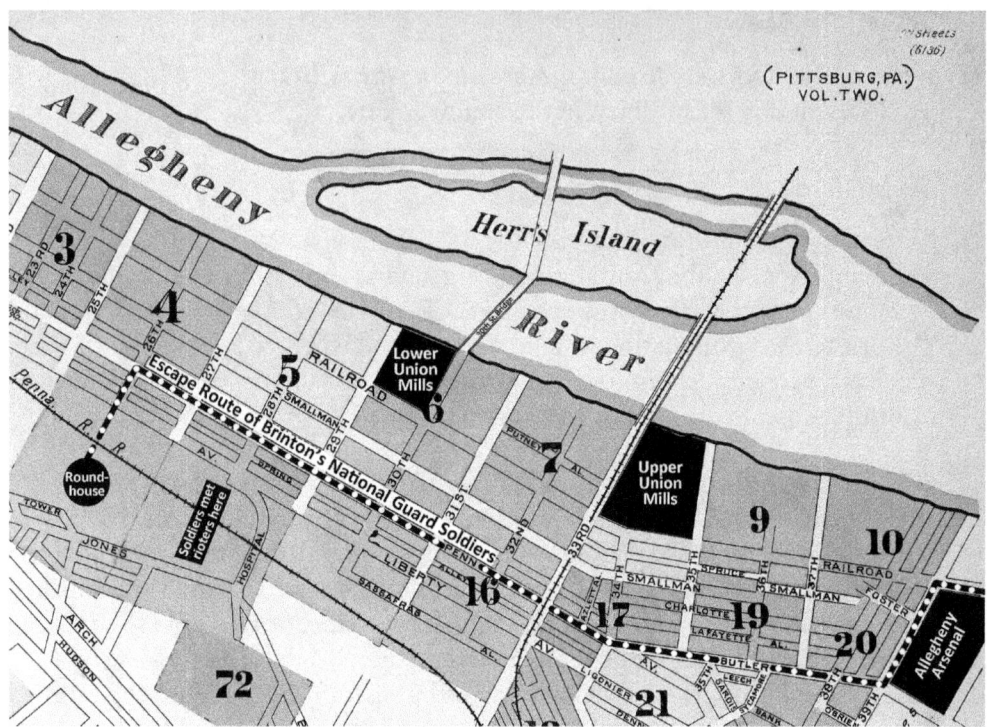

Locations of the 1877 Railroad Strike. Note Carnegie, Kloman & Company's Lower and Upper Union Mills along the Allegheny River. This area of Pittsburgh is referred to as the Strip District because it is composed of a narrow strip of buildable land between the Allegheny River and a nearby steep hillside (adapted from Sanborn Fire Insurance Map of Pittsburgh of 1893).

freight and passenger cars. Ironically, the rioters never touched the Westinghouse air brake factory at 25th Street and Liberty Avenues, even though the brakes made there contributed to significant job losses among railroad brakemen.

Finally, the prize, the magnificent four-story Union Depot and Hotel, was set on fire at about 3:30 p.m. on Sunday, July 22. *Harper's Weekly* reported,

> "The Union Depot is on fire!" was an announcement that spread like a flash of lightning throughout the city, and thousands of people at once crowded all the avenues leading to the scene. The people seemed entirely reckless of the danger in their wild anxiety to see the sight. The hillside above the depot was covered with people thick as leaves upon forest trees. Every available point of view was taken up. Hundreds climbed to the high tower in City Hall, and from that altitude had a magnificent view of the scene.[13]

Harper's Weekly from August 11, 1877, reported on the riots:

> The news of the slaughter of the mob spread through the city like wild-fire, and produced the most intense excitement. The streets were rapidly crowded, and the wildest rumors prevailed. When the news reached the large number of rolling-mill hands and workmen in the various shops of the city, they were excited to frenzy, and by eight o'clock the streets of the central portion of the city were alive with them. A large crowd broke into the manufactory of the Great Western Gun-Works, and captured 200 rifles and a quantity of small-arms, and various other crowds sacked all the other places in the city where arms were exposed for sale, getting about 300 more.[14]

Union Depot and Hotel burning, Pittsburgh, Pennsylvania, July 22, 1877 (*Harper's Weekly*, August 11, 1877. Engraving by M.B. Leiser).

Away from the fires, hundreds of men, women, and children ransacked intact freight cars. The August 11 *Harper's* article continued with a description of the chaos:

> Men armed with heavy sledges, keeping ahead of the fire which was running west toward the Union Depot, broke open the cars, and threw the contents to the crowds below. The street was almost completely blockaded by persons laboring to carry off the plunder they had gathered together. In hundreds of instances wagons were pressed into service to enable thieves to get away with their goods. Some of the scenes, notwithstanding the terror which seemed to paralyze peaceable and orderly

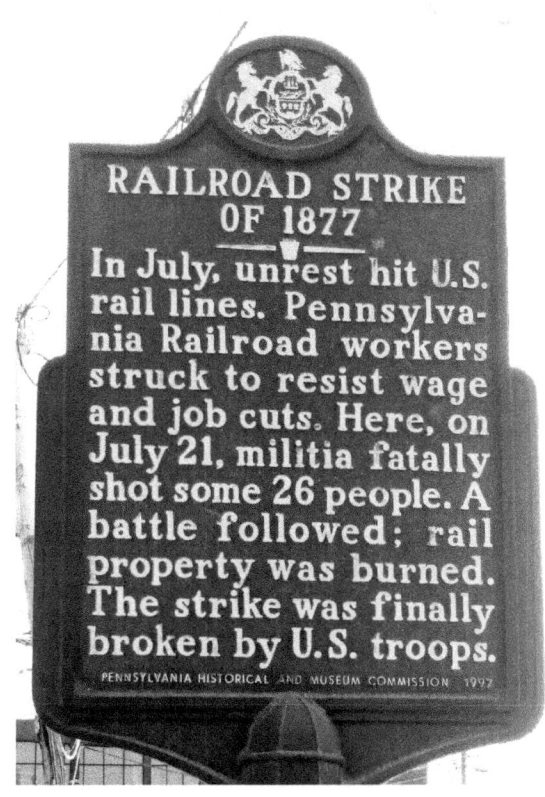

Historical marker at 28th Street and Liberty Avenue, commemorating the 1877 Railroad Strike (photograph by the author).

citizens, were ludicrous in the highest degree.... A woman, carrying an infant, would be rolling a barrel of flour along the sidewalk, using her feet as the propelling power.... Boys hurried through the crowd with large-sized family Bibles as their share of the plunder, while scores of females utilized aprons and dresses to carry flour, eggs, dry-goods, etc.... In one place where barrels of flour had been rolled from the cars and over the wall to the street below, breaking with the fall, heaps of flour were piled up several feet in depth.[15]

The Strike Spreads Across the Country

Because the roots of unrest affected rail workers throughout the nation, disturbances, blockades of trains, and strikes spread across the entire country. As a vital rail hub, Chicago became the target of the Workingmen's Party, which had been organized in Philadelphia in 1876. On Monday, July 23, 1877, leaders Philip Van Patten and Albert Parsons led a rally of 30,000 unemployed Civil War veterans and others on Chicago's Market Street. As a result, local businesses boarded up their storefronts, and the Chicago Board of Trade hired Pinkerton guards to watch over businesses and affluent neighborhoods. The violence started on Tuesday, July 24, and increased through the week. By the end of the rioting, 30 people had died.

Widespread but less violent demonstrations occurred as far south as Galveston and as far west as San Francisco.[16] The transcontinental railroad had spawned a transcontinental labor movement. In the summer of 1877, over 100,000 workers had gone on strike.[17] As a result, freight stopped moving on half of the nation's 75,000 miles of railroad track.[18] The railroad strike of 1877 marked the beginning of labor violence in the United States, but it would be far from the end.

Casualties and Cost

Back in Pittsburgh, which had seen the most destruction in the country, city leaders and businessmen were totaling up the damage. The human cost was enormous. An estimated 53 rioters were killed, 109 injured, and 139 arrested. Eight soldiers lost their lives, and another 15 were wounded.

About 1,600 freight cars, 55 passenger cars, and 104 locomotives were destroyed, along with machine shops and railroad offices.[19] In addition, almost two square miles of the city were devastated by fire. Various sources estimated the total damage to be between $4 and $10 million.

Recovery by the PRR

Sporadic disturbances continued for the next two days. Finally, on July 28, Pennsylvania Governor Hartranft accompanied fresh militiamen from Philadelphia along with 16 companies of federal troops. The soldiers protected PRR employees as they cleared the debris and rebuilt the train tracks.[20]

Robert Pitcairn testified about the repairs:

26th Street Roundhouse after the fire, Pittsburgh, Pennsylvania (Wikimedia Commons).

I had orders to repair the damage, and try to get the main track through to the Union depot as quickly as possible, to gather up the force then scattered through the city, and the men who had gone to their homes, to repair the track and get to Union depot as quickly as possible.

I went to the mayor and asked him if we would commence work there if he would give protection. He said he would.

By Mr. Larrabee:

Q. *What day was that?*

A. I think Thursday. I was gathering up the men, but was cautioned by some of the citizens not to go out and work too brash in the beginning—not to take too many men about the ruins to clear them off, but to commence moderately, explaining the feeling of the city, how matters were not quiet there, and that delayed me some days. I met Governor Hartranft at Blairsville before I left, going to Harrisburg. After he came here we got a large force.[21]

Tom Scott agreed to meet with the strikers to negotiate their grievances. The 1877 Annual Report of the PRR stated, "It is hoped that the present depression will

Remains of freight cars in the Union Depot, 1877 (Wikimedia Commons).

soon end and that with improved results a higher rate of compensation can be paid to your employees."[22]

On July 30, 1877, 11 days after the order to "shape up a double-header" had been posted, the railroads passing through Pittsburgh began again to operate. A tenuous peace returned to the Pennsylvania Railroad.

Aftermath

The railroad strike of 1877 brought fundamental changes to American politics and labor-management relations. From under 10,000 miles of track in 1850, there were over 75,000 miles by 1877. But even with this explosive growth, emigration from

Europe to America and migration from farms to urban areas kept the labor supply well above the demand. Because the individual worker was not a scarce commodity, companies had little incentive to meet employees' needs. While labor unions were declared legal in the 1842 *Commonwealth v. Hunt* Supreme Court ruling, public opinion of unions was negative prior to the Great Railroad Strike of 1877. But the strike changed perceptions. It was the first labor movement to jump state boundaries and extend nationwide. Labor became a political and societal force in the years following the strike.

New labor leaders emerged from the carnage of the 1877 strike. Terence Vincent Powderly's Knights of Labor learned how to influence public opinion by turning workers' outrage into effective protests. Under his leadership, membership in the Knights reached 700,000. Powderly opposed strikes, preferring boycotts and negotiation to obtain an eight-hour day, better wages, and improved working conditions.

Eugene Debs had been a member of the Brotherhood of Locomotive Firemen before being laid off in the Panic of 1873.[23] After the 1877 strike, he told Brotherhood members, "(R)ecent strikes, which terrified an entire nation … are the last means … after all peaceful efforts to obtain justice have failed."[24]

Likewise, Samuel Gompers, founder of the American Federation of Labor, favored negotiation, at least at the initial stages of a disagreement. He blamed the violence and eventual failure of the Great Railroad Strike of 1877 on the lack of organized labor. Gompers believed that unions could provide the discipline and strength for workers to negotiate successfully.[25]

Despite the preference of these and other labor leaders for negotiation, strikes became more prevalent and violent in the late 1880s and 1890s. The turmoil culminated in the 1894 Pullman Palace Car Company strike, which stopped railroad traffic across the nation and left 25 people dead.[26]

Political Impact

The Great Railroad Strike of 1877 also impacted the political scene. Initially focused on the nation's currency, the Greenback Party broadened its base by changing its name to the Greenback-Labor Party. As such, it advocated laws reducing labor hours and prohibiting convict labor. As a result, it received over one million votes in the 1878 election and placed 14 members in Congress.[27]

The Workingmen's Party of the United States was formed in 1876 and gained members by rallying support for the striking railroad workers. In the 1878 elections, its charismatic leader, Albert Parsons, polled eight thousand votes for county clerk in Chicago but lost by a narrow margin. In December 1878, the party became the Socialist Labor Party and remained a minority party under various names until 2011.[28]

While the minor parties faded away, labor issues advanced in importance in the two major parties. The first Labor Day celebration was in September 1882, in conjunction with the General Assembly of the Knights of Labor in New York City. In June 1894, President Grover Cleveland declared Labor Day an official federal holiday to be celebrated on the first Monday in September.[29]

In 1884, Congress established the Bureau of Labor to investigate "relations between labor and capital, the wages and hours of labor, the conditions of the labor classes ... strikes, and ... the causes thereof."[30]

Although the Great Railroad Strike of 1877 gained nothing for the workers who participated, it did lead to long-term political and societal changes. Soon after the strike ended, a commentator in the *Washington Capital* wrote, "Those who understand the forces at work in American society already know that America will never be the same again. For decades, yes centuries to come, our nation will feel the effects of the tidal wave that swept over it for two weeks in July."[31]

12

Marriage and Divorce

> *"Great marriages are made in heaven—but so are thunder and lightning."*
>
> —Dee Compere

On May 19, 1879, John Pitcairn returned from an extended European trip. Later that month, he chose to attend the General Convention of the New Church in New York City rather than the celebration marking the opening of the Tidewater Oil pipeline in Coryville, Pennsylvania. That decision signaled a shift in Pitcairn's focus that would take him in new and unforeseen directions.

Romance

On June 6, 1879, John was back at the Continental Hotel in Philadelphia. Eighteen years earlier, as a 20-year-old, he had met here with Allan Pinkerton and president-elect Abraham Lincoln to plan Lincoln's trip to his inauguration in Washington, D.C. Now, John was in town to handle pipeline business and attend an Academy of the New Church celebration.

In the afternoon, John, now 38 and an experienced world traveler, called on his friend from his previous visits to the city, Dr. George R. Starkey. There he renewed his acquaintance with the doctor's eldest daughter, Gertrude, who was 24. They had first met in March 1877 at an Academy meeting in Philadelphia when Gertrude was 21.

The rest of June was a mixture of business, New Church activities, and walks in nearby Fairmount Park with Gertrude and her friends.

In September, Gertrude traveled by train with Bishop Benade to Pittsburgh to visit with her pen pal, Maria Hogan. Maria, born in 1850, was the daughter of Catherine "Kittie" Morrison Hogan and Thomas Hogan and the maternal first cousin of Andrew Carnegie.

John Pitcairn met them in Pittsburgh and wrote of the visit:

> I took the two girls up to see the Oil Regions last week and surprised them by going through to Niagara Falls. We left Wednesday morning and returned on Saturday evening. The weather was charming and we had a delightful time.[1]

Gertrude wrote of her visit to the Falls:

In the evening we saw the falls and the fountains in the park, illuminated with white and colored lights. The beauty of the effect produced was very fascinating to us.[2]

In early December 1879, John asked Gertrude to be his wife. She refused, but sweetly.

Afterward, John wrote to Gertrude:

Windsor Hotel, New York

December 10, 1879

My dear friend,

...I thank you for your words to me. You remarked that you said more than you intended. You did not say too much. Always speak to me thus openly.... I think I understood the full intent and meaning of your words—are the real ones.

Your type is rare, I only wish there were more women in the world like you, not that you do not have your evils to overcome—for who has not—but there is a genuine honesty of purpose that is sure to bring you happiness; if not in this world certainly in the next.

You _are_ a dear good girl and—I was going to say that I love you—well so I do, not as a lover; but as one dear friend may love another.

Sincerely yours,

Jno. Pitcairn Jr.[3]

Gertrude responded the next day, saying that her belief in Swedenborg's high ideal of marriage as laid out in *Conjugal Love* required her to examine her affections carefully in order to "live up to the principles we hold in regard to marriage" and she found that her feelings did not have the interior depth required, but proposed that "we commence a new volume of our friendship prepared to love and help each other as never before."[4]

End of Romance

In 1880, shortly after his trip escorting Gertrude Starkey to Pittsburgh, Bishop William Benade stunned John Pitcairn and his other New Church compatriots by announcing that his wife, Amelia "Emily" Davis, was divorcing him. The couple, married on October 4, 1846, had four children, but the divorce should not have been surprising because they had been living apart since 1864 when William moved to Pittsburgh to pastor a New Church there. But Benade's statement also conveyed the startling news that he was planning to remarry.

Two Marriage Surprises

Swedenborg's writings describe several acceptable reasons for a married couple to separate, but only adultery was grounds for divorce and the right of the injured party to remarry. Benade's announcement caused much concern among the New Church leaders. Benade produced one or two Swedenborg passages that seemed to justify his remarriage, leading to a general feeling of acceptance but not approval.

Bishop Benade's new wife was to be Annie Barnes, a former teacher in the Academy's Cherry Street School in Philadelphia. Benade, 64, and his bride, 61, were married by the Rev. J.P. Stuart on September 28, 1881, in the Philadelphia home of the bride's mother.

Eight months later, another surprising marriage took place. Dr. George Rogers Starkey, John Pitcairn's long-time friend from Philadelphia, had been a widower since his wife, Caira, died on May 20, 1881. Almost exactly one year later, on May 22, 1882, George married again. His new wife was Margaret Pitcairn, John's sister. George Starkey was 52, and Margaret had just turned 44. As a result, John Pitcairn was placed in the unusual position of courting Gertrude Starkey, his sister's stepdaughter. The rather convoluted relationships are shown in the "Hourglass Chart for John Pitcairn Jr. and Gertrude Starkey" in Appendix I.

Back to Europe

John Pitcairn could not attend his sister's wedding to George Starkey because he was once again off to Europe. He departed on April 15, 1882, to negotiate a loan for the Union Oil Company. But as was his usual practice, he took every opportunity to attend New Church locations and discuss New Church doctrine with anyone who would listen.

While in London, John met fellow Pittsburgher George Westinghouse, who was promoting his air brake system for British railroads. He also learned that a boyhood chum, Harry Phipps, had rented an estate complete with servants at Norbiton, about 30 minutes from Waterloo station. John stayed there on at least two separate occasions. Andrew Carnegie also stayed with the Phipps family but was away during John's visits.

John's pursuit of a loan for the Union Oil Company did not go well. Union's much larger competitor, the Standard Oil Company, had planted a newspaper article critical of Union Oil and then made sure it was forwarded to London to dissuade financiers there from loaning money to Union. Facing that negative publicity and the likelihood of obtaining the money from a U.S. source, John left for the States via the liner *Servia* on June 4, 1882. He arrived home on June 12.[5]

Money and Love

From Pitcairn's papers, we have an accounting of his assets. The most significant holdings were in H.L. Taylor Company ($400,000) and Loyal Hanna Coal and Coke Company ($140,500). His total wealth at the end of 1882 was almost $747,000. John was the primary source of finances for the Academy of the New Church. In 1883, he contributed $17,800.[6]

In mid–1883, John entered into a new venture, one that would be the capstone of his business career. He invested in a new company called "The New York Plate Glass Company." The following month, James H. Shields, the company's secretary, wrote John to thank him for his investment and to say that the company would soon be moving from New York to Creighton, Pennsylvania.[7] The next chapter will explore the evolution of John Pitcairn's new venture.

An even more significant change in John's life soon followed. At the end of August 1883, Gertrude Starkey wrote to John, inviting him to visit her family during their vacation at Taughannock Falls in upstate New York. They met there on September 9, and he proposed marriage again. Almost four years after rejecting his previous proposal, Gertrude accepted.

After more than six years of courtship, it surprised no one when John and Gertrude announced their engagement. At a New Church betrothal ceremony on October 31, 1883, they formally confirmed their intention to be married. John presented Gertrude with a ruby and diamond engagement ring.

The couple planned a January 4, 1884, wedding (it actually took place on January 8). It was to be a double wedding, shared with Gertrude's sister, Cara, and her fiancée, Robert Glenn.

The Weddings

The weddings occurred at the House of Worship of the Advent in Philadelphia. It was a dark and snowy night, and the snow covered ice from the rain that had fallen earlier in the day. The only accounts of the weddings are letters written by young Adolph L. Tafel and Dr. Ernest Farrington. Adolph tells us that his father, Louis H. Tafel, performed the marriage ceremony for Robert Glenn and Cara Starkey, followed by Bishop William Benade doing the same for John Pitcairn and Gertrude Starkey. He further reported "they had everything, oysters raw or fried, chicken salad, ice cream, coffee, etc." Farrington's letter assures that there was plenty of champagne to toast the brides and grooms. Much was made of John's new mother-in-law also being his sister.[8]

On his wedding day, John was two days short of 43 years old; Gertrude was 28. Both had solid training in Swedenborgian theology and complete dedication to their marriage.

Gertrude was a slim and very pretty brunette of medium height. She was artistic and loved the outdoors. Her mother had been a helpless invalid for several years, so Gertrude gained extensive experience as a household manager and hostess.[9]

Honeymoon for Five

John and Gertrude made their first home at 634 North 16th Street in Philadelphia. They stayed there for three weeks before departing from New York on February 2 on the German liner *City of Berlin* to Liverpool. They were not alone. Also on board were Gertrude's younger sister, Dora, and John's younger brother, Hugh, as

John and Gertrude Pitcairn traveled to their wedding in this carriage. The streets were filled with snow and slush, the sidewalks were slippery, and the gutters were almost impassable (photograph by the author; courtesy of Cairnwood Estate).

well as Hugh's wife, Anna. The voyage was far from smooth, as near-hurricane force winds buffeted the ship almost as soon as she left New York harbor.

On arrival in England, John, ever the businessman, contacted the office of the Inman Steamship Company to discuss supplying coal for their vessels. The contact paid off, and John wrote instructions to D.M. Watt, manager of the Loyal Hanna Coal and Coke Company at Connellsville.

As the rest of the party had no foreign travel experience, John acted as a tour guide, focusing on the tourist sights attractive to first-time visitors. The group stayed almost a month in London and Paris before heading to southern France. From there, they visited Monaco and the famous Casino before crossing into northern Italy.

At Pisa, they saw the Leaning Tower and toured the adjacent cathedral, then rode on donkeys up the side of Mount Vesuvius. John had seen the dormant volcano from shipboard in mid–1878 when he and Bishop Benade toured Egypt and the Holy Land.

Further south, they boarded a small boat to enter the Blue Grotto on the Isle of Capri. Then, back on the mainland, the tourists went to Rome and visited St. Peter's Square in what would later become the Vatican.

The artist in Gertrude was thrilled by the statues and paintings of Florence. The Uffizi Gallery, the Pitti Palace, and the Medici Chapels all held treasures beyond belief. They toured the Duomo with Brunelleschi's gravity-defying dome, the adjacent 278-foot campanile (bell tower), and the Baptistery of St. John featuring Ghiberti's "Gates of Paradise" doors.

Then it was on to Venice, where John treated the group to the enchanting moonlight gondola ride he and Walter Childs had experienced while touring in 1874.

They returned to Paris on April 30, then on May 1 traveled to Holland, where they met Bishop Benade and his new wife. Throughout May, the travelers explored The Hague, including extended tours of the Mauritshuis museum, which featured over 800 of the finest Dutch paintings. At the Museum of Antiquities in Leiden, John examined the impressive Egyptian exhibit and a small collection of Swedenborg books, including an original edition of *True Christian Religion* published in Amsterdam in 1771.

The four Pitcairns and Dora Starkey left Holland on June 10; sailed up the Rhine to Cologne, Wiesbaden, and Mannheim; and then rode overland to Heidelberg, arriving there on June 21. By June 25, they were in Zurich and then traveled southwest to Brienz, a woodworking center.

After visiting the Jungfrau Mountain, called the Top of Europe, and witnessing an avalanche there, the party returned to Paris. There, Bishop Benade conducted Sunday services on July 20 and 27. At the latter service, he inducted four new members into the Academy of the New Church. Later that day, Benade dedicated an Academy school with six students.

The "honeymoon plus three" returned to London in early August and then traveled to Birmingham on August 11 to attend the General Conference of the British New Church. The only news of interest from the conference was that Dr. Rudolph Tafel was given permission to establish his New Church Educational Institute. While benign on its face, his separate training facility signaled a coming split between Tafel and the Academy of the New Church.

After a nearly eight-month honeymoon, the travelers sailed from Liverpool on September 13 and arrived in New York on September 21, 1884.[10]

Divorce

John Pitcairn had been baptized as a member of the New Church when he was eight years old. He attended his first General Convention of the New Church in Portland, Maine, when he was 27. In 1880, when he was 39, he was appointed to the executive council of the New Church's Pennsylvania Association and named a lay delegate to the General Convention that same year. In 1883, he was elected chairman of the Council of the Laity in the Pennsylvania Association. In that post, John was in charge of managing the money used to support the entire organization.

The General Convention was the ruling body of the New Church and was composed of societies and associations (combinations of societies) in various geographical locations. The largest was the Massachusetts Association, and the Pennsylvania Association had the largest percentage of Academy of the New Church members.

The 1883 conference of the General Convention made two changes to placate divergent views within the New Church. First, each Association was now permitted to make its own regulations regarding its clergy. Second, the geographical boundaries on Associations were eliminated. In response, the Pennsylvania Association reorganized as the General Church of Pennsylvania with William Benade as its bishop.

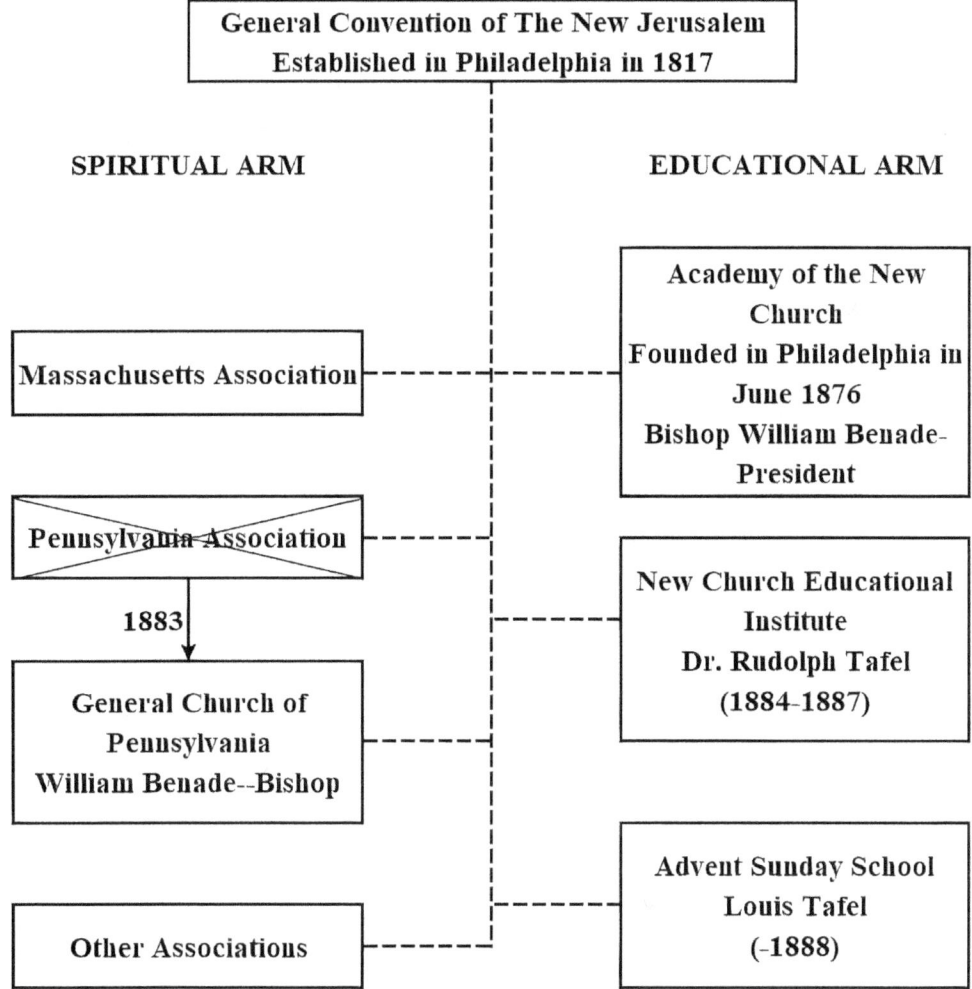

Organization of the New Church, 1817–1888 (compiled by the author).

This newfound independence reduced tensions but also led to divergent viewpoints and practices.

The first open split involved Dr. Rudolph Tafel. Tafel had established the New Church Educational Institute in 1884 and, in 1887, was up for election as president of the General Conference of the British New Church. However, he had ignored letters from and had openly criticized the Academy of the New Church. On February 26, 1887, Rudolph Tafel was dropped from the rolls of the Academy.

The second issue involved corporal punishment at the Academy Boys' School. In December 1887, the school's headmaster punished two 14-year-old boys who had consistently disobeyed instructions by whipping them with rattan reeds. The Rev. Louis Tafel (Rudolph Tafel's brother), the uncle of one of the boys, accused the headmaster of brutality. The dispute escalated. Bishop Benade announced that Academy Boys' School students were not to attend the Advent Sunday school operated by Louis Tafel. Tafel retaliated by removing his children from the Academy Boys' School and enrolling them in a Quaker school. Others of his supporters did the same, reducing the Academy Boys' School enrollment by 20 students. On November 2, 1888, Louis Tafel resigned from the Academy of the New Church.

John Pitcairn and four other members of the Advent Society, which oversaw Tafel's Advent Sunday school, drew up a series of four charges against Louis Tafel. Under the General Church of Pennsylvania regulations, all the clergy of that body considered the charges and examined the evidence. The clergy found the charges valid, and in an open meeting of the Advent Society, Bishop Benade removed Tafel from his positions within the General Church of Pennsylvania. Tafel's supporters, about half of those in attendance, walked out in anger, denouncing both the Academy of the New Church and the General Church of Pennsylvania.[11]

At its annual meeting the following summer, the General Convention censured the Academy and voted to support Louis Tafel. John Pitcairn, caught in the middle of strong and opposing viewpoints, did what he could to maintain civility, but the stage was set for a divorce between the Academy of the New Church and the General Convention.

13

Glass and Gas

"The magic of the window is not in itself but in the view it shows outside!"
—Mehmet Murat ildan

In mid–1883, John Pitcairn had invested in the fledgling New York Plate Glass Company and then learned the company was moving to Creighton, Pennsylvania. He decided to visit the plant site and meet the owner, John Ford. Pitcairn soon learned that Ford had been planning to use coal for fuel.

Because he had pioneered natural gas transportation by pipeline and owned the controlling interest in a gas company, Pitcairn convinced Ford that gas would be a cleaner and more reliable choice. As glass manufacturing requires precise temperature control for each step, gas would prove to be a far better alternative than coal.

John Baptiste Ford and the Glass Industry

The American plate glass industry originated with John Baptiste Ford, born November 17, 1811, in a log cabin in Danville, Kentucky. During the War of 1812, John Ford's father, Jonathan, joined the Kentucky Volunteer Homespun Regiment to fight the British at New Orleans and never came home. John's mother apprenticed him to a Danville saddle maker when he was 12, but John chafed at the stern discipline and ran away at age 14 to settle in Greenville, Indiana, on the Ohio River. There he met a farm girl, Mary Bower, who taught him to read and write. John and Mary were married in 1831 when John was 20 and Mary was 25.

The young couple had seven children, the first five of whom died between the ages of five days and 15 years. The last two children, Edward Ford, born in 1843, and Emory Low Ford, born in 1846, grew to adulthood and worked in the family business. Emory graduated from Duff's Mercantile College in Pittsburgh, founded by Peter Duff in 1841 as the first business college in America, in June 1864. When John visited his son in Pittsburgh, he and Emory toured some of the many glass factories in the city, primarily on the South Side (then called Birmingham).[1]

Inspired by what they had seen in Pittsburgh, the Fords established a small glass factory near their New Albany, Indiana, home. Starting in 1865, the New Albany Glass Works manufactured bottles and jars. John Ford had previously owned a small iron foundry and rolling mill, the Ohio Falls and New Albany Rolling Mills. He believed that he could apply his knowledge of rolling iron to roll glass into sheets for windows. At that time, all window glass was imported from Europe because no one in the U.S. had the knowledge or equipment to manufacture it.

Ford initially failed, but in 1867, with a larger facility and skilled workers from England, he successfully rolled the first plate glass in the United States and installed it in the window of John Hieb's tailor shop on Pearl Street in New Albany.

Artist's rendering of the installation of the first American-made plate glass window at John Hieb's tailor shop in New Albany, Indiana (courtesy of Floyd County Historical Society).

However, competition from overseas drove Ford out of business, and he left New Albany in 1873.² But he remained convinced he could make a fortune in the plate glass business. At age 70 and with $100 loaned to him by George Schmitt, one of his former workers, he found three New Yorkers to back his venture. On May 17, 1881, they incorporated the New York Plate Glass Company and planned their first factory in Camden, New Jersey. But before starting construction, they learned of an initiative by the Commonwealth of Pennsylvania to encourage out-of-state companies to manufacture metals and glass.

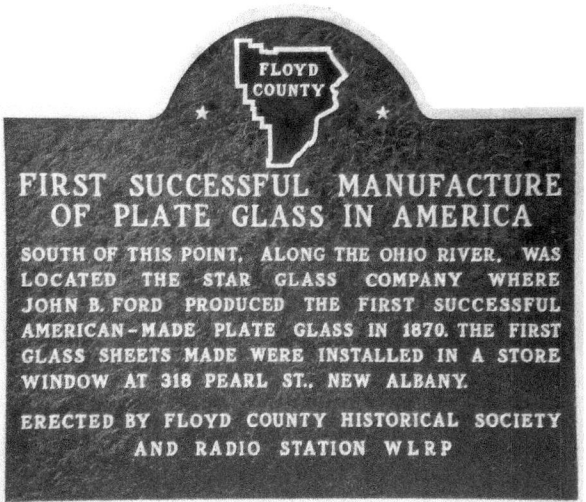

Historical marker commemorating first plate glass manufacture in America (courtesy of Floyd County Historical Society).

Ford had previously identified Creighton, Pennsylvania, as an attractive site. On the Allegheny River 20 miles northeast of Pittsburgh, Creighton had the raw materials Ford needed: large deposits of glass sand, grinding sand, limestone, clay, and coal for fuel. Soon, Camden was scratched and Creighton, Pennsylvania, became the site for the new glass factory.³

John Baptiste Ford (1811–1903), left; John Pitcairn (1841–1916).

From Sand to Glass

In addition to gas for fuel, John Ford needed something else from John Pitcairn—investment money. Despite knowing little about the manufacture or demand for plate glass, Pitcairn invested $27,000. He also accepted John Ford's offer of

$150,000 more in stock when the plant became operational. Ford and Pitcairn reincorporated the New York Plate Glass Company into the Pittsburgh Plate Glass Company (PPG) on August 24, 1883. Once the new company was formed, the three New York investors sold most of their interests back to the company.[4]

PPG had no shortage of customers, as domestically produced plate glass was in high demand. John Ford and his sons Edward and Emory provided the technical knowledge to make plate glass, and John Pitcairn supplied essential business acumen. As a major shareholder, director, and later vice president, Pitcairn urged the construction of a new, larger, and more efficient plant. Looking back in January 1889, he said of the Creighton works:

Historical marker for Pittsburgh Plate Glass Company, located at One PPG Place in Pittsburgh (photograph by the author).

> The Creighton works were put up in a very hasty manner.... As to the business, it is true they had a business, but it was in such condition that you couldn't begin to supply the wants of the trade, and we had to turn off customers all the time, and there was business there for any first-class concern....We have never sent out an agent to solicit any business; it has come to us.[5]

Although Pitcairn disparaged the size and construction of the Creighton facility, it was a behemoth. It included furnaces to melt glass, roll it into 20-foot × 13-foot plates, and polish, grind, and transport it to storage warehouses. Its casting and grinding houses each measured 310 × 290 feet, almost large enough to contain a football field. Annealing ovens to remove stress from the glass measured 16 × 44 feet, and iron casting tables were 20 × 13.5 feet. In addition, two cranes could lift enormous pots of molten glass from the furnaces.

John Pitcairn continued to push for a new glass factory. The market for plate glass seemed insatiable, and PPG knew how to manufacture it. He placed a plan to add a new factory before the board of directors, and they approved it. However, when John suggested that PPG build the plant themselves instead of contracting it out, John Scott, whom Pitcairn had brought into the company, objected. A group of minority stockholders agreed with Scott, fearing the company would be overextended. Although Pitcairn and the Fords controlled the majority of the company stock, Pitcairn was unwilling to override the will of the minority stockholders.

Instead, he convinced the Fords to abide by a "one man–one vote" policy so that even large stockholders would have only one vote on issues.

John Baptiste Ford was no longer affiliated with the company in any managerial role but retained a strong interest in its success. So when the stockholders decided against PPG building a new factory themselves, he suggested another approach. How about if he and John Pitcairn established an ad hoc company to build the new facility and then sold the completed operation to PPG?

John Pitcairn saw merit in Ford's proposal, but in late 1883, he had other things on his mind, specifically his upcoming marriage to Gertrude Starkey. Pitcairn urged Ford to delay construction until he and Gertrude returned from their honeymoon.

John Ford, now 72, was impatient, so while John and Gertrude were on their European honeymoon, he started constructing the new glass plant using his own money. When Pitcairn returned and saw what Ford had done, he became concerned lest the new, large, and efficient factory become a competitor to PPG. Ford assured him that was not his intention, so Pitcairn bought a one-half share in the venture.

At a PPG board of directors meeting on July 2, 1886, John Ford and John Pitcairn presented the following proposition:

> To the Board of Directors of the Pittsburgh Plate Glass Company:
>
> We hereby propose ... to sell ... to you our new plate glass works situate in the borough of Tarentum ... with all property ... appurtenant thereto for eleven hundred and twenty thousand dollars ($1.12 million) payable in stock of your company.... The property consists of about fifteen acres of land ... having thereon the glass works proper, also twenty-five building lots ... near ... works with double frame dwelling houses erected thereon, also the gas right...
>
> J.B. Ford
>
> John Pitcairn[6]

After a 60-day grace period required by the company bylaws, the PPG stockholders met on September 6, 1886, to consider Ford and Pitcairn's offer. With a selling price reduction to $1 million, the stockholders accepted the proposal with no dissenting votes. The Tarentum plant, soon called Works No. 2, became part of PPG. After achieving full staffing, Works No. 2 became twice as efficient and productive as the Creighton plant.

Labor Relations

John Baptiste Ford was a hands-on manager who inspired loyalty among his employees. Despite the limited success of the New Albany venture, several of Ford's workers there willingly followed him to the PPG plants. While John Ford no longer had any official position within the company, his sons, Emory and Edward, were managers and retained Ford's favorable image with the PPG employees. John Pitcairn was less visible since he spent most of his time in Philadelphia. Even so, he was viewed as a fair and just manager with his drive for profits balanced by concern for his workers. Thus, in contrast to the steel and railroad industries, PPG was relatively free of labor disagreements.

Two Lives

Since his wedding to Gertrude Starkey on January 8, 1884, John Pitcairn had been leading two lives, one in Philadelphia and the other in Pittsburgh. His life in Philadelphia centered on his wife and the Academy of the New Church. John and Gertrude's first child, Raymond Pitcairn, was born in Philadelphia on April 18, 1885. One year later, Walter Childs Pitcairn was born on April 23, 1886, but survived for only just over one month. Their third child, Vera, arrived 13 months after Walter on May 30, 1887.

Later that year, John was deeply saddened to hear of the death of Annie Benade, the second wife of his pastor and traveling companion, Bishop William Benade, on November 19, 1887.[7]

John Pitcairn's Pittsburgh life focused on the Pittsburgh Plate Glass Company. After four years of building new and ever-larger plants to keep up with the demand for plate glass, Pitcairn was able to leave the company's day-to-day operation to Edward and Emory Ford and John Pitcairn's cousin, Artemas Pitcairn.

From the beginning of 1888, John Pitcairn lived in Philadelphia and commuted to Pittsburgh via the Pennsylvania Railroad whenever company business dictated.

Family and Church

As a bachelor in the 1870s, John Pitcairn had traveled the world. Now that he had a family, he was anxious to share similar experiences with them. Their first trip was to Paris in May and June 1888, and then to Switzerland (probably Sonnenberg, west of Lucerne) until September. Two young women from the New Church accompanied the family to help with the children (Raymond was three, and Vera was one).

Early in 1889, John wrote to his closest friend, Walter Childs, of an uncharacteristically speculative move that he had made:

> And now I have just about time enough to tell you about some property I have purchased with a view to moving out of the City and as a possible location for the Academy.
>
> Land in the vicinity of Philadelphia is being taken up so rapidly that Robert Glenn thought I ought to secure some. On the line of the Pennsylvania Railroad for fifteen miles out—the fashionable locality—property sells for from $1,500 to $5,000 an acre.
>
> About a mile from the station on the Second Street Turnpike there was a property of 35 acres for sale which I purchased about two weeks ago. It has fine woods on it and is said to be the highest ground in Montgomery County and is a beautiful sight [sic] for a residence. This purchased, we wanted some more and I bought 49 acres adjoining at $350 per acre; and I still want a little more.[8]

The Robert Glenn mentioned as encouraging the purchase was John Pitcairn's brother-in-law. Glenn had married Cara Starkey in a double wedding shared with John and Gertrude in 1884. Cara and Gertrude were sisters.

John Pitcairn and Robert Glenn eventually accumulated over 450 acres in the Montgomery County area.

In 1889, the Pitcairns replicated their 1888 vacation. May and the first three weeks of June were spent in Paris before proceeding to Sonnenberg, Switzerland, for the balance of the summer.

On July 17, word came that Bishop Benade, John's close friend and pastor, had suffered a stroke while visiting in London. John and his companion, Eugene Schreck, started for London immediately. They arrived to find Benade's condition "very discouraging"[9] and stayed to provide help and encouragement until August 10. By then, Benade had recovered, and there was no more danger of death or paralysis. John and Eugene returned to Sonnenberg, where they stayed until late September before returning to the U.S. by way of Paris.

More Glass Factories

Building glass factories made John Ford, now 75, a happy man. As soon as the Tarentum factory was up and running, the J.B. Ford Company started a new and more ambitious project. That company, which began as a partnership between John Ford and John Pitcairn, now included Edward Ford, Emory Ford, and Artemas Pitcairn, John's cousin. Artemas, called "Teem" by John, was an attorney who shared John's Swedenborgian religion and his strict business and personal ethics. He had been elected to the PPG board of directors in 1884 and would later become vice president of PPG.

J.B. Ford Company's new focus was a larger, more advanced, and more self-contained plate glass factory and a surrounding model industrial town to be called Ford City. The factory and new town were to be on the Allegheny River, 24 road miles northeast of Tarentum. The plant and dwelling houses for workers and management cost almost $1.2 million to build and, on July 1, 1889, were purchased by PPG for $1.5 million. In addition to the manufacturing facility, there were six-room and eight-room houses and one twelve-room house for the superintendent. Building lots were provided for several religious denominations to build churches. Later in 1889, John Pitcairn financed a four-room frame

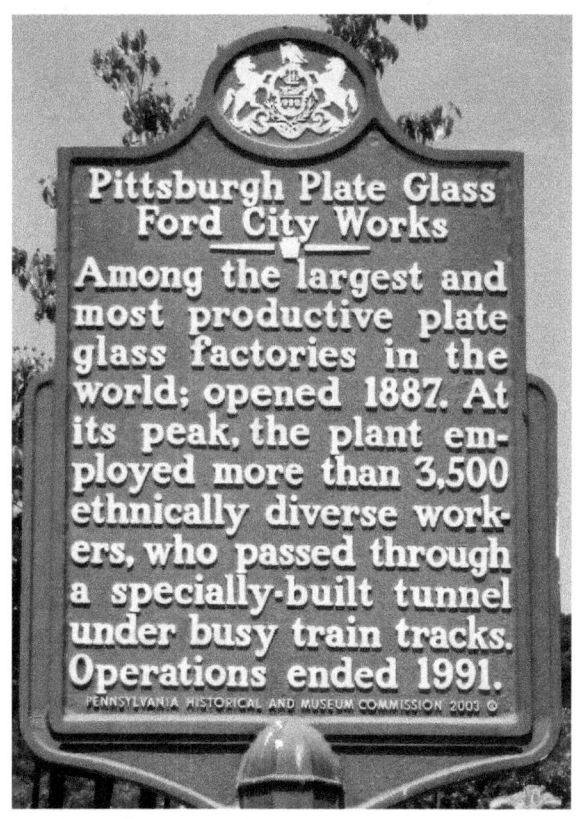

Historical marker commemorating the Ford City Works of Pittsburgh Plate Glass. The plant operated from 1887 to 1991 (photograph by the author).

schoolhouse, and PPG built 12 brick double houses, with each half containing four rooms. In addition, John Ford commissioned a town hall, including a library.

In 1891, on John Ford's 80th birthday, Ford City residents staged a grand celebration with banners, a parade, and speeches. The highlight was the unveiling of a statue honoring Ford, paid for by employees in the glass plants he had built. Each employee volunteered a day's pay to fund the statue.

Even with its three glass works at Creighton, Tarentum, and Ford City, PPG could not satisfy the demand for plate glass. As a result, another plant was built in Ford City in 1891 and another before 1895.

But by 1895, the manufacturing capacity of PPG and its competitors outstripped the demand. As a result, factories of several rival companies became available at low prices. Although John Ford and his sons objected, John Pitcairn held the majority of the PPG shares and, for once, exerted his will. As a result, PPG purchased the following facilities:

- The Crystal City Plate Glass Company in Crystal City, Missouri;
- The Diamond Plate Glass Company, with plants in Kokomo and Elwood, Indiana;
- The Howard Plate Glass Company in Walton, Pennsylvania:
- The American Silica Sand Company in Akron, Ohio; and
- The Charleroi Plate Glass Company and the Charleroi Coal Company in Charleroi, Pennsylvania.

With these acquisitions, PPG produced about two-thirds of the plate glass manufactured in America.

Statue of John Baptiste Ford. The dedication plaque reads "ERECTED IN HONOR OF JOHN B. FORD, THE FATHER OF THE PLATE GLASS INDUSTRY IN AMERICA, BY THREE THOUSAND EMPLOYEES ON THE EIGHTIETH ANNIVERSARY OF HIS BIRTH NOVEMBER 17, 1891" (photograph by the author).

How Should Glass Be Sold?

Almost from the beginning of the plate glass industry in America, the National Plate Glass Association had acted as the middleman between glass manufacturers and their ultimate customers. The NPGA distributed virtually all plate glass sold in the U.S., whether manufactured in the country or overseas. But some direct-to-customer sales by PPG prompted a letter from the NPGA that was discussed at the October 23, 1895, PPG board meeting. The letter read in part, "… requesting this company confine its sales of plate glass to members of their association or to make them a discriminating price."

The PPG board decided to upend the historic glass distribution model and provide better market visibility and higher profits for the company. The board minutes reported:

> *Resolved:* that the request of the New York members of the National Plate Glass Association, having been fully and carefully considered by the Board, we deem it unwise to grant the same for the reason that such action on our part would in the end militate against our interest and be prejudicial to the trade and against public policy.[10]

That carefully worded statement is legalese for "Go pound sand!"

The NPGA responded by marching on Washington and accusing PPG of being a trust and restraining trade. But PPG's lobbyist, E.A. Hitchcock, nullified their self-serving claims.

A board committee backed by John Pitcairn established a new PPG Commercial Department to replace the external organization acting as a middleman. That department would be responsible for warehousing, sales, and marketing plate glass in the U.S. Salesmen were instructed to build a detailed customer database, including planned projects, schedules, responsible architects, competitors for glass sales, and likely quotes from those competitors.

By 1906, Pitcairn reported to PPG stockholders that 20 warehouses had been established in major U.S. cities and that the volume of business had increased by a factor of five.

Management Split

At the stockholders' meeting of February 2, 1897, Edward and Emory Ford declined to stand for reelection as officers of PPG. Their refusal confirmed what the rumor mill had been saying for many months—they were leaving the company. The reasons for their departure were widely debated, and Gladish, in his biography of John Pitcairn, provides his well-reasoned opinion.[11]

Potential reasons for the split included:

- PPG's jettisoning of the National Plate Glass Association as the distributor for its plate glass;
- Differing business philosophies between John Pitcairn (conservative) and the Fords (boost the stock price by borrowing money to pay larger dividends);

- The Fords' desire to build a competing plate glass business. This desire became a reality in 1899 with the founding of the Edward Ford Plate Glass Company, headquartered in Rossford, Ohio.

Gladish concludes that the last two items were related and led to the management split. If the board could be convinced to borrow money to raise the dividend rate, the stock price would inevitably climb. Then the Fords could sell their shares at the enhanced price, providing the funds they needed to start a new glass venture. The difference in business philosophy was short-term gain vs. long-term benefit.

The two sides sent competing circulars to the stockholders, and a proxy fight was underway. John Pitcairn bought all the company's shares that he could without disturbing the market. By the time of the annual meeting in February 1897, both sides were entrenched. But the Fords had both miscalculated and failed to carry out their most basic responsibilities.

By declining to stand for reelection, they ceded management of the company to John Pitcairn and his allies. But even more damaging was the failure of PPG secretary Emory Ford to issue the necessary published call for a special meeting to be held after the regular stockholders' meeting. Therefore, that special meeting, which was to determine whether or not to borrow money to pay dividends, could not be held as planned. Thus, the decision on borrowing had to be delayed and would be resolved by the newly elected officers, all Pitcairn allies. John Pitcairn was named president (pro tem) and chairman of the board, and his cousin, Artemas Pitcairn, was chosen vice president.

PPG lost the knowledge and experience of the Ford family and would face competition from their new company in two years. That new company, the Edward Ford Plate Glass Company, would merge with the Libbey-Owens Sheet Glass Company in 1930 to form the Libbey-Owens-Ford Glass Company. L-O-F became one of the largest glass manufacturers in the world.

Growth of PPG

In 1900, to broaden PPG's product line, John and Artemas Pitcairn purchased the Patton Paint Company of Milwaukee, Wisconsin. Soon after, they added the brush business of Rennous, Kleinle & Company; the Pitcairn Varnish Company; the Corona Chemical Company; and the Red Wing Linseed Oil Company. By diversifying into different but related product lines, the Pitcairns reduced PPG's dependence on glass.[12]

In 1907, the company became one of the first corporations to develop a profit-sharing plan for its employees. At the time, John Pitcairn reiterated his conservative business philosophy:

> The strength of your company is in a large measure due to the conservative policy which has actuated the Management from its inception, when the properties were taken over at actual cost. In all manufacturing plants liberal provision should be made for depreciation and for improved processes. Failure often results from neglecting to provide for such changing conditions.

As is well-known, there never has been watering or inflation in the Company's assets … your properties were never in a more satisfactory condition than now, and the selling price of the stock is in no way indicative of its actual value.

John Pitcairn's final report as chairman of the board, written in 1916, stated:

Your Board of Directors takes this opportunity to express its appreciation to the faithful services of the factory superintendents, warehouse managers, their assistants, and employees, and of their loyal support of the general management.

Respectfully submitted,

John Pitcairn

Chairman of the Board of Directors[13]

John Pitcairn remained as chairman of the board of PPG until his death on July 22, 1916. The company prospered under his and subsequent leadership. Dividends have been paid annually from 1899 to the present day (2025), with consecutive dividend growth for the past 50 years.

PPG buildings in Pittsburgh. Set on 5.5 acres, a 635-foot, 40-story tower is flanked by one 14-story building and four six-story buildings covered with 19,750 pieces of glass totaling nearly one million square feet (photograph by the author).

14

Antediluvian Johnstown

> *"The attractions of Johnstown as a place of summer resort for the residents of the large cities are not appreciated—either at home or abroad."*
> —James Moore Swank

On September 1, 1769, a 19-year-old Amish farmer named Joseph Schantz arrived in Philadelphia on the ship *Nancy and Suckey*. Schantz was from Amtsbezirk, Konolfingen, Canton Bern, Switzerland, and had sailed from London.

Twenty-four years later, on September 30, 1793, Schantz bought about 140 acres in the Allegheny Mountains of western Pennsylvania from James McLanahan. Schantz paid the equivalent of $2,150 at the time, about $8.50 per acre. Finally arriving at the site of his purchase in 1794, he built a log cabin at the present-day intersection of Vine and Levergood Streets in Johnstown, planted an orchard, and began to clear land for farming.

By 1800, Schantz had cleared about 30 acres and laid out a village with 141 lots, ten streets, and six alleys. Some of Schantz's planning is evident in today's Johnstown. What he designated as "all the piece of ground called the Point, lying between the two rivers or creeks aforesaid shall be reserved for common and public amusements for the use of the said town and its future inhabitants forever"[1] is now Point Stadium. He planned to build a courthouse in Central Park if his settlement became the county seat. But on March 26, 1804, Cambria County was formed, and Ebensburg, not Johnstown, was named the county seat.

In geography, Johnstown is a scale model of Pittsburgh, with two rivers meeting at a point to form a third. In Pittsburgh, those rivers are the Allegheny and the Monongahela, which merge to form the Ohio. In Johnstown, the Little Conemaugh and the Stony Creek combine to form the Conemaugh. After many twists and turns, the Conemaugh River eventually empties into the Allegheny across from Freeport, Pennsylvania.

Joseph Schantz, whose name had been anglicized on deeds by courthouse recorders to Joseph Johns, called his settlement Conemaugh Old Town and registered it in Somerset on November 1, 1800. Unfortunately, Schantz (then known as Johns) died on January 18, 1813, so he did not live to see his settlement, renamed Johnstown in 1834.[2]

The year 1834 was pivotal to the newly renamed settlement. March 18, 1834, saw the opening of the Pennsylvania Main Line Canal from Philadelphia to Pittsburgh, including the Allegheny Portage Railroad from Hollidaysburg to Johnstown.

14. Antediluvian Johnstown

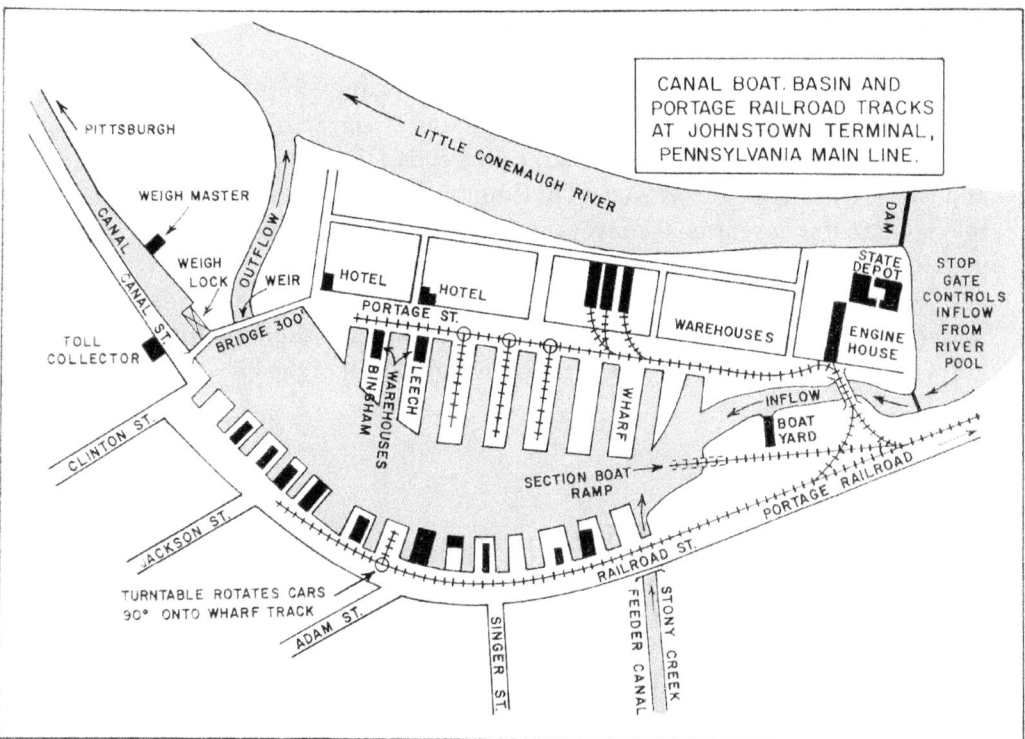

Junction between the Western Division of the Pennsylvania Main Line Canal (on the left, to Pittsburgh) and the Allegheny Portage Railroad (on the right). The three or four portions of a westbound packet boat from the Allegheny Portage Railroad, such as the Pitcairns were riding, would be reassembled and enter the water at the Section Boat Ramp (author's collection).

For 55 years, from 1834 until May 1889, Johnstown prospered. At its peak in the summer, the Allegheny Portage Railroad carried 100 canal boats daily, each holding up to 10 tons of freight and passengers.[3] As much as 1,000 tons of goods and hundreds of people passed through Johnstown in a single day. But of course in the winter months when the canal froze, no canal boats moved.

The diagram of the canal basin shows two hotels and three warehouses. They represent just a portion of the facilities required for Johnstown to handle the influx of supplies and humans, mostly headed west to Pittsburgh and beyond.

William Latshaw reported in 1836,

> It is scarcely necessary to add that the Borough of Johnstown is situated at the head of Canal Navigation on the Great Western Division of the Pennsylvania Canal. It has within the last three or four years trebled its population and is destined ere long to become a place of considerable and manufacturing business. The water power in the neighborhood of the town is among the greatest, west of the Alleghenies, and the beds of Bituminous Coal, that lay in the adjoining hills, are inexhaustible, offering inducements to capitalists that are rarely found.[4]

In 1836, Johnstown's total revenue from the canal, including tolls and other charges, was $125,000. Revenue rose to $147,000 in 1839. For the next 12 years, Johnstown was a boat and rail center that attracted people, wealth, and industry. The population reached 1,260 in 1850.[5]

Pitcairns Travel Through Johnstown

Ten-year-old Robert Pitcairn and his parents and siblings first encountered Johnstown in October 1846 as immigrants en route from Scotland to Allegheny City, Pennsylvania. Because Johnstown marked the end of the Allegheny Portage Railroad and the beginning of the Western Division of the Pennsylvania Main Line Canal, they rode an unconventional conveyance, one-third or one-fourth of an 82-foot-long packet boat lashed to a railroad flatcar.

Twenty years later, the Portage Railroad and Main Line Canal would be gone, replaced by the mainline of the Pennsylvania Railroad. Robert Pitcairn, then 30 years old, would be the superintendent of that vital link of the PRR.

Cambria Iron Works

Two milestones made 1852 another turning point for Johnstown. First, the mainline of the Pennsylvania Railroad was completed through the town on December 10 of that year. Although the railroad would continue to use the Allegheny Portage Railroad to connect to Hollidaysburg for two more years, the impending demise of the Allegheny Portage Railroad and Pennsylvania Main Line Canal was apparent to all.

Second, the Cambria Iron Works received a Pennsylvania charter on June 29, 1852.

The area around Johnstown held mineral riches, including iron ore and coal, that supplied several small stone blast furnaces. But the Cambria Iron Works was to be far more extensive than an isolated furnace and would produce iron rails for the growing railroad industry.

A March 27, 1853, newspaper article painted a rosy future for the Cambria Iron Works and Johnstown:

> We were not at all mistaken in saying that this Company will expend half a million of dollars in Johnstown this summer. It will be the making of the place. People should buy lots soon and build as we think the entire salable property in town will all be bought up during the summer. Pittsburg was once as small a place as Johnstown, and the time may come when Johnstown will be as large as Pittsburg. No reason can be given why it should not be as great a business place.[6]

Unfortunately, financial issues interrupted the construction of the Cambria Iron Works, so on May 21, 1855, six Philadelphia investors, including Charles S. Woods and Daniel Johnson Morrell, each contributed $30,000 to form Wood, Morrell and Company. The new company leased the Cambria Iron Works for a period of five years.[7]

Born on August 8, 1821, in North Berwick, Maine, Daniel Morrell was a successful dry goods merchant in Philadelphia with no iron-making experience. However, the new operators of the Cambria Iron Works decided he was the best candidate to revive the floundering facility in Johnstown, so Morrell moved there in 1855.

By 1856, the Cambria Iron Works, operated by Wood, Morrell and Company and managed by Daniel J. Morrell, employed 1,500 men. By 1870, that number grew to 4,000; 2,500 in the mills and shops and 1,500 in the mines. By 1889, Cambria Iron had about 7,000 workers, and the population of Johnstown exceeded 20,000.

Cambria Iron became a leader in producing iron rails for the railroads. In one week during May 1859, the facility completed 722 tons of rails, and after the Civil War, weekly output increased to 1,000 tons.[8]

Bessemer Process Comes to Johnstown

In the late 1860s, a few U.S. plants started using the Bessemer process to efficiently convert iron into steel. Daniel Morrell recognized that steel rails would be more durable than iron rails, so he started the difficult job of convincing the owners of Cambria Iron to install two six-ton Bessemer converters. It took him eight years.

Alexander Holley, the expert who would later create the Edgar Thomson Works for Andrew Carnegie, was hired to design the new Bessemer plant in Johnstown. Finally, on July 12, 1871, Cambria Iron produced their first Bessemer steel for rails.[9]

Plaque in Johnstown commemorating the Cambria Iron Company. Cambria Iron was recognized as an industry leader in technological innovations (photograph by the author).

King of Johnstown

The energetic Daniel Morrell was also heavily involved in activities outside of Cambria Iron:

- President of the local gas and water company from 1860 to 1884;
- President of the First National Bank of Johnstown from 1863 to 1884;
- President of the Johnstown City Council for many years;
- President of the American Iron and Steel Institute in 1879;
- Republican U.S. Representative from 1867 to 1871;
- Chairman of the U.S. House Committee on Manufactures in the Fortieth and Forty-first Congresses; and
- Commissioner of the Paris Exposition of 1878.[10]

Morrellville Borough, west of Johnstown, is named for him.

Historian David McCullough described Morrell's home and reputation:

> He lived on Main Street in the finest house in Johnstown, a tall brick house with a mansard roof, painted white and set among gardens and shade trees on a lawn that took up a full city block. He had the only greenhouses in town, a full-time gardener, and all his property was enclosed with an ornamental iron fence. Children used to gather by the fence after school, hoping for a chance to look at him. "Whatever Mr. Morrell wants, well that's it," they heard at home. He was the king of Johnstown.[11]

In 1878, Cyrus Elder, the Cambria Iron Works chief counsel, recognized Morrell's contributions to Johnstown:

Daniel Johnson Morrell: "The King of Johnstown" (1821–1885) (Library of Congress).

> When Mr. Morrell came to Johnstown the mud in the streets was often bottomless; now the streets are well paved with stone. Bridges over the rivers which were of wood are now of iron. The once gloomy ways are lighted with gas, the wooden market sheds are replaced with handsome public buildings and school houses have been erected through his munificent aid. The citizens know him as the promoter of all these improvements, the organizer and chief officer of the Savings Bank, the National Bank, the Gas Company, the president of the active spirit in municipal affairs.[12]

Abusing the Environment

In 1860, James Moore Swank, editor of the *Cambria Tribune*, extolled the virtues of Johnstown as a vacation destination:

> The attractions of Johnstown as a place of summer resort for the residents of the large cities are not appreciated—either at home or abroad. Someday we will write a "leader" on the subject which, we have no doubt, will have the effect of immediately filling the town with strangers. Our scenery is grand beyond description, neighboring streams large and numerous; drives good; women beautiful and accomplished; men all gentlemen and scholars; hotels as good as the best.[13]

By 1880, the idea of vacationing in Johnstown would seem ludicrous. In his 1940 dissertation, "A History of Johnstown," Nathan Shappee describes the scene greeting an 1880s visitor arriving by train from Pittsburgh:

As the traveler entered the Conemaugh gorge the smoke of the mills palled the eastern view. As his train passed Dornick Point, the smoke and fires of a company brick plant at Coopersdale gleamed on the left. A company railroad, busy with trains and cars loaded with brick and iron, paralleled the Pennsylvania Railroad across the river to the north. When the traveler crossed the stone bridge, the greatest view of the works was at his left. Four blast furnaces roared night and day. The boom of the rolling mill pounded against his ears. Showers of sparks created the only beauty of the scene. Bessemer retorts grumbled into an angry roar as they spit out the impurities of molten metal held in their hot mouths.[14]

Pittsburgh was long known as the Smoky City and "Hell with the Lid Taken Off,"[15] but in the 1880s, Johnstown was not much better.

The boundaries of Johnstown are tightly defined and confined by nature. Steep mountains limit the space available for building homes, stores, factories, hospitals, schools, and streets to about 2,500 acres. The only way to expand the buildable area was to encroach on the river banks. If the Cambria Iron Works had slag to dump, the river banks were a nearby depository. If the citizens needed garbage dumps or sewer outlets, the rivers were the obvious choice. By 1887, "The Stonycreek from Chestnut Street to the Point was one continuous garbage dump where 'loud and pestiferous stinks' prevailed."[16]

Some conversion of rivers to filled land was more intentional. When the Pennsylvania Railroad required more space, it filled in the canal. Then it sold the obsolete canal basin to the Cambria Iron Works, which promptly converted it to useable land. In 1873, the PRR filled in the Conemaugh River near Franklin Street to obtain space for more freight tracks. All over town, rivers and canals narrowed or disappeared, becoming the sites for railroad tracks, factories, and even houses.

But the cost of narrowing the rivers would eventually have to be paid. Even sustained moderate rainfall caused water to spill from the diminished river channels into the streets. What would happen if heavy rain persisted for more than 24 hours?

15

South Fork Fishing & Hunting Club

"The thing for the rich man to do was to divide his life into two parts. The first part should be for acquisition, the second for distribution. At this stage the gentlemen of the South Fork Fishing and Hunting Club were attending strictly to the first part."
—David McCullough

In July 1853, Robert Pitcairn started working for the Pennsylvania Railroad at a job obtained for him through his friend, Andrew Carnegie. Robert's duties were as a telegrapher and assistant ticket agent at Mountain House, Pennsylvania, where the Allegheny Portage Railroad joined the recently built Pennsylvania Railroad.

Most of Robert's long career with the PRR would be centered in Pittsburgh. But in 1881, he would return to a beautiful remnant of the Pennsylvania Main Line Canal (PMLC) as a member of the South Fork Fishing & Hunting Club.

History of the South Fork Dam and Lake Conemaugh

As discussed in Chapter 1, the PMLC comprised an 82-mile railroad connecting the eastern canal to Philadelphia and two canal segments separated by the Allegheny Portage Railroad. Soon after the line opened in 1834, it was discovered that rainfall during the dry season was inadequate to keep the canal segments operational. With so much invested in building the PMLC, a solution to the water problem was mandatory.

In April 1835, the Pennsylvania Legislature approved $100,000 to survey and begin constructing two dams, one to supply water to the Western Division Canal between Pittsburgh and Johnstown and one for the Juniata Division Canal between Hollidaysburg and Columbia. Sylvester Welsh, the principal engineer for the western division of the PMLC, identified suitable locations for both dams in 1835, and the state legislature authorized the Canal Commissioners to commence work on February 18, 1836. The western dam's site was on the south fork of the Little Conemaugh River, so the structure became known as the South Fork Dam.

Political disputes and lack of funds delayed the start of dam construction until the spring of 1840. Work continued at a low level because of insufficient money and stopped entirely on May 1, 1841. Five years later, on January 3, 1846, an appropriation of $20,000 allowed work on the western dam to restart. However, a spring flood damaged other portions of the canal system, and resources were shifted to remedy those problems.

Another appropriation of $45,000 on April 15, 1851, allowed the stuttering project to resume again. Finally, further funding of $55,000 on May 4, 1852, resulted in enough progress to permit the closing of the discharge pipes and filling of the reservoir. By early September, the lake was 40 feet deep at the dam. Some of that water was released to keep the Western Division Canal full enough to operate. Thus, the South Fork Dam fulfilled its objective.

When filled to its design depth, Lake Conemaugh, created and restrained by the dam, was almost three miles long, one mile wide, up to 72 feet deep, covered over 400 acres, and held back 16 million tons of water.[1]

Obsolete at Completion

The Pennsylvania Railroad completed its all-rail link from Philadelphia to Pittsburgh in 1854, making the Allegheny Portage Railroad obsolete. On August 1, 1857, the Pennsylvania Railroad purchased the entire Pennsylvania Main Line Canal, and its supporting structures and equipment. The PRR operated the Pittsburgh-to-Johnstown Canal until 1863 but then abandoned it. With the Western Division Canal closed, its water supply from Lake Conemaugh was no longer needed.

It Happened Before

"South Fork Dam Breaks; Floods Johnstown" might have been the newspaper headline on July 26, 1862. But because the breach in the South Fork Dam formed

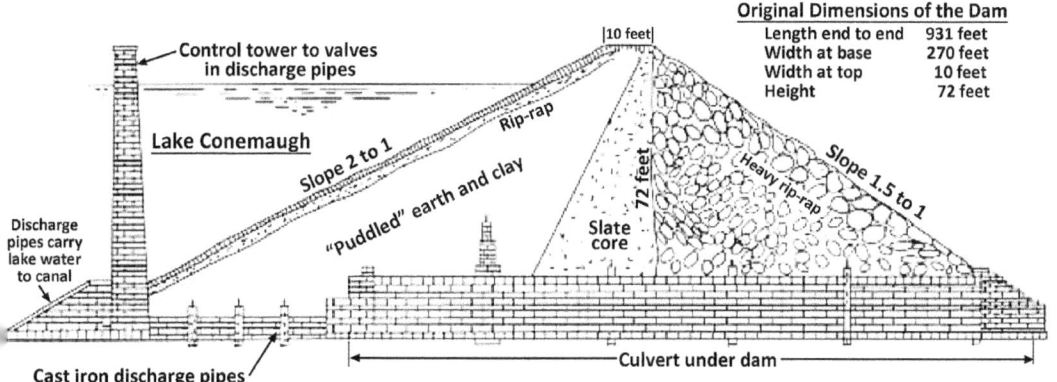

Original design of the South Fork Dam by Morris, 1841. Before construction, the stone control tower was replaced by a wooden structure (original 1841 diagram adapted by the author).

slowly and Lake Conemaugh was far from full, water in the Little Conemaugh River rose just three feet. By the time it reached Johnstown, the increase was almost too small to notice.

Why did the dam fail? In his thoroughly researched 2019 study of the 1889 Johnstown Flood, Neil Coleman suggests scavengers might have climbed through the culvert under the dam to reach the drainage pipes. Once there, they would have access to metallic lead that sealed the joints between sections of the drainage pipes and filled the spaces where the pipes entered the culvert. They could then sell the valuable lead to junk dealers. With the lead removed, water could seep around the pipes and erode the soil supporting the drainage culvert.[2]

Whatever the cause, the stone culvert through the base of the dam collapsed in 1862. With that support gone, the embankment itself slowly collapsed, opening the way for water from the lake to flow through. The breach in the dam was triangular, with a width at the top of 200 feet and a depth of 50 feet.

Because of the gradual collapse, it took 11 hours for the lake to drain. As with any earthen dam, flow over or through the structure carries away more material and thus accelerates the failure of the entire dam. No one knew that this small flood would be a precursor and contributor to a monstrous and fatal flood 37 years later. Because the dam was useless to the PRR, they did not repair the break.

The dam and lake stood unused until March 25, 1875, when the PRR sold 500 acres, including the dam and partially drained lake, to a former employee, John Reilly, for $2,500.[3] Reilly had just been elected to the U.S. House of Representatives, where he served from March 4, 1875, to March 3, 1877. After his House term ended, Reilly returned to Altoona, rejoining the PRR as superintendent of transportation.

Benjamin Ruff and the Club

Benjamin Franklin Ruff, born in 1829, was a former railroad tunnel contractor, coke salesman, and real estate broker. Based on the obsolete and damaged South Fork Dam, Ruff planned to create a summer resort for some wealthy Pittsburgh friends.

Ruff formed the South Fork Fishing & Hunting Club of Pittsburgh on May 19, 1879. The club was capitalized at $10,000 in $100 shares. Ruff bought eight shares himself and convinced his friend, Henry Clay Frick, to subscribe for six shares. Fourteen other prominent Pittsburghers subscribed for two shares each, making a total of 42 shares sold. Frick became the spokesman and promoter for the Club. Ruff served as Club president until he died on March 29, 1887.

In November 1879, the owners sought a charter for a nonprofit corporation from the Allegheny County Court of Common Pleas. Despite the dam and lake being in Cambria County, Judge Edwin B. Stowe signed the Allegheny County charter on November 17, 1879. By incorporating in Allegheny County, the owners prevented Cambria County authorities and residents from learning the details of their project.[4]

At this point, Ruff had a chartered organization and members but no dam or lake. That shortcoming was remedied when John Reilly transferred ownership of the damaged dam, the partial lake, and 500 acres of land to the South Fork Fishing & Hunting Club of Pittsburgh for $2,000 on March 15, 1880.[5]

Irresponsible actions created more links in the fatal chain, culminating in the Johnstown Flood of 1889. In late 1879, either Reilly, Ruff, or perhaps both removed the 60 to 70 tons of cast iron drainage pipes that ran under the dam. In a later hearing on the causes of the Johnstown Flood, Robert Pitcairn testified that the former owner, John Reilly, had removed and sold the pipes. Other evidence indicates that workers hired by Ruff removed the cast iron. Coleman's 2019 book on the dam and flood postulates that Ruff's workers removed the pipes while Reilly still owned the property, sold them, and gave the proceeds to Reilly in partial payment for the land and dam. Regardless of who removed the pipes, the dam was left with no way to lower the water level of the lake behind it.

As neither the PRR nor Reilly had repaired the damaged dam after the 1862 breach, it was left for Benjamin Ruff to rebuild the structure. According to David McCullough in his classic 1968 book, *The Johnstown Flood*, Ruff boarded up the stone culvert (where the drainage pipes had been) and dumped "every manner of local rock, mud, brush, hemlock boughs, hay, just about everything at hand. Even horse manure was used in some quantity."[6]

A further crucial change to the dam was to lower its height by about three feet. Most commentators claim that the lowering was to make the top wide enough to accommodate a two-lane carriage road. However, Coleman's study suggests a more likely reason was to provide Ruff with readily accessible material to fill the old breach.[7]

Whatever the reason, the lowered top of the dam was then just seven feet above the spillway's surface, insufficient to prevent a rapidly rising lake from flowing over the top. Such overtopping of an earthen dam almost always results in the total failure of such a structure.

In another compromise to save money, Ruff used smaller rocks to cover the dam's downstream face instead of the heavy riprap specified in the original plans.

To access the east side of the lake, the owners built a wooden bridge across the spillway. The final factor in compromising the dam's integrity was the installation of heavy bars and screens

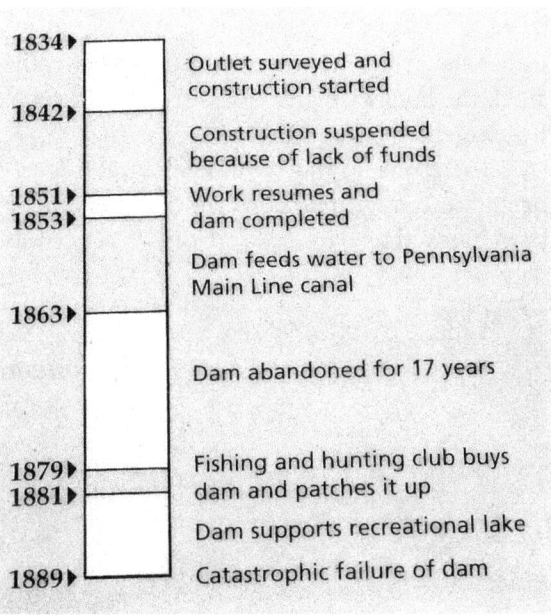

Condensed history of the South Fork Dam (photograph by the author at the Johnstown Flood National Memorial).

Lake Conemaugh behind South Fork Dam. Note on the left the bridge over the spillway and the A-shaped debris catcher behind the spillway (courtesy of National Park Service, Harpers Ferry Center, Commissioned Art Collection, artist Lloyd Kenneth Townsend).

under the bridge to prevent the escape of valuable fish. The Club had spent $1,000 to stock the lake with black bass from Lake Erie, and the screens would preserve that investment.[8]

There was no way to lower the water level in the lake, the height of the dam had been reduced with no corresponding lowering of the spillway, and the spillway had been blocked by bars and screens. Disaster was inevitable.

Map of the dam and spillway before the flood; a bridge across the spillway had a screen below it to keep fish from escaping. That screen became clogged by debris and held back the rising water, which eventually overtopped the sunken center portion of the dam, causing its collapse (adapted by the author from a display at the dam site).

Membership

The original plans for the South Fork Fishing & Hunting Club called for no more than 100 members and their families, and the initiation fee was $100.

The Club opened for guests in July 1881. Its purpose was to provide members, their families, and guests a sanctuary from Pittsburgh's noise, heat, and dirt. The first page of the ledger book from the Club reveals that H.C. Frick and Robert Pitcairn, with four others, visited the Club on August 25, 1881.

A list of members, probably by date of joining, is shown below. The two pages include 60 people, including B.F. Ruff (#1), H.C. Frick (#26), Robt. Pitcairn (#34), Thos. M. Carnegie (#49), A. Carnegie (#55), and D.J. Morrell (#57).

The two pages shown are all that exist today, but it seems likely that other members were listed on a subsequent page since lost to posterity.

126 Members

1 B F Ruff
2 C C Hussey
3 H Hartley
4 Jno D Hunt
5 H Holdship
6 M B Suydam
7 J J Lawrence
8 C B Shea
9 Jno B Jackson
10 O McClintock
11 W L "
12 F J "
13 Jno F Wilcox
14 B Shaw
15 F Semple
16 F B Laughlin
17 W F Fundenberg
18 W T Dunn
19 D C Phillips
20 E J Unger
21 H C Yeager
22 D R Ewart
23 C A Carpenter
24 C J Clarke
25 Thos S "
26 H C Frick
27 F S Bissell
28 R C Gray
29 Jno Caldwell Jr
30 Jno W Chalfant
31 Jno K Ewing (Uniontown)
32 H J Brunot (Greensburgh)
33 Jas McGregor
34 Robt Pitcairn
35 Wm Mullins
36 W A McIntosh
37 Geo B Roberts
38 W C Taylor
39 E A Myers
40 W K Woodwell
41 Jos R "
42 A C Crawford
43 Durbin Horne
44 A V Holmes
45 O F Wharton
46 J B White
47 Jno A Harper
48 Geo W Hope
49 Thos M. Carnegie
50 Jesse Lippincott
51 Jas M. Schoonmaker
52 J. G. Schwartz
53 Lewis Irwin
54 Wm Rea
55 A. Carnegie
56 Saml Rea
57 D.J. Morrell (Johnstown)
58 H. Sellers McKee
59 Calvin Wells
60 Aaron French

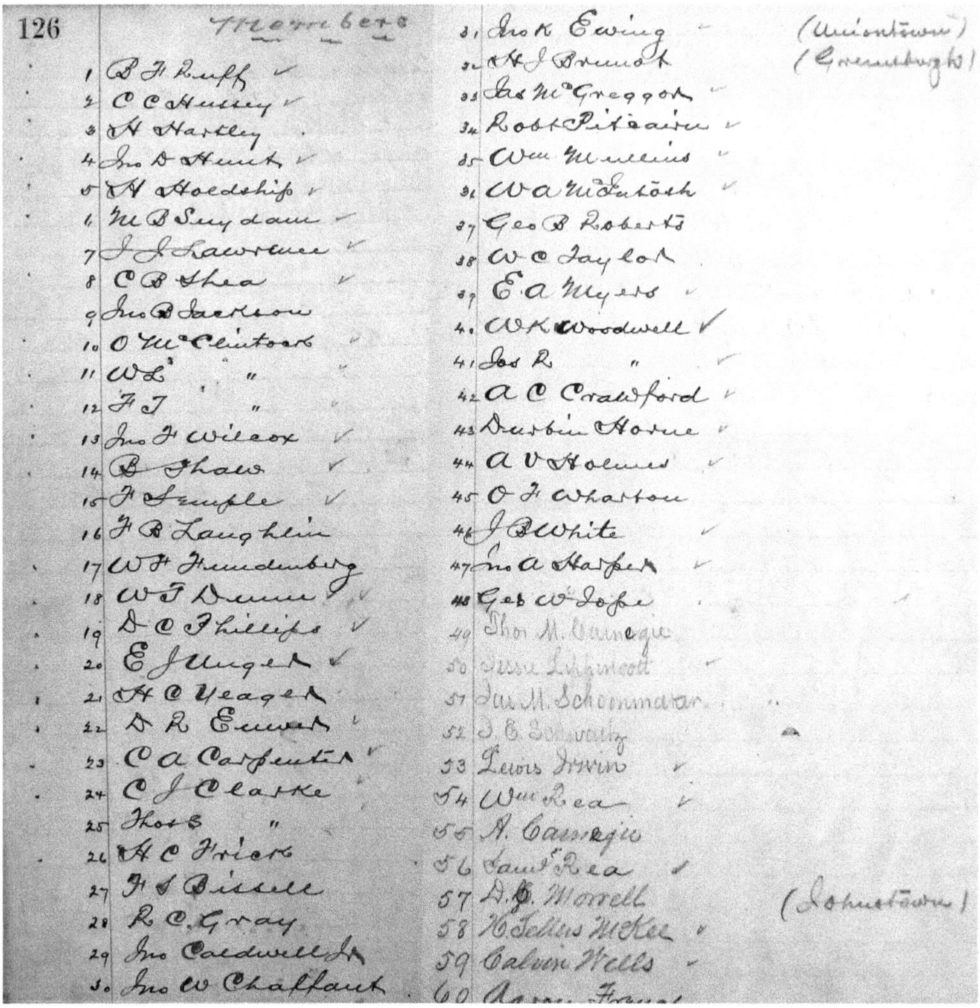

Member list, South Fork Fishing & Hunting Club (courtesy of Neil Coleman; original ledger is in the archives of Heritage Johnstown).

By 1889, the Club had at least 61 member families, primarily wealthy industrialists, businessmen, bankers, and attorneys from the East End of Pittsburgh. Among the better-known names were:

- Andrew Carnegie, steel magnate and later an outstanding philanthropist, and his brother, Thomas;
- Henry Clay Frick, coke magnate and chairman of Carnegie Steel Company;
- Henry Phipps, Jr., chairman of Carnegie Steel Company before Frick;
- Philander Chase Knox, personal attorney for Carnegie and Frick, who would serve as U.S. attorney general under Presidents William McKinley and Theodore Roosevelt, U.S senator from Pennsylvania (twice), and U.S. secretary of state under President William Howard Taft;
- John G.A. Leishman, vice chairman of Carnegie Brothers and then president of Carnegie Steel Company. Leishman later became a U.S. ambassador, first to Switzerland and then to three other countries;
- John Caldwell, Jr., treasurer of George Westinghouse's Philadelphia Company and trustee of Carnegie Institute;
- Durbin Horne, head of Pittsburgh department store, Joseph Horne and Company;
- Daniel J. Morrell, head of the Cambria Iron Company in Johnstown;
- Andrew W. Mellon, banker and future U.S. secretary of the treasury under Presidents Harding, Coolidge, and Hoover;
- William Thaw, one of the 100 wealthiest Americans and father-in-law of Thomas Carnegie's son, George Lauder Carnegie;

Unknown artist's rendition of the original South Fork Fishing & Hunting Club clubhouse (photograph taken by the author at the clubhouse on June 28, 2021).

15. South Fork Fishing & Hunting Club

South Fork Fishing & Hunting Club clubhouse, circa 1888. The gabled building to the left is the original structure, completed in 1881, and the larger section to the right is the Annex, completed in about 1887. The Annex is still standing, but the original section burned down in 1930 (University of Pittsburgh Library System, Historic Pittsburgh collection).

Philander Chase Knox cottage. This cottage was built in 1885 and Andrew Carnegie probably stayed here when he visited the Club. Knox owned the home until 1904 and it is now privately owned (photograph by the author).

- Samuel Rea, future president of the Pennsylvania Railroad; and
- Robert Pitcairn, superintendent of the Pittsburgh Division of the Pennsylvania Railroad and close friend of Andrew Carnegie.

The three-story, 47-bedroom clubhouse featured a 150-seat dining room.

There were also 16 privately owned "cottages" that were actually large houses. Wealthy members built the cottages on land leased from the Club. The first was built in 1872, before the Club's existence, and the last in 1888. Nine houses are still standing, six in private hands and three owned by the National Park Service.[9] Andrew Carnegie did not own a cottage, but if he visited the lake, he likely stayed at the one owned by his personal attorney, Philander Chase Knox.

The Club's water fleet included two steam-powered boats, many sailboats and canoes, and boathouses. There was an annual regatta, theatricals, and musical performances to entertain the visitors.[10]

The lake on the mountaintop functioned as a getaway for the hard-working, wealthy Pittsburghers, easy enough to reach but far enough away to forget the burdens of the city. But other than Daniel J. Morrell and his family and guests, no one from Johnstown could enjoy Lake Conemaugh.

16

The Johnstown Flood—Part 1

"The water by now, from one end of town to the other, was anywhere from two to ten feet deep.
　It was already higher than the '87 flood, making it, by noon at least, Johnstown's worst flood on record."

—David McCullough

The Flood City

The 1862 flood was not the first in Johnstown; the rise in water level from that first dam break was too small to even qualify as a flood. The first acknowledged flood occurred in 1808 when a small dam on Stony Creek failed. In 1847, another dam on Stony Creek ruptured. Neither of these failures caused substantial damage. In 1875, heavy rains caused the Conemaugh River to rise two feet in one hour. From 1808 to 1977, Johnstown suffered through 21 floods, three of them severe.

Chronological List of Johnstown Floods
(* denotes major floods)

1808	1818	1837	1861	1880	1884	1907
1816	1819	1847	1867	1881	1887	1936*
1817	1820	1859	1875	1883	1889*	1977*

Johnstown is known as the Flood City. Several local merchants include Flood City in their names, and there is even an annual Flood City Music Festival. Why is Johnstown so prone to flooding?

Topography

Part of the answer is simple and obvious. The town is at the junction of two narrow mountain valleys. All the drainage from rainfall on those mountains flows into two rivers, the Little Conemaugh and the Stony Creek. These two rivers merge in the middle of Johnstown to form the Conemaugh River.

As one who grew up in Johnstown and has continued to monitor the weather

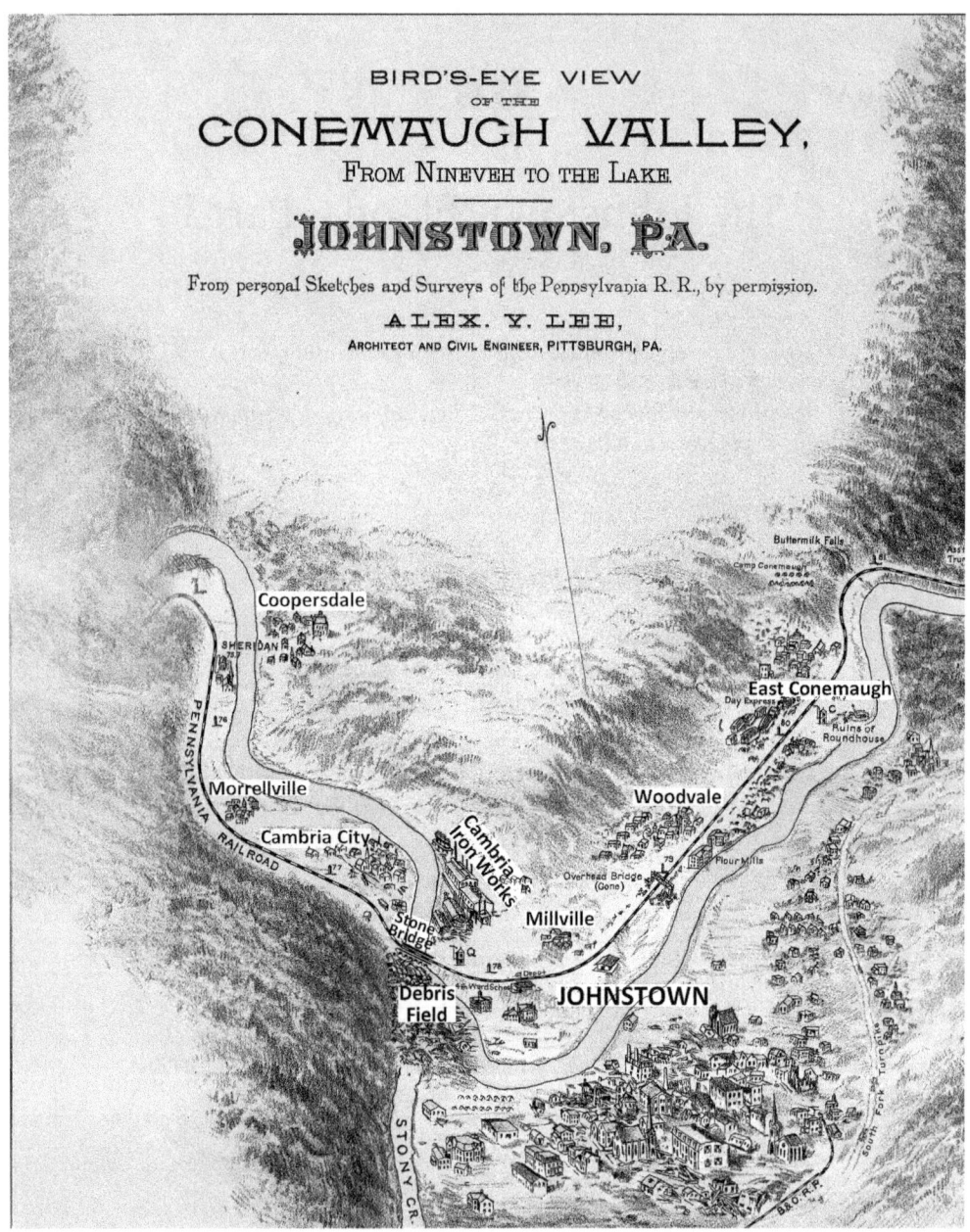

Above and opposite: "From Nineveh to the Lake." Map from 1889 by Alex Y. Lee (Library of Congress).

there, I have the impression that rainstorms hover over the area. Although difficult to quantify, another aspect of the topography might explain the long duration of storms.

To the west of Johnstown is a gap in the mountain range called the Conemaugh Gap or Packsaddle. Storms approaching from the west are funneled through that gap into the Johnstown basin and then trapped by the ridge of mountains to the east.

16. The Johnstown Flood—Part 1

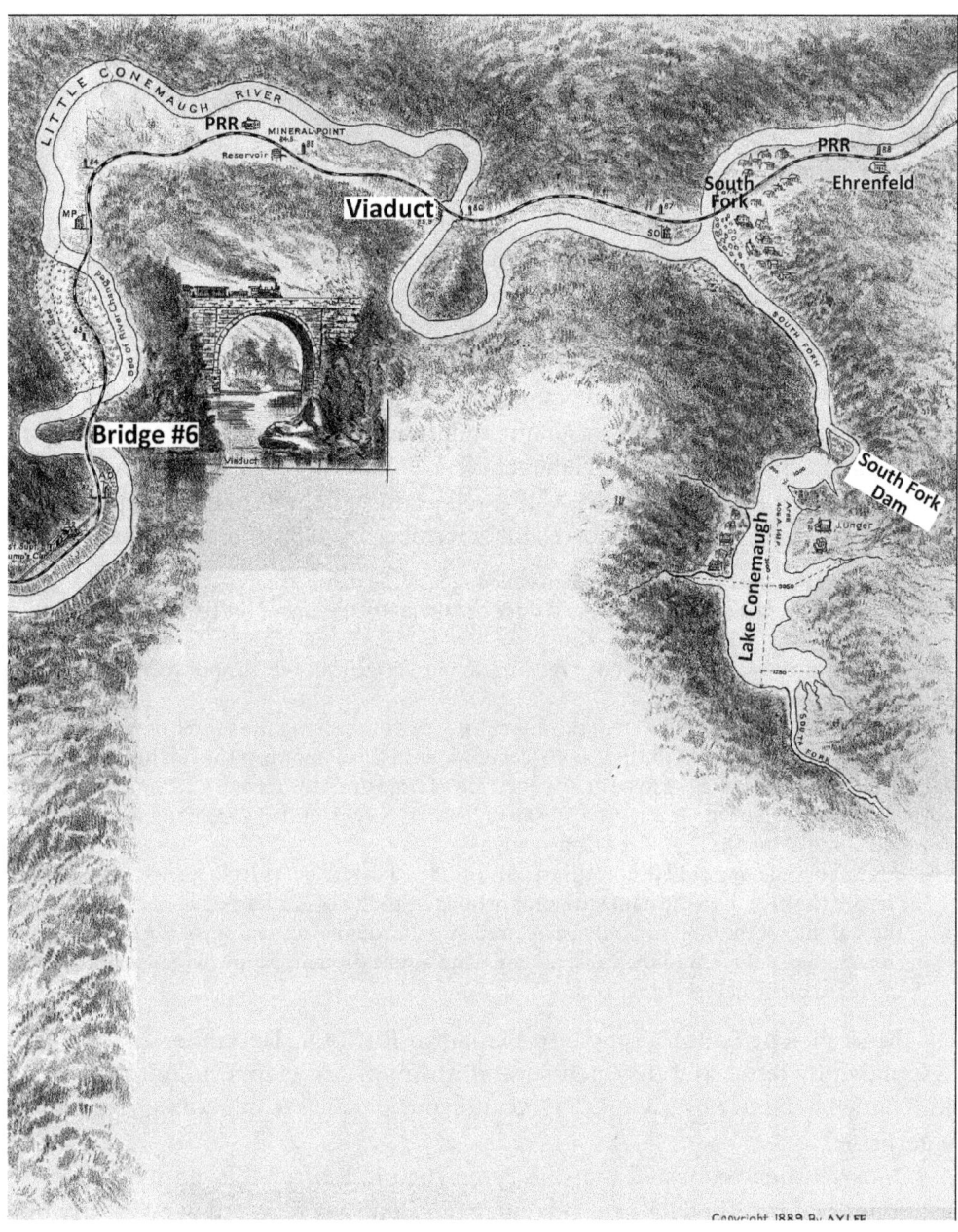

The resulting rainfall can exceed five inches per day and last for several days. Such was the case for the major floods of 1889, 1936, and 1977.

The 1889 map on these pages illustrates the topography of the area. At that time, Johnstown and the adjacent suburbs were home to about 22,000 people (most authors claim Johnstown's population in 1889 was 30,000, but Shappee reported 20,639 in 1890[1]). On the map, shaded regions denote mountains. Lake Conemaugh and the South Fork Dam appear at the far right. Johnstown is at the lower left on the map. Following the Little Conemaugh River west from the dam to the city reveals that steep mountains constrain the river to a narrow channel until it reaches the eastern portion of the suburb at East Conemaugh. In other words, excess water has no place to go until it approaches Johnstown. In 14 miles of river, the water descends 400 feet.

Worries and Warnings

Daniel Morrell, the general manager of the Cambria Iron Works and "King of Johnstown," became a member of the South Fork Fishing & Hunting Club primarily to monitor activities there, especially regarding the dam's safety.

With extensive modifications to the South Fork Dam underway, Morrell sent his chief engineer and second-in-command, John Fulton, to inspect the dam. Fulton, his assistant W.A. Fellows, club members Colonel B.J. Unger and C.A. Carpenter, and Pittsburgh engineer N.M. McDowell examined the dam in November 1880.

Fulton sent his report to Morrell on November 26, 1880. It read, in part:

> There appear to me two serious elements of danger in the dam:
> 1st. The want of a discharge pipe to reduce or take the water out of the dam for needed repairs.
> 2nd. The unsubstantial method of repair, leaving a large leak, which appears to be cutting the new embankment.
> As the water cannot be lowered, the difficulty arises of reaching the source of the present destructive leaks. At present there is 40 feet of water in the dam, when the full head of 60 feet is reached, it appears to me to be only a question of time until the former cutting is repeated. Should this break be made during a season of flood, it is evident that considerable damage would ensue along the line of the Conemaugh.
> It is impossible to estimate how disastrous this flood would be, as its force would depend on the size of the breach in the dam with proportional rapidity of discharge.
> The stability of the dam can only be assured by a thorough overhauling of the present lining on the upper slope, and the construction of an ample discharge pipe to reduce or remove the water to make necessary repairs.[2]

Morrell sent Fulton's report to Benjamin Ruff. On December 2, 1880, Ruff responded by letter and disputed several unimportant errors in Fulton's report. Ruff ended his letter by saying, "[Y]ou and your people are in no danger from our enterprise."

Morrell then requested that the Pennsylvania Railroad have their engineers examine the dam. The PRR sent two engineers, but they reported opposite findings on the dam's safety.

Frustrated but powerless, Morrell wrote again to Ruff:

> We do not wish to put any obstruction in the way of your accomplishing your object in the reconstruction of the dam; but we must protest against the erection of a dam at that place, that will be a perpetual menace to the lives and property of those residing in the upper valley of the Conemaugh from its insecure construction. In my judgement there should have been provided some means by which the water could be let out of the dam in case of trouble, and I think that you will find it necessary to provide an outlet pipe or gate before any engineer could pronounce the job a safe one. If this dam could be securely reconstructed with a safe means of driving off the water in case any weakness manifests itself, I should regard the

accomplishment of this work a very desirable one, and if some arrangement could be made with your Association by which the store of water in this reservoir could be used in time of great drouth in the mountains, this Company would be willing to cooperate with you in the work, and contribute liberally toward making the dam absolutely safe.[3]

Despite the intense attention, nothing significant was done in the next eight and a half years to resolve the dangers uncovered by Fulton's inspection.

Mere Mortals

Daniel Morrell was the general manager of the Cambria Iron Works for 29 years, but due to poor health, he retired in 1884. He died on August 20, 1885, at 64, and is buried in the central pride of place at Grandview Cemetery above Johnstown.

John Fulton succeeded Morrell as general manager of the Cambria Iron Works in 1886. Cyrus Elder, chief counsel for Cambria Iron, took Morrell's membership in the South Fork Fishing & Hunting Club.

A Great Lakes freighter named the SS *Daniel J. Morrell* was launched to honor Morrell on August 22, 1906. Unfortunately, the ship met the same tragic fate that would later befall the legendary SS *Edmund Fitzgerald* when she broke apart in a severe storm on Lake Huron on November 29, 1966.[4]

Benjamin Franklin Ruff died on March 29, 1887, in Pittsburgh. Neither Morrell nor Ruff lived to see the disaster wrought by Lake Conemaugh and the South Fork Dam.

Pay the Piper

Light to moderate rain fell all afternoon on May 30, 1889, then called Decoration Day, but at about 11:00 p.m., pouring rain started. Very few South Fork Fishing & Hunting Club members were in residence, as the "season" would not begin for another three weeks. That day, the rainfall in western Pennsylvania was the heaviest ever recorded in the area, six to eight inches in 24 hours.

Numerous mountain streams, all overflowing their banks, fed Lake Conemaugh, which rose one inch every ten

Monument to the Morrell Family in the center of Grandview Cemetery, Johnstown (photograph by the author).

minutes. Logs, stumps, and other debris clogged the fish screens and prevented excess lake water from draining over the spillway. There was no place for the deluge of water to go but over the top of the dam.

At about noon on May 31, the telegraph agent at South Fork, just below the dam, received an excited visitor. The agent, Emma Ehrenfeld, recognized the man but could hardly believe his story. He said a man came from the lake and told him, "It's rising very fast and there's danger of the reservoir breaking."[5]

Emma knew she could not send the message to Johnstown because there was a break in the lines somewhere to the west. But she could reach Mineral Point, the next station to the west, so she sent a telegram to W.H. Pickerell, the operator there. Together they composed a message addressed to the yardmaster at East Conemaugh, J.C. Walkinshaw, and the division head, Robert Pitcairn. The actual telegram is lost to posterity, but the message said something like, "SOUTH FORK DAM LIABLE TO BREAK: NOTIFY THE PEOPLE OF JOHNSTOWN TO PREPARE FOR THE WORST."

Pickerell wrote out the message and sent it by foot with a trackman named William Reichard. Reichard walked as far west as Buttermilk Falls, where he handed the message to his boss, L.L. Rusher, who was foreman of the Division. Rusher started to walk to East Conemaugh to deliver the message in person, but when he got to the next tower, called the "AO" tower, he found that the telegraph lines to the west were operational. The AO tower operator, R.W. Shade, sent the message by wire to Walkinshaw at East Conemaugh and to telegraph agent Frank Deckert in Johnstown. Deckert forwarded the warning to Charles Culp at the Union Depot in Pittsburgh. Culp later said he took it right over "and laid it on Mr. Pitcairn's table in front of him." The message arrived on Pitcairn's desk at about 1:00 p.m.[6] Pitcairn immediately boarded his private railroad car and headed to Johnstown.

Two other telegraph messages warning Johnstown of the coming calamity followed. One, sent at 1:52 p.m. and arriving in Johnstown around 2:00 p.m., and also lost in the flood, said something to the effect of "WATER IS NOW RUNNING OVER THE TOP OF LAKE DAM IN CENTER AND WEST SIDE AND IS BECOMING DANGEROUS." The third and final telegram was sent at 2:25 p.m. and reported, "AGENT JOHNSTOWN—DAM IS BECOMING DANGEROUS AND MAY POSSIBLY GO." This telegram reached Johnstown telegraph operator Frank Deckert at 2:44 p.m. Deckert alerted operator Hettie Ogle at the Johnstown Western Union office, and she notified the Pittsburgh office. Unfortunately, it would be the last telegram she would ever send, as the oncoming water wiped out her office, and her body was never recovered.

At 3:15 p.m., Hettie Ogle called George Swank, editor of the *Johnstown Tribune* newspaper, to say that she had been told that the South Fork Dam was getting worse all the time and that the danger of its breaking was increasing momentarily. Swank later wrote, "The town sat down with its hands in its pockets to make the best of a very dreary situation. All … had got out of reach of the flood that could and there was nothing to do but wait; and what impatient waiting it was."[7]

Despite heroic efforts by workers and residents, at 11:30 a.m. on May 31, water started to flow over the dam. Between 2:50 and 2:55 p.m., the dam's center disintegrated, and the resulting 200-foot-wide gap drained the lake within an hour. Then, carrying before it trees, small bridges, houses, dead animals, and assorted rubbish, the 60-foot-high wall of water rushed down the valley through the town of South Fork.

Because they were built on a hillside well above the river channel, many homes in South Fork remained untouched by the water. But the rushing water picked up debris from lower down the hill, including railroad ties and rolling stock, trees, and bushes. When the flood reached the first river loop, it tore out virgin timber, oak, beech, and chestnut trees over 100 feet tall. Some of those massive trees lodged across the 80-foot arch of the stone Conemaugh Viaduct, which the PRR had opened in 1852. The trees and debris behind

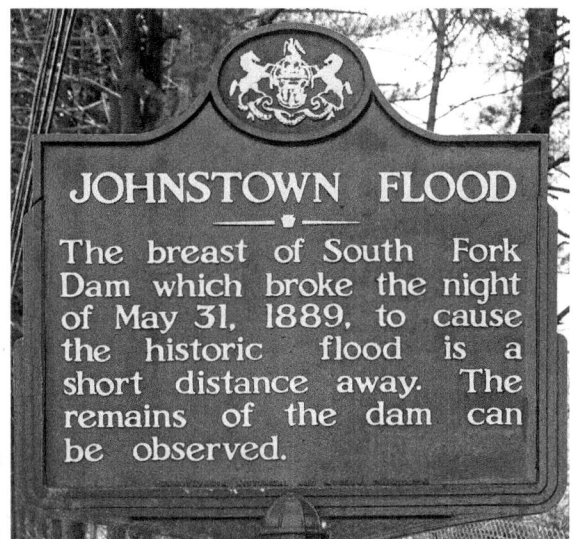

Historical marker near the site of the South Fork Dam (photograph by and courtesy of Mike Wintermantel).

them formed a new but temporary dam, and the water depth rose to about 67 feet. At 40 feet wide at its base and 28 feet wide at the top, the massive viaduct was strong. But its large stones were laid on top of each other without mortar between them, so it was no match for water comprising one-fifth of Lake Conemaugh's volume.

The viaduct collapsed, releasing the debris and water. Neil Coleman has calculated that the water flow rate when the viaduct failed would have been similar to the initial flow when the dam broke. The jam at the viaduct renewed the power of the flood.[8] Over 14 million tons of water roared at speeds up to 40 miles per hour down the narrow river channel, destroying everything in its path, picking up a dozen or more locomotives, some weighing as much as 50 tons,[9] along with several hundred railroad freight and passenger cars. A hundred or more houses and their terrified and doomed occupants added to the jumble of debris at the front of the surging water.[10]

The scene at the viaduct was repeated on a somewhat smaller scale at Bridge #6 (see map earlier in this chapter). Flood water pushing debris in front of it, slowed by the oxbow in the river, piled up at the bridge until the pressure demolished the barrier. Once again, the pent-up water, suddenly released, sped along its destructive path toward East Conemaugh, just 1.5 miles away.

The Gautier Mill of Cambria Iron Works was the next target and yielded many miles of barbed wire to the fatal mix.

At 4:07 p.m., after decimating the eastern suburbs of East Conemaugh and Woodvale, the torrent hit Johnstown.[11]

Eyewitness accounts of traumatic events can be exaggerated, but a story from Victor Heiser, who was 16 years old at the time, gives compelling testimony to the suddenness and power of the flood waters. He reported on his experiences during the Johnstown Flood:

Conemaugh Viaduct of the Pennsylvania Railroad in calmer times. Debris carried by the flood blocked the arch, forming a temporary dam and a lake almost 70 feet deep (author's collection).

All during the latter part of May 1889, a chill rain had been descending in torrents upon the Conemaugh Valley. The small city of Johnstown, walled in by precipitous Pennsylvania hills, was invaded by high water which stood knee deep in front of my father's house on Washington Street.

During the afternoon of the thirty-first, the overflow from the river crept steadily higher, inch by inch, through the streets of the town. Although it had not yet reached the stable, which stood on higher ground than the house, my father became concerned over the safety of his fine pair of horses which were tied in their stalls, and suggested that I make a dash for the stable and unfasten them. The rain was falling so hard that I was almost drenched as I plowed my laborious way through the two feet of water.

I had loosed the horses and was about to leave the shelter of the doorway when my ears were stunned by the most terrifying noise I had ever heard in my sixteen years of life. The dreadful roar was punctuated with a succession of tremendous crashes. I stood for a moment, bewildered and hesitant. I could see my mother and my father standing at an upper window in the house. My father, frantic with anxiety over my safety, was motioning me urgently toward the top of the building. Fortunately, I had made a passageway only a few days before to the red tin roof, so that some necessary repairs could be made. Thus it was only a matter of seconds before I was up on the ridge.

From my perch I could see a huge wall advancing with incredible rapidity down the diagonal street. It was not recognizable as water, it was a dark mass in which seethed houses, freight cars, trees, and animals. As this wall struck Washington Street broadside, my boyhood home was crushed like an eggshell before my eyes, and I saw it disappear.[12]

What Victor Heiser was seeing was not a normal flood, in which the water rises more or less continuously over time. Instead, it was tsunami-like, with a violent wall of roaring water hitting all at once. And this wall of water pushed before it all manner of debris, from dead bodies to houses, railroad cars, and locomotives.

Heiser continues:

I wanted to know how long it would take me to get to the other world, and in the split second before the stable was hit, I looked at my watch. It was exactly four-twenty.

But, instead of being shattered, the big barn was ripped from its foundations and began to roll, like a barrel, over and over. Stumbling, crawling, and racing, I somehow managed to keep on top.

Lying on my belly, I bumped along on the surface of the flood, which was crushing, crumbling, and splintering everything before it. The screams of the injured were hardly to be distinguished above the awful clamor; people were being killed all about me.

I was borne headlong toward a jam where the wreckage was already piling up between a stone church and a three story brick building. Into this hurly burly I was catapulted. The pressure was terrific. A tree would shoot out of the water; a huge girder would come thundering down. As these trees and girders drove booming into the jam, I jumped them desperately, one after another. Then suddenly a freight car reared up over my head; I could not leap that. But just as it plunged toward me, the brick building gave way, and my raft shot out from beneath the freight car like a bullet from a gun.

There was nothing I could do for anybody....

I was carried on toward the narrows below the city where the tracks of the Pennsylvania Railroad crossed both valley and river on a high embankment and bridge. When the twisted, interlaced timbers ahead of me struck the stone arches, they plugged them tight, and in the powerful recoil my raft was swept back behind the hill which had saved the lower part of the town from complete destruction and left many buildings standing.[13]

Heiser searched for his parents for two weeks, viewing hundreds of corpses as they arrived at multiple temporary morgues established around the shattered town. He finally found his mother's body and had it buried in the family plot at Grandview Cemetery. His father's body was later found and also buried there.[14]

Heiser mentions a stone arch bridge that stopped the forward progress of the floodwaters. Tragically, the thirty-acre debris field behind that bridge caught fire, and the victims who did not drown were incinerated. He commented on the horrific scene at the stone bridge:

As I approached the railway embankment, I saw that it had given way in the night and allowed the water to rush unimpeded toward Pittsburgh and the Mississippi. The consequent subsidence of the flood had left in front of the stone bridge several acres of wreckage in which many people were still imprisoned. This inflammable material had caught fire. I can still hear the maddened shrieks of the men, women and children, as the flames approached. I joined the rescue squads and we struggled for hours trying to release them from this funeral pyre,

The Schultz home with an extra tree. Six people were inside when the Johnstown flood hit; all survived (Wikimedia Commons).

Burning debris field at the PRR Stone Arch Bridge, 1889 (1890 lithograph, Library of Congress).

but our efforts were tragically hampered by the lack of axes and other tools. We could not save them all. It was horrible to watch helplessly while people, many of whom I actually knew, were being devoured in the holocaust.[15]

Victor Heiser later attended Jefferson Medical College in Philadelphia and became a renowned physician specializing in international public health issues.

The Stone Arch Bridge as it appeared in 2021 (photograph by the author).

He was associate director of the Rockefeller Foundation and was credited with saving 100,000 lives a year through his organization of sanitation and preventive medicine in the Philippine Islands. He wrote a best-selling book about his experiences, *An American Doctor's Odyssey: Adventures in Forty-Five Countries*. Heiser lived to age 99 and is buried next to his parents at Grandview Cemetery in Johnstown.[16]

Tombstone of Victor George Heiser (February 5, 1873– February 27, 1972), Grandview Cemetery, Johnstown, Pennsylvania (photograph by the author).

17

The Johnstown Flood—Part 2

> *"Oh, it seemed to me as if all the destructive elements of the Creator had been turned loose at once in that awful current of water: in less than two hours Conemaugh lake was dry; and its fearful burden of water was speeding on towards its thousands of victims in the cities below."*
>
> —Elias J. Unger

Pitcairn Heads to Johnstown

Robert Pitcairn left for Johnstown shortly after 1:00 p.m. on May 31, 1889, alarmed by the telegram he had just received about the South Fork Dam. He had first become aware of the dam in 1853 when he worked as an assistant ticket agent for the Pennsylvania Railroad near Hollidaysburg at the east end of the Allegheny Portage Railroad. Then, when it first broke in 1862, resulting damage to the PRR brought the dam into sharper focus. And now, as a member of the South Fork Fishing & Hunting Club, he had a personal interest in the dam.

The 53-year-old Pitcairn had traveled the route from Pittsburgh to Johnstown hundreds of times. He started from the Union Station in Pittsburgh and passed within three blocks of his home at the corner of Amberson and Ellsworth Avenues in Shadyside. Just two blocks further south sat Shadyside Presbyterian Church, where he had been an elder for years. A few miles further east, at the Homewood Station, he would pass Solitude, the home of his friend and business partner, George Westinghouse. Pitcairn was a director in several Westinghouse companies.

The tracks skirted the giant Union Switch & Signal facility in Swissvale, another Westinghouse company, before entering the Monongahela River valley at Braddock, the location of the massive Edgar Thomson Works of another friend, Andrew Carnegie. A bit further on, the route passed more Westinghouse properties: the East Pittsburgh Works of Westinghouse Electric and the Wilmerding plant of Westinghouse Air Brake. Further east, he would pass through the towns of Irwin and Greensburg.[1]

At Latrobe, the tracks bridged Loyalhanna Creek, and Pitcairn was alarmed to see the creek was already over its banks. Twelve miles further east, at the base of Chestnut Ridge, the scope of the problem became more evident. The Conemaugh River had flooded the fields and woodland. As the train progressed further upstream

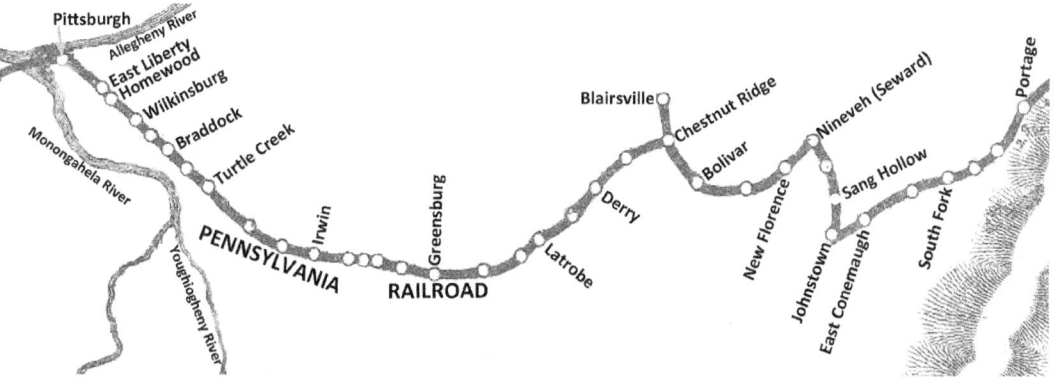

PRR Mainline from Pittsburgh to Portage. Robert Pitcairn followed this route in response to warnings that the South Fork Dam was in jeopardy of failing. His journey ended at Sang Hollow because the tracks were impassable beyond that point (created by the author).

along the Conemaugh, the flooding increased. Bolivar, New Florence, Nineveh (now Seward)—each town revealed higher water. Then the train entered the Conemaugh Gap, a 1,500-foot-deep gorge carved by the Conemaugh River on its path from Johnstown. Their progress stopped at a tower named Sang Hollow, about four miles west of Johnstown.

The time was 4:05 p.m., two minutes before the wall of water arrived at Johnstown.

Pitcairn climbed the Sang Hollow tower to determine the reason for the stoppage. The operator said the telegraph lines to Johnstown were down, and he could not allow them to proceed without clearance. Pitcairn was about to overrule him and proceed when debris in the river caught his eye. Initially, he saw pieces of broken wood, but that was soon followed by a man riding the trash pile. Then there were more people, some clinging to telegraph poles, some to damaged buildings, some trying to swim. Pitcairn and the other men on the train tried to help. By dark, they had counted 119 people rushing by, dead and alive. They had managed to rescue seven.

Pitcairn ordered the train back to New Florence, but before leaving Sang Hollow, he sent news of the disaster to the Pittsburgh *Commercial Gazette*. By 8:00 p.m. on May 31, 1889, the outside world was starting to learn of the devastation at Johnstown.

After returning to New Florence, Pitcairn composed a more detailed report but waited to send it pending further news. That news came in the form of a man, W.N. Hays, who had walked the four miles from Johnstown to Sang Hollow and then sent a telegram to New Florence. Hays said that Johnstown was "literally wiped out" and that the debris at the stone arch bridge was 40 feet high and burning. Accordingly, Pitcairn sent an order to "collect all the men from the western lines, and material to repair the damage."[2] He also completed and sent a detailed report to the newspapers, as follows:

> To the Editor of the *Commercial Gazette*,
>
> In going to the trouble, with water west of Lilly's, I could get no further than Sang Hollow. Our tracks west of this point are also obstructed. While at Sang Hollow, over 100 men,

women and children passed there on debris; seven were recovered at Sang Hollow, two at Conemaugh Furnace and two here.... From my supervisor who was at Johnstown, I learn that Johnstown is literally wiped out. Our track between Johnstown and Conemaugh is filled with buildings and drift forty feet high or more, which is on fire. All our tracks as I have said are badly blocked between Sang Hollow and Johnstown. I fear there will be terrible suffering among those saved, which should be relieved as soon as possible. In the interest of humanity, I think a public meeting should be called early tomorrow to send food, clothing, etc., to those poor people, which we will be glad to forward to Johnstown and neighborhood as soon as we can get a clear track there.

Robert Pitcairn

The resulting newspaper story notified the public:

Pittsburgh, Penn. May 31—

A rumor, loaded with horror, holds this city in dreadful expectancy tonight. It is said that the bursting of a reservoir, just above Johnstown, a flourishing place in Cambria County, had flooded the town and swept at least 200 of her citizens to death. The news is of a very uncertain character, there being no communication with the district where the flood is reported to have occurred, all the wires being down ...There is no way to get to the scene of the disaster and full particulars are not expected tonight.[3]

The reality was far worse than the early speculation.

At about 4:00 a.m. on June 1, Pitcairn decided to take the train back to Pittsburgh. He and the remaining passengers headed west while news reporters who had arrived in town started walking east toward the remnants of Johnstown.

Devastation

It took two weeks for the Johnstown *Weekly Tribune* to resume publishing. Editor George Thompson Swank printed two articles. The first, titled "Before the Reservoir Came," reported his observations from his front window as the water rose in the streets:

As we write at noon, Johnstown is again under water, and all about us the tide is rising. Wagons have for hours been passing along the streets carrying people from submerged points to places of safety, and boats, floating as jauntily as on the bosom of a river, have traversed the thoroughfares in the lower end of town, removing pent-up inmates from homes to which partial ruin has come thrice in as many years. The streets up and back as far as Jackson are running with the yellow devastating flood. A most exasperating state of affairs, and one for which there ought to be a remedy.

From 7 o'clock on the water rose. People who were glad they "didn't live down town" began to wish they didn't live in town at all. On the water crept, and on, up one street and out another, across the imaginary lines between the many boroughs, until at last there was "consolidation," and the same wet blanket covered all. Eighteen inches an hour the Stonycreek rose for a time, and the Conemaugh about as rapidly. The narrow banks were filled to overflowing and the town took what the channels could not carry.

Many of our citizens had not gone to their employment at all, feeling the imminence of danger. But in the end all that they could do was to move things from the cellar, and then move things to the upper floors. Others who had left their homes were soon cut off from them by the water, and thus on both and all sides of the flood there were anxious hearts.

So the hours wore on, full only of excitement for some, but of hard fatiguing work and increasing distress for many others. Now would run over the town a rumor of a man drowned, of horses perishing, of daring rescuers or reckless adventurers nearly losing their lives, and the hello bell in the central office was hot with the impatient jingle of repeated calls. Johnstown, Cambria, the upper boroughs—wherever the telephone line runs—at the end of each wire was a worried listener or a man or woman excitedly asking somebody else how it fared with them. What a blessing the telephone was, and how, if it could feel, it must have tingles with modest thoughts of its great usefulness.[4]

Swank's second story, published in the same edition of the paper, captured the scene on the morning after the flood hit:

Then came the real awakening. We must learn the truth the shortest and quickest way. We must find our friends or their bodies. We must live, so out poured the saved. But soon they realized their helplessness. People went miles over debris, at the risk of life and limb, to find no sign of their homes. Where houses had stood was bare ground, or perhaps the wreck of a house that the day before had stood miles away. The Cambria Mills were wrecked—not hopelessly, but badly wrecked. The Gautier and Woodvale mills were gone, and so was every business house in town,—or, if the building remained, the merchant moved among us, a tramp like the rest. Freight cars, carried long distances, stood in the streets. At one place was a locomotive that had ridden on the bosom of the flood like a toy. Here was a big hotel, filled with people, when the water came, nothing left of it—even the cellar to be dug over again. Strong brick blocks mowed down like our colored farmer used to cut the grass in the Park. Hands of the dead stuck out of the ruins. Dead everywhere you went, their arms stretched above their heads almost without exception—that last instinct of humanity grasping at a straw. Whole families swept away—here and there, three generations. Whole families saved—the mockery of fate.

Where to go, what to do, no one could tell. The survivors were moving, but they knew not whither. Over and under the wrecks they went, in and out of the ruins,—hoping, dreading to find a friend. The bridges were gone and the rivers divided us. In parts of town there was still a waste of waters. Food there was none except up on the hills, and even there the prudent housewives had depended upon Saturday's marketing for their supplies, and their charitable hearts were sore because they could not feed the hungry.

The Pennsylvania Railroad was blocked both ways; the B.&O. to the south was stuck, and we might as well for the first few hopeless, helpless hours have been in the Alps, with glaciers all about us, and crevasses, and death.[5]

Damage to Robert Pitcairn's Pennsylvania Railroad facilities was beyond belief. Thirty-three engines that had been at home in the roundhouse were strewn in a haphazard line stretching for a mile. Eighteen passenger cars and 315 freight cars floated by the flood stood dumbly in the streets with no rails in sight. Parts of railroad cars would be excavated as late as 1900. Utilities—Johnstown Street Railway Company and its 68 horses, Johnstown Gas Company, Johnstown Water Company—all were totally destroyed.

A brief newspaper story from Philadelphia reported:

One walks across a desolate sea of mud in which are interred many human bodies. It was once the handsome portion of the town. The cellars are filled with mud, so that a person who has never seen the city can hardly imagine that houses ever stood where they did. Four streets solidly built up with houses have been swept away. Nothing but a small two-story frame house remains. It was near the edge of the wave and thus escaped, although one side was torn off. The walk up to the wreck of houses was interrupted in many places by small branch streams. Along the route were strewn tin utensils, pieces of machinery, iron pipes, and wares of every conceivable kind. In the midst of the wreck, a clothing store dummy, with a hand in the position of beckoning to a person, stands erected and uninjured.[6]

Donations Pour In

At 1:00 p.m. on Saturday, June 1, a mass meeting was held at Pittsburgh's Old City Hall. Robert Pitcairn reported what he had seen and then urged the crowd to help, saying, "Gentlemen, it is not tomorrow you want to act, but today; thousands of lives were lost in a moment, and the living need immediate help." The response was overwhelming:

> Then there was a call for contributions, and the storm of checks and bank notes began. Fives, tens, fifties and thousands flooded the chairman's table. Treasurer Thompson's hands were filled and Mayor McCallin held out both of his. In a minute more, H.I. Gourley was called to his assistance. The three men stood there for half an hour and the crowd kept both hands busy. It was almost impossible to keep track of the contributions. "Whose $25 is this?" cried Mr. Thompson. And a moment later—"Somebody laid this one hundred-dollar bill down here—who was it?" Business men and their employees, distillers and doctors of divinity, saloon keepers and prohibitionists, vied with each other. Differences of creed and condition disappeared in the generous rivalry of charity. There was no speech making, no oratory but the golden eloquence of cash. Big and little contributions got applause, so long as they were in proportion to the means of the giver. For almost an hour, at the rate of a thousand dollars a minute, the storm of money poured down upon the table, until $48,116.70 had been received.[7]

The South Fork Fishing & Hunting Club donated $3,000 and 1,200 blankets. About half of the club members contributed money, most notably Andrew Carnegie, who gave $5,000; Henry Clay Frick, who donated $5,000; and William Thaw, $3,000. George Westinghouse, who was not a club member, donated $15,000, more than the other three combined.

People and organizations from every state in the U.S. provided over $3.6 million for the relief effort. Contributions from 12 foreign countries added another $141,301.[8] In addition to the money, people and organizations sent goods—food, clothes, furniture, and tools. The Pennsylvania Flood Relief Commission estimated that 1,408 railroad carloads of goods, weighing 17 million pounds, had been sent to Johnstown.[9]

The first of those goods came from Pittsburgh, where wagons went through the city collecting food and clothing, which were then loaded aboard train cars. PRR crews had been at work rebuilding the track from Sang Hollow to the now-infamous stone arch bridge. The first train out from Pittsburgh had 20 full cars along with 75 volunteers of the "Pittsburgh Relief Committee," 12 reporters, and 18 police. The relief train left Pittsburgh at 4:30 p.m. on Saturday, June 1. Stalled freight trains along the line and a 400-foot washout east of Sang Hollow delayed the train. It crept through the ruins of Coopersdale, Morrellville, and Cambria City and arrived at the stone arch bridge in Johnstown on the morning of Sunday, June 2.[10] The scene that greeted the men was surreal:

> The scene there beheld was horrible beyond description. Across the north end of the bridge, where the railroad embankment had been, swept a foul and loathsome torrent 800 feet wide.

Along the east side bridge was the jagged mass of debris rising twenty feet above the tracks, crackling and smoking and filling the air with the unmistakable odor of burnt flesh. Beyond this, where Johnstown had once been was a lake, a great stretch of sandy plain and here and there clusters of partly wrecked houses. About and between these houses was piled, often fifty feet high, every form of wreckage the flood produced, locked together by hundreds of feet of wire and packed by the water into an inextricable mass.[11]

Building rebuilt by Andrew Carnegie as a library, now the Johnstown Flood Museum. The office-residence of Mrs. Hettie Ogle, the Western Union operator who transmitted messages about the precarious state of the South Fork Dam, was behind this library. Both buildings were reduced to a pile of debris by the flood (photograph by the author).

The "Great Bronze Plate" above the door of the Johnstown Public Library (photograph by the author).

Aftermath

The 1889 Johnstown Flood, with an official death toll of 2,209, remained the worst civilian disaster in the United States until the 1900 Galveston hurricane. Of those who died, 777 bodies were never identified and were buried in the "Plot of the Unknown" in Grandview Cemetery above and west of the city.

The flood destroyed 1,600 homes and four square miles of the downtown area and caused $17 million in property damage.

Johnstown poet Isaac G. Reed captured the anguish of the tragedy:

> Many thousand human lives—
> Butchered husbands, slaughtered wives
> Mangled daughters, bleeding sons,
> Hosts of martyred little ones,
> (Worse than Herod's awful crime)
> Sent to heaven before their time;
> Lovers burnt and sweethearts drowned,
> Darlings lost but never found!
> All the horrors that hell could wish,
> Such was the price that was paid for—fish!

Plot of the Unknown at Grandview Cemetery, Johnstown, Pennsylvania. The inscription on the statue reads, "IN MEMORY OF THE UNIDENTIFIED DEAD FROM THE FLOOD MAY 31, 1889" (photograph by the author).

17. The Johnstown Flood—Part 2

> An hour of flood, a night of flame,
> A week of woe without a name,
> A week when sleep with hope had fled,
> While misery hunted for its dead;
> A week of corpses by the mile,
> A long, long week without a smile,
> A week whose tale no tongue can tell,
> A week without a parallel!
> All the horrors that hell could wish,
> Such was the price that was paid for—fish![12]

Rebuilding Johnstown

Robert Pitcairn put his PRR crews to work as soon as the floodwaters receded. Washouts had occurred along the banks of the Little Conemaugh and Conemaugh Rivers from South Fork in the east to Sang Hollow west of Johnstown. Three miles of track and their supporting embankments were gone. Bridge #6 and the massive viaduct had to be replaced by wooden trestles. In five days, the PRR crews reopened the line from Pittsburgh to Johnstown, and by June 14, the workers had accomplished what looked impossible and restored rail service from Pittsburgh, through Johnstown, to Altoona.

On those trains flowed tons of relief supplies, including lumber, furniture, barrels of quicklime, embalming fluid, and pitch. Foodstuffs such as potatoes from

Temporary trestle to replace the Conemaugh Viaduct, 80 feet high and 400 feet long. Regular rail traffic resumed 14 days after the flood, on June 14, 1889 (photograph from Allegheny Portage Railroad NHS Archive).

Washington state, flour from Minneapolis, a thousand loaves of bread baked by prisoners at Pennsylvania's Western Penitentiary, coffee from Pittsburgh, and 20,000 pounds of ham from Cincinnati relieved all fears about how to feed the survivors. The train yards in Johnstown were filled with food and supplies of all kinds.

Before Johnstown's rebuilding could begin, the massive amount of rubble, some carried from as far away as South Fork, had to be hauled away. A city of 20,000 people, with their houses and possessions, was now filthy, contaminated debris.[13]

Governor James Addams Beaver sent the state militia to keep order, and 55 undertakers came to take care of the dead.[14]

Clara Barton and a small party of Red Cross workers arrived on Wednesday, June 5, via a B&O rail link from Rockwood in Somerset County, Pennsylvania. Fifty more Red Cross doctors, nurses, and other workers came soon after to mount the most significant peacetime relief effort of the American Red Cross.

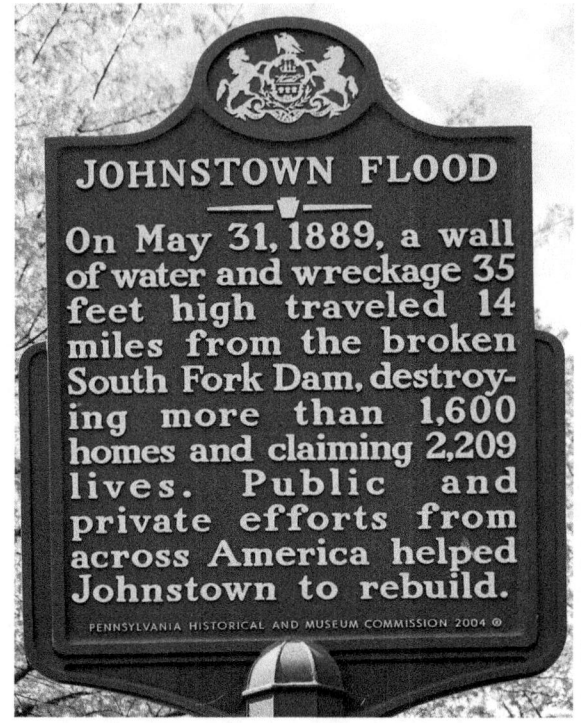

Historical marker commemorating the May 31, 1889, Johnstown Flood (photograph by and courtesy of Mike Wintermantel).

Clarissa Harlowe (Clara) Barton was born on Christmas Day, 1821, in North Oxford, Massachusetts. On an 1869 trip to Geneva, Switzerland, she learned of the Red Cross movement and worked for the Red Cross in Europe through 1872. Back in the United States in 1873, she began work to establish an American branch of the organization. It took eight years and appeals to two U.S. presidents (Rutherford B. Hayes and Chester A. Arthur) before Barton held the first meeting of the American Red Cross in her Washington, D.C., home on May 21, 1881.

The first work of the American Red Cross was during an 1881 fire in Michigan, followed by the 1884 floods on the Ohio River, a famine in Texas in 1887, and a tornado in Illinois in 1888. But the reputation and fame of Barton, then 67, and the American Red Cross were established by their tireless work at Johnstown in 1889. Barton and her volunteers toiled in Johnstown for five months.[15]

The Philadelphia chapter of the Red Cross and Dr. Frances Malone, with her Yellow Cross workers, focused on providing medical relief. Clara Barton's most crucial work was distributing furniture, beds, mattresses, and utensils and providing lodging in "Red Cross Hotels" to the many who had lost their homes.

Amazingly, the size of Johnstown was unaffected by the disaster. After such a calamity, it would not be surprising to see people desert the scene, never to return. But the city's growth continued unabated, possibly because the feared dam was gone, never again to devastate the city.

However, the population of Johnstown did begin to decline after World War II, and today stands just below 20,000, very close to where it was at the time of the 1889 flood.

Blame

After the shock and numbness of the disaster abated, resentment and outrage took their place. Newspaper reporters interviewed South Fork residents and found uniform bitterness about Benjamin Ruff's shoddy rebuilding of the dam and the superior attitude of the Club members in dealing with the locals. By contrast, those very few Club members who did talk with the press either claimed that the dam was sound or doubted that the South Fork Dam was the one that collapsed. Those positions proved false when investigators reached the dam site.

American Red Cross historical marker located at Peoples Natural Gas Park in Johnstown (photograph by the author).

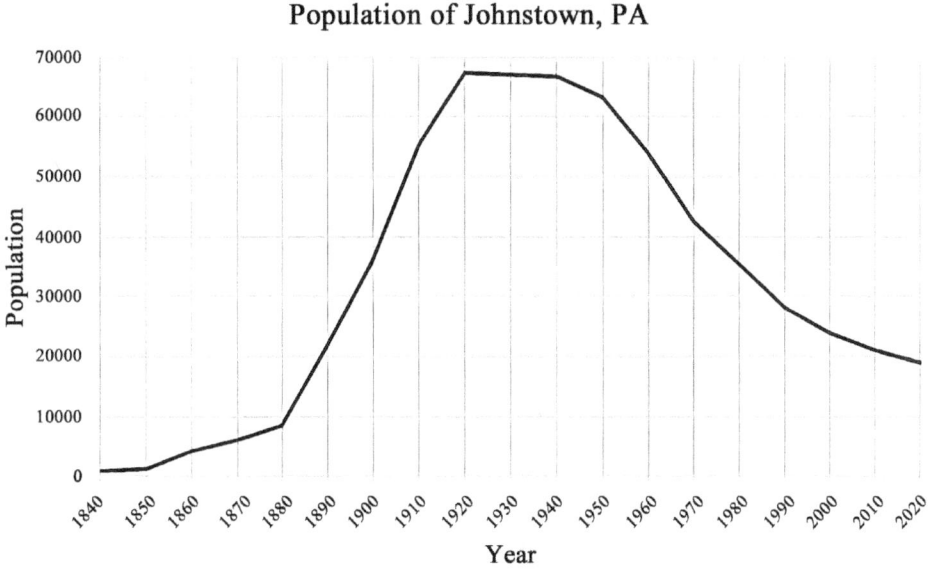

Johnstown population (data from U.S. Decennial Census via Wikipedia).

Panorama of Johnstown, 2004. The Little Conemaugh River is in the center; the Stony Creek is at the bottom and right. These two rivers meet to the left of Point Park to form the Conemaugh River, just before flowing under the Stone Arch Bridge where the debris field formed and burned in the 1889 flood. (courtesy of the Johnstown Area Historical Association).

Two coroner's juries were convened; the first was in Westmoreland County to examine the cause of death of the 121 bodies recovered at Nineveh. The second was in Cambria County to determine the cause of death of one victim, Mrs. Ellen Hite. Both juries visited the dam site and heard dozens of witnesses.

While the investigations were still underway, the *New York Sun* published the following headline on its June 5, 1889, front page:

CAUSE OF THE CALAMITY
The Pittsburgh Fishing Club
Chiefly Responsible
The Waste Gates Closed
When the Club Took
Possession

On June 7, the Westmoreland County coroner's jury returned its verdict: "death by violence due to the flood caused by the breaking of the dam at the South Fork Reservoir." That conclusion had already been reached by every thinking adult in the area.

The day before, the Cambria County jury had reached the same decision and went further to assess blame:

> death by drowning caused by the breaking of the South Fork dam.... We further find, from the testimony and what we saw on the ground that there was not sufficient water weir, nor was the dam constructed sufficiently strong nor of proper material to withstand the overflow; and hence we find the owners of said dam were culpable in not making it as secure as it should have been, especially in view of the fact that a population of many thousands were in the valley below; and we hold that the owners are responsible for the fearful loss of life and property resulting from the breaking of the dam.[16]

Newspapers in New York, Cincinnati, Chicago, and elsewhere pounced on the verdict, with headlines such as "THE CLUB IS GUILTY" and "An Engineering Crime."

Anger directed against the Club members, who had the temerity to build and enjoy a lake in the mountains without adequately maintaining the dam that held it back, rose to a fever pitch.

ASCE Investigation

At their annual meeting on June 5, 1889, the American Society of Civil Engineers (ASCE) appointed a committee of four to investigate the cause of the South Fork Dam collapse and subsequent flood. Members were Max J. Becker, Alphonse Fteley, James B. Francis, and William E. Worthen. Francis was a hydraulic engineer and most qualified to determine what precipitated the dam's failure. Still, as president of ASCE, Becker acted as the de facto chairman of the committee.

After visits to the dam site and the path of the flood waters as far as Johnstown, the committee completed its report on January 15, 1890, and submitted it to the ASCE. However, Becker, as outgoing president of ASCE, sealed the report. The incoming president was William P. Shinn, formerly general manager of Edgar

Thomson Works until 1879. Shinn allowed Becker to retain control of when the report would be released.

Refusing to release the committee's report was highly unusual and was opposed by the other committee members. The committee's findings could have impacted the safety of other large dams, as well as the design of future dams.

The 1890 annual ASCE convention was held at the Mountain House Hotel in Cresson, Pennsylvania. The organizers, including Robert Pitcairn, offered excursions to Johnstown and other area locations but not to the nearby South Fork Dam site. Thus, despite pressure from many ASCE members including report author James Francis, the committee report on the South Fork dam failure remained sealed.

Finally, the long-awaited report was released at the following year's convention in May 1891. The meeting was held at Lookout Mountain above Chattanooga, Tennessee, far from the South Fork Dam. James Francis presented the report; the other three committee members, including Max Becker, the former ASCE president, were not in attendance. The report concluded:

> The (South Fork) Hunting and Fishing Club (*sic*), in repairing the breach of 1862, took out the five sluices (drainage pipes) in the dam, lowered the embankment about 2 feet, and subsequently, partially obstructed the wasteway (spillway) by gratings, etc., to prevent the escape of fish. These changes materially diminished the security of the dam, by exposing the embankment to overflow, and consequent destruction, by floods of less magnitude than could have been borne with safety if the original construction of 1851–1853 had been adhered to; but in our opinion they cannot be deemed to be the cause of the late disaster, as we find that the embankment would have overflowed and the breach formed if the changes had not been made. It occurred a little earlier in the day on account of the changes, but we think the result would have been equally disastrous, and possibly even more so....[17] [Explanatory words added by Coleman.]

Why did it take so long for the ASCE report to be released? Neil Coleman's authoritative book, *Johnstown's Flood of 1889: Power over Truth and the Science Behind the Disaster* provides the following answer:

> The Pittsburgh men covered their tracks well, but enough is now known to see their intentions. The Club members wanted to control the message in the formal ASCE engineering report, which they believed would carry great weight in the judgment of history. But the evidence shows that Robert Pitcairn, and through him other members, worked to suppress and whitewash the ASCE investigation, a report by some of the most prominent hydraulic engineers in the country. These actions to distort history are also part of the Johnstown Flood legacy.[18]

Litigation

Survivors filed several suits against the South Fork Fishing & Hunting Club for negligence in the modifications made to the dam and inadequate maintenance. However, attorneys Philander Knox and James Hay Reed, both Club members, successfully argued that the flood was a natural disaster that was an act of God. Therefore, no one was held legally responsible for the South Fork Dam's failure and resulting destruction and loss of life.[19]

That result seems ridiculous in light of what we know today. First, the missing drain pipes at the bottom of the dam, whoever removed them, made maintenance of the dam impossible and therefore contributed to its failure. Second, Benjamin Ruff's repairs of the 1862 breach, unsupervised by any qualified engineer, were inadequate. Third, Ruff's lowering of the top of the dam, with no corresponding reduction in the spillway elevation, violated dam safety principles. Finally, the fish screen blocking the spillway forced excess water over the top of the dam. All of these factors argue for the liability of Ruff and the members of the South Fork Fishing & Hunting Club.

But things were different in 1889. Three factors allowed the millionaires of the Club to escape punishment. First, they were rich and powerful. It would be difficult for any jury convened in Pittsburgh to rule against the men who employed their family members, friends, and themselves.

Second, the ASCE committee report concluded that the dam breach would have occurred even if Ruff had not made all the compromising revisions to the dam. However, a more recent and undoubtedly less biased analysis by Coleman suggests that if the dam had been rebuilt to the original specifications, including the installation of a second (emergency) spillway, it would have withstood the rapidly rising water.[20]

Third, before the Johnstown Flood, natural disasters caused by human activity were not punishable by a court of law. Extraordinary as that sounds, such was the practice in the U.S. before the flood. Based on this principle, no damages could be awarded.

Soon after the flood, jurists and legislators began to look at legal practices in other countries, especially England. There, a series of reservoir failures led to Ryland's Law, which states that negligence does not need to be proven for a person, organization, or company to be found liable for a natural disaster caused by man-made structures. Had a U.S. version of Ryland's Law been in force, the South Fork Fishing & Hunting Club, and perhaps its individual members, including Andrew Carnegie, Robert Pitcairn, and Henry Clay Frick, would have had to pay restitution to the Johnstown Flood victims. Shugerman, in his 2000 *Yale Law Journal* article, says, "three of the states most widely recognized for their rejection of *Rylands*—New York, New Jersey, and Pennsylvania—reversed their stance on *Rylands* in the 1890s, soon after the Johnstown Flood."[21]

18

Unintended Consequences

> *"The law of unintended consequences pushes us ceaselessly through the years, permitting no pause for perspective."*
> —Richard Schickel

R.P. Remains R.P.

Before the Great Railroad Strike of 1877, Robert Pitcairn's employees had liked and respected him. That was still true after the strike. PRR historian William Bender Wilson says of him:

> Robert Pitcairn was a leader of men and possessed in pre-eminent degree the qualities that endear a leader to his subordinates. He inspired them not only with confidence in themselves, but with faith in him. They knew that he was master of the theory and practice of railroad operations; they had unwavering confidence in his knowledge of what was the right thing to do, the right time to do it and in his ability to achieve success.
>
> He believed his men had no superiors, or even peers, in the world. He taught them, corrected them, helped them, and, if need be, defended them. In return, his men gave him their unswerving loyalty and their undying devotion.[1]

Because of his employees' enduring confidence in him, Pitcairn was able to continue as general agent and superintendent of the Pittsburgh Division of the PRR with even greater success after the 1877 strike.

In addition to being liked and respected by his employees in the Pittsburgh Division, Robert Pitcairn was a leader in the railroad industry as a whole. In 1883, he represented the PRR at the General Time Convention, which standardized time in the U.S. and established four time zones. The *Indianapolis Sentinel* declared, "The sun will be requested to rise and set by railroad time."[2]

For many years, Pitcairn was chairman of the American Railway Association Committee on Train Rules. Under his leadership, the committee developed the complex rules essential to guarantee the safe and efficient operation of the complex nationwide rail network.[3]

As railroad traffic grew, Pitcairn saw the need to build a rail yard in a less crowded area outside of the congestion in Pittsburgh. In January 1889, he announced the construction of a new rail yard on 215 acres of land in the Turtle Creek Valley near Wall Station, Pennsylvania, 12 miles east of Pittsburgh. Building the facility required changing the course of Turtle Creek, separating the passenger and freight mainlines by moving the passenger tracks to the north, and situating the yard on reclaimed bottom land.[4]

A rail yard consists of multiple interconnected railroad tracks used to sort, arrange, and store loaded and unloaded railroad cars and locomotives. Trains are assembled and held in the rail yard until one or more locomotives are attached and then depart. Switcher engines move the railroad cars, sometimes assisted by gravity.

In addition to the switching yards, there were two engine roundhouses, machine shops, a lumber yard, power plant, and cabinet, upholstery, and paint shops so the facility could build, service, and repair all types of rolling stock.

Building lots were laid out to accommodate homes for railroad workers. By 1890, the village grew and became known as Walurba, denoting a suburb of Wall. The rail yard also grew, eventually becoming the most extensive rail yard in the world, at one time employing nearly 10,000 people. The Wall Yard, with 20 miles of track, opened on April 22, 1892.[5]

In 1894, the residents decided to form their own community. The village was incorporated as a borough and adopted Pitcairn as its name. On December 6, 1897, at the request of the Borough Council, the PRR changed the name of its depot from Walurba to Pitcairn.

Because of a lack of service by local electric companies, the Pitcairn Council issued $20,000 in bonds in 1898 to finance its own electric plant and distribution

Pitcairn, Pennsylvania 1901. Turtle Creek separates Pitcairn Borough from the railroad yards (Library of Congress).

system. In November 1901, at Robert Pitcairn's urging, the PRR approved $35,000 to build a YMCA in Pitcairn.[6]

In 1955, the Borough of Pitcairn merged its school system with that of neighboring Monroeville. The merged system became the Gateway Union School District in 1960.[7] (On a personal note, my wife taught in the Gateway Union School District in 1967, and we had a Pitcairn, Pennsylvania, address.)

Shadyside Presbyterian Church

Robert Pitcairn and his family continued their active participation in the affairs of Shadyside Presbyterian Church. Following is a tabulation of Robert's official roles at the church:

Robert Pitcairn's Service to Shadyside Presbyterian Church

Position	Dates
Sunday School Superintendent	Intermittently for 12 years total, starting in September 1868 and ending in March 1903
Deacon	April 27, 1873, to his death in 1909; 36 years total
President of Board of Trustees	1881 to 1882
Ruling Elder	April 2, 1882, to his death in 1909; 27 years total

Alarming news met the Shadyside congregation when they assembled for worship on Sunday, April 8, 1888. A notice on the church doors read, "Services in the Chapel—This building is unsafe." Expert opinions from a building inspector, a contractor, a stonemason, a local architect, a civil engineer, and even the original architect confirmed that the building, especially the massive tower, was unsafe. Inferior construction methods and water damage from underground springs appeared to be the causes.

A building committee immediately started planning to raise funds for a new building. But the pastor, John Morville Richmond, opposed a new church, especially one as elaborate as was being proposed by the building committee. Dr. Richmond resigned, and a new building, the third one in 23 years, was completed in 1890.

Despite the turmoil, Robert Pitcairn persevered. He said in July 1891, "I feel that I can with truth say ... to the promoters of this great enterprise, which has so blessed this neighborhood—those conservative men and women who gave up their beloved and cherished [church] homes, denominational preferences, and saw that their duty was at home and with their neighbors ... and now I expect to live and die in my adopted church home, and can say with truth, that everything I am and have I owe to the Shadyside Presbyterian Church."[8]

In 1920, well after the deaths of both Robert and Elizabeth, new stained glass was installed in the windows of the Shadyside Presbyterian Church. Among those windows was one titled *The Feeding of the Five Thousand*, which was dedicated "In Loving Memory of Robert Pitcairn and Elizabeth Rigg Pitcairn."[9]

18. *Unintended Consequences* 161

The third Shadyside Presbyterian Church building (completed in 1890) as it appeared in 2021 (photograph by the author).

"The Feeding of the Five Thousand" stained glass window at Shadyside Presbyterian Church (photograph courtesy of Tim Engleman).

A Fateful Trip with a Friend

Robert Pitcairn first met George Westinghouse in 1869, when the 23-year-old Westinghouse was pitching his inventive railroad air brake system. Robert was impressed both with the air brake and with Westinghouse and agreed to serve on the original board of directors of the Westinghouse Air Brake Company. The two men remained friends and business partners for the rest of their lives.

On December 23, 1885, George Westinghouse, his brother Herman Westinghouse, Robert Pitcairn, and four others applied for a charter for a corporation called the Westinghouse Electric Company (WEC). The charter was granted on January 8, 1886, and WEC quickly became one of the dominant companies in the electrical equipment industry.[10]

George Westinghouse and Robert Pitcairn both lived within walking distance of the Pennsylvania Railroad mainline on the east side of Pittsburgh. At 6:30 p.m. on June 24, 1892, they left New York City together, bound for home aboard Westinghouse's private railcar, *Glen Eyre*. The ten-hour trip was usually uneventful but turned tragic soon after midnight.

In heavy rain, the two sections of the Western Express No. 9 approached Harrisburg, Pennsylvania, at about 12:30 a.m. The first section, composed of a baggage car, an express car, three day coaches, and *Glen Eyre* in the rear, stopped for a few minutes to permit some shifting in the train yards.

On board *Glen Eyre* with Westinghouse and Pitcairn was a porter, W.H. Woodyard, and a cook. As the first section of the train started forward, the second section, with two baggage cars and five Pullman sleeper cars, failed to stop as it should have and plowed into *Glen Eyre* at 40 miles per hour, telescoping it into the rest of the train. Pitcairn, Westinghouse, the porter, and the cook all escaped with only minor injuries, but 12 passengers in the day coaches were killed and 23 injured. The accident destroyed *Glen Eyre*. The coroner's jury determined that negligence by the 22-year-old novice operator working the Steelton tower caused the accident. Failures by the flagman on the first section and the engineer of the second section also contributed to the disaster.[11]

Dining with the President

William McKinley was inaugurated as the 25th president of the United States on March 4, 1897. He campaigned on a platform advocating "sound money" and high tariffs and was popular with industrialists such as Pitcairn and Westinghouse. McKinley and George Westinghouse were close friends, having first met in 1890. As chairman of the Ways and Means Committee of the House of Representatives, McKinley had consulted Westinghouse about pending legislation for the protection of railroad workers.[12]

Eight months after his inauguration, McKinley and his wife, Ida, visited Pittsburgh to celebrate the second anniversary of the founding of the Carnegie Cultural Complex in the Oakland district. As usual, Andrew Carnegie was out of town but sent a formal welcome letter to the distinguished guests. Other Pittsburgh residents were happy to take up the slack. As the *Bulletin*, Pittsburgh's society magazine, noted: "Pittsburgh has opportunities to entertain the president of the United States too infrequently not to make the most of them when they do come. When the president is accompanied by his wife … added importance is given the visit … the day was given over to as many social entertainments as could possibly be crowded into it."[13]

Just after 11:00 a.m., the McKinleys arrived at Union Station in Pittsburgh and were greeted by deafening cheers from a massive crowd. Upon disembarking from the Pullman car, *Cleopatra*, the president was driven by horse carriage around the downtown business area. His destination was Beechwood Hall, the palatial home of William F. Frew, head of the Carnegie Library Commission. There McKinley dined with a small but select group of Pittsburgh's leading men, including Henry Clay Frick.

Meanwhile, Mrs. McKinley remained on the train to the Shadyside depot, where almost 300 women greeted her. From there, she rode in a carriage driven by Elizabeth Pitcairn and pulled by her matched pair of chestnut geldings, whimsically named McKinley and Hobart for the president and vice president (Garret Augustus Hobart). Their destination was the Pitcairn house, Cairncarque.

Willa Cather, poet, novelist, journalist, and later Pulitzer Prize–winner, attended the gathering and published her impressions in the Nebraska *Lincoln-Courier*.

> Never before was I present at anything so gorgeous. It was one of those rare things that are not overdone and yet leave nothing to be wished for. The floral decorations were from New York and Sherry of New York did the catering. Everything moved on velvet wheels. Outside the house the grounds and streets were packed with people under the charge of a score of policemen but inside there were just guests enough to fill the rooms comfortably. The parlors were simply lined with chrysanthemums of that magnificent pink variety which was named after Mrs. Robert Pitcairn. The dining rooms were in green palms and ferns, no flowers visible except the gorgeous American beauties on the tables. But the staircase was the chef-d'œuvre. It is some twelve feet wide with a big curve toward the top. The white and gold chrysanthemums were so thick upon it as to only leave room for people to descend two abreast. I should hate to count the thousands of blossoms on that stairway. Presently two boys in livery descended to make sure the way was clear. Then the orchestra began playing the waltz song from Gounod's Roméo et Juliette very softly, and Mrs. McKinley came down the staircase on Mrs. Pitcairn's arm, between the serried ranks of chrysanthemums under the soft light that fell through the stained-glass windows.[14]

After their respective luncheons, President and Mrs. McKinley and the assembled guests united for a Founders' Day gala at the Carnegie Music Hall in nearby Oakland.

A glittering dinner at Cairncarque, followed by the first concert of the season back at Carnegie Music Hall, completed the president's visit. Guests at the dinner included Pittsburgh royalty:

Mr. and Mrs. William Frew
Mr. and Mrs. Henry Clay Frick
Mr. and Mrs. William Thaw
Mr. and Mrs. Christopher McGee

Mr. and Mrs. Philander Knox
Mr. and Mrs. George Westinghouse
Mr. and Mrs. Robert Pitcairn

President McKinley was impressed by the transformation of Pittsburgh from an industrial center "to rank as one of the great literary, art, musical, and educational cities of the United States."[15]

President McKinley returned to Pittsburgh and Cairncarque on August 28, 1899. The occasion was to welcome the return of the Tenth Pennsylvania Volunteers from their service in the Spanish-American War. Robert Pitcairn and President McKinley rode together in the first carriage of the parade honoring the soldiers.[16]

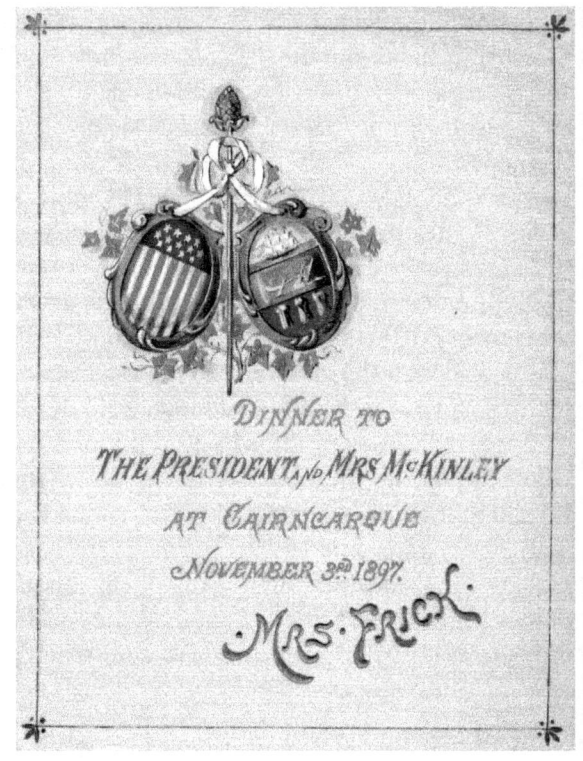

Cover of dinner program at Cairncarque, November 3, 1897 (courtesy of the Senator John Heinz History Center).

A New Job for Uncle Robert

On January 1, 1902, Robert Pitcairn was promoted to resident assistant to the president of the Pennsylvania Railroad Company. Richard Lincoln O'Donnel, who had been assistant superintendent, took over as superintendent of the Pittsburgh Division, a post that Pitcairn had held for over 36 years.[17] As a token of their esteem, the Pittsburgh Division employees presented a grandfather clock valued at $2,000 to Pitcairn in January 1903.

Many years earlier, Pitcairn had been instrumental in establishing the PRR's policy that employees with 25 or more years of service had to retire with a pension upon reaching age 70. Pitcairn believed the plan would allow old men to spend their later years "without care or responsibility."[18]

Little did he know that he would be the first to feel the effects of the policy. Robert would reach the retirement age stated in the policy on May 6, 1906. As reported in the December 18, 1905, *Pittsburgh Press*, Pitcairn assured that he had no thought of retiring and that the story had no foundation.[19] He argued his case with PRR President A.J. Cassatt, stating that he had not intended for the retirement mandate to apply to himself. But two days after the initial newspaper story, the Lancaster, Pennsylvania, *New Era* reported that Pitcairn said, "How could I, being one of the sponsors of that idea, seek to be made an exception when the rule became operative in my case. No, boys, I am ready to quit."[20]

Thus, Robert Pitcairn was forced to retire from his $25,000 per year post on May 31, 1906. He had served the Pennsylvania Railroad for 53 years.[21]

On the occasion of his retirement, Robert Pitcairn's old and enduring friend, Andrew Carnegie, wrote,

> Two East Ninety-first Street, New York
> Sunday Morning, May 13th, 1906
>
> My dear Bob,
>
> So sorry that I sail before the evening of retirement arrives.
>
> Well, my fellow "seventy year old," those who lay down the armor, not who put it on, are the people who can boast. They have fought the fight and won.
>
> You have done this and now comes the final triumph of all—a dignified, calm, old age, for at seventy we enter upon a new stage.
>
> All that of active business must be dismissed.
>
> To become an old man gracefully is our only true aim. You do not need to grab for more dollars—they would add nothing worth while. The benefit of your experience on committees for public good will be valuable. All you do should have reference to others, individuals, or the community as a whole.
>
> "We have climbed the hill the gither."
>
> I welcome you to begin the last ascent and then, no more. We shall have lived our lives on earth, let us allure ourselves as with enchantments hoping there's another where old age comes not.
>
> With every good wish, my dear, dear friend of boyhood.
>
> Always yours,
> Andy[22]

Carnegie later wrote,

> No man was more devoted to his duties on the Pennsylvania Railroad than Robert Pitcairn. His whole life was given to it. I was one who tried hard to have an exception made in his case regarding the rule that compelled retirement at a certain age. I felt sure that he would never be happy after retirement. He came to visit us at Skibo, and I found such was the case; nothing appeared to interest him; his life's work was done. Fortunately he was made a trustee of the Hero Fund and I believe that his work there prolonged his life.[23]

Robert Pitcairn did have interests outside of the Pennsylvania Railroad, as indicated by the following list of activities: "He was a director of 11 corporations, a presidential elector for three presidents, a member of city commissions, a Past Master of Hailman Lodge of Free and Accepted Masons, and Past Grand Commander of the Knights Templar of Pennsylvania. He was a Director of Western Theological Seminary and Vice Moderator of the (Presbyterian) Assembly in 1901."[24] In addition, Pitcairn was vice president of Westinghouse Air Brake and Union Switch & Signal Companies. He was also a director and second vice president of Fidelity Title & Trust Company.[25]

But Carnegie was right; nothing captured Pitcairn's interest and attention as the PRR did.

Susan Blanche Pitcairn

Susan Blanche Pitcairn, Robert and Elizabeth's youngest daughter (born March 19, 1868), married Victor Lee Crabbe on December 2, 1897. The couple had two daughters: Elizabeth, born April 5, 1900, and Susan Lee, born October 3, 1903. The Crabbe family lived at Cairncarque with Robert and Elizabeth Pitcairn.

After briefly teaching at Shadyside Academy, Victor Crabbe joined the Carbon Steel Company and was promoted until he reached top management.

Victor was returning home from a hearing in New York City on May 11, 1905, aboard the Pennsylvania Railroad's Cleveland & Cincinnati Express. Near Harrisburg, Pennsylvania, at about 1:00 a.m., an eastbound freight train suffered a burst airbrake hose, resulting in several cars falling across the adjacent passenger tracks. Soon after, with no time to stop, the ten-car passenger train carrying Victor and hundreds of others plowed into the wrecked freight cars. The boiler of the passenger locomotive blew up and ignited a fire. Six minutes later, the flames reached a freight car carrying 5,000 pounds of dynamite, which exploded with an enormous roar. Flames immediately engulfed the pile of freight and passenger cars.

The crash and explosions threw the passengers, most of whom had been sleeping, from their berths. Many landed outside the train, some in the nearby Susquehanna River. Twenty people, including Victor Lee Crabbe, died in the wreck and flames, and 125 were hospitalized.[26]

Imagine the shock at Cairncarque, where Robert and Elizabeth attempted to comfort their daughter, Susie, and her two young daughters. Robert Pitcairn had to be thinking back 13 years to June 24, 1892. On that early morning, at almost the exact location, he and his friend, George Westinghouse, had been involved in a fatal train accident. Robert and George were fortunate to walk away unhurt. But Victor Crabbe, Robert's son-in-law, had not been so lucky.

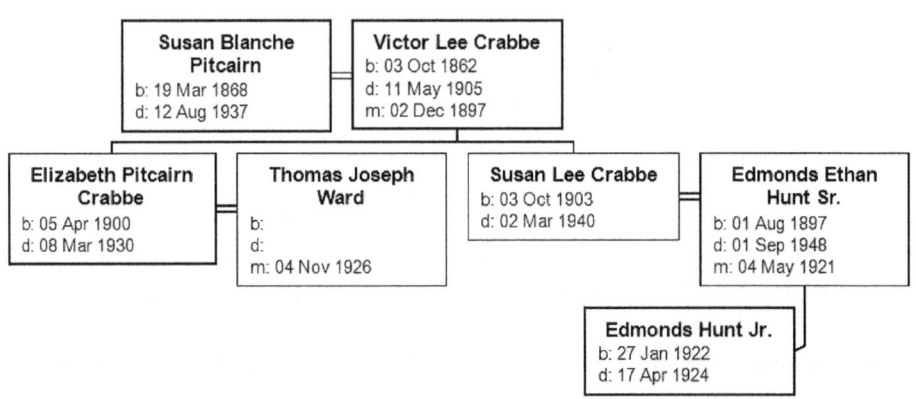

Descendant chart for Susan Blanche Pitcairn (compiled by the author).

End of a Fruitful Life

On June 20, 1907, just over a year after his forced retirement from the PRR, Robert Pitcairn suffered a severe accident. He was at the corner of Forbes Avenue and Craig Street in the Oakland section of Pittsburgh, preparing to board a streetcar to return home from the Carnegie Institute. A bicyclist collided with Pitcairn, knocking him down and landing with his cycle on top of him. Robert managed to board the next streetcar to return home but was in great pain when he arrived. His daughter summoned Dr. Patterson, who remained with his patient all night. By morning, Pitcairn's right arm and shoulder were so swollen that further diagnosis was hindered. Robert recovered from his injuries, but his family continued to worry about his physical and emotional health.[27]

Robert Pitcairn died at age 73 at his Pittsburgh home, Cairncarque, on July 25, 1909, three years after his retirement. His funeral service, led by the Rev. Doctor J. Kinsey Smith of Shadyside Presbyterian Church, was held at the family home. Pallbearers included George Westinghouse and Richard B. Mellon.[28]

Robert had been "R.P." to his employees and friends, But he had an even more personal nickname, one that he appreciated more as he grew older. His obituary in the *Pittsburgh Post-Gazette* reported, "He was 'Uncle Robert' to many who had no personal acquaintance with him at all, but who grew to like him by hearing those who did know him talk about the man."[29]

After her husband's death, Elizabeth Pitcairn became quite active in suffragette causes around Pittsburgh and hosted related events at Cairncarque. With a dozen other women who owned automobiles, she drove around Pittsburgh with placards supporting women's right to vote. In June 1915, more than 3,000 people gathered on the lawn at Cairncarque to party and dance for women's suffrage.[30]

Elizabeth died at her son's Pasadena, California, home on April 13, 1917. Robert and Elizabeth are interred in a mausoleum at Pittsburgh's Homewood Cemetery near their Shadyside home.

In her will, Elizabeth bequeathed $5,000 each to her three daughters and three of her grandchildren. In addition, her personal belongings were distributed to her daughter, Susan Pitcairn Crabbe, and two granddaughters. The balance of the estate was placed in trust with the Fidelity Title & Trust Company.[31]

Pitcairn-Crabbe Foundation

Robert and Elizabeth Pitcairn's granddaughter, Susan Lee Crabbe Hunt, signed her last will and testament on May 20, 1939, less than a year before her death in March 1940. In that document, she created the Pitcairn-Crabbe Foundation to commemorate her mother and her grandparents. The Allegheny County Court of Common Pleas incorporated the Pitcairn-Crabbe Foundation as a nonprofit corporation on December 23, 1940.

As stated in Susan Hunt's will, "The income of the said Corporation shall be applied in equitable proportions through approved institutions, organizations and

Pitcairn mausoleum in Homewood Cemetery, Pittsburgh, Pennsylvania (photograph by the author).

individuals for religious and church work, for Christian education, for community welfare, and, generally, for the relief of distress and the improvement of the spiritual and material condition of humanity, especially in the Commonwealth of Pennsylvania." The Foundation's board of directors is the board of trustees of Shadyside Presbyterian Church.

Mrs. Hunt's initial bequest was worth nearly $1 million. The funds and grants have been managed to preserve the purchasing value of the grants to account for inflation.

Grants of the Pitcairn-Crabbe Foundation

Years	Total Grants	Average per Year
1942–1951	$585,000	$58,500
1952–1970	$1,943,000	$102,260
1971–1985	$2,970,800	$198,060
1986–1999	$4,000,500	$285,750
2000–2020	$7,767,000	$369,860
TOTAL	$17,266,300	$218,561

As of the end of 2020, the asset value of the Foundation was $15,130,000. Robert and Elizabeth Pitcairn's fortune continues to benefit their beloved community.[32]

19

Into the Country—Bryn Athyn

"The city reveals the moral ends of being and sets the awful problem of life.
  The country soothes us, refreshes us...."
—Edwin Hubbel Chapin

In early 1889, John Pitcairn wrote to his friend, Walter Childs, about his purchase of 84 acres north of Philadelphia. The land was near Alnwick Grove, an excursion park built in the 1870s by the Philadelphia, Newtown & New York Railroad. By 1909, as the map on the next page shows, the Pitcairns, the Glenns, and the New Church owned over 450 acres in the area.

Other members of the New Church had been coming to Alnwick Grove for a decade before John Pitcairn started buying property there. On the bank of Pennypack Creek, the park included a large pavilion for dancing, many picnic tables, and a three-quarter-mile-long lake for swimming, boating, and fishing, all shaded by trees. It was an ideal spot to escape the dirt and congestion of Philadelphia. In 1880, "on June 19th the Academy held its third annual celebration in the picnic grounds near Alnwick Grove, Pa."[1]

New Church Community and Cairnwood

At the annual June 19 celebration of the New Church in 1892, John Pitcairn stated his intentions for the land he and Robert Glenn had been buying near Alnwick Grove:

> I hope that another school year in the city may be our last, and that all is necessary to do in order to move ... may be done by October of next year.... We all look forward to this movement with bright anticipation; but ... coming into closer contact ... may bring temptation. The trials we shall have, however, will be useful, and I hope that the closer relations into which we shall come may be the beginning of a choir with us and thus a preparation for a life in heaven.
>   Communities as a rule fail. Failure has been predicted of this movement, but we do not believe there will be failure. Principles of the Academy are to be ultimate, and we believe that the truths which we have, and which we will endeavor to ultimate will protect us from errors which have caused the failure of other communities.
>   Then let us be prepared for the trials that will come, and not be too sanguine that when we

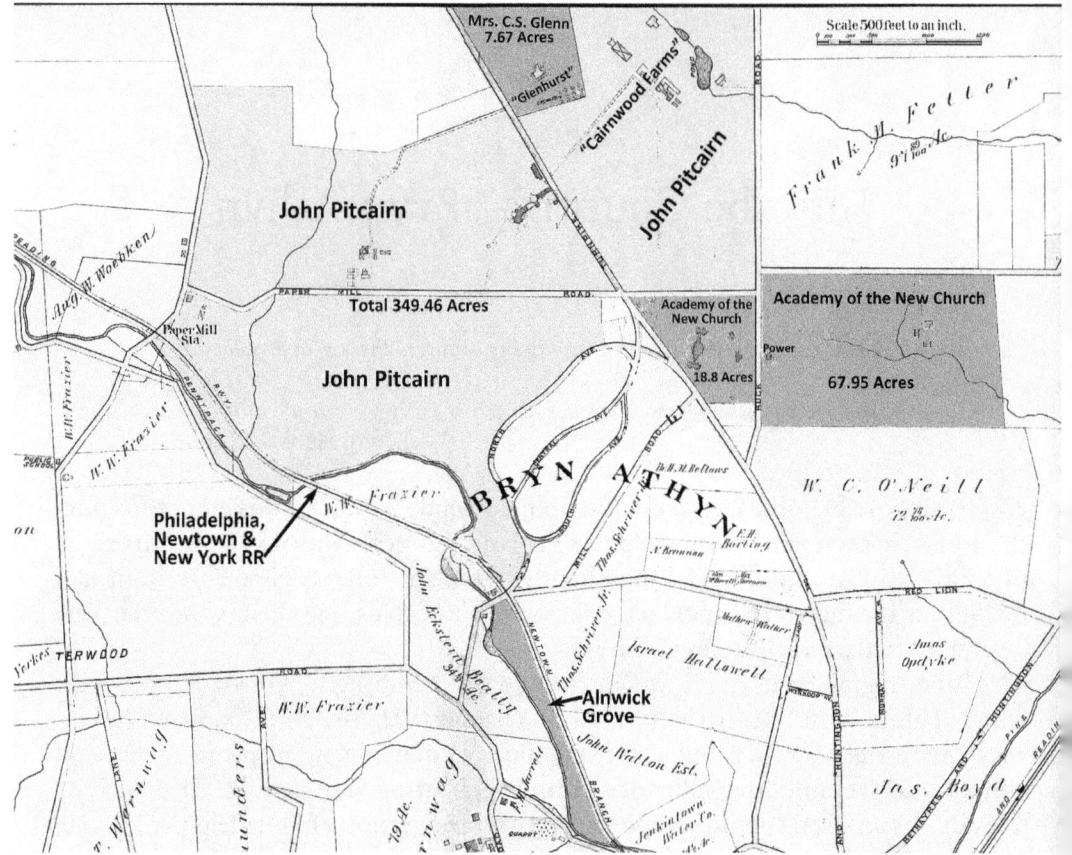

1909 map of the Huntington Valley region north of Philadelphia; shaded areas show the properties purchased by John and Gertrude Pitcairn, as well as by Mrs. C.S. Glenn (1909 map adapted by the author).

get out here into the country we are going to live a heavenly life. Do not be deceived by the rosy features you may have seen in the newspapers about our movement, nor expect all the external advantages money can bring.... We do not contemplate anything on a grand scale. Our buildings will be modest, but we hope to have those things which are necessary for the uses that are to be performed.[2]

Not far from the site of the celebration in Alnwick Grove, a new home for the John Pitcairn family, to be called Cairnwood, was under construction. Cairnwood was designed by the respected New York City architectural firm of Carrère & Hastings in the Beaux-Arts style, which blended "influences from classical Greek and Roman architecture with French Renaissance inspirations."[3] The estate, consisting of the main house, an adjacent courtyard, a garden house, and a formal garden, took three years to build and was completed in 1895.

The gardens and grounds for Cairnwood were designed by the famous New York firm of Olmsted, Olmsted, and Eliot (OOE).[4] While Cairnwood was under construction, OOE was also planning the grounds of the 1893 World's Columbian Exposition (the "White City") in Chicago.

Before Cairnwood was completed, John and Gertrude Pitcairn welcomed their

19. Into the Country—Bryn Athyn

fifth child, Theodore, on November 5, 1893. Their fourth child, Thelemasou, had been born on October 29, 1890, but survived less than a day.

On May 22, 1895, New Church Bishop William Frederic Pendleton dedicated the house and grounds at Cairnwood. The formal part of the ceremony was conducted in the chapel on the third floor of the octagonal turret that seated 25 people. Bishop Pendleton read from the Gospels and Swedenborg's *Arcana Coelestia* (Secrets of Heaven).

The total cost of the Cairnwood complex was $161,600.[5]

By the time the Pitcairns occupied Cairnwood, a New Church school had convened, first at the home of Charles S. Smith, then at Glenhurst, the mansion of Robert Glenn, John Pitcairn's brother-in-law. By October 1895, the school classes moved to a clubhouse commissioned by John Pitcairn. The clubhouse became a church on Sundays.

Cairnwood Estate circa 1920 (courtesy of Academy of the New Church Archives, Photograph Collection–ANC Buildings).

Downfall of Bishop Benade

As John Pitcairn had foreseen at the New Church Celebration of 1892, the church would face trials.

In the mid–1880s, Bishop William Benade had advocated a two-church concept—the General Church of the Advent, an external church focused on worship services for the general church membership, and the Academy, an internal church focused on the education of future leaders. The two-church idea received only reluctant acceptance among New Church religious authorities.

After Benade's stroke in 1889, he made a slow recovery. A young woman and New Church adherent named Kate Gibbs had nursed Benade back to health after his stroke.

The two stayed in contact, and on April 23, 1894, Benade married Kate, his third wife, at the Burton Road Church in London. The bishop was 78 years old, and Kate was 44. The couple returned to Philadelphia late in 1894.

But Bishop Benade was becoming more and more authoritarian, confrontational, and paranoid. In 1893, he proclaimed himself to be the Lord's chief representative and thus able to determine the divine will among men. He dissolved the Council of the Laity, which had been managing the secular affairs of the New Church. He dismissed former friends and colleagues, suspecting them of disloyalty. Despite once favoring the move of the Academy from Philadelphia to the Huntington Valley location, he now vehemently opposed it. Finally, he turned against Bishop William F. Pendleton, who had taken up the slack while Benade recovered from his stroke.

In early 1897, five priests resigned from Benade's leadership and asked Bishop Pendleton to organize them under his leadership. Pendleton reluctantly agreed and formed the General Church of the New Jerusalem with the Academy as its educational arm. The new organization operated out of Huntington Valley buildings.

Benade orally offered his resignation, then rescinded his offer and continued to claim his old position and salary. Finally, John Pitcairn had to take action against his old friend and mentor. On June 1, 1897, Pitcairn introduced a resolution:

> *Whereas*, The Corporation ... has notified Bishop Benade of the discontinuance of his salary on and after June 1st, 1897, and
> *Whereas*, Bishop Benade has appealed to the Corporation ... therefore be it
> *Resolved*, That this Corporation sees no reason why the action of its Board of Directors should in any way be reversed or modified.

After being duly seconded, the resolution carried unanimously.

In private, John Pitcairn made sure his old friend had a comfortable living during the seven remaining years of his life, the last five spent in London from 1900 until his death on May 22, 1905, at the age of 88. Kate Gibbs Benade died on March 13, 1931.[6]

With the proxy battle at PPG, which culminated in February 1897 with the ouster of Edward and Emory Ford, and the unfortunate need to oust his old friend, Bishop Benade, in June 1897, the year was full of turmoil for John Pitcairn. But a blessing, in the form of son Harold Frederick Pitcairn, arrived on June 20, 1897.

A Community Grows

With the ouster of Bishop Benade, the New Church became formally known as the General Church of the New Jerusalem (but still informally called the New Church), and the educational arm remained the Academy. Both organizations officially moved from Philadelphia to the area around Alnwick Grove.

Real-world problems immediately intruded. With the increasing population inspired by the New Church and Academy, mundane issues such as water, food, roads, housing, fire and police protection, health care, and community buildings had to be addressed. So John Pitcairn turned to Robert Glenn, with his real estate and development expertise, to be the community administrator.

Based on their success with the Cairnwood grounds, Robert retained Olmsted, Olmsted, and Eliot to design the roads, building lots, walkways, and plantings for

Earthly Marriage—To Be Continued in Heaven

John and Gertrude Pitcairn were deeply devoted to one another. While en route to Europe, John wrote, on April 10, 1897,

> My darling One, Peace be with thee! I read a few evenings ago the two chapters in *Heaven and Hell* (on) Innocence and Peace, and I was wishing that I could have read these numbers with you. They are so beautiful.... You have been almost constantly in my active thought since I left home, and I ... long to know just how you are doing. I do so love you.[7]

Sadly, Gertrude died of peritonitis from a burst appendix less than a year later, on March 27, 1898. She was just 42 years old, and her early death stunned John Pitcairn.

In replying to a letter of condolence, John wrote,

> my heartfelt thanks for your kind and sympathetic letter of April 27th. The Lord in His wisdom has taken my dear one from earth.... I have never been so grateful for His Divine revelation and promise that those "who are interiorly united cannot be rent asunder by the death of either." A few days before my dear wife left this world she was reading in *Divine Providence* 73. She also wrote to a friend a short time ago, "The other world may seem a long way off but in reality the time is short for any of us."

John Pitcairn never remarried.

Gertrude's early death left John Pitcairn with four children to care for: Raymond, age 12; Vera, age 10; Theodore, age four; and Harold, nine months. To help with the children and the management of Cairnwood, John sent for Maria Hogan, whom he had met in 1879 when he took Gertrude Starkey and Maria to Niagara Falls. Maria was a New Church member in Pittsburgh and the cousin of Andrew Carnegie. She had also been Gertrude's best friend, as confirmed by the many letters the two had exchanged through the years.

Maria quickly became the beloved "Aunt Rydie" to the Pitcairn children. She stayed in Bryn Athyn for the rest of her life and died there on April 17, 1926, at age 75.[8]

Bryn Athyn

In early May 1898, a group of residents met to form an association to lead the development of the new community. Robert Glenn was elected president, and he, with four others, formed a board of control.

But the community lacked a name. The search for a name continued for over a year, with candidates including "Bonnie Brae," "Collyn," "Ridgemont," and "Swedenborg." Finally, "Hillbrook" was chosen in May 1899 but was abandoned when it failed to gain community support. Eventually, Bishop Pendleton studied a Welsh dictionary and proposed the name "Bryn Athyn." Translated from Welsh to English,

Bryn Athyn train station built by the Philadelphia, Newtown & New York Railroad. The station is now the Bryn Athyn post office (photograph by the author).

it means "Hill of Cohesion" or "Hill of Unity." On September 25, 1899, the Village Association approved the new name, hoping the community would live up to its meaning.[9]

Now that the new location of the Academy and the New Church had an official name, construction began. The decade from 1901 to 1910 witnessed the construction of seven buildings of the Academy of the New Church at Bryn Athyn.

Construction on Benade Hall, a classroom building named for the ousted but still-loved bishop, was started in September 1900. It would also serve as a chapel until a proper church building could be constructed.

At the dedication of Benade Hall on April 6, 1902, John Pitcairn laid out his vision for both the building and the Academy:

> It is the purpose of the Academy, as the Divine Providence opens the way, to establish a university for the elementary and academic education of the youth of the Church, in the Doctrines and Principles of the New Church, in the Languages, ancient and modern, and in the Sciences.
>
> From the beginning it has been the desire and hope of the founders of the Academy ... to have a building adequate to the uses intended. In the fullness of time the Lord provided the men and the means that made this building possible, and it now becomes my duty and my privilege to deliver to you, as the representative and president of the corporation of the Academy of the New Church, the deed for this property, free of encumbrance, covering the land and the buildings erected thereon, to be used for the purposes and uses defined in the charter of that body; and may the Lord bless and prosper the Academy of the New Church, and the men engaged in its uses ever be faithful to their trust.[10]

Benade Hall as it appears today. The building suffered a serious fire in 1948, was rebuilt and opened in 1950, and is now the center for Information and Admissions (photograph by the author).

Between 1901 and 1905, Glenn Hall (girls' dormitory), Stuart Hall (boys' dormitory), a dining hall, and a heating plant were completed. In 1909, John Pitcairn announced the construction of a library and museum. Finally, De Charms Hall (elementary school) was completed in 1910.[11] Buildings to house all grades in a nearly complete facility, sitting on a spacious and lovely campus, were in place thanks to the generosity of one man, John Pitcairn. In addition to covering day-to-day expenses, he provided a $400,000 endowment for the Academy.[12]

20

Life Goes On

"Death is not the opposite of life, but a part of it."
—Haruki Murakami

Vaccination

Epidemics of diseases such as bubonic plague, smallpox, typhus, cholera, influenza, and COVID-19 have brought suffering and death to humanity throughout history.

Smallpox has been traced back to Egyptian Pharaoh Ramses V, who died in 1157 BC. It is caused by a virus that most likely came from rodents. "In May 1980, the World Health Assembly, the governing body of the World Health Organization, officially certified the global elimination of smallpox, the first-ever eradication of a disease in human history." The victory over smallpox is the result of work by Edward Jenner in the 1790s that led to a safe and effective vaccine against the disease.[1]

A relatively small epidemic of smallpox hit Pennsylvania in 1904. Of the 606 smallpox deaths in the U.S. in the last half of that year, two-thirds were in Pennsylvania.

At the beginning of the 1905–1906 school year, the state commissioner of health told schools in the commonwealth that, based on state law, all schoolchildren must be vaccinated against smallpox. He warned that local school officials had no authority to override the state law.[2]

Then as now, many people opposed vaccination, especially mandated vaccination. Opposition was most vigorous among adherents of homeopathic medicine, a belief common to New Church members. For various reasons, including that his son Raymond had contracted blood poisoning from a vaccination, John Pitcairn became a vocal and influential opponent.

Bishop W.F. Pendleton, the Academy president, had no choice but to obey the Pennsylvania law. But several Academy teachers and board members, including Pitcairn, favored defying the state. The division threatened the New Church, with members on both sides of the issue holding strong opinions.

The intense debate over compulsory vaccination split the community and inspired a song:

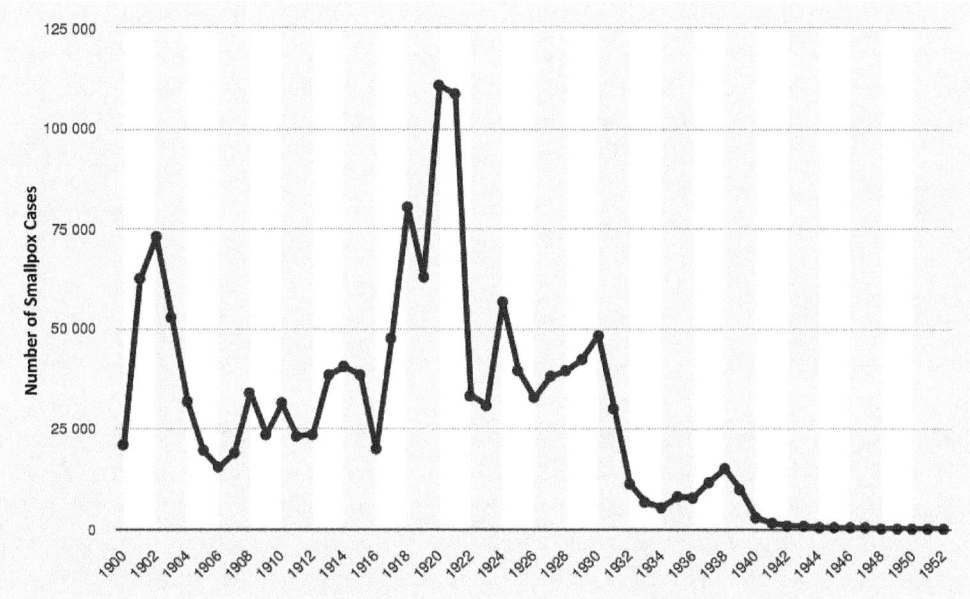

Number of Smallpox cases reported in the United States (Our World in Data, 2018).

> For it's Vaccination, Abomination,
> Anti-Vaccinationists only can be saved!
> Or, Vaccination, we uphold the nation,
> The laws of Uncle Sam must be obeyed.
> This once peaceful little hamlet,
> Is now torn by bitter strife
> All harmony is turned to discord,
> And dissensions mar our life.[3]

Finally, on March 22, 1906, Pitcairn agreed to keep his vaccine opposition separate from the New Church. But he continued his fight against vaccinations in Pennsylvania and the country as a whole. He funded an anti-vaccine periodical and became president of the National Anti-Vaccination League. On March 5, 1907, John addressed the Committee on Public Health and Sanitation of the Pennsylvania Legislature. His rational arguments persuaded the legislature to repeal the law making vaccination mandatory, but the governor vetoed their action.

Undaunted, Pitcairn continued his fight. In May 1910, the *Ladies' Home Journal* published his article, "The Fallacy of Vaccination." At the time, *Ladies' Home Journal*, edited by Edward W. Bok, was one of the most popular magazines in the country, with readership in the millions.[4] In his paper, Pitcairn traced the history of vaccination back to 1721, highlighted the dangers and failures of vaccination, denied its efficacy, and protested compulsory vaccination as infringing on personal freedom. In addition, he cited medical professionals who had initially favored vaccination but, after their own research, turned against it. John also appealed to the writings of Swedenborg, which he interpreted as opposing the introduction of foreign substances into the blood.

The *Ladies' Home Journal* article was well organized and free of emotional appeals. It was so well received that Pitcairn had the article republished in 1911 by the Anti-Vaccination League of America. A companion article by Dr. Jay Frank Schamberg presented the counter-arguments for vaccination. The 48-page book, *Both Sides of the Vaccination Question*, is still available in several U.S. libraries.

John Pitcairn paid more than lip service to the cause, leaving $10,000 in his will for the anti-vaccination effort.

Tragedy and Joy

In early July 1910, John Pitcairn and his 16-year-old son, Theodore, joined 1,300 other delegates in London for an International Swedenborg Congress. Meanwhile, back at Bryn Athyn, John's 25-year-old son, Raymond, was courting Mildred Glenn. Mildred was the daughter of John's late close friend and brother-in-law, Robert Glenn. John's daughter, Vera, 23, was planning an automobile tour of New England.

A *New Church Life* article described Vera as "young, vivacious, beautiful, and generous, the warm-hearted friend of newborn babies and their mothers," with a great love "for the spiritual things of the Church."[5] On July 13, Vera left with her friends for the New England adventure. But on July 15, at Port Jervis, New York, she fell ill with abdominal pain, later diagnosed as appendicitis. Summoned by telegram, her brothers Raymond and Harold arrived with a doctor and nurse on Saturday, July 16. The young woman rallied, and Harold wrote, "Vera is getting better." But on Friday, July 22, Vera succumbed to the same disease, peritonitis, that had claimed her mother 12 years earlier.[6]

Raymond sadly notified his father and the Church family at large, resulting in a sea of condolences for John. Then Raymond sailed to London to join his father and brother, where he provided the details of Vera's last days. He also told them of his engagement to Mildred Glenn, news that must have brought joy among the intense sorrow that John was feeling.

Confident that he would soon be reunited with his beloved wife and daughter, John Pitcairn continued what he had been doing before the tragic news. He entertained New Church friends at luncheons and dinners and even attended a British General Church Assembly at Colchester, 66 miles northeast of London. The three Pitcairn men returned to Bryn Athyn in early September.

Raymond Pitcairn married Mildred Glenn on December 29, 1910. They moved into Cairnwood and lived there with John.

God Builds a Church

By 1907, the congregation of 300 members was taxing the capacity of Benade Hall. A small committee started to think about a dedicated church building. As usual, John Pitcairn accelerated the process by depositing money, in this case $30,000, into the building fund in 1908. But even with that stimulation, little happened until 1912, when the Philadelphia architectural firm of Lawrence Visscher

Boyd was charged with drawing plans. Their concept, submitted in the spring of 1912, showed a solid, rather plain structure that failed to excite those who favored a soaring Gothic style. Raymond Pitcairn, in particular, desired a more inspired design, so his father charged him with creating something better than the Boyd effort.

Raymond consulted with Ralph Adams Cram, the prolific and influential Boston-based architect of collegiate and ecclesiastical buildings, often in the Gothic Revival style.

John gave Raymond free rein in the planning and execution of the new building. John himself continued his work for Pittsburgh Plate Glass, often combined with a resumption of his world travels.

War

In mid–1914, war in Europe seemed inevitable. But John Pitcairn, as Chairman of the PPG Board, had regularly visited all PPG plants, and it was time to examine the Courcelles plate glass factory near Brussels, Belgium.

John arrived in Paris on June 29, 1914, and met with the plant manager, Richard Melchers. The pair first toured a rival French plate glass factory and then proceeded to Courcelles. After inspecting the factory, Pitcairn traveled to Aix-la-Chapelle (also known as Aachen), where he took the waters at the spa once enjoyed by Charlemagne.

But everything in Europe was in turmoil. On the day before John arrived in Paris, the assassination of Archduke Franz Ferdinand launched an unstoppable series of events. Civilian travel in Europe was effectively suspended, and one month later, July 28, 1914, marked the start of World War I.

On August 2, Germany demanded free passage through Belgium so it could invade France. When Belgium refused, Germany invaded Belgium, thus disrupting all banking transactions and placing the Courcelles glass factory behind enemy lines. Richard Melchers, the Courcelles manager, cabled Pitcairn with an urgent request for 25,000 Belgian francs to pay the 700 workers at Courcelles. John requested and received the francs from America, but with no way to deliver the money, the 73-year-old Pitcairn waited in London.

On October 14, John embarked on a journey to deliver the money to Melchers. It was a convoluted trip, made possible only because the United States had not yet entered the war. First, John received a letter of introduction from the U.S. ambassador to Britain, addressed to the U.S. ambassador at Brussels. The letter explained John's mission and vouched for his character. John was also given government documents under seal for the Brussels legation, thus granting him official status.

The next day, Thursday, October 15, John traveled to Tilbury, near the mouth of the Thames, where he boarded a ship to carry him across the English Channel the following morning. On Friday, he reached Vlissingen, Holland, and finally, via another boat, The Hague.

The U.S. minister at The Hague provided more sealed papers for Brussels. John also requested and received endorsement of his journey from the German minister to The Hague. A friend at The Hague arranged a private automobile trip from Rotterdam to Antwerp. On Sunday morning, October 18, John and four other passengers—two Dutch, one Belgian, and one German—left Rotterdam. John carried the 25,000 francs and diplomatic envelopes on his lap.

German officers examined passports and papers at the Belgian border; such inspections continued on the way to Antwerp. Despite John's offer of additional money, his driver refused to continue to Brussels and dropped John at an Antwerp hotel. A hotel employee had access to a car and agreed to drive John to Brussels. But first, John had to obtain a permit to continue from the German governor of Antwerp. He succeeded in his quest and, while doing so, heard a German band playing in a public square and saw a German regiment marching by.

At 3:00 p.m., still on Sunday, October 18, John and a German officer departed for Brussels. About halfway to their destination, the car broke down, and John and the German began to walk. Fortunately, the German officer hailed a German military vehicle carrying an army surgeon to Brussels. Upon arrival in the city, the two Germans disembarked and told the driver to deliver John to his destination, the apartment of Richard Melchers.

John delivered the 25,000 francs to Melchers, and they spent the evening discussing John's perilous journey and the war. In the morning, he visited the Brussels legation to deliver the papers he had been given. When he asked for a car to get him out of Belgium, the U.S. ambassador replied that the Germans controlled all vehicles. So John proceeded to the consul's office, where a young American obtained a car, gasoline, a driver, and a permit from the German governor of Brussels. Somehow, John left Belgium and arrived in Liverpool, England, in time to board the RMS *Lusitania* on Saturday, October 24.

John's journey home was rough and stormy, but he got home safely. Less than seven months later, on May 7, 1915, going from New York bound for Liverpool, a German U-boat sank the *Lusitania*, resulting in the loss of 1,197 lives, including 123 Americans, and moving the U.S. closer to declaring war on Germany.

John Pitcairn arrived back at Bryn Athyn on October 31, 1914.

Around South America

John Pitcairn never stood still. At the turn of the new year, he visited two local New Church assemblies in Kitchener and Toronto, Canada. Then, on January 21, 1915, with his son Theodore and the chairman of the Commercial Department of PPG, he set sail on a voyage around South America.

The Dutch ship *Kroonland* suffered multiple cancellations before sailing because of hostile naval actions south of Santiago, Chile, and near the Falkland Islands. But the voyage continued with 240 passengers.

The Panama Canal had opened for navigation on August 15, 1914, and the *Kroonland*, with the Pitcairns aboard, was the first large ship to pass through its locks. On the west coast of South America, the ship docked long enough for those interested to ascend the 13,000 feet to Lake Titicaca at the border of Bolivia and Peru. Of course, John Pitcairn, age 74, participated in the climb. After a voyage that encountered no hostile warships, John and Theodore returned to Bryn Athyn on April 12, 1915.

Bryn Athyn Incorporates

One week after John and Theodore arrived home, the Village Association of Bryn Athyn petitioned the Montgomery County Court of Quarter Sessions for incorporation as a borough within Moreland Township. The area to be included covered 467 acres and had 400 residents. Presiding Judge Aaron S. Swartz delivered a favorable decision on the application, noting that the settlement had a public library with 25,000 volumes and "extensive college and school buildings ... of high standard and efficiency." He also commented that Bryn Athyn Cathedral, when completed, "will be one of the finest church buildings in this county." He granted the formal decree of incorporation on February 8, 1916.[7]

Final Trips

Two more trips rounded out John Pitcairn's later life. The first, with his two younger sons, Theodore, 21, and Harold, 18, took them to Canada's rugged and rocky Gaspe Peninsula. The Gaspe is known for its 200,000 gannet seabirds, the largest North American colony, and its four national parks. But John and his sons did not go for the birds or the parks but for the fish. The expedition lasted two weeks, from July 17 through August 1, 1915, and sapped much of John's remaining strength.

The second and final trip was by car during the first two weeks of September 1915. John and three New Church friends toured the Adirondacks and White Mountains of New York, Vermont, and New Hampshire.

Illness and Death

Soon after returning from the automobile journey, John Pitcairn came down with a severe cold that worsened to pneumonia, complicated by asthma and heart trouble. He remained in his room, mostly in bed, for the balance of 1915.

In 1916, John gradually gained strength. The annual New Church General Assembly in June marked his first public appearance that year. At the General Church Corporation meeting on June 17, John took his place in a wheelchair behind a heavy oak table. As president, he called the meeting to order, and, despite his failing health, allowed himself to be reelected president of the corporation.

In late June, John's doctors told him that his heart ailment was incurable but that he could survive months or even years with proper care. However, that prognosis proved optimistic. On Saturday, July 22, 1916, just after 7:00 a.m., John Pitcairn died at age 75.

Tombstones of John and Gertrude Pitcairn in Bryn Athyn Cemetery (photograph by the author).

Remembrances of John Pitcairn

A multitude of tributes followed John Pitcairn's death, but three captured the essence of the man.

First, at a memorial service the day after his death, Bishop William Pendleton, his old friend, commented on John's restraint in influencing New Church affairs despite his overwhelming financial support:

> No one as far as I know has ever been so willing to do so much for the work of the Church, and at the same time recognize the freedom of the members of the Church. Although he gave so much ... yet when we met together in the Board of Directors, he sat there as one of us, considering the uses of the Church ... the members of the Church should be as free as he was ... in deciding on expenditures of money for the uses of the Church.
>
> It has certainly been of the Lord's Providence that he has been raised up to do what he has done. We all recognize the Providence of the Lord in raising up Father Benade to do what he did, and next to that it seems to me the most wonderful Providence—a layman who would stand for those principles and provide the means for carrying them out.[8]

Second, at their first meeting after John's passing, the board of directors of Pittsburgh Plate Glass called John "the controlling personality in the organization." They further stated that the company's success was mainly due to his genius for organization, trust in men, encouraging appreciation of their services, and constant personal interest and touch.[9]

Third, at a meeting of the Executive Committee of the General Church of the New Jerusalem held at Bryn Athyn on February 10, 1917, the following resolutions were adopted unanimously:

WHEREAS: On Saturday, July 22, 1916, our brother, Mr. John Pitcairn, for many years the president of the General Church of the New Jerusalem and Chairman of its Executive Committee, was, by the merciful Providence of the Lord, called to the spiritual world; therefore be it

RESOLVED: That this Executive Committee and the entire General Church of the New Jerusalem have, in the death of Mr. John Pitcairn, sustained a well nigh irreparable loss.

RESOLVED: That by his departure this Executive Committee is bereft of one who, for sixteen years, has been its honored and trusted Chairman and its wisest counselor.

RESOLVED: That, individually, we deeply feel the loss of a friend whose spiritual qualities of mind and heart, sincerity, justice, executive ability and unvarying and refined courtesy as a gentleman were such as to win our enduring admiration and deep affection.

RESOLVED: That our General Church has cause to mourn for one who, despite the pressure of unusually extensive worldly responsibilities, was conspicuous for faithful, prompt and willing attendance at the various meetings of the Church, whether of devotional, doctrinal, business or social character; whose presence was ever felt as a strength, and who gave himself to the Church as willingly even as he gave material support.

RESOLVED: That the Executive Committee and the entire General Church have reason to be profoundly grateful to the Lord that our departed brother, the generous benefactor of our Church, was so long spared to us, to guide by his counsel and to inspire by his example.

RESOLVED: That also we are deeply grateful for the consolation brought by those Divine Revelations, the study and application of which so characterized the earthly life of our departed brother, feeling assured that he is now supremely happy in continuing the work that was his life's love, and which we may confidently believe will, in ways hereafter to be known to us, benefit the Church even more than his bodily presence could accomplish.

RESOLVED: That our most heartfelt sympathy is extended to Mr. Pitcairn's family, to whom our Secretary is hereby requested to transmit an engrossed [*sic*] copy of these resolutions.[10]

21

Pitcairns After John

"Your descendants shall gather your fruits."
—Virgil

Completion of the Cathedral

After the death of John Pitcairn, construction of the Bryn Athyn Cathedral continued. John and Gertrude's eldest son, Raymond, had been working with Boston-based architect Ralph Adams Cram, but in 1917 Cram withdrew from the project. There is no official reason for Cram's departure, but he likely grew tired of dealing with an untrained but wealthy and stubborn client who could not read architectural drawings.

Raymond persevered and brought medieval construction techniques to the building of the cathedral. On-site workshops for stone carvers, woodworkers, metalsmiths, and stained-glass artists allowed designers and craftsmen to collaborate and influence the design. Although all the work was done on-site, materials were sourced from all over the world, including gneiss granite from a nearby quarry.[1]

To give the massive cathedral a sense of life and movement, Raymond avoided straight lines by adding curves in the walls and elevation changes in the floors. Because of his inability to read and interpret conventional architectural drawings, he relied on large-scale models so that he and the artisans could study, review, and embellish their designs.

The stained-glass windows are unique. The glass was made by the medieval method of melting sand with metallic oxides and various pigments and then creating glass discs of varying thicknesses. This technique resulted in exceptionally bright and intense colors.

The major construction of the cathedral was finished in 1919, and it was dedicated on October 5 of that year. However, several features took much longer to complete. The Ezekiel Tower, located south of the main tower, was built from 1920 to 1926. The Choir Hall to the north was finished and dedicated in 1929. The Michael Tower, adjoining the Choir Hall, took until the 1950s to complete. The first stained glass was blown in 1922, and the final stained-glass window was completed and installed in the 1960s.[2]

Intentional or not, the Gothic spires of the Bryn Athyn Cathedral, built in 1919, are reflected in the PPG Buildings in Pittsburgh, designed by Philip Johnson and John Burgee and completed in 1984. Both structures are breathtaking and reach to the sky.

Raymond Pitcairn

Based on his experience with the cathedral, Raymond Pitcairn built a summer home named Glen Tonche in 1928. Nicknamed "Zeus of the Catskills," the 18,000 square-foot compound still sits on 35 acres atop Mount Tonche in Ulster County, near Woodstock, New York. In 2012, Glen Tonche was listed for sale for $8 million.[3]

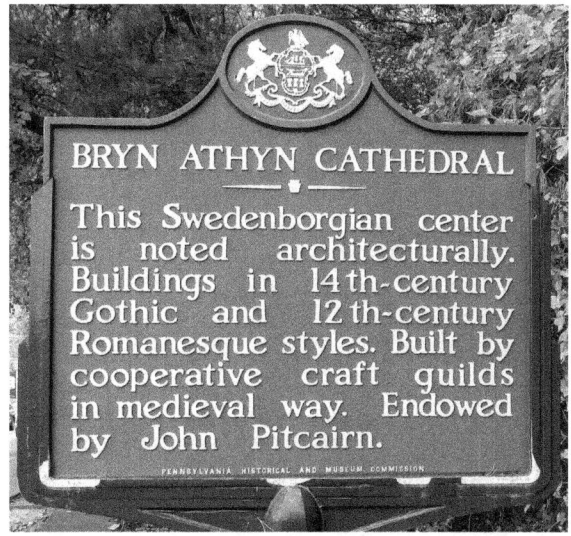

Historical marker commemorating the Bryn Athyn Cathedral (photograph by the author).

Starting in 1928, Raymond also built Glencairn as a family home in Bryn Athyn, with the same techniques used for the Bryn Athyn Cathedral.

Bryn Athyn Cathedral is the Episcopal seat of the General Church of the New Jerusalem (courtesy of Larry Lamb via Wikimedia Commons).

Bryn Athyn Cathedral (1919); Main PPG Building (1984) (photographs by the author).

As early as 1922, Raymond contemplated another building at Bryn Athyn, not as a family home but as a more modest "studio" to display his ever-growing collection of medieval stained glass and sculpture. He had acquired many of these items to inspire the artisans working on the cathedral. But Raymond was an inveterate collector who continued adding artifacts from Mesopotamia, ancient Egypt, classical Greece, Rome, and other cultures to his private museum.

Raymond's artistic interests also extended to the performing arts. He was a skilled amateur musician and often sponsored small concerts for his Bryn Athyn neighbors at Cairnwood. So the "studio" for displaying his art collection grew to include a music hall, later called the Great Hall.

His dedication to his family and commitment to his religious ideals led to the final purpose for the new structure, a home for his wife and children. "So the building began, and as it progressed, Raymond's plans were enlarged in order that he might indulge his artistic ability in decorating with the beautiful symbolisms upon which his home life was based—a New Church home in every sense."[4]

Raymond, Mildred, and the youngest four of their nine children moved from Cairnwood into Glencairn in 1939, 11 years after the start of construction.

After Raymond and his family vacated Cairnwood, it provided a residence for various Pitcairn family members. In 1945, Raymond's daughter, Gabriele; her husband, the Rev. Willard Pendleton; and their children moved in and stayed until 1980. At that time, Cairnwood was donated to the Academy of the New Church. The Academy now rents out Cairnwood for events and as a conference center.[5]

Raymond Pitcairn was "a lawyer by profession, an architect by choice, and a businessman by force of circumstances."[6] He served as a delegate to the Pennsylvania convention to ratify the Twenty-First Amendment (repealing Prohibition) and

Glencairn Museum (photograph by the author).

also to the 1956 Republican National Convention. In addition, Raymond was a personal friend of President Dwight D. Eisenhower.[7]

Raymond died on July 12, 1966. Mildred remained in Glencairn until her death on June 23, 1979. In 1980, Glencairn and its contents were donated to the Academy of the New Church. Since 1982, it has served as a museum to educate visitors about the history of religion, using art and artifacts from various cultures and time periods.[8]

Theodore Pitcairn

Theodore Pitcairn, the middle son of John and Gertrude Pitcairn, received a bachelor of theology degree from the Academy of the New Church Theological School in June 1918.

He started buying paintings as a hobby, and in 1921, he saw a pastel portrait of a young girl, *Marijke with White Feather Fan*, by Dutch painter Philippe Smit. Theodore purchased the picture and asked to meet the model. She was Marijke Urban, born on September 7, 1905. When they met, Marijke was 16. Five years later, in 1926, Theodore and Marijke married.

Theodore and Marijke had nine children between 1927 and 1942. Pitcairn later built a studio at his Bryn Athyn estate for Philippe Smit and bought most of his paintings.

Art collecting soon became more of a business for Theodore, with acquisitions of paintings by El Greco, Monet, Rembrandt, and van Gogh. In 1967, he sold a Monet, *La terrasse à Sainte-Adresse*, to the New York Metropolitan Museum of Art for $1.4 million. He had bought the painting for $11,000 in 1926.[9]

Theodore worked with church missions in Africa, teaching theology to students in South Africa and Basutoland (now Lesotho). In addition, he served as pastor of the Durban Society in Natal, South Africa.

Theodore and his family lived in Bryn Athyn on their 100-acre country estate called Dientjehame, complete with barns and livestock. It was decorated with rare rugs, ancient sculptures, antiques from around the world, and his collection of paintings. He also owned a home at Cape Cod.[10]

Marijke with White Feather Fan, Philippe Smit, 1921 (© Fonds de dotation Philippe Smit, Paris, courtesy of Mrs. Eshowe Pitcairn-Pennink, photo: Christopher Burke Studios).

Although trained in theology at the Academy, Theodore started to question the New Church doctrine around 1929. After increasingly contentious and emotional meetings (Theodore described them as "violent") among church leaders, in 1937, he and several others broke from the General Church of the New Jerusalem (New Church) over those doctrinal issues. They formed the Lord's New Church Which is Nova Hierosolyma (usually called Lord's New Church). The studio built for Philippe Smit now serves as the chapel for the Lord's New Church.

During a March 25, 1971, doctrinal class, Theodore said of the split:

> In this connection, you might say that the essential difference between the Academy and the General Church is that we believe that the Divine goods and truths can be in man, thus that the Lord can be in man, while the General Church took the position, particularly at that time, that the Divine, the goods and truths when they entered man, were only human.[11]

Theodore's explanation does little to clarify the theological differences or justify the splitting of a church that was already struggling. But the underlying reasons for church splits are often obscure.

In 1967, Theodore wrote *My Lord and My God: Essays on Modern Religion*, the

Bible, and Emanuel Swedenborg, an exploration of the spiritual problems facing mankind and the solution to those problems based on the word of God.

The New Church and the Lord's New Church headquarters are both in Bryn Athyn, and the two are often confused with each other. To add to the confusion, there is a third Swedenborgian religious organization, the General Convention of the New Jerusalem. Some information on the three branches is tabulated below.[12]

Swedenborgian Organizations

Name	Headquarters	Founded	Membership U.S.	Membership Outside of U.S.
General Convention of the New Jerusalem	11 Highland Ave. Newtonville, MA 02460	1817	1,601 in 2001	294 in 2001
General Church of the New Jerusalem (New Church)	1100 Cathedral Road Bryn Athyn, PA 19009	1897	7,052 in 2009	
The Lord's New Church Which Is Nova Hierosolyma (Lord's New Church)	1725 Huntingdon Rd. P.O. Box 7 Bryn Athyn, PA 19009	1937	Three congregations in the U.S.	Congregations in Holland, Japan, Sweden, Ukraine, and South Africa

Another organization, the Swedenborg Foundation in West Chester, Pennsylvania, publishes, preserves, and promotes the principles of Emanuel Swedenborg through spiritual growth books and webcasts.[13]

Theodore Pitcairn died in Bryn Athyn at age 80 on December 17, 1973. His wife, Marijke (Urban) Pitcairn, died on November 10, 1978, at age 73.[14]

Lord's New Church Chapel; originally built as a studio/home for Philippe Smit (photograph by the author).

Harold Pitcairn

The youngest of John and Gertrude's children, Harold Pitcairn, was born June 20, 1897, at Bryn Athyn. Just nine months later, on March 27, 1898, Gertrude died, and John invited her best friend, Maria Hogan, to move to Cairnwood to care for Harold and his three siblings.

On December 17, 1903, on the sand dunes of North Carolina, two bicycle mechanics from Dayton, Ohio, Wilbur and Orville Wright, made the first controlled, sustained flight in a heavier-than-air aircraft.[15] That 59-second, 852-foot flight would transform the world and set the course of Harold Pitcairn's life.

Harold and the other Pitcairn children attended school at the Academy of the New Church on property adjacent to Cairnwood. Except for the tragic loss of his mother, his life was idyllic. His neighbors were all friends and relatives, and his playground was the estate with massive lawns, formal gardens, greenhouses, and a pergola. But Harold's world was shaken when his sister, Vera, died in 1910. With no mother to comfort him, a father consumed by business, and an older brother, Theodore, who did not want Harold to restrain his adventures, Harold became more withdrawn and shy.[16]

But at age 15, Harold saw his first real airplane. While visiting relatives in Atlantic City, he was amazed by a Curtiss flying boat soaring above the beach surf. He watched from the boardwalk as the plane took off, climbed to level flight, and landed on the water, only to repeat the cycle again and again. On returning to Bryn Athyn, he and a friend commandeered the rear portion of the carriage house, where they built a full-sized glider. In the summer of 1913, Harold's first flight ended with pilot and plane in a crumpled heap on the ground.[17] But the flying bug had bitten Harold.

John Pitcairn regarded Harold's interest in aeronautics as a hobby. But he sought to build his son's confidence and self-esteem by arranging an apprenticeship for him in the summer of 1914 at the Curtiss Aircraft factory in Hammondsport, New York. There, he bent and glued wooden framing structures and learned firsthand how airplanes were built.

Two years later, in 1916, Harold enrolled in formal flying lessons at the Curtiss Flying School in Newport News, Virginia. But on July 22, Harold's dream summer ended when his father died. When Harold returned home for the funeral, his brother Raymond made it clear that Harold should give up flight school and complete his formal education to prepare for work in the family businesses. Harold reluctantly enrolled in the Wharton School of Business at the University of Pennsylvania in Philadelphia.[18]

Somewhat bored with his studies, Harold continued to make aircraft drawings and dream of flying. His drawings now were different, as he focused on rotary-wing aircraft, similar to what we now call helicopters.

At the end of World War I, Harold married his childhood sweetheart, Clara Davis, on January 21, 1919. Harold was 22, and Clara was 23. Like his older brothers, he and Clara would have nine children. A chart showing the 27 children of Raymond, Theodore, and Harold Pitcairn (the grandchildren of John and Gertrude Pitcairn) is included in Appendix I.

Cairncrest, the estate of Harold and Clara (Davis) Pitcairn (photograph by the author).

Harold, Clara, and their family later moved to Cairncrest, an estate they built in Bryn Athyn between 1925 and 1928.

Harold's fascination with flying and airplanes never abated. In October 1923, he bought a Farman biplane and housed it in a small hanger east of Bryn Athyn. The following year, he purchased two adjacent farms, and there established a flying service and flight school named Pitcairn Aviation. He officially opened the Pitcairn Flying Field on November 2, 1924.[19]

By February 1926, Harold's ambitions had outgrown the small Bryn Athyn field, so he purchased farmland to the west near Willow Grove, Pennsylvania. Pitcairn Field No. 2 became the new home of Pitcairn Aviation. A new company, Pitcairn Aircraft, Inc., occupied the Pitcairn Flying Field facility in Bryn Athyn, where it would design, manufacture, and sell aircraft and engines to the commercial market. A third company, Pitcairn Aeronautics, Inc., also managed by Harold, was to design and develop rotary-wing aircraft.

The National Air Races were to be held September 4–13, 1926, at Model Farms Field in Philadelphia, coincident with the 150th anniversary of the signing of the Declaration of Independence. Pitcairn entered the same airplane in two events: the efficiency race and the 100-mile speed race. After winning the efficiency race with a small engine, mechanics swapped in a more powerful engine, and the plane won the speed race. With these victories, the name Pitcairn became well known in the world of aviation.[20]

Air Mail Service

In early 1918, President Woodrow Wilson signed the order establishing air mail service in the United States. The first air mail flight took place on May 15, 1918. As the service grew, railroad interests complained that the government-sponsored flights were hurting their business. As a result, the Kelly Act of 1925 encouraged commercial aviation providers to take over air mail service.

In December 1926, Harold applied for and, on January 28, 1927, was awarded an overnight airmail route linking New York, Philadelphia, Baltimore, Washington, and Atlanta. That contract led to the establishment of airports in several southern cities:

- Richmond, Virginia (Richard E. Byrd Field, now Richmond International Airport);
- Greensboro–Winston-Salem–High Point, North Carolina (Lindley Field, now Piedmont Triad International Airport);
- Spartanburg, South Carolina (now Spartanburg Downtown Memorial Airport); and
- Atlanta, Georgia (Candler Field, now Hartsfield-Jackson Atlanta International Airport).[21]

On May 1, 1928, Pitcairn Aviation inaugurated its regularly scheduled air mail service.[22]

By the end of 1927, Pitcairn Aircraft had designed two different planes for airmail service on 12 U.S. and two Canadian routes. In all, he sold 40 aircraft, flew 20,000 sightseeing passengers, instructed 200 flight students, and operated 23 airplanes flown by 35 pilots.

Pitcairn autogiro NC-12681 at St. Hubert, Quebec, August 19, 1932 (courtesy of A.E. [Ted] Hill via Wikimedia Commons).

On December 18, 1928, Harold made the first U.S. flight of an autogiro, a rotary-wing aircraft that employs a propeller for forward motion and a freely rotating rotor for lift, the precursor of today's helicopter.

Harold sold his airline route and planes to a syndicate of Curtiss Wright and General Motors executives on July 10, 1929. In 1934, that company became Eastern Airlines, one of the "Big Four" legacy airlines (American, TWA, United, and Eastern) that dominated passenger airline service in the U.S. for nearly 50 years.[23]

Eastern faced a series of financial difficulties starting in 1987. Competition from low-cost carriers such as JetBlue and serious labor disputes beginning in 1989 led to a filing for bankruptcy protection in March 1989. Finally, Eastern stopped flying on January 19, 1991.[24]

Harold Pitcairn and his associates received the 1930 Collier Trophy, presented by President Herbert Hoover at the White House, for developing and applying the autogiro. The trophy is awarded annually "for the greatest achievement in aeronautics or astronautics in America, with respect to improving the performance, efficiency, and safety of air or space vehicles, the value of which has been thoroughly demonstrated by actual use during the preceding year."[25]

Most of Pitcairn Field No. 2 in Horsham was transferred to the U.S. Navy during World War II and is now the Willow Grove Naval Air Station.

Pitcairn pursued the development of rotary-wing aircraft until 1948 and held 30 patents in the technology.[26]

Left: Harold Pitcairn at the White House with the 1930 Collier Trophy and his autogiro in the background; right: historical marker commemorating Harold Pitcairn (photograph by the author).

Tragic End

Harold Pitcairn died of a gunshot wound on April 23, 1960, just after leading 450 guests in celebrating his brother Raymond's 75th birthday. Several books and at least one professional presentation have examined Harold's death, but there is no definitive answer about whether it was suicide or an accident.[27]

After Harold's wife, Clara Davis Pitcairn, died on May 24, 1964, their Cairncrest estate was donated to the church and is now used as the international headquarters of the Church of the New Jerusalem.[28]

Based on a patent infringement suit filed in 1951, the Supreme Court in 1978 affirmed Pitcairn's autogiro patents and awarded his estate $32 million in damages.[29]

Keep It in the Family

John Pitcairn accumulated great wealth through his railroad, oil, and glass activities. During his lifetime, he provided the vast majority of the financial support for the Swedenborgian Church of the New Jerusalem. As his life approached the end, he wanted to ensure that his children and future descendants would not only prosper but be able to maintain the church's facilities and work.

While concerns for the financial well-being of descendants are understandable, it is difficult to achieve. The problem is multifaceted, having both mathematical and behavioral components.

Simple Math

John Pitcairn's problem, and that of any wealthy person trying to pass on their riches, is that the number of descendants can grow much faster than the wealth. Both grow exponentially, but slight differences in the exponents lead to significant mismatches between the number of descendants and the money available. The net result is that large estates are usually subdivided until they become irrelevant.

John Pitcairn died in 1916. Seven years later, in 1923, his three sons, Raymond, Theodore, and Harold, formed the Pitcairn Company to manage their $16 million inheritance.

In 1990, there were 334 living descendants, and the fortune had grown to $1.3 billion. However, many family members had withdrawn their entire share of the assets and no longer participated. As of 1990, just 115 adult family members were still company members, so their per capita assets were $11.3 million.[30]

As of 2015, the Pitcairn family fortune was $1.7 billion, making them number 149 on the Forbes list of America's richest families.[31] In 2016, there were 672 family members, so the asset value per member had dropped to about $2.5 million. But that result is still outstanding among multigenerational family businesses. For example, at a family reunion of 120 Vanderbilt descendants in 1973, not one was a millionaire.[32]

Human Nature

The behavioral component of leaving a large amount of money to one's descendants is challenging to quantify. There is always the risk that having a fortune will eliminate ambition. The likely result is captured in the proverbial saying, "Shirtsleeves to shirtsleeves in three generations." An even more descriptive version, and one possibly more relevant to the Pitcairns, is the Scottish saying : "The father buys, the son builds, the grandchild sells, and his son begs."[33]

Based on the accomplishments of his sons, John Pitcairn proved that it is possible to leave a fortune to family members without stifling their initiative and productivity.

At least one of the later descendants, Elizabeth Pitcairn, John's great-granddaughter and Theodore's granddaughter, has been incredibly successful. Born December 5, 1973, Elizabeth is a classical violinist who performs worldwide on her red Stradivarius. The violin was built in 1721 by Antonio Stradivari and was nicknamed the Red Mendelssohn. It was purchased for her in 1990 (for a reported $1.7 million) at auction at Christie's London. The convoluted history of the violin inspired the movie *The Red Violin*, which won the Academy Award for Best Musical Score in 1999.[34]

Appendix II discusses a November 2021 visit to Bryn Athyn, where my wife and I met Elizabeth and several other Pitcairn descendants.

Epilogue and Retrospection

"Study the past if you would define the future."
—Confucius

What has happened to the two enormous companies in which Robert and John Pitcairn invested so much of their time and energy? It has been over a century since the men died, so it is no surprise that their companies have seen monumental changes.

First, let us review the fortunes and misfortunes of the Pennsylvania Railroad and Pittsburgh Plate Glass. After examining the evolution of the companies, we will take one last look at the lives of Robert and John. What can we learn from them and how should they be remembered?

Pennsylvania Railroad

The Pennsylvania Railroad, once the largest corporation in the world, the crucible for both Scottish lads and Robert's lifetime employer, prospered for a century. However, it declined in importance after World War II, as oil pipelines, freight transport by trucks on the interstate highway system, and passenger air travel expanded. By 1968, close to bankruptcy, the PRR merged with its old rival, the equally challenged New York Central, to become the Penn Central Railroad. The Penn Central continued to struggle, and in 1970 it filed for the largest bankruptcy in U.S. history to date. Amtrak was created on May 1, 1971, and nationalized passenger train operations. Consolidated Rail Corporation (Conrail), owned by the U.S. government, took over railroad properties and operation of the Penn Central and six other railroads on April 1, 1976.

Today, the Norfolk Southern RR and CSX Transportation operate as freight carriers over much of what was the PRR.[1] One landmark from the glory days of J. Edgar Thomson (PRR chief engineer and later president) is the Horseshoe Curve. It remains the indispensable east-west link for freight and passenger rail traffic.[2]

Pittsburgh Plate Glass

John Pitcairn's Pittsburgh Plate Glass Company has been a far more consistent performer than the Pennsylvania Railroad.

The Fortune 500 list of the largest U.S. corporations was first issued in 1955, and PPG ranked 68. Below is a graph of PPG's Fortune 500 rankings from 1955 to 2020.

In 1995, the Fortune 500 added about 90 service companies to its list, thus significantly degrading the rankings of non-service companies. For example, PPG went from 93 in 1994 to 183 in 1995. To artificially remove that offset, I have adjusted the rankings of PPG after 1994 by subtracting 90. This adjustment, although not official, makes the rankings comparable for all years. PPG is one of only 52 companies that have remained on the Fortune 500 list since its inception.[3]

PPG diversified into paint and coatings in 1928 when it bought Ditzler Color Company. To further emphasize its broader product lines, Pittsburgh Plate Glass became PPG Industries on December 19, 1968. By September 2018, PPG Industries divested the last of its glass and fiberglass operations. With over 47,000 employees at 156 facilities in 52 countries, it now focuses on paint, coatings, adhesives, and chemicals.[4] PPG corporate headquarters remain in the glass tower at One PPG Place in downtown Pittsburgh.

Glass to Beer

Pittsburgh Plate Glass built its first plant in Creighton, Pennsylvania, in 1883. However, as the glass business evolved, the facility became obsolete, and PPG sold its interest in the Creighton facility to a private investment firm in 2016. In 2017, Mexico's Vitro S.A.B. de C.V. acquired the plant but announced its closing in November of that year.[5]

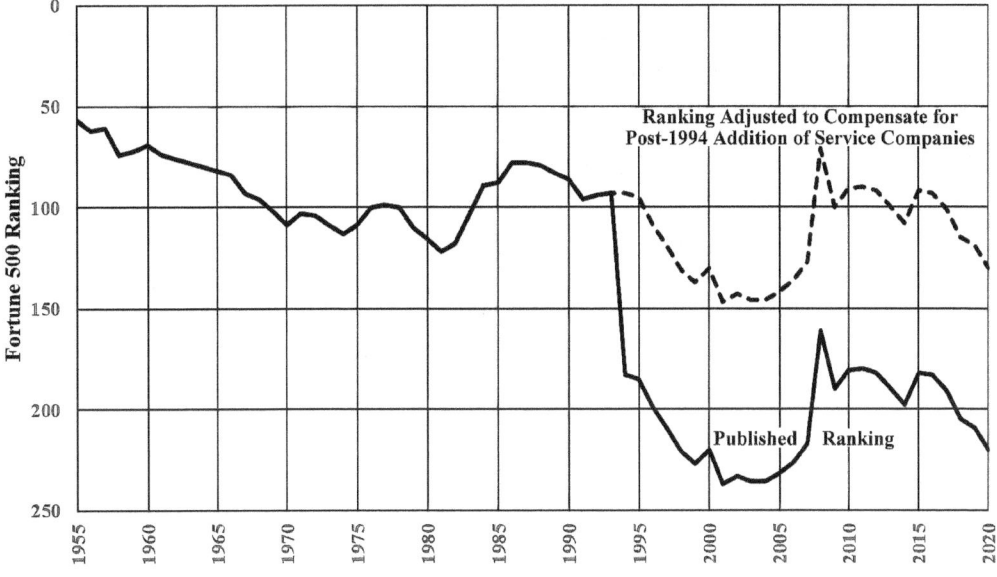

PPG ranking in the *Fortune* 500.

However, the site is gaining new life thanks to Cliff Forrest. Forrest, who bought the Pittsburgh Brewing Company in 2018, has implemented grand plans to reinvigorate the Iron City Beer franchise. He purchased the PPG Creighton facility and installed a state-of-the-art brewery and other facilities on the 42-acre site. As of late 2022, 400 cans of beer per minute were rolling off the automated production line.[6]

Two Men from Scotland

How can we encapsulate the lives of these two lads from Scotland who grew into men in America with wealth beyond their imaginations?

Both started their lives in the United States as impoverished immigrant youth living in Allegheny City, across the Allegheny River from Pittsburgh. Their early religious training was based on Swedenborgian doctrines. Both Pitcairns dedicated significant amounts of time and money to their respective faiths, Robert to the Presbyterian Church and John to the Swedenborgian New Church.

Following Andrew Carnegie's lead, Robert and John worked for the Pennsylvania Railroad. From that beginning, their paths diverged somewhat, but they persevered and accumulated enormous wealth.

Robert Pitcairn

Robert Pitcairn was focused and dedicated, and the Pennsylvania Railroad was his focal point for 53 years. His final position was resident assistant to the president of the Pennsylvania Railroad Company. "Uncle Robert" retired in 1906 only because of a company retirement policy he had advocated.

Despite his involvement in the violent and deadly railroad strike in 1877 and the disastrous Johnstown Flood of 1889, Robert remained well respected by employees and the general public. After replacing Andrew Carnegie as superintendent of the Western (Pittsburgh) Division of the PRR in 1865, he never seriously considered any promotion requiring him to move from his beloved Pittsburgh.

Robert started his family early. He was 20 when he married 15-year-old Elizabeth Rigg in 1856. He and Elizabeth had four children, and they remained married until he died in 1909 at age 73.

In addition to the PRR and his family, Robert's passion was his Shadyside Presbyterian Church. He served there in various leadership positions from the church's founding in 1866 until his death. The congregation fondly remembered his contributions and honored him and his wife with an impressive stained-glass window.

John Pitcairn

While Robert Pitcairn concentrated on his railroad career, family, and church, his younger brother John had multiple interests. Like Robert and the Carnegies, John started with the PRR but stayed in that industry only until he was 30. Then he moved on to the burgeoning and wealth-generating oil business, engaging in drilling, refining, and pipelines.

In 1883, by serendipity, 42-year-old John Pitcairn met 71-year-old John Baptiste Ford. Together, they founded and grew the Pittsburgh Plate Glass Company into the dominant U.S. manufacturer of glass and glass products.

John Pitcairn was an efficient and respected manager, but his passion was his Swedenborgian New Church. So once he had made his fortune and traveled the world, he focused on building that organization.

John married, later in life, a much younger woman. He was two days shy of his forty-third birthday when he and Gertrude Starkey, then 28, were wed in 1884. The couple had five children, one of whom died in infancy.

John and Gertrude worked as a team to grow the New Church, and her death in 1898 at age 42 left him heartbroken. After that, John never remarried and spent all his energy on traveling and his church.

While the New Church has never achieved a large number of adherents, the homes, the magnificent cathedral, and the college at Bryn Athyn remain as testimony to John Pitcairn's incredible achievements.

Nature or Nurture?

With their almost identical origins and early experiences, it is instructive to compare significant aspects in the lives of the two lads as they became two men.

- Both Pitcairn brothers were firmly devoted to God and church.
- Robert married young, while John waited until middle age to wed.
- Both had just one wife and four or more children.
- Robert was risk-averse; John was a risk-taker.
- Robert stayed close to home; John traveled extensively and often.
- Both became incredibly wealthy and lived in mansions.
- Robert retained his money within the family for two generations and then dispersed much of it; John, through his sons, kept most of his wealth within the family.
- Both Pitcairn brothers are almost universally revered.

So, what accounts for the life outcomes of the Pitcairn brothers, heredity or environment? Of course, both played a part, along with fortuitous timing and good luck. Their shared history, growing up poor as young immigrants in a rapidly expanding country, instilled a desire and provided an opportunity for something better—escape from the city's pollution, better housing, and more money. With perseverance, both were extraordinarily successful in achieving those goals.

In each of my books, I say, "I hate biographies. They always end badly." But I continue to be drawn to the lives of fascinating people, those who persevere through difficult times and those who leave a lasting legacy. Following these two lads has shown me how, despite similar initial conditions, small decisions can lead to highly divergent outcomes. How can we apply that insight to our own lives?

Appendix I:
Pitcairn Family Trees

The following four charts present the family trees of Robert, John, and Hugh Pitcairn, as well as the grandchildren of John Pitcairn. Information was compiled from multiple genealogy sources, including Ancestry.com, FamilySearch.com, Wikitree.com, MyHeritage.com, and FindaGrave.com.

Appendix I: Pitcairn Family Trees

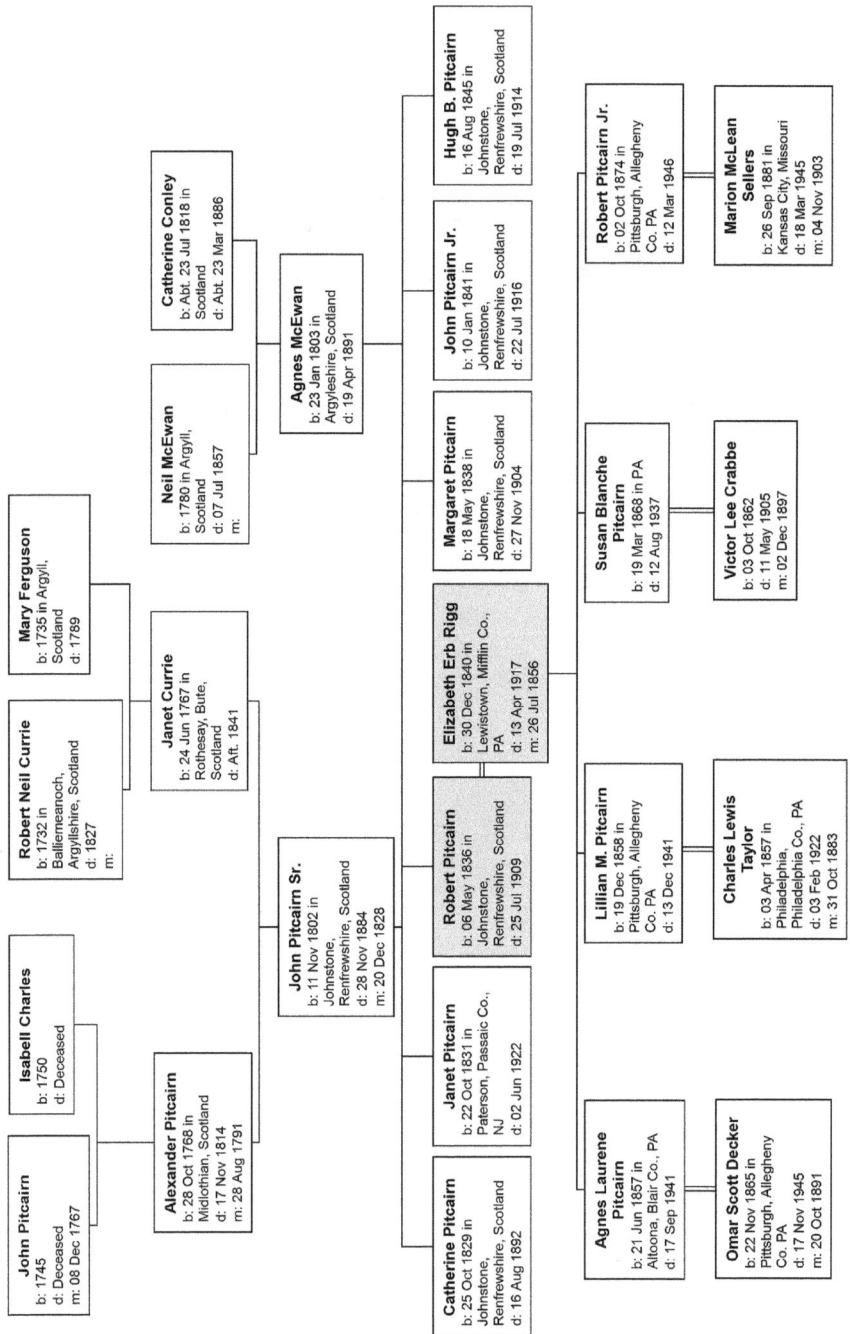

Hourglass chart for Robert Pitcairn (compiled by the author).

Appendix I: Pitcairn Family Trees

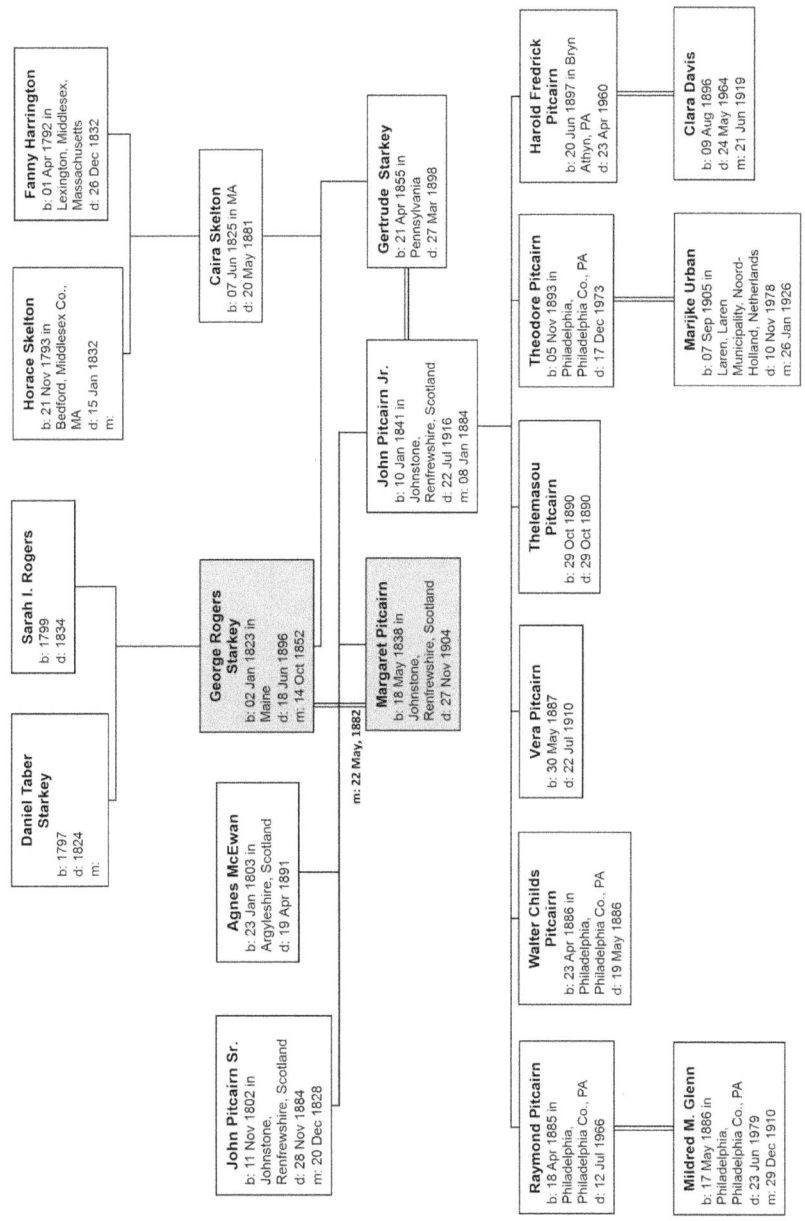

Hourglass chart for John Pitcairn Jr. and Gertrude E. Starkey (compiled by the author).

Appendix I: Pitcairn Family Trees

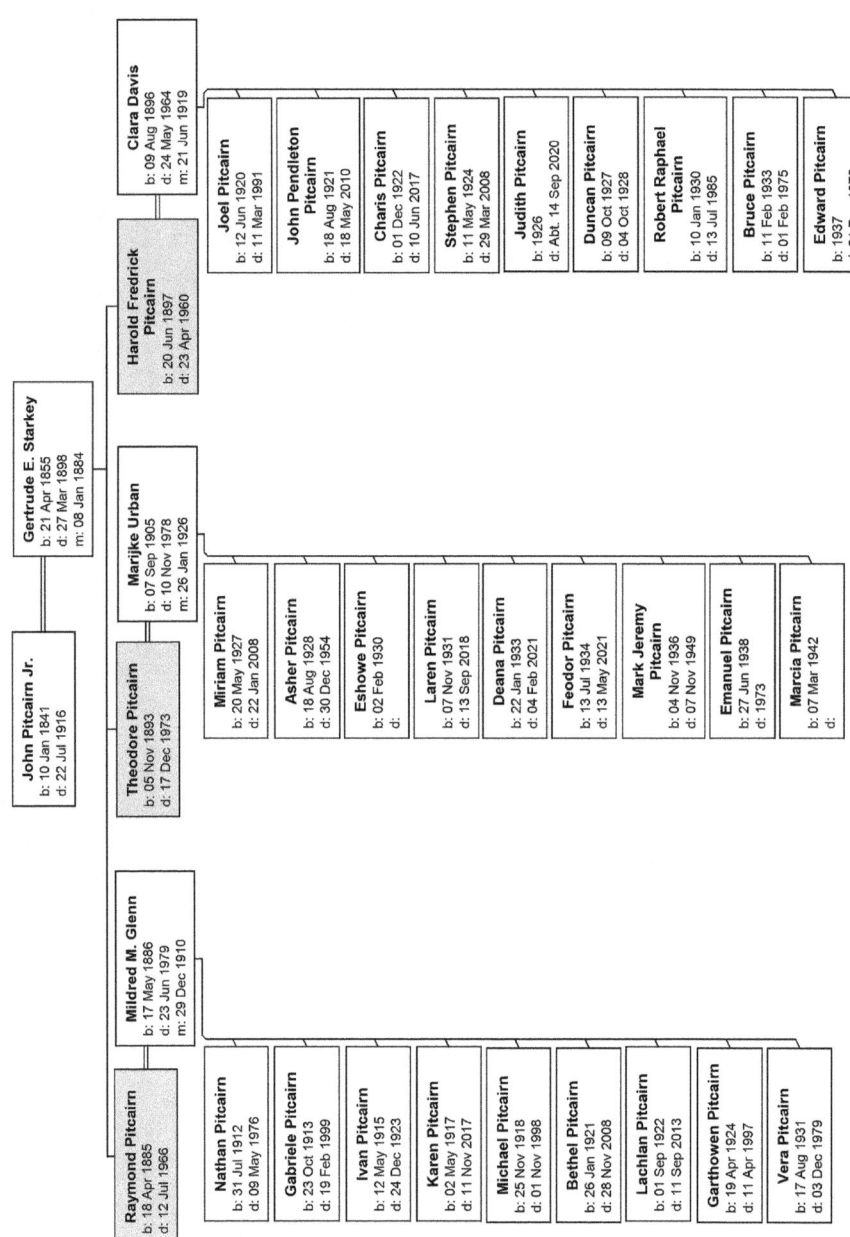

Descendant chart for John Pitcairn Jr. and Gertrude Starkey Pitcairn (compiled by the author).

Appendix I: Pitcairn Family Trees

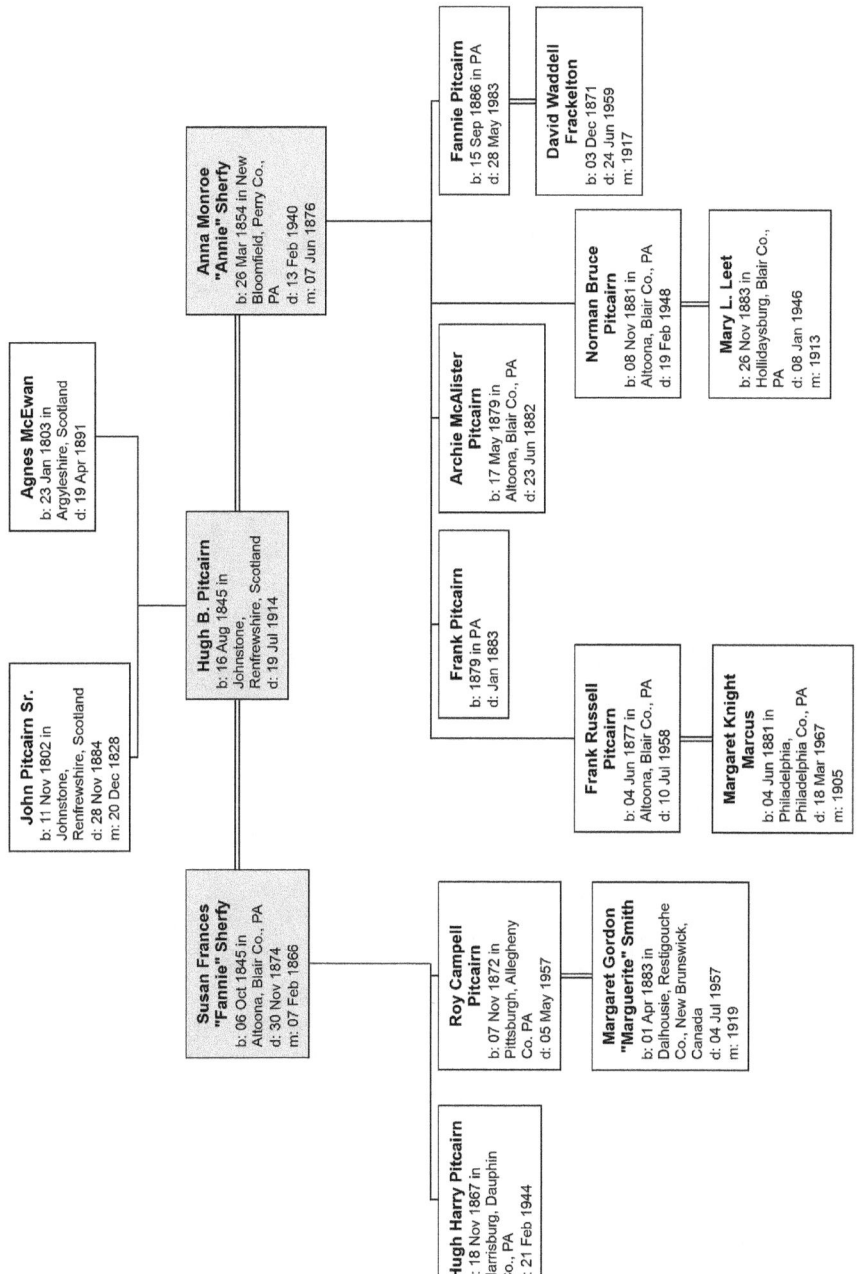

Hourglass chart for Hugh B. Pitcairn (compiled by the author).

Appendix II:
Visiting Bryn Athyn

In early November 2021, my wife and I visited Bryn Athyn. We stayed in the Fetters Mill Bed & Breakfast run by a delightful couple, a grandson of Harold and his wife. They were able to fill us in on Pitcairn family history.

Bryn Athyn with Cairnwood at top right, Glencairn at top left, and the Bryn Athyn Cathedral at lower center (aerial photograph of the Bryn Athyn Historic Landmark District courtesy of Bryn Athyn Cathedral).

Bryn Athyn is a hidden gem. I lived in Pennsylvania for the first 41 years of my life, including 20 years in eastern Pennsylvania, and had never heard of it. Although just 14 miles northeast of center-city Philadelphia, Bryn Athyn is uncrowded, with tree-covered rolling hills and large homes.

We focused our visit on the three significant buildings: Cairnwood, the home of John Pitcairn and his family; Glencairn, the home of the Raymond Pitcairn family; and the Bryn Athyn Cathedral. In 2008, the National Park Service designated all three sites as National Historic Landmarks. Our tours of each location were enhanced by friendly and knowledgeable guides who were passionate about what they were showing us.

Cairnwood is a historic house-museum available for wedding receptions and other private affairs. In addition to the main house, our guide, Lisa Parker-Adams, showed us the Garden House and Carriage House. The Carriage House is where Harold Pitcairn built his early gliders; it now contains several horse-drawn carriages that belonged to John and Gertrude Pitcairn, along with Raymond Pitcairn's vintage Packard automobile.

Glencairn, with 90+ rooms, was built as a home for Raymond's family and a

From left: Elizabeth Pitcairn with "Felix," Gjilberta Lucaj, and Louise Thomas in the Great Hall at Glencairn (photograph by the author).

museum for the massive array of ancient artifacts collected by John, Raymond, and Theodore on their many overseas journeys. The building features enormous and intricate stained-glass windows that would be equally at home in a medieval church. The central tower provides views of the countryside and the distant Philadelphia skyline.

The stone, glass, and metalwork of the cathedral, both inside and outside, testify to the skill of the artisans who resided on-site during the multiyear construction. The massive yet delicate central tower is reminiscent of Gloucester Cathedral in England, built in 679.

In addition to the featured buildings, one of our guides took us to the Bryn Athyn Cemetery as well as Cairncrest, the former home of the Harold Pitcairn family. Cairncrest is now the administrative center for the Church of the New Jerusalem and is not open to the public.

We also visited the Lord's New Church, founded by Theodore Pitcairn, just 1.3 air miles from the Bryn Athyn Cathedral.

The highlight of our trip to Bryn Athyn came at the end when world-renowned violinist Elizabeth Pitcairn (Theodore's granddaughter) presented a recital in the Great Hall of Glencairn. Two other incredible artists, Irish-born pianist Dr. Louise Thomas and Albanian-born cellist Gjilberta Lucaj, played with Elizabeth. Elizabeth and Louise performed selections from Beethoven, Elgar, Saint-Saëns, and Gershwin. Then, after an intermission, they were joined by Gjilberta to perform Felix Mendelssohn's Piano Trio in D minor, Op. 49. This last selection was especially appropriate, as Elizabeth's Stradivarius is called the Red Mendelssohn. She nicknamed it "Felix," after the composer.

Chapter Notes

Introduction

1. Churella, Albert J. 2012. *The Pennsylvania Railroad, Volume 1—Building an Empire, 1846–1917*. Philadelphia: University of Pennsylvania Press, 501.

Chapter 1

1. n.d. *People of Medieval Scotland 1093–1371*. https://www.poms.ac.uk/record/source/902/.
2. Pitcairn, Sheila. 2004. *The Pitcairn Family*. February 19. http://www.pitcairnfamily.com/index.htm.
3. n.d. "Perthshire Pitcairns: Family Branch 7_Perthshire_Sheet 2." Royal Dunfermline. http://www.royaldunfermline.com/Resources/Genealogy/FB7/FAMILY_BRANCH7_PERTHSHIRE_SHEET-2.pdf.
4. n.d. "Helen Pitcairn Rush." Find a Grave. https://www.findagrave.com/memorial/36990363/helen-rush.
5. n.d. "John Pitcairn (1803–c1884)." Familypedia. https://familypedia.fandom.com/wiki/John_Pitcairn_(1803-c1884).
6. Bentley, Elizabeth Petty. 2000. "Passenger arrivals at the Port of New York, 1830–1832: From customs passenger lists." https://archive.org/details/passengerarrival0000bent/page/788/mode/2up.
7. Odhner, C. Th. 1917. "John Pitcairn, A Biography." *New Church Life*, January: 3–6. https://newchristianbiblestudy.org/bundles/ncbsw/ondeck/english/new-church-life/1917_HTML.htm.
8. Gibson, Samantha. n.d. "Panic of 1837." *Digital Public Library of America*. https://dp.la/primary-source-sets/the-panic-of-1837#tabs.
9. 1846. "John Pitcairn." My Heritage. October 1. https://www.myheritage.com/research/record-10373-763929/john-pitcairn-in-atlantic-gulf-ports-passenger-list-card-index; Green, Harry. 2010. "Ship Venice." Immigrant Ship Transcribers Guild. February 10. https://www.immigrantships.net/v12/1800v12/venice18461001.html.
10. Klein, Theodore B. 1901. *The Canals of Pennsylvania and the System of Internal Improvements*. William Stanley Ray.
11. Drago, Harry Sinclair. 1972. *Canal Days in America*. New York: Bramhall House; Ilisevich, Robert D., and Carl K. Burkett, Jr. 1985. "The Canal Through Pittsburgh: Its Development and Physical Character." *Western Pennsylvania Historical Magazine*, October: 353.
12. Rhoads, Willard B. 1960. "The Pennsylvania Canal." *Western Pennsylvania Historical Magazine*, September: 203–238.
13. Swank, James M. 1845. "Annual Report of the Board of Canal Commissioners of Pennsylvania with accompanying documents." 253–254.
14. Rhoads 1960; Shank, William H. 1965. *The Amazing Pennsylvania Canals*. York, PA: Historical Society of York County; n.d. "Main Line of Public Works." Wikipedia. https://en.wikipedia.org/wiki/Main_Line_of_Public_Works#Eastern_Division_Canal.
15. n.d. "Great Pennsylvania Canal." Living Places. https://www.livingplaces.com/PA/Pennsylvania_Canal.html.
16. Stephenson, Clarence D. 1961. *Pennsylvania Canal—Indiana & Westmoreland Counties*. Marion Center, PA: Stephenson.
17. n.d. "Crossing the Alleghenies." Stories from PA History. https://explorepahistory.com/story.php?storyId=1-9-A; Holzwarth, Larry. 2020. "See 1842 America Through Charles Dickens' Eyes." *History Collection*, January 14. https://historycollection.com/see-1842-america-through-charles-dickens-eyes/20/.
18. Jones, Diana Nelson. 2007. "The Day the City of Allegheny Disappeared." *Pittsburgh Post-Gazette*, December 9. https://www.post-gazette.com/local/city/2007/12/09/The-day-the-City-of-Allegheny-disappeared/stories/200712090229.

Chapter 2

1. Jones 2007; Brown, David M. 2007. "Society marks 1907 annexation of Allegheny City." *Trib Live*, July 28. https://archive.triblive.com/news/society-marks-1907-annexation-of-allegheny-city/.
2. n.d. *History of the Pittsburgh Public Water Supply (1801 to Present)*. https://slideplayer.com/

slide/1519050/; Nasaw, David. 2006. *Andrew Carnegie*. New York: Penguin, 31.

3. Wall, Joseph Frazier. 1970. *Andrew Carnegie*. Pittsburgh: University of Pittsburgh Press; Nasaw 2006.

4. Nasaw 2006, 14.

5. n.d. "Shorter Catechism." Orthodox Presbyterian Church. https://www.opc.org/sc.html.

6. Nasaw 2006, 17.

7. Nasaw 2006, 25.

8. National Archives and Records Service. 1957. "Passenger lists of vessels arriving at New York, 1820–1897." https://archive.org/details/passengerlistsoo0074unix/page/n820/mode/1up.

9. Nasaw 2006, 26.

10. National Archives and Records Service 1957, 825.

11. n.d. "Robert Logan Anderson." Find a Grave. https://www.findagrave.com/memorial/101414676/robert-logan-anderson.

12. Nasaw 2006, 27.

13. Young, Patrick. 2011. "1848: The Year that Created Immigrant America." Long Island Wins, March 18. https://longislandwins.com/news/national/1848-the-year-that-created-immigrant-america/.

14. n.d. "Immigrant Population." USA Facts. https://usafacts.org/data/topics/people-society/immigration/immigration-and-immigration-enforcement/immigrants/.

15. Nasaw 2006, 27–29.

16. *Baltimore Sun*. 1906. "Potter for Sixty Years." November 10: 7.

17. n.d. "William P Morris (Morrison)." Geni.com. https://www.geni.com/people/William-Morris/6000000023133489968?through=6000000030551501053.

Chapter 3

1. History.com Editors. 2022. "Morse Code & the Telegraph." *History*. August 12. https://www.history.com/topics/inventions/telegraph; Branch, E. Douglas. 1938. "The Coming of the Telegraph to Western Pennsylvania." *Pennsylvania History*, January: 21–29.

2. Thompson, Robert Luther. 1947. *Wiring a Continent: The History of the Telegraph Industry in the United States, 1832–1866*. Princeton: Princeton University Press; n.d. "Henry O'Reilly." Wikipedia. https://en.wikipedia.org/wiki/Henry_O%27Reilly; Branch.

3. Cox, Lucille T. 1939. "Former Potter Here 'Started' Young Carnegie." *East Liverpool (OH) Evening Review*, April 13, 10.

4. Carnegie, Andrew. 1920. *Autobiography of Andrew Carnegie*. London: Constable & Co.

5. Carnegie, 39–42.

6. Carnegie, 48–49.

7. Carnegie, 57–58.

Chapter 4

1. Henderson, Bruce. 1987. *Window to Eternity*. West Chester, PA: Swedenborg Foundation. 15.

2. *Time*. 1954. "Religion: The Great Swede." June 28. http://content.time.com/time/subscriber/article/0,33009,860897,00.html; Simonton, Dean Keith. 2017. "The Science of Genius." *Scientific American*, March. https://www.scientificamerican.com/article/the-science-of-genius2/; Najera, Jesus. 2020. "Young Polymaths." Medium. https://medium.com/young-polymaths/in-their-20s-leonardo-da-vinci-5655c3d8ef82.

3. Henderson 1987, 17–19.

4. 2021. "Swedenborg's Life." Swedenborg Foundation. https://swedenborg.com/emanuel-swedenborg/about-life/.

5. Manlove, Colin. 1992. *Swedenborg: Heaven and Hell*. London: Palgrave Macmillan.

6. Cunningham, John M. n.d. "Emanuel Swedenborg, Swedish Philosopher." *Britannica*. https://www.britannica.com/biography/Emanuel-Swedenborg/His-theology.

7. Henderson 1987, 23; Sigstedt, Cyriel. 1952. *The Swedenborg Epic: The life and works of Emanuel Swedenborg*. Bookman Associates. http://swedenborgdigitallibrary.org/ES/epic43.htm. 269.

8. Henderson 1987, 23–24.

9. Sigstedt 1952.

10. Henderson 1987, 25; Sigstedt 1952, 381.

11. Holzinger, Kay. 2002. *Encyclopedia of Cults, Sects, and New Religions*. Edited by James R. Lewis. Amherst: Prometheus Books.

12. Cunningham.

13. n.d. *Who Was Swedenborg?* Performed by Jonathan Rose. https://www.youtube.com/watch?time_continue=480&v=HEa0e8AcS78&feature=emb_title.

14. *Who Was Swedenborg?*

15. Swedenborg, Emanuel. 1952. *A Brief Exposition of the Doctrine of the New Church*. London: Swedenborg Society. 88.

16. Adams, Hannah. 1817. *A Dictionary of All Religions and Religious Denominations, Jewish, Heathen, Mahometan and Christian, Ancient and Modern*. 4th ed. New York: James Eastburn and Company. 203.

17. Ankerberg, John. 1999. "Swedenborg Foundation." *John Ankerberg Show*. August 14. https://jashow.org/articles/swedenborg-foundation/.

18. 2020. "New Church (Swedenborgianism) vs Evangelical Christianity." YouTube. August 23. https://www.youtube.com/watch?v=KxCyq3Sw72I.

19. Alston, David. n.d. "James Glen." Slaves & Highlanders. https://www.spanglefish.com/slavesandhighlanders/index.asp?pageid=497813.

20. Alston.

21. Wiley, Samuel T., ed. 1891. *Biographical and historical cyclopedia of Indiana and Armstrong counties, Pennsylvania*. Philadelphia: J.M. Gresham & Co. 296–298.

22. Bayley, Rev. Dr. Jonathan. n.d. "Mr. Glen,

And the Introduction of the New Church into America." New Church Worthies. http://www.newchurchhistory.org/articles/jb1884/15_Mr_Glen.php.
  23. Emerson, Ralph Waldo. 1896. *Swedenborg; or, The Mystic.* https://emersoncentral.com/texts/representative-men/swedenborg-the-mystic/.
  24. Keller, Helen. 1927. *My Religion.* New York: Swedenborg Foundation. 17, 29.
  25. n.d. "Was Johnny Appleseed a Real Person?" *Britanica.* https://www.britannica.com/story/was-johnny-appleseed-a-real-person.
  26. Odhner 1917, 7.
  27. Bayley, Rev. Dr. Jonathan. n.d. "Johnny Appleseed, Who Made a great part of his Religion to Spread the New Church and Plant Apple-trees in the Western States of America." New Church Worthies. http://www.newchurchhistory.org/articles/jb1884/16_Johnny_Appleseed.php.
  28. Odhner 1917, 3–6.
  29. Odhner 1917, 12.
  30. Gladish, Richard R. 1989. *John Pitcairn: Uncommon Entrepreneur.* Bryn Athyn, PA: Academy of the New Church. 5.
  31. n.d. "William Henry Benade, Sr." Geni.com. https://www.geni.com/people/William-Benade-Sr/6000000020572608292?through=6000000020573068673.
  32. Gladish, Richard R. 1984. *Bishop William Henry Benade—Founder and Reformer.* Bryn Athyn, PA: Academy of the New Church.
  33. Gladish 1984.

Chapter 5

  1. Baer, Christopher T. n.d. "A General Chronology of the Pennsylvania Railroad Company, Its Predecessors and Successors and Its Historical Context." Pennsylvania Railroad Technical & Historical Society. http://www.prrths.com/newprr_files/Hagley/PRR_hagley_intro.htm.
  2. Carnegie 1920, 63–64.
  3. n.d. "Thomas Alexander Scott." Find a Grave. https://www.findagrave.com/memorial/11428591/thomas-alexander-scott.
  4. Editors of Encyclopaedia Britannica. 2021. "J. Edgar Thomson—American engineer and businessman." *Britannica.* May 23. https://www.britannica.com/biography/J-Edgar-Thomson.
  5. Baer n.d.
  6. Wilson, William Bender. 1899. *History of Pennsylvania Railroad Company.* Vol. 1. Philadelphia: Henry T. Coates & Company.
  7. "Pennsylvania Railroad." n.d. Wikipedia. https://en.wikipedia.org/wiki/Pennsylvania_Railroad; "John Edgar Thomson." n.d. Wikipedia. https://en.wikipedia.org/wiki/John_Edgar_Thomson; "Horseshoe Curve (Pennsylvania)." n.d. Wikipedia. https://en.wikipedia.org/wiki/Horseshoe_Curve_(Pennsylvania).
  8. "Gallitzin Tunnel." n.d. Wikipedia. https://en.wikipedia.org/wiki/Gallitzin_Tunnel; Alexander, Edwin P. 1971. *On the Main Line: The Pennsylvania Railroad in the 19th Century.* New York: Bramhall House.
  9. Wikipedia, "Gallitzin Tunnel."
  10. 1874. *Biographical Encyclopaedia of Pennsylvania of the Nineteenth Century.* Philadelphia: Galaxy Publishing Company.
  11. Wilson, William Bender. 1900. *General Superintendents of the Pennsylvania Railroad Division, Pennsylvania Railroad Co.* Philadelphia: Kensington Press.
  12. Gladish 1989, 11.
  13. Odhner 1917, 82; Gladish 1989, 7–12.
  14. Odhner 1917, 83.
  15. n.d. "Elizabeth Erb (Rigg) Pitcairn (1841)." WikiTree. https://www.wikitree.com/wiki/Rigg-138.
  16. Pitcairn, Robert. 1858. "Letter to John Pitcairn, Jr." Fort Wayne, Indiana, October.
  17. Wilson, William Bender. 1913. *Robert Pitcairn 1836-1909: In Memoriam.* Holmsburg, PA. https://digital.library.pitt.edu/islandora/object/pitt%3A00c679529m/viewer#page/6/mode/2up. 13–16.
  18. Gladish 1989, 12; "John Pitcairn, Jr." n.d. Wikipedia. https://en.wikipedia.org/wiki/John_Pitcairn_Jr.
  19. Schotter, H.W. 1927. *The Growth and Development of the Pennsylvania Railroad Company: A Review of the Charter and Annual Reports of the Pennsylvania Railroad Company 1846 to 1926, Inclusive.* Philadelphia: Allen, Lane & Scott; "Allegheny Portage Railroad." n.d. Wikipedia. https://en.wikipedia.org/wiki/Allegheny_Portage_Railroad.
  20. Schotter 1927.
  21. n.d. "Pennsylvania Canals—1846." Pennsylvania Historical & Museum Commission. http://www.phmc.state.pa.us/portal/communities/documents/1776-1865/pennsylvania-canals.html.
  22. "Gallitzin Tunnel," Wikipedia.
  23. Schotter 1927, 10; "John Edgar Thomson," Wikipedia.

Chapter 6

  1. n.d. "Abraham Lincoln." Wikipedia. https://en.wikipedia.org/wiki/Abraham_Lincoln#1860_presidential_election.
  2. Stashower, Daniel. 2013. "The Unsuccessful Plot to Kill Abraham Lincoln." *Smithsonian Magazine.* February. https://www.smithsonianmag.com/history/the-unsuccessful-plot-to-kill-abraham-lincoln-2013956/.
  3. Stashower 2013.
  4. Odhner 1917, 86–87; Gladish 1989.
  5. Gladish 1989, 20; Stashower 2013; Ewbank, Douglas. 2009. "Enoch Lewis's Tale of Intrigue." Powelton History Blog: A Collective Biography of a Philadelphia Neighborhood. August 15. https://poweltonhistoryblog.blogspot.com/2009/08/enoch-lewis-tale-of-intrigue.html.
  6. History.com Editors. 2019. "Secession." History.com. June 7. https://www.history.com/

topics/american-civil-war/secession; "American Civil War." n.d. Wikipedia. https://en.wikipedia.org/wiki/American_Civil_War#Secession_crisis; Baer n.d.; n.d. "Smithsonian American Art Museum." *How the Railroad Won the War.* https://americanexperience.si.edu/wp-content/uploads/2015/02/How-the-Railroad-Won-the-War.pdf; Burns, Adam. 2023. "Railroads In The Civil War: Maps, Facts and Statistics (North vs South)." American-Rails.com. June 7. https://www.american-rails.com/civil.html.
    7. Finseth, Ian Frederick. 2006. *The American Civil War—An Anthology of Essential Writings.* New York: Routledge–Taylor & Francis Group. 176.
    8. Baer n.d.; Nasaw 2006.
    9. Pitz, Marylynne. 2012. "Allegheny Arsenal Explosion: Pittsburgh's worst day during the Civil War." *Pittsburgh Post-Gazette*, September 16. https://www.post-gazette.com/life/lifestyle/2012/09/16/Allegheny-Arsenal-Explosion-Pittsburgh-s-worst-day-during-the-Civil-War/stories/201209160145.
    10. Carnegie 1920.
    11. Carnegia 1920, 99.
    12. Bates, David Homer. 1907. *Lincoln in the Telegraph Office.* London: Century Company. 22, 25.
    13. Carnegie 1920; Nasaw 2006, 71–74.; Baer n.d.
    14. Baer n.d., see 1862 and 1863 secs.
    15. Gladish 1989, 22; Odhner 1917, 88. Mechanicsburg Museum Association. "Cumberland Valley Railroad & Mechanicsburg." MechanicsburgMuseum.org. http://www.mechanicsburgmuseum.org/cvrr.html.
    16. Klein, Christopher. 2022. "Abraham Lincoln's Funeral Train: How America Mourned for Three Weeks." History.com. February 8. https://www.history.com/news/abraham-lincoln-funeral-train.

Chapter 7

    1. Odhner 1917, 89.
    2. n.d. "Renovo, Pennsylvania." Wikipedia. https://en.wikipedia.org/wiki/Renovo,_Pennsylvania.
    3. Gladish 1989, 30.
    4. Gladish 1989, 34.
    5. Gladish 1989, 37.
    6. Gladish 1989, 38.
    7. *The New York Times*. 1864. "Pennsylvania Oil Region." December 20: 1. https://timesmachine.nytimes.com/timesmachine/1864/12/20/78995901.pdf.
    8. Gladish 1989, 41.
    9. Gladish 1989, 42.
    10. Gladish 1989, 43.
    11. Dolson, Hildegarde. 1959. *The Great Oildorado—The Gaudy and Turbulent Years of the First Oil Rush: Pennsylvania, 1859–1880.* New York: Random House. 289.
    12. n.d. "Oil refinery." Wikipedia. https://en.wikipedia.org/wiki/Oil_refinery.
    13. Helfman, Harold M. 1950. "Twenty-Nine Hectic Days: Public Opinion and the Oil War of 1872." *Pennsylvania History: A Journal of Mid-Atlantic Studies*, April: 121–138.
    14. Tarbell, Ida Minerva. 1904. *The History of the Standard Oil Company.* Vol. I. New York: McClure, Phillips & Co. 56.
    15. Hawke, David Freeman. 1980. *John D.: The Founding Father of the Rockefellers.* New York: Harper & Row.
    16. Tarbell 1904, 36–37.
    17. Helfman 1950, 126. Citation from Tidioute *Commercial*, February 27, 1872.
    18. Gladish 1989, 71–72.
    19. Gladish 1989, 80.
    20. Gladish 1989, 90–91.

Chapter 8

    1. Belfour, Stanton. 1966. *Centennial History of the Shadyside Presbyterian Church.* Pittsburgh, PA: Davis & Warde, Inc.
    2. Engleman, Timothy C. 2016. *Liturgy: A Reflection on Shadyside Presbyterian Church.* Pittsburgh, PA: Shadyside Presbyterian Church.
    3. 1868. "Minutes of Session." Pittsburgh, PA: Shadyside Presbyterian Church, July 9.
    4. 1869. "Minutes of Session." Pittsburgh, PA: Shadyside Presbyterian Church, January 28.
    5. *Railroad Age Gazette.* 1909. "A Letter of the Late Robert Pitcairn." October 29: 816–817.
    6. Leonard, John, ed. 1907. *Who's Who in Pennsylvania: A Biographical Dictionary of Contemporaries.* Vol. 2. New York: L.R. Hammersly; n.d. "Hugh Pitcairn." Wikipedia. https://en.wikipedia.org/wiki/Hugh_Pitcairn; n.d. "Dr Hugh B. Pitcairn." Find a Grave. https://www.findagrave.com/memorial/14409791/hugh-b-pitcairn.
    7. Bender 1913.
    8. Bender 1913.
    9. Westinghouse, George. 1910. "History of the Air Brake." *The Electric Journal*, Jan. 1911, 227–236; Huber, William R. 2022. *George Westinghouse—Powering the World.* Jefferson, NC: McFarland.
    10. Wilson 1913.

Chapter 9

    1. Gladish 1984, 217–219.
    2. Gladish 1989, 91.
    3. Odhner 1917, 289–301, 415.
    4. Gladish 1989, 122.
    5. Huber, William R. 2020. *Adolph Sutro—King of the Comstock Lode and Mayor of San Francisco.* Jefferson, NC: McFarland.
    6. Carnegie, Andrew. 1884. *Round the World.* New York: Charles Scribner's Sons. 11–12.
    7. Huber 2020.
    8. Huber 2020.
    9. Gladish 1989, 128.
    10. Huber 2020.
    11. Gladish 1989, 136.

12. Gladish 1989.
13. Gladish 1989, 137.
14. Odhner 1917, 517.
15. Odhner 1917, 522.
16. Gladish 1989, 150–151.
17. Dorman, Peter F. n.d. "Akhenaten." *Britannica*. https://www.britannica.com/biography/Akhenaten; Etheredge, Laura. n.d. "Aton." *Britannica*. https://www.britannica.com/topic/Aton; Etheredge, Laura. n.d. "Tell el-Amarna." *Britannica*. https://www.britannica.com/place/Tell-el-Amarna.
18. Gladish 1989, 152–155.
19. Odhner 1917, 530; Gladish 1989, 156.
20. Odhner 1917, 533.
21. Gladish 1989, 156–162.
22. n.d. "Law Against Adultery." SwedenborgStudy.com. https://www.swedenborgstudy.com/books/H.Lj.Odhner_Ten-Commandments/adultery.html.
23. *Glencairn Museum News*. 2015. "The Purchase of the Lanzone Egyptian Collection (1878)." August 31. https://glencairnmuseum.org/newsletter/august-2015-the-purchase-of-the-lanzone-egyptian-collection.html; Gyllenhaal, Ed. 2012. "From Parlor to Castle: The Egyptian Collection at Glencairn Museum." Glencairn Museum. July 19. https://glencairnmuseum.org/articles/2012/7/19/from-parlor-to-castle-the-egyptian-collection-at-glencairn-m.html.
24. n.d. "1879: Tidewater Pipe Company-World's 1st Successful Oil Pipeline." Smethport History. http://www.smethporthistory.org/coryville/oilarticle.html.

Chapter 10

1. n.d. "*Munn v. Illinois* (1877): An Important Granger Case." U-S-History.com. https://www.u-s-history.com/pages/h855.html.
2. 1887. "Interstate Commerce Act Is Passed." United States Senate. February 4. https://www.senate.gov/artandhistory/history/minute/Interstate_Commerce_Act_Is_Passed.htm.
3. Dray, Philip. 2010. *There Is Power In a Union*. New York: Anchor Books.
4. n.d. "Financial Panic of 1873." U.S. Department of the Treasury. https://home.treasury.gov/about/history/freedmans-bank-building/financial-panic-of-1873; n.d. "Panic of 1873." Wikipedia. https://en.wikipedia.org/wiki/Panic_of_1873; n.d. "The Panic of 1873." *American Experience*. https://www.pbs.org/wgbh/americanexperience/features/grant-panic/.
5. Skrabec, Jr., Quentin. 2007. *George Westinghouse: Gentle Genius*. New York: Algora Publishing.
6. Johnston, Robert D. n.d. "Rutherford B. Hayes: Campaigns and Elections." UVA Miller Center. https://millercenter.org/president/hayes/campaigns-and-elections; Kilgore, Ed. 2020. "The Last Time a Contested Presidential Election Nearly Tore the Country Apart." *Intelligencer*. September 7. https://nymag.com/intelligencer/2020/09/the-last-time-a-contested-election-tore-the-country-apart.html; Monroe, James. 1893. "The Hayes-Tilden Electoral Commission: How Congress Settled the Disputed Electoral Count in the Presidential Election of 1876." *The Atlantic*. October. https://www.theatlantic.com/magazine/archive/1893/10/the-hayes-tilden-electoral-commission/523971/.
7. Woodward, Comer Vann. 1951. *Reunion and Reaction: The Compromise of 1877 and the End of Reconstruction*. Vol. 10. Boston: Little, Brown and Company; n.d. "Compromise of 1877." Wikipedia. https://en.wikipedia.org/wiki/Compromise_of_1877; n.d. "Wormley Conference." *Britannica*. https://www.britannica.com/event/Wormley-Conference.
8. Nast, Thomas. 1878. "Cipher Mumm(er)y." *Harper's Weekly*. November 2. https://www.harpweek.com/09Cartoon/BrowseByDateCartoon.asp?Month=November&Date=2#top.
9. Chernow, Ron. 2015. "John D. Rockefeller and the Great Railroad Strike of 1877." Mr. Jensen's U.S. History Website. October 3. https://waverlyhs.weebly.com/us-history-blog-may-2015---may-2016/john-d-rockefeller-and-the-great-railroad-strike-of-1877.
10. 2016. "Industrialization and the Working Class: The Great Railroad Strike." Digital History. https://www.digitalhistory.uh.edu/disp_textbook_print.cfm?smtid=2&psid=3189; Przybylek, Leslie. 2017. "Picturing Protest: The Great Railroad Strike of 1877." The Heinz History Center. July 18. https://www.heinzhistorycenter.org/blog/western-pennsylvania-history/picturing-protest-great-railroad-strike-1877; Aler, F. Vernon. 1888. *History of Martinsburg and Berkeley County, West Virginia*. Hagerstown, MD: Mail Publishing Company; 1877. "B&O Railroad Strike of 1877 (from Martinsburg Statesman)." West Virginia Archives & History. July 24. https://archive.wvculture.org/history/labor/bandostrike01.html.
11. Aler 1988, 300–313.
12. Pinkerton, Allan. 1878. *Strikers, Communists, Tramps and Detectives*. New York: G.W. Carleton & Company.
13. *New York Times*. 1877. "The Fifth's March to Camden." July 22: 1. https://timesmachine.nytimes.com/timesmachine/1877/07/22/issue.html.
14. Pinkerton 1878, 166–196; *New York Times*. 1877. "The Riot in Baltimore—Scene During the Fight." July 22: 1. https://timesmachine.nytimes.com/timesmachine/1877/07/22/issue.html.

Chapter 11

1. 1878. *Report of the Committee Appointed to Investigate the Railroad Riots in July 1877*. Harrisburg, PA: Lane S. Hart, State Printer. https://archive.org/details/reportcommittee03goog/page/n23/mode/2up. 22–23.
2. *Report of the Committee*, 63.
3. *Report of the Committee*, 140.
4. *Report of the Committee*, 73–74.
5. *Report of the Committee*, 70.

6. *Report of the Committee*, 59.
7. *Report of the Committee*, 63.
8. Pinkerton 1878, 232–234.
9. *Report of the Committee*, 68–69.
10. *Report of the Committee*, 68–69.
11. Dray, Philip. 2010. *There Is Power in a Union*. New York: Anchor Books. 110–111; *Harper's Weekly*. 1877. "The Great Strike." August 11. http://www.catskillarchive.com/rrextra/sk7711.Html.
12. Progressive Labor Party. n.d. "The Pittsburgh Insurrection of 1877." Marxists.org. https://www.marxists.org/history/erol/1960-1970/insurrection.pdf. 11.
13. Dray 2010, 110–111; *Harper's Weekly* 1877.
14. *Harper's Weekly* 1877.
15. *Harper's Weekly* 1877.
16. Dray 2010, 114–119.
17. 1997. "Railroad Strike of 1877 Historical Marker." Explore PA History. September 23. http://explorepahistory.com/hmarker.php?markerId=1-A-1C1.
18. 2002. "Great Strike of 1877." UE News. June. http://www.ranknfile-ue.org/uen_1877.html.
19. *Report of the Committee*, 68.
20. *Report of the Committee*, 72.
21. *Report of the Committee*, 71.
22. "Railroad Strike of 1877 Historical Marker" 1997.
23. Piper, Jessica. 2013. "The Great Railroad Strike of 1877: A Catalyst for the American Labor Movement." *The History Teacher*, November; n.d. "Terence Powderly." Ohio History Central. https://ohiohistorycentral.org/w/Terence_Powderly; n.d. "Eugene V. Debs." AFL-CIO. https://aflcio.org/about/history/labor-history-people/eugene-debs; Editors of Encyclopaedia Britannica. n.d. "Samuel Gompers—American Labour Leader." *Britannica*. https://www.britannica.com/biography/Samuel-Gompers.
24. Salvatore, Nick. 1982. *Eugene V. Debs: Citizen and Socialist*. Urbana: University of Illinois Press. 36–37.
25. Mandel, Bernard. 1963. *Samuel Gompers*. Yellow Springs, OH: Antioch Press. 25.
26. Piper 2013.
27. Piper 2013; n.d. "Greenback movement." *Britannica*. https://www.britannica.com/event/Greenback-movement.
28. Piper 2013; n.d. "Socialist Labor Party of America." Wikipedia. ttps://en.wikipedia.org/wiki/Socialist_Labor_Party_of_America; n.d. "Workingmen's Party of the United States." Wikipedia. https://en.wikipedia.org/wiki/Workingmen%27s_Party_of_the_United_States.
29. n.d. "Labor Day." Wikipedia. https://en.wikipedia.org/wiki/Labor_Day.
30. Piper 2013; Grossman, Jonathan, and Judson Maclaury. 1975. "Creation of the Bureau of Labor Statistics." *Monthly Labor Review*, February: 25.
31. Foner, Philip Sheldon. 1977. *Great Labor Uprising of 1877*. New York: Pathfinder Press. 230.

Chapter 12

1. Gladish 1989, 183.
2. Starkey, Gertrude. 1877. "Letter." John and Gertrude Pitcairn Papers. Glencairn Museum Archives, September.
3. Pitcairn, John. 1879. "Letter to Gertrude Starkey." John and Gertrude Pitcairn Papers. Glencairn Museum Archives, December 10.
4. Starkey, Gertrude. 1879. "Letter to John Pitcairn." John and Gertrude Pitcairn Papers. Glencairn Museum Archives, December 11.
5. Gladish 1989, 185–188.
6. Gladish 1989, 189, 206.
7. Gladish 1989, 216.
8. Gladish 1989, 221.
9. Gladish 1989, 220–223.
10. Odhner 1917, 645–650.
11. 1891. "College Letter No. IX." New Church History. April 1. https://www.newchurchhistory.org/articles/collegeletters/april1st1891.php.

Chapter 13

1. n.d. "John Baptiste Ford." Wikipedia. https://en.wikipedia.org/wiki/John_Baptiste_Ford; n.d. "History of PAPSA." PAPSA. https://papsa.org/history.html; Warnes, Kathy. n.d. "Another Ford—John Baptiste Ford—Builds Downriver History." Meandering Michigan History. https://meanderingmichiganhistory.weebly.com/another-ford-john-baptiste-ford-builds-downriver-history.html; *Glassworker*. 1920. "Pittsburgh Glass Factories in 1870." November 27: 11–12. https://reference.insulators.info/publications/view/?id=7392.
2. n.d. "GLASS WORKS." Floyd County Library. https://floydlibrary.org/wp-content/uploads/2016/07/1.09-Glass-Works.pdf.
3. Aiken, William Earl. 1957. *The Roots Grow Deep*. Cleveland: Lezius-Hiles Company.
4. n.d. "Guide to the PPG Industries Inc. Ledgers and Photographs 1883–1981." Historic Pittsburgh—The John Heinz History Center. https://historicpittsburgh.org/islandora/object/pitt%-3AUS-QQS-mss667/viewer; n.d. "PPG Industries." Wikipedia. https://en.wikipedia.org/wiki/PPG_Industries; Gladish 1989, 245–247.
5. Gladish 1989, 247–248.
6. Gladish 1989, 254 (PPG Board Minutes. July 2, 1886. 33–36).
7. Gladish 1984, 48, 383–384.
8. Gladish 1989, 291–292.
9. Gladish 1989, 291.
10. Gladish 1989, 269.
11. Gladish 1989, 271–279.
12. 1923. *Glass, Paints, Varnishes and Brushes: Their History, Manufacture, and Use*. Pittsburgh, PA: Pittsburgh Plate Glass Company.
13. Gladish 1989, 283–284.

Chapter 14

1. Shappee, Nathan Daniel. 1940. "A History of Johnstown and the Great Flood of 1889: A Study of Disaster and Rehabilitation." Unpublished Doctoral Dissertation, University of Pittsburgh, Pittsburgh, PA. https://digitalarchives.powerlibrary.org/papd/islandora/object/papd%3Aacacc-jtf_1036. 24.
2. Hall, K. 2023. "Joseph Schantz Johns." *MyHeritage*. February 1. https://www.myheritage.com/research/record-1-773791621-2-502511/joseph-schantz-johns-in-myheritage-family-trees; Shappee 1940; n.d. "First Village." JohnstownPA. https://www.johnstownpa.com/History/hist05.html; n.d. "Set Present Pattern." JohnstownPA. https://www.johnstownpa.com/History/hist06.html.
3. Holzwarth, Larry. 2020. "America's First Technological Titan that Changed the Course of History." History Collection. May 15. https://historycollection.com/americas-first-technological-titan-that-changed-the-course-of-history/15/.
4. Shappee 1940 (William Latshaw. 1836. *Johnstown Democrat*, April 26. Quoted on 43).
5. n.d. "Borough Incorporated." JohnstownPA. https://www.johnstownpa.com/History/hist10.html.
6. Shappee 1940 (*Johnstown Cambrian*. 1853. April 1. Quoted on 63).
7. n.d. "Iron Age." JohnstownPA. https://www.johnstownpa.com/History/hist11.html; Cutcliffe, Stephen H. 1990. "Cambria Iron Company." In *The Encyclopedia of American Business History and Biography*. Facts on File; Shappee 1940, 65.
8. Shappee 1940, 67.
9. 2022. "Daniel Johnson Morrell (1821–1885)." *Johnstown Flood*. February 6. https://www.nps.gov/jofl/learn/historyculture/daniel-johnson-morrell.htm; Shappee 1940, 92; Cutcliffe 1990.
10. n.d. "Morrell, Daniel Johnson 1821–1885." *Biographical Directory of the United States Congress*. https://bioguide.congress.gov/search/bio/M000964.
11. McCullough, David. 1968. *The Johnstown Flood*. New York: Simon & Schuster. 67–68.
12. Shappee 1940 (Cyrus Elder. 1878. "Testimonial to Daniel J. Morrell." Philadelphia. 37–40. Quoted on 68).
13. Shappee 1940 (James Moore Swank. 1860. *Cambria Tribune*, July 26. Quoted on 11).
14. Shappee 1940, 97.
15. n.d. "Pittsburgh." SteelCactus. https://www.steelcactus.com/OLDPGH1.html.
16. Shappee 1940, 201.

Chapter 15

1. Coleman, Neil M. 2019. *Johnstown's Flood of 1889: Power over Truth and the Science behind the Disaster*. Cham, Switzerland: Springer International Publishing AG.
2. Coleman 2019, 27–28.
3. 1875. "Pennsylvania Railroad Company to John Reilly." Cambria County Deed Book. Vol. 38. Ebensburg, PA, March 29. 56–58.
4. Shappee 1940, 213; Unrau, Harlan D. 1979. *Historic Structure Report; The South Fork Dam; Historical Data; Johnstown Flood National Memorial; Pennsylvania; Package No. 124*. National Park Service. https://irma.nps.gov/DataStore/DownloadFile/474407. 62–64.
5. 1880. "John Reilly, et. nx., to South Fork Hunting and Fishing Club of Pittsburgh." Cambria County Deed Book. Vol. 43. Ebensburg, PA, March 15. 319–322.
6. McCullough 1968, 55.
7. Coleman 2019.
8. 2021. "Benjamin Franklin Ruff." *Johnstown Flood*. National Park Service. February 20. https://www.nps.gov/jofl/learn/historyculture/benjamin-franklin-ruff.htm; McCullough 1968.
9. Bosley, Doug. 2020. "The Cottages of the South Fork Fishing & Hunting Club." *Johnstown Flood*. National Park Service. September 3. https://www.nps.gov/jofl/learn/historyculture/the-cottages-of-the-south-fork-fishing-and-hunting-club.htm.
10. n.d. "Club and the Dam." Johnstown Area Heritage Association. https://www.jaha.org/attractions/johnstown-flood-museum/flood-history/the-club-and-the-dam/.

Chapter 16

1. Shappee 1940, 67
2. McCullough 1968, 73–74.
3. Shappee 1940, 218–219; McCullough 1968, 74–75.
4. n.d. "SS *Daniel J. Morrell*." Wikipedia. https://en.wikipedia.org/wiki/SS_Daniel_J._Morrell.
5. McCullough 1968, 93–94.
6. McCullough 1968, 95–98.
7. Telegrams and description from display at the Johnstown Flood National Memorial, South Fork, PA;
McCullough 1968, 94–96.
8. Coleman 2019.
9. n.d. "Pennsylvania Railroad interview transcripts about the safety of the dam." Johnstown Area Heritage Association. https://www.jaha.org/education-materials/flood-museum-materials/pennsylvania-railroad-interview-transcripts-about-the-safety-of-the-dam/.
10. McCullough 1968, 126.
11. McCullough 1968.
12. Heiser, Victor George. 1936. *An American Doctor's Odyssey: Adventures in Forty-Five Countries*. New York: W.W. Norton.
13. Heiser 1936.
14. 2023. "Burial Records." *Johnstown Flood*. National Park Service. January 7. https://www.nps.gov/jofl/learn/burial-records.htm.
15. Heiser 1936.
16. n.d. "Victor Heiser." Wikipedia. https://en.wikipedia.org/wiki/Victor_Heiser.

Chapter 17

1. n.d. "Passenger Trains in America." Travegeo.com. https://travegeo.com/Passenger_trains_in_America#.
2. Coleman 2019, 55.
3. *Pittsburgh Commercial Gazette.* 1889. June 1.
4. Swank, George Thompson. 1889. "Before the Reservoir Came." *Johnstown Weekly Tribune*, June 14.
5. Swank 1889.
6. *Philadelphia Evening Bulletin.* 1889. June 3.
7. *Pittsburgh Times.* 1889. June 3.
8. n.d. "Relief Effort." Johnstown Area Heritage Association. https://www.jaha.org/attractions/johnstown-flood-museum/flood-history/the-relief-effort/; McCullough 1968, 224–225.
9. Shappee 1940, 334.
10. McCullough 1968, 199; Shappee 1940, 308.
11. McMaster, John Bach. 1933. "The Johnstown Flood." *Pennsylvania Magazine of History and Biography.* 329.
12. Shannon, B. Clay. n.d. *Still Casting Shadows: A Shared Mosaic of U.S. History, 1620–1913.* Vol. I. https://archive.org/details/StillCastingShadowsASharedMosaicOfU.s.HistoryVol.I1620-1913, 404; Kline, Stevie, and Joyce Mason. 2013. *National History Day Topic: The Johnstown Flood.* November 7.
13. "Relief Effort"; McCullough 1968, 225–229.
14. Shappee 1940, 305.
15. n.d. "American Red Cross." Wikipedia. https://en.wikipedia.org/wiki/American_Red_Cross; n.d. "Clara Barton." Wikipedia. https://en.wikipedia.org/wiki/Clara_Barton#American_Red_Cross; Coleman 2019, 55.
16. McCullough 1968, 245–246.
17. Coleman 2019, cited on 96–97.
18. Coleman 2019, 185.
19. "Johnstown Flood." n.d. Wikipedia. https://en.wikipedia.org/wiki/Johnstown_Flood.
20. Coleman 2019, 184.
21. Nanez, Karina. 2017. "The Johnstown Flood of 1889: A Preventable Disaster." StMU Research Scholars. December 9. https://stmuscholars.org/the-johnstown-flood-of-1889-a-preventable-disaster/; Shugerman, Jed Handelsman. 2000. "The Floodgates of Strict Liability: Bursting Reservoirs and the Adoption of *Fletcher v. Rylands* in the Gilded Age." *Yale Law Journal*, 333–377. https://openyls.law.yale.edu/bitstream/handle/20.500.13051/9337/21_110YaleLJ333_2000_2001_.pdf.

Chapter 18

1. Bender 1913, 26–27.
2. 1883. "Sun will be requested to rise and set by railroad time." Environment & Society Portal. November 21. http://www.environmentandsociety.org/exhibitions/cbq-railroad/sun-will-be-requested-rise-and-set-railroad-time.
3. *Rule Book of The American Railway Association.* 1905. https://babel.hathitrust.org/cgi/pt?id=nyp.33433007752037&seq=1.
4. Baer n.d., 1889 sec.
5. Baer 1790–1989; Chandler, Louis A. 2012. *A History of Patton Township (Monroeville and Pitcairn) Pennsylvania.* Monroeville: Monroeville Historical Society.
6. Baer n.d.
7. Seibel, Kurt. n.d. "Was George Washington Here?" *Pitcairn Borough.* https://pitcairnborough.us/index.php/about-us/pitcairn-history; 2021. "Welcome to Pitcairn Borough." *Pitcairn Borough.* https://pitcairnborough.us/; n.d. "Pitcairn, Pennsylvania." Wikipedia. https://en.wikipedia.org/wiki/Pitcairn,_Pennsylvania.
8. Belfour, Stanton. 1966. *Centennial History of The Shadyside Presbyterian Church.* Pittsburgh: Davis & Warde, Inc.
9. Belfour 1966, 95–96.
10. Huber 2022.
11. Baer n.d., see 1892 sec. "Dauphin County Pennsylvania News: 1892 Harrisburg Train Wreck." Genealogy Trails. June 26. http://genealogytrails.com/penn/dauphin/news/1892wreck.html.
12. Leupp, Francis E. 1919. *George Westinghouse: His Life and Achievements.* Boston: Little, Brown, and Company.
13. Morris, Sue. 2021. "Partying with the Presidents: Part Two." The Frick Pittsburgh. February 18. https://www.thefrickpittsburgh.org/Story-Partying-with-the-Presidents-Part-Two.
14. Morris 2021.
15. Morris 2021.
16. *East Liverpool (OH) Evening Review.* 1899. "The Tenth Home." August 28: 1A.
17. Baer n.d.; *Railway Age Gazette.* 1911. "Railway Officers." 708.
18. Wilson 1913, 29.
19. *Pittsburgh Press.* 1905. "Denies he will retire." December 18: 8.
20. *New Era* (Lancaster, PA). 1905. "Pitcairn to Leave P.R.R." December 20: 6.
21. *Philadelphia Inquirer.* 1906. "Investigation Proves Red Flag to Pitcairn." May 25: 4.
22. Wilson 1913, 27–28.
23. Wilson 1913, 29.
24. Belfour 1966, 55.
25. *Pittsburgh Daily Post.* 1906. "Cassatt Here for Conference." May 3: 2.
26. *Pittsburgh Daily Post.* 1905. "Victor L. Crabbe." May 12: 2; *Butte Inter Mountain.* 1905. "Score Dead, Five Score Are Hurt." May 11: 1, 11.
27. *Pittsburgh Press.* 1907. "Robert Pitcairn in Serious Condition; Run Down by Cyclist." June 21: 1.
28. *The Index.* 1909. "Deaths: Pitcairn." July 31: 3; *The New York Times.* 1909. "Robert Pitcairn Dies in Pittsburg." July 26.
29. *Pittsburgh Post-Gazette.* 1909. "'R.P.' and 'Uncle Robert;' How He Earned the Titles." July 26: 6.
30. Pitz, Marylynne. 2017. "The Next Page: The Ladies of Section 14." *Pittsburgh Post-Gazette*, July 30.
31. *Pittsburgh Post-Gazette.* 1917. "Pitcairn Will Leaves Estate in Trust." July 20: 9.

32. Belfour 1966, 120–121; n.d. Pitcairn-Crabbe Foundation. https://www.pitcairn-crabbe.org/; Engleman, Timothy C. 2022. *Spiritual & Material History of the Pitcairn-Crabbe Foundation*. Pittsburgh: Pitcairn-Crabbe Foundation.

Chapter 19

1. Gyllenhaal, Ed and Kirsten H. 2006. "Early Maps of Bryn Athyn, Pennsylvania, a New Church Community." New Church History. January 25. http://www.newchurchhistory.org/articles/bamaps/bamaps.php.
2. Gladish 1989, 293–294. (Quoted from *College Letters*, June 20, 1892. 12.)
3. 2018. "Estate." Cairnwood. https://cairnwood.org/the-estate/.
4. Old York Road Historical Society. 2002. *Morelands and Bryn Athyn*. Charleston, SC: Arcadia Publishers. 117.
5. Gladish 1989, 298–299.
6. Gladish 1989, 305–308; n.d. "Bishop William Henry Benade." Ancestry.com. https://www.ancestry.com/genealogy/records/bishop-william-henry-benade-24-2ypn2m; Gladish 1984, 447–449, 568; n.d. "William Henry Benade, Sr." Geni.com.
7. Gladish 1989, 315.
8. n.d. "Maria Carnegie Hogan." Find a Grave. https://www.findagrave.com/memorial/51478851/maria-carnegie-hogan.
9. Gladish 1989, 313–314; Gyllenhaal, Ed and Kirsten. 2010. "The Naming of Bryn Athyn (1899)." New Church History. February 23. http://www.newchurchhistory.org/funfacts/index4976.html?p=528.
10. Gladish 1989, 325.
11. 2016. "Hill of Unity: The Founding of Bryn Athyn Borough." *Glencairn Museum News*. April 22. https://glencairnmuseum.org/newsletter/2016/4/15/a-hill-of-unity-the-founding-of-bryn-athyn-borough.
12. Gladish 1989, 322–323.

Chapter 20

1. Ochmann, Sophie, and Max Roser. 2018. "Smallpox." Our World in Data. https://ourworldindata.org/smallpox.
2. Gladish 1989, 330.
3. King, Cairn. 2006. "Vaccination Abomination, or Vaccination Upholds the Nation?" New Church History. April 13. https://www.newchurchhistory.org/articles/ck2006/ck2006.php#Top.
4. n.d. "Ladies' Home Journal." Wikipedia. https://en.wikipedia.org/wiki/Ladies%27_Home_Journal#History.
5. Gladish 1989, 345–346.
6. Gladish 1989, 345–346.
7. 2016. "Hill of Unity: The Founding of Bryn Athyn Borough." *Glencairn Museum News*. April 22. https://glencairnmuseum.org/newsletter/2016/4/15/a-hill-of-unity-the-founding-of-bryn-athyn-borough.
8. Gladish 1989, 413.
9. Gladish 1989, 414.
10. Odhner 1917, 243–244.

Chapter 21

1. Old York Road Historical Society 2002, 119.
2. Cheney, Jim. 2023. "Visiting Bryn Athyn Cathedral: Pennsylvania's European Cathedral." UncoveringPA. January 31. https://uncoveringpa.com/visiting-bryn-athyn-cathedral; Glenn, E. Bruce. 1971. "Bryn Athyn Cathedral: The Building of a Church." New Church History. http://www.newchurchhistory.org/articles/cathedral/01cathedralmain.php; n.d. "Bryn Athyn Cathedral." Wikipedia. https://en.wikipedia.org/wiki/Bryn_Athyn_Cathedral.
3. Toy, Vivian S. 2012. "Zeus of the Catskills." *New York Times*, June 17: 2. https://www.nytimes.com/2012/06/17/realestate/zeus-of-the-catskills.html.
4. Gaskill, Jennie. 1977. *Biography of Raymond Pitcairn*. Bryn Athyn, PA: Self-published. 102; 2022. "Why Did Raymond Pitcairn Build Glencairn? From Cloister Studio to Castle." Glencairn Museum News. February 23. https://glencairnmuseum.org/newsletter/2022/2/22/why-did-raymond-pitcairn-build-glencairn-from-cloister-studio-to-castle.
5. Old York Road Historical Society 2002, 117.
6. Gaskill 1977, 155.
7. n.d. "Raymond Pitcairn." Wikipedia. https://en.wikipedia.org/wiki/Raymond_Pitcairn; Old York Road Historical Society 2002, 123.
8. n.d. "The History of the Museum." Glencairn Museum. https://glencairnmuseum.org/history-of-the-museum; Old York Road Historical Society 2002, 123.
9. Fowle, Farnsworth. 1973. "Rev. Theodore Pitcairn, 80, Dies: Art Collector and Philanthropist." *New York Times*, December 19: 46. https://timesmachine.nytimes.com/timesmachine/1973/12/19/91060061.html.
10. Linder, Lee. 1967. "Work by Monet Is Sold by Cleric to Aid Charity." *Times-Tribune*, December 24: 21.
11. Pitcairn, Theodore. 1971. "The History of The Lord's New Church which is Nova Hierosolyma." Bryn Athyn, PA, March 25.
12. n.d. "Swedenborgian Groups." Encyclopedia.com. https://www.encyclopedia.com/religion/encyclopedias-almanacs-transcripts-and-maps/swedenborgian-groups; n.d. "General Church of the New Jerusalem (1890—Present)." Association of Religious Data Archives (ARDA). https://www.thearda.com/us-religion/group-profiles/groups?D=363.
13. n.d. Swedenborg Foundation. https://swedenborg.com/.
14. n.d. "Theodore Pitcairn." Wikipedia. https://en.wikipedia.org/wiki/Theodore_Pitcairn.

15. History.com Editors. 2023. "Wright Brothers." History.com. June 13. https://www.history.com/topics/inventions/wright-brothers.
16. Russell, David Lee. 2013. *Eastern Air Lines: A History, 1926–1991*. Jefferson, NC: McFarland. 4.
17. Smith, Frank Kingston. 1981. *Legacy of Wings, The Harold F. Pitcairn Story*. Aronson. 19–23.
18. Russell 2013, 5.
19. Russell 2013, 7.
20. Smith 1981, 75–80.
21. Serling, Robert J. 1980. *From the Captain to the Colonel: An Informal History of Eastern Airlines*. New York: Dial Press. 17–18.
22. Smith 1981, 113–114.
23. Russell 2013, 2.
24. Finlay, Mark. 2022. "What Caused Eastern Air Lines' 1991 Shutdown?" *Simple Flying*. January 18. https://simpleflying.com/eastern-air-lines-1991-shutdown/; Old York Road Historical Society 2002.
25. n.d. "Collier Trophy." National Aeronautic Association (NAA). https://naa.aero/awards/awards-and-trophies/collier-trophy.
26. Smith 1981.
27. *New York Times*. 1960. "Harold Pitcairn Takes Life at 62." April 24: 81. https://timesmachine.nytimes.com/timesmachine/1960/04/24/99490571.html; O'Brien, Kathryn E. 1978. *The Great and the Gracious on Millionaires' Row: Lake George in its Glory*. North Country Books; Smith 1981; Gunther, Carl R. 2009. *Harold F. Pitcairn: Aviator, Inventor, and Developer of the Autogiro*. Bryn Athyn, PA: Bryn Athyn College Press; Charnov, Bruce H. 2020. *Life and Mysterious Death of Harold F. Pitcairn: Was it Suicide?* Produced by Vertical Flight Society. https://www.youtube.com/watch?v=rHhQRFRxlIs.
28. Old York Road Historical Society 2002.
29. n.d. "Harold Frederick Pitcairn." Wikipedia. https://en.wikipedia.org/wiki/Harold_Frederick_Pitcairn; n.d. "Eastern Air Lines." Wikipedia. https://en.wikipedia.org/wiki/Eastern_Air_Lines; n.d. "Pitcairn Aircraft Company." Wikipedia. https://en.wikipedia.org/wiki/Pitcairn_Aircraft_Company.
30. Sheeline, William E. 1990. "Managing a Clan Worth $1 Billion." *Fortune*, June 4.
31. *Forbes*. 2015. "2015 America's Richest Families Net Worth: Pitcairn family." July 1. https://www.forbes.com/profile/pitcairn/?sh=45e2f3601c07.
32. Simonoff, Evan, and Caren Chesler. 2016. "Pitcairn Today." *Private Wealth*, September 12. https://www.fa-mag.com/news/pitcairn-today-28888.html?section=49.
33. Jinsky, Dawn. 2020. "Shirtsleeves to shirtsleeves: Breaking the family business cycle." Plante Moran. February 5. https://www.plantemoran.com/explore-our-thinking/insight/2013/10/shirtsleeves-to-shirtsleeves-breaking-the-family-business-cycle.
34. n.d. "The Red Violin." Wikipedia. https://en.wikipedia.org/wiki/The_Red_Violin.

Epilogue and Retrospection

1. n.d. "Amtrak." Wikipedia. https://en.wikipedia.org/wiki/Amtrak#Formation; n.d. "Conrail." Wikipedia. https://en.wikipedia.org/wiki/Conrail; n.d. "Penn Central Transportation Company." Wikipedia. https://en.wikipedia.org/wiki/Penn_Central_Transportation_Company#Bankruptcy.
2. 2020. "History of the Pennsylvania Railroad." Model Train Stuff. October 22. https://blog.modeltrainstuff.com/the-history-of-the-pennsylvania-railroad/; n.d. "Penn Central Transportation Company." Wikipedia.
3. Perry, Mark J. 2019. "Only 52 U.S. Companies Have Been on the Fortune 500 Since 1955, Thanks to the Creative Destruction That Fuels Economic Prosperity." AEIdeas. May 22. https://www.aei.org/carpe-diem/only-52-us-companies-have-been-on-the-fortune-500-since-1955-thanks-to-the-creative-destruction-that-fuels-economic-prosperity/.
4. n.d. "PPG Industries." Wikipedia. https://en.wikipedia.org/wiki/PPG_Industries.
5. Gannon, Joyce. 2018. "After more than a century, Pittsburgh Glass Works' plant in Creighton is shutting down." *Pittsburgh Post-Gazette*, August 16. https://www.post-gazette.com/business/career-workplace/2018/08/16/Pittsburgh-Glass-Works-Creighton-plant-closing-PPG-East-Deer-car-windshields-production/stories/201808150038.
6. Schooley, Tim. 2020. "Cliff Forrest's firm closes on buying Pittsburgh Brewing property." *Pittsburgh Business Times*, February 3. https://www.bizjournals.com/pittsburgh/news/2020/02/03/forrests-firm-closes-on-buying-brewery.html; Schooley, Tim. 2021. "A shot to go with Iron City Beer? Pittsburgh Brewing Company to add distillery to new brewery." *Pittsburgh Business Times*, August 31. https://www.bizjournals.com/pittsburgh/news/2021/08/27/pittsburgh-brewing-co-to-add-distillery.html; Cerilli, Richard. 2021. "Corridors of Opportunity panelists on what's happening along Route 28." *Pittsburgh Business Times*, September 13. https://www.bizjournals.com/pittsburgh/news/2021/09/07/corridors-of-opportunity-route-28-panelists.html; Hanz, Joyce. 2022. "Pittsburgh Brewing Co. settles into its state-of-the-art new home of Iron City Beer in East Deer." *TRIB Live*. September 8. https://triblive.com/local/valley-news-dispatch/brewing-underway-at-pittsburgh-brewing-co-in-east-deer/.

Bibliography

"Abraham Lincoln." Wikipedia. https://en.wikipedia.org/wiki/Abraham_Lincoln.

Adams, Hannah. 1817. *A Dictionary of All Religions and Religious Denominations, Jewish, Heathen, Mahometan and Christian, Ancient and Modern*. 4th ed. New York: James Eastburn and Company.

Aiken, William Earl. 1957. *The Roots Grow Deep*. Cleveland: Lezius-Hiles Company.

Aler, F. Vernon. 1888. *Aler's History of Martinsburg and Berkeley County, West Virginia*. Hagerstown, MD: Mail Publishing Company. https://babel.hathitrust.org/cgi/pt?id=yale.39002014909098&seq=13.

"Alexander III of Scotland." Wikipedia. https://en.wikipedia.org/wiki/Alexander_III_of_Scotland.

Alexander, Edwin P. 1971. *On the Main Line: The Pennsylvania Railroad in the 19th Century*. New York, NY: Bramhall House.

"Allegheny County's Toxic Ten." 2003. *PennEnvironment*. April 4. https://environmentamerica.org/pennsylvania/center/resources/allegheny-countys-toxic-ten/.

"Allegheny Portage Railroad." Wikipedia. https://en.wikipedia.org/wiki/Allegheny_Portage_Railroad.

Alston, David. n.d. "James Glen." *Slaves & Highlanders*. https://overtown.org.uk/cw/Charles_Waterton/pdf/James%20Glen%20Slaves%20and%20Highlanders%20on%20Spanglefish.pdf.

"American Civil War." Wikipedia. https://en.wikipedia.org/wiki/American_Civil_War.

"American Red Cross." Wikipedia. https://en.wikipedia.org/wiki/American_Red_Cross.

"Amtrak." Wikipedia. https://en.wikipedia.org/wiki/Amtrak.

Ankerberg, John. 1999. "Swedenborg Foundation." *John Ankerberg Show*. August 14. https://jashow.org/articles/swedenborg-foundation/.

"B&O Railroad Strike of 1877 (from Martinsburg Statesman)." 1877. West Virginia Archives & History. July 24. https://archive.wvculture.org/history/labor/bandostrike01.html.

Baer, Christopher T. n.d. "A General Chronology of the Pennsylvaina Railroad Company, Its Predecessors and Successors and Its Historical Context." Pennsylvania Railroad Technical & Historical Society. http://www.prrths.com/newprr_files/Hagley/PRR_hagley_intro.htm

Baltazar, Lyndon. 2013. "Airmail Comes of Age." Federal Aviation Administration History Office. https://www.faa.gov/sites/faa.gov/files/about/history/milestones/Airmail_Comes_of_Age.pdf.

Bates, David Homer. 1907. *Lincoln in the Telegraph Office*. London: Century Company.

Bayley, Rev. Dr. Jonathan. n.d. "JOHNNY APPLESEED, Who Made a great part of his Religion to Spread the New Church and Plant Apple-trees in the Wereseren States of America." New Church Worthies. http://www.newchurchhistory.org/articles/jb1884/16_Johnny_Appleseed.php.

Bayley, Rev. Dr. Jonathan. n.d. "Mr. Glen, And the Introduction of the New Church into America." New Church Worthies. http://www.newchurchhistory.org/articles/jb1884/15_Mr_Glen.php.

Belfour, Stanton. 1966. *Centennial History of the Shadyside Presbyterian Church*. Pittsburgh, PA: Davis & Warde, Inc.

"Benjamin Franklin Ruff (1829–1887)." 2021. Johnstown Flood. National Park Service. February 20. https://www.nps.gov/jofl/learn/historyculture/benjamin-franklin-ruff.htm.

Bentley, Elizabeth Petty. 2000. "Passenger arrivals at the Port of New York, 1830–1832 : from customs passenger lists." https://archive.org/details/passengerarrival0000bent/page/788/mode/2up.

Biographical Encyclopaedia of Pennsylvania of the Nineteenth Century. 1874. Philadelphia: Galaxy Publishing Company.

"Bishop William Henry Benade." Ancestry.com. https://www.ancestry.com/genealogy/records/bishop-william-henry-benade-24-2ypn2m.

"Borough Incorporated." JohnstownPA. https://www.johnstownpa.com/History/hist10.html.

Bosley, Doug. 2020. "The Cottages of the South Fork Fishing & Hunting Club." Johnstown Flood. National Park Service. September 3. https://www.nps.gov/jofl/learn/historyculture/the-cottages-of-the-south-fork-fishing-and-hunting-club.htm.

Bosley, Edward R. "Pitcairn, Robert Jr., House,

Pasadena, CA." *Pacific Coast Architecture Digest (PCAD)*. https://pcad.lib.washington.edu/building/16331/.

Branch, E. Douglas. 1938. "The Coming of the Telegraph to Western Pennsylvania." *Pennsylvania History*, January: 21–29.

Brignano, Mary. 2012. "Carnegie tapped efficient steelmaker to head new Hero Fund." *imPULSE--A Periodic Newsletter of the Carnegie Hero Fund Commission*, March: 5–6, 9.

Brodt, Zach. "Harwick Mine Explosion." Archives & Manuscripts @ Pitt. https://pittarchives.tumblr.com/post/108822300464/harwick-mine-explosion.

Brown, David M. 2007. "Society marks 1907 annexation of Allegheny City." *Trib Live*. July 28. https://archive.triblive.com/news/society-marks-1907-annexation-of-allegheny-city/.

"Bryn Athyn Cathedral." Wikipedia. https://en.wikipedia.org/wiki/Bryn_Athyn_Cathedral.

Buffett, Warren. 2021. "Grow." *Leave your children some money, but 'not enough that they can do nothing.'* June 25. https://grow.acorns.com/warren-buffett-leaving-money-to-kids/.

"Burial Records." 2023. *Johnstown Flood*. National Park Service. January 7. https://www.nps.gov/jofl/learn/burial-records.htm.

Burns, Adam. 2023. "Railroads In The Civil War: Maps, Facts and Statistics (North vs South)." *American-Rails.com*. June 7. https://www.american-rails.com/civil.html.

Butte Inter Mountain. 1905. "SCORE DEAD, FIVE SCORE ARE HURT." May 11: 1, 11. https://www.newspapers.com/image/348792289/.

Carnegie, Andrew. 1920. *Autobiography of Andrew Carnegie*. London: Constable & Co. https://www.gutenberg.org/files/17976/17976-h/17976-h.htm#FNanchor_17_17.

Carnegie, Andrew. 1884. *Round the World*. New York, NY: Charles Scribner's Sons. https://play.google.com/books/reader?id=CQQIAAAAQAAJ&hl=en&pg=GBS.PA11.

Cerilli, Richard. 2021. "Corridors of Opportunity panelists on what's happening along Route 28." *Pittsburgh Business Times*, September 13. https://www.bizjournals.com/pittsburgh/news/2021/09/07/corridors-of-opportunity-route-28-panelists.html.

Chandler, Louis A. 2012. *A History of Patton Township (Monroeville and Pitcairn) Pennsylvania*. Monroeville, PA: Monroeville Historical Society.

Charnov, Bruce H. 2020. *Life and Mysterious Death of Harold F. Pitcairn: Was it Suicide?* Produced by Vertical Flight Society. https://www.youtube.com/watch?v=rHhQRFRxlIs.

Cheney, Jim. 2023. "Visiting Bryn Athyn Cathedral: Pennsylvania's European Cathedral." *UncoveringPA*. January 31. https://uncoveringpa.com/visiting-bryn-athyn-cathedral.

Chernow, Ron. 2015. "John D. Rockefeller and the Great Railroad Strike of 1877." *Mr. Jensen's U.S. History Website*. October 3. https://waverlyhs.weebly.com/us-history-blog-may-2015---may-2016/john-d-rockefeller-and-the-great-railroad-strike-of-1877.

Churella, Albert J. 2012. *The Pennsylvania Railroad, Volume 1—Building an Empire, 1846–1917*. Philadelphia: University of Pennsylvania Press.

"Clara Barton." Wikipedia. https://en.wikipedia.org/wiki/Clara_Barton.

"Club and the Dam." Johnstown Area Heritage Association. https://www.jaha.org/attractions/johnstown-flood-museum/flood-history/the-club-and-the-dam/.

Coleman, Neil M. 2019. *Johnstown's Flood of 1889: Power Over Truth and the Science Behind the Disaster*. Cham, Switzerland: Springer International Publishing AG.

"College Letter No. IX." 1891. New Church History. April 1. https://www.newchurchhistory.org/articles/collegeletters/april1st1891.php.

"Collier Trophy." National Aeronautic Association (NAA). https://naa.aero/awards/awards-and-trophies/collier-trophy.

"Compromise of 1877." Wikipedia. https://en.wikipedia.org/wiki/Compromise_of_1877.

"Conrail." Wikipedia. https://en.wikipedia.org/wiki/Conrail.

"Crossing the Alleghenies." Stories from PA History. https://explorepahistory.com/story.php?storyId=1-9-A.

Cunningham, John M. "Emanuel Swedenborg, Swedish Philosopher." *Britannica*. https://www.britannica.com/biography/Emanuel-Swedenborg/His-theology.

Cutcliffe, Stephen H. 1990. "Cambria Iron Company." In *The Encyclopedia of American Business History and Biography*. Facts on File.

"Daniel Johnson Morrell (1821–1885)." 2022. Johnstown Flood. February 6. https://www.nps.gov/jofl/learn/historyculture/daniel-johnson-morrell.htm.

"Dauphin County Pennsylvania News: 1892 Harrisburg Train Wreck." 1892. Genealogy Trails. June 26. http://genealogytrails.com/penn/dauphin/news/1892wreck.html.

Dolson, Hildegarde. 1959. *The Great Oildorado—The Gaudy and Turbulent Years of the First Oil Rush: Pennsylvania, 1859–1880*. New York: Random House.

Dorman, Peter F. "Akhenaten." *Britannica*. https://www.britannica.com/biography/Akhenaten.

"Dr Hugh B. Pitcairn." Find a Grave. https://www.findagrave.com/memorial/14409791/hugh-b-pitcairn.

Drago, Harry Sinclair. 1972. *Canal Days in America*. New York: Bramhall House.

Dray, Philip. 2010. *There Is Power In a Union*. New York: Anchor Books.

East Liverpool (OH) Evening Review. 1899. "The Tenth Home." August 28: 1A.

"Eastern Air Lines." Wikipedia. https://en.wikipedia.org/wiki/Eastern_Air_Lines.

Editors of Encyclopaedia Britannica. 2021. "J. Edgar Thomson—American engineer and businessman." *Britannica*. May 23. https://www.britannica.com/biography/J-Edgar-Thomson.

Editors of Encyclopaedia Britannica. "Samuel Gompers: American labour leader." *Britannica*. https://www.britannica.com/biography/Samuel-Gompers.

"1879: Tidewater Pipe Company-World's 1st Successful Oil Pipeline." Smethport History. http://www.smethporthistory.org/coryville/oilarticle.html.

"Elizabeth Erb (Rigg) Pitcairn (1841)." WikiTree. https://www.wikitree.com/wiki/Rigg-138.

Emerson, Ralph Waldo. 1896. *Swedenborg; or, The Mystic*. https://emersoncentral.com/texts/representative-men/swedenborg-the-mystic/.

Engleman, Timothy C. 2016. *Liturgy: A Reflection on Shadyside Presbyterian Church*. Pittsburgh, PA: Shadyside Presbyterian Church.

Engleman, Timothy C. 2022. *Spiritual & Material History of the Pitcairn-Crabbe Foundation*. Pittsburgh, PA: Pitcairn-Crabbe Foundation.

"Estate." 2018. Cairnwood. https://cairnwood.org/the-estate.

Etheredge, Laura. "Aton." *Britannica*. https://www.britannica.com/topic/Aton.

Etheredge, Laura. "Tell el-Amarna." *Britannica*. https://www.britannica.com/place/Tell-el-Amarna.

"Eugene V. Debs." AFL-CIO. https://aflcio.org/about/history/labor-history-people/eugene-debs.

Ewbank, Douglas. 2009. "Enoch Lewis's Tale of Intrigue." Powelton History Blog: A Collective Biography of a Philadelphia Neighborhood. August 15. https://poweltonhistoryblog.blogspot.com/2009/08/enoch-lewiss-tale-of-intrigue.html.

Finlay, Mark. 2022. "What Caused Eastern Air Lines' 1991 Shutdown?" Simple Flying. January 18. https://simpleflying.com/eastern-air-lines-1991-shutdown/.

Finseth, Ian Frederick. 2006. *The American Civil War—An Anthology of Essential Writings*. New York: Routledge–Taylor & Francis Group.

"First Village." JohnstownPA. https://www.johnstownpa.com/History/hist05.html.

"Float Glass Process." Science Direct. https://www.sciencedirect.com/topics/engineering/float-glass-process.

Foner, Philip Sheldon. 1977. *Great Labor Uprising of 1877*. New York: Pathfinder Press.

Forbes. 2015. "2015 America's Richest Families Net Worth: Pitcairn family." July 1. https://www.forbes.com/profile/pitcairn/?sh=45e2f3601c07.

"Fortune 500." 2021. Fortune. https://fortune.com/fortune500/2021/search/?name=Steel.

"Fortune 500 1955." CNN Money. https://money.cnn.com/magazines/fortune/fortune500_archive/full/1955/1.html.

Fowle, Farnsworth. 1973. "Rev. Theodore Pitcairn, 80, Dies: Art Collector and Philanthropist." *New York Times*, December 19: 46. https://timesmachine.nytimes.com/timesmachine/1973/12/19/91060061.html?pageNumber=46.

Frazier, Reid. 2021. "US Steel cancels $1B upgrade to Pittsburgh plants." State Impact Pennsylvania. April 30. https://stateimpact.npr.org/pennsylvania/2021/04/30/us-steel-cancels-1b-upgrade-to-pittsburgh-plants/.

Fulton, John. *Meetings of the Diretors of the Cambria Library Association, 1878–1893*. Vol. III. Johnstown, PA.

"Gallitzin Tunnel." Wikipedia. https://en.wikipedia.org/wiki/Gallitzin_Tunnel.

Gannon, Joyce. 2018. "After more than a century, Pittsburgh Glass Works'plant in Creighton is shutting down." *Pittsburgh Post-Gazette*, August 16. https://www.post-gazette.com/business/career-workplace/2018/08/16/Pittsburgh-Glass-Works-Creighton-plant-closing-PPG-East-Deer-car-windshields-production/stories/201808150038.

Gaskill, Jennie. 1977. *Biography of Raymond Pitcairn*. Bryn Athyn, PA: Self-published.

Gearhart Brothers Services. "Stackhouse Park Abandoned Mine Reclamation." Pennsylvania Department of Environmental Protection. https://files.dep.state.pa.us/mining/Abandoned%20Mine%20Reclamation/AbandonedMinePortalFiles/Accomplishments/OSM11_1052_101.1_Stackhouse_Park.pdf.

"General Church of the New Jerusalem (1890–Present)." Association of Religious Data Archives (ARDA). https://www.thearda.com/us-religion/group-profiles/groups?D=363.

Gibson, Samantha. "Panic of 1837." Digital Public Library of America. https://dp.la/primary-source-sets/the-panic-of-1837#tabs.

Gladish, Richard R. 1984. *Bishop William Henry Benade—Founder and Reformer*. Bryn Athyn, PA: Academy of the New Church.

Gladish, Richard R. 1989. *John Pitcairn: Uncommon Entrepreneur*. Bryn Athyn, PA: Academy of the New Church.

"GLASS WORKS." Floyd County Library. https://floydlibrary.org/wp-content/uploads/2016/07/1.09-Glass-Works.pdf.

Glass, paints, varnishes and brushes—their history, manufacture, and use. 1923. Pittsburgh, PA: Pittsburgh Plate Glass Company. https://archive.org/details/GlassPaintsVarnishesAndBrushesTheirHistoryManufactureAndUse/page/n7/mode/2up?view=theater.

Glassworker. 1920. "Pittsburgh Plate Glass Factories in 1870." November 27: 11–12. https://reference.insulators.info/publications/view/?id=7392.

Glencairn Museum News. 2015. "The Purchase of the Lanzone Egyptian Collection (1878)." August 31. https://glencairnmuseum.org/newsletter/august-2015-the-purchase-of-the-lanzone-egyptian-collection.html.

Glenn, E. Bruce. 1971. "Bryn Athyn Cathedral: The Building of a Church." New Church History. http://www.newchurchhistory.org/articles/cathedral/01cathedralmain.php.

"Great Pennsylvania Canal." Living Places. https://www.livingplaces.com/PA/Pennsylvania_Canal.html.

"Great Strike of 1877." 2002. UE News. June. http://www.ranknfile-ue.org/uen_1877.html.

Green, Harry. 2010. "Ship Venice." Immigrant Ship Transcribers Guild. February 10. https://www.immigrantships.net/v12/1800v12/venice18461001.html.

"Greenback Movement." *Britannica*. https://www.britannica.com/event/Greenback-movement.

Gregersen, Erik. "United States Steel Corporation." *Britannica*. https://www.britannica.com/topic/United-States-Steel-Corporation.

Grossman, Jonathan and Judson Maclaury. 1975. "Creation of the Bureau of Labor Statistics." *Monthly Labor Review*, February: 25.

"Guide to the PPG Industries Inc. Ledgers and Photographs 1883–1981." Historic Pittsburgh—The John Heinz History Center. https://historicpittsburgh.org/islandora/object/pitt%3AUS-QQS-mss667/viewer.

Gunther, Carl R. 2009. *Harold F. Pitcairn: Aviator, Inventor, and Developer of the Autogiro*. Bryn Athyn, PA: Bryn Athyn College Press.

Gyllenhaal, Ed. 2012. "From Parlor to Castle: The Egyptian Collection at Glencairn Museum." Glencairn Museum. July 19. https://glencairnmuseum.org/articles/2012/7/19/from-parlor-to-castle-the-egyptian-collection-at-glencairn-m.html.

Gyllenhaal, Ed and Kirsten. 2010. "The Naming of Bryn Athyn (1899)." New Church History. February 23. http://www.newchurchhistory.org/funfacts/index4976.html?p=528.

Gyllenhaal, Ed and Kirsten H. 2006. "Early Maps of Bryn Athyn, Pennsylvania, a New Church Community." New Church History. January 25. http://www.newchurchhistory.org/articles/bamaps/bamaps.php.

Hall, K. 2023. "Joseph Schantz Johns." *MyHeritage*. February 1. https://www.myheritage.com/research/record-1-773791621-2-502511/joseph-schantz-johns-in-myheritage-family-trees?indId=externalindividual-da2f04ed60159ae36eea831f9eb1fbea&trn=partner_Geni&trp=logged_out_matches_module.

Hanz, Joyce. 2022. "Pittsburgh Brewing Co. settles into its state-of-the-art new home of Iron City Beer in East Deer." *TRIB Live*. September 8. https://triblive.com/local/valley-news-dispatch/brewing-underway-at-pittsburgh-brewing-co-in-east-deer/.

"Harold Frederick Pitcairn." Wikipedia. https://en.wikipedia.org/wiki/Harold_Frederick_Pitcairn.

Harper's Weekly. 1877. "The Great Strike." August 11. http://www.catskillarchive.com/rrextra/sk7711.Html.

Haseleu, Stacey J. 2012. *Understanding Why the South Fork Dam Failed*. Dissertation, Pittsburgh, PA: Chatham University.

Hawke, David Freeman. 1980. *John D. : The Founding Father of the Rockefellers*. New York: Harper & Row.

Heiser, Victor George. 1936. *An American Doctor's Odyssey: Adventures in Forty-Five Countries*. New York: W.W. Norton.

"Helen Pitcairn Rush." Find a Grave. https://www.findagrave.com/memorial/36990363/helen-rush.

Helfman, Harold M. 1950. "Twenty-Nine Hectic Days: Public Opinion and the Oil War of 1872." *Pennsylvania History: A Journal of Mid-Atlantic Studies*, April: 121–138.

Henderson, Bruce. 1987. *Window to Eternity*. West Chester, PA: Swedenborg Foundation.

"Henry O'Reilly." Wikipedia. https://en.wikipedia.org/wiki/Henry_O%27Reilly.

Hero. https://www.merriam-webster.com/dictionary/hero.

"Hill of Unity: The Founding of Bryn Athyn Borough." 2016. Glencairn Museum News. April 22. https://glencairnmuseum.org/newsletter/2016/4/15/a-hill-of-unity-the-founding-of-bryn-athyn-borough.

"Historical Timeline." Carnegie Hero Fund Commission. https://www.carnegiehero.org/about/historical-timeline/.

"History of PAPSA." PAPSA. https://papsa.org/history.html.

"History of the Carnegie Hero Fund Commission." Carnegie Hero Fund Foundation. https://www.carnegiehero.org/about/history/;.

"History of the Museum." Glencairn Museum. https://glencairnmuseum.org/history-of-the-museum.

"History of the Pennsylvania Railroad." 2020. Model Train Stuff. October 22. https://blog.modeltrainstuff.com/the-history-of-the-pennsylvania-railroad/.

History of the Pittsburgh Public Water Supply (1801 to Present). https://slideplayer.com/slide/1519050.

History.com Editors. 2022. "Morse Code & the Telegraph." History.com. August 12. https://www.history.com/topics/inventions/telegraph.

History.com Editors. 2019. "Secession." History.com. June 7. https://www.history.com/topics/american-civil-war/secession.

History.com Editors. 2023. "Wright Brothers." History.com. June 13. https://www.history.com/topics/inventions/wright-brothers.

Holzinger, Kay. 2002. *Encyclopedia of Cults, Sects, and New Religions*. 2nd. Edited by James R. Lewis. Amherst: Prometheus Books.

Holzwarth, Larry. 2020. "America's First Technological Titan that Changed the Course of History." History Collection. May 15. https://historycollection.com/americas-first-technological-titan-that-changed-the-course-of-history/15/.

Holzwarth, Larry. 2020. "See 1842 America Through Charles Dickens' Eyes." History Collection. January 14. https://historycollection.com/see-1842-america-through-charles-dickens-eyes/20/.

"Horseshoe Curve (Pennsylvania)." Wikipedia. https://en.wikipedia.org/wiki/Horseshoe_Curve_(Pennsylvania).

Huber, William R. 2020. *Adolph Sutro—King of the Comstock Lode and Mayor of San Francisco*. Jefferson, NC: McFarland.

Huber, William R. 2022. *George Westinghouse—Powering the World*. Jefferson, NC: McFarland.

"Hugh Pitcairn." Wikipedia. https://en.wikipedia.org/wiki/Hugh_Pitcairn.

Ilisevich, Robert D., and Carl K. Burkett Jr. 1985. "The Canal Through Pittsburgh: Its Development and Physical Character." *Western Pennsylvania Historical Magazine*, October: 351–371.

"Immigrant Population." USA Facts. https://usafacts.org/data/topics/people-society/immigration/immigration-and-immigration-enforcement/immigrants/.

Index. 1909. "Deaths: Pitcairn." July 31: 3. https://www.google.com/books/edition/The_Index/lmlJAQAAMAAJ?hl=en&gbpv=1&bsq=Victor%20Lee%20Crabbe.

"Industrialization and the Working Class: The Great Railroad Strike." 2016. Digital History. https://www.digitalhistory.uh.edu/disp_textbook_print.cfm?smtid=2&psid=3189.

"Interstate Commerce Act Is Passed." 1887. United States Senate. February 4. https://www.senate.gov/artandhistory/history/minute/Interstate_Commerce_Act_Is_Passed.htm.

"Iron Age." JohnstownPA. https://www.johnstownpa.com/History/hist11.html.

Jinsky, Dawn. 2020. "Shirtsleeves to shirtsleeves: Breaking the family business cycle." Plante Moran. February 5. https://www.plantemoran.com/explore-our-thinking/insight/2013/10/shirtsleeves-to-shirtsleeves-breaking-the-family-business-cycle.

"John Baptiste Ford." Wikipedia. https://en.wikipedia.org/wiki/John_Baptiste_Ford.

"John Edgar Thomson." Wikipedia. https://en.wikipedia.org/wiki/John_Edgar_Thomson.

"John Pitcairn (1803-c1884)." Familypedia. https://familypedia.fandom.com/wiki/John_Pitcairn_(1803-c1884).

"John Pitcairn." 1846. My Heritage. October 1. https://www.myheritage.com/research/record-10373-763929/john-pitcairn-in-atlantic-gulf-ports-passenger-list-card-index.

"John Pitcairn, Jr." Wikipedia. https://en.wikipedia.org/wiki/John_Pitcairn_Jr.

"John Reilly, et. nx., to South Fork Hunting and Fishing Club of Pittsburgh." 1880. Cambria County Deed Book. Vol. 43. Ebensburg, PA, March 15. 319–322.

Johnston, Robert D. "Rutherford B. Hayes: Campaigns and Elections." UVA Miller Center. https://millercenter.org/president/hayes/campaigns-and-elections.

"Johnstown Flood." Wikipedia. https://en.wikipedia.org/wiki/Johnstown_Flood.

"Johnstown Flood Museum." Johnstown Area Heritage Association. https://www.jaha.org/attractions/johnstown-flood-museum/visitor-information/online-tour/.

Jones, Diana Nelson. 2007. "The Day the City of Allegheny Disappeared." *Pittsburgh Post-Gazette*, December 9. https://www.post-gazette.com/local/city/2007/12/09/The-day-the-City-of-Allegheny-disappeared/stories/200712090229.

Kanchwala, Hussain. 2021. "How Is Glass Made?" ScienceABC. January 4. https://www.scienceabc.com/innovation/how-is-glass-made.html#the-history-of-making-glass.

Keller, Helen. 1927. *My Religion*. New York: Swedenborg Foundation.

Kilgore, Ed. 2020. "The Last Time a Contested Presidential Election Nearly Tore the Country Apart." *Intelligencer*, September 7. https://nymag.com/intelligencer/2020/09/the-last-time-a-contested-election-tore-the-country-apart.html.

King, Cairn. 2006. "Vaccination Abomination, or Vaccination Upholds the Nation?" New Church History. April 13. https://www.newchurchhistory.org/articles/ck2006/ck2006.php#Top.

Klein, Christopher. 2022. "Abraham Lincoln's Funeral Train: How America Mourned for Three Weeks." History.com. February 8. https://www.history.com/news/abraham-lincoln-funeral-train.

Kline, Stevie, and Joyce Mason. 2013. *National History Day Topic: The Johnstown Flood*. November 7.

"Labor Day." Wikipedia. https://en.wikipedia.org/wiki/Labor_Day.

"Ladies' Home Journal." Wikipedia. https://en.wikipedia.org/wiki/Ladies%27_Home_Journal.

"Largest (non-government) employers in Pa. and elsewhere: From medical centers to Walmart." 2019. PennLive. March 15. https://www.pennlive.com/life/2019/03/from-medical-systems-to-universities-and-walmart-the-largest-non-government-employer-in-pa-and-every-other-state.html.

"Law Against Adultery." SwedenborgStudy.com. https://www.swedenborgstudy.com/books/H.Lj.Odhner_Ten-Commandments/adultery.html.

Leonard, John, ed. 1907. *Who's Who in Pennsylvania: A Biographical Dictionary of Contemporaries*. Vol. 2. New York, NY: L.R. Hammersly.

Leupp, Francis E. 1919. *George Westinghouse: His Life and Achievements*. Boston: Little, Brown and Company.

Linder, Lee. 1967. "Work by Monet Is Sold By Cleric to Aid Charity." *Times-Tribune*, December 24: 21. https://www.newspapers.com/article/the-times-tribune-rev-theodore-pitcairn/71658771/.

Locklin, Kristy. 2022. "Pittsburgh Brewing Co. on tap to be one of the biggest brewers on the East Coast." NextPittsburgh. January 27. https://nextpittsburgh.com/latest-news/pittsburgh-brewing-co-on-tap-to-be-one-of-the-biggest-brewers-on-the-east-coast/.

"Main Line of Public Works." Wikipedia. https://en.wikipedia.org/wiki/Main_Line_of_Public_Works#Eastern_Division_Canal.

Mandel, Bernard. 1963. *Samuel Gompers*. Yellow Springs, OH: Antioch Press.

Manlove, Colin. 1992. *Swedenborg: Heaven and Hell*. London: Palgrave Macmillan.

"Maria Carnegie Hogan." Find a Grave. https://www.findagrave.com/memorial/51478851/maria-carnegie-hogan.

McCullough, David. 1968. *The Johnstown Flood*. New York: Simon & Schuster.

McMaster, John Bach. 1933. "The Johnstown Flood." *Pennsylvania Magazine of History and Biography*, 329.

Mechanicsburg Museum Association. "Cumberland Valley Railroad & Mechanicsburg." MechanicsburgMuseum.org. http://www.mechanicsburgmuseum.org/cvrr.html.

"Minutes of Session." 1869. Pittsburgh, PA: Shadyside Presbyterian Church, January 28.

"Minutes of Session." 1868. Pittsburgh, PA: Shadyside Presbyterian Church, July 9.

"Mission of the Carnegie Hero Fund Commission." Carnegie Hero Fund Commission. https://www.carnegiehero.org/about/mission/.

Monroe, James. 1893. "The Hayes-Tilden Electoral Commission: How Congress settled the disputed electoral count in the presidential election of 1876." *The Atlantic*, October. https://www.theatlantic.com/magazine/archive/1893/10/the-hayes-tilden-electoral-commission/523971/.

"Morrell, Daniel Johnson 1821–1885." Biographical Directory of the United States Congress. https://bioguide.congress.gov/search/bio/M000964.

Morris, Sue. 2021. "Partying with the Presidents: Part Two: McKinley Comes to Pittsburgh." The Frick Pittsburgh. February 18. https://www.thefrickpittsburgh.org/Story-Partying-with-the-Presidents-Part-Two.

"*Munn v. Illinois* (1877): An Important Granger Case." U-S-history.org. https://www.u-s-history.com/pages/h855.html.

Najera, Jesus. 2020. "Young Polymaths." *Medium*. https://medium.com/young-polymaths/in-their-20s-leonardo-da-vinci-5655c3d8ef82.

Nanez, Karina. 2017. "The Johnstown Flood of 1889: A Preventable Disaster." StMU Research Scholars. December 9. https://stmuscholars.org/the-johnstown-flood-of-1889-a-preventable-disaster/.

Nasaw, David. 2006. *Andrew Carnegie*. New York: Penguin Press.

Nast, Thomas. 1878. "Cipher Mumm(er)y." *Harper's Weekly*. November 2. https://www.harpweek.com/09Cartoon/BrowseByDateCartoon.asp?Month=November&Date=2#top.

National Archives and Records Service. 1957. "Passenger lists of vessels arriving at New York, 1820–1897." https://archive.org/details/passengerlists00074unix/page/n820/mode/1up?q=Glasgow.

"New Church (Swedenborgianism) vs Evangelical Christianity." 2020. YouTube. August 23. https://www.youtube.com/watch?v=KxCyq3Sw72I.

New Era (Lancaster, PA). 1905. "Pitcairn to Leave P.R.R." December 20: 6.

New York Times. 1877. "The Fifth's March to Camden." July 22: 1. https://timesmachine.nytimes.com/timesmachine/1877/07/22/issue.html.

New York Times. 1960. "Harold Pitcairn Takes Life at 62." April 24: 81. https://timesmachine.nytimes.com/timesmachine/1960/04/24/99490571.html?pageNumber=81.

New York Times. 1864. "Pennsylvania Oil Region." December 20: 1. https://timesmachine.nytimes.com/timesmachine/1864/12/20/78995901.pdf?pdf_redirect=true&ip=0.

New York Times. 1877. "The Riot in Baltimore—Scene During the Fight." July 22: 1. https://timesmachine.nytimes.com/timesmachine/1877/07/22/issue.html.

New York Times. 1909. "Robert Pitcairn Dies in Pittsburg." July 26.

O'Brien, Kathryn E. 1978. *The Great and Gracious on Millionaires' Row: Lake George in its Glory*. North Country Books.

Ochmann, Sophie and Max Roser. 2018. "Smallpox." *Our World in Data*. https://ourworldindata.org/smallpox.

Odhner, C. Th. 1917. "John Pitcairn, A Biography." *New Church Life*, January: 3–6. https://newchristianbiblestudy.org/bundles/ncbsw/ondeck/english/new-church-life/1917_HTML.htm.

"Oil refinery." Wikipedia. https://en.wikipedia.org/wiki/Oil_refinery.

Old York Road Historical Society. 2002. *Morelands and Bryn Athyn*. Charleston, SC: Arcadia Publishers.

"Passenger Trains in America." Travegeo.com. https://travegeo.com/Passenger_trains_in_America#.

"Penn Central Transportation Company." Wikipedia. https://en.wikipedia.org/wiki/Penn_Central_Transportation_Company.

"Pennsylvania Canals—1846." Pennsylvania Historical & Museum Commission. http://www.phmc.state.pa.us/portal/communities/documents/1776-1865/pennsylvania-canals.html.

"Pennsylvania Railroad." Wikipedia. https://en.wikipedia.org/wiki/Pennsylvania_Railroad.

"Pennsylvania Railroad Company to John Reilly." 1875. Cambria County Deed Book. Vol. 38. Ebensburg, PA, March 29. 56–58.

"Pennsylvania Railroad interview transcripts about the safety of the dam." Johnstown Area Heritage Association. https://www.jaha.org/education-materials/flood-museum-materials/pennsylvania-railroad-interview-transcripts-about-the-safety-of-the-dam/.

People of Medieval Scotland 1093–1371. https://www.poms.ac.uk/record/source/902/.

Perry, Mark J. 2019. "Only 52 US Companies Have Been on the Fortune 500 Since 1955, Thanks to the Creative Destruction That Fuels Economic Prosperity." AEIdeas. May 22. https://www.aei.org/carpe-diem/only-52-us-companies-have-been-on-the-fortune-500-since-1955-thanks-to-the-creative-destruction-that-fuels-economic-prosperity/.

"Perthshire Pitcairns: Family Branch

7_Perthshire_Sheet 2." Royal Dunfermline. http://www.royaldunfermline.com/Resources/Genealogy/FB7/FAMILY_BRANCH7_PERTHSHIRE_SHEET-2.pdf.

Philadelphia Evening Bulletin. 1889. June 3.

Philadelphia Inquirer. 1906. "Investigation Proves Red Flag to Pitcairn." May 25: 4.

Pinkerton, Allan. 1878. *Strikers, Communists, Tramps and Detectives.* New York: G.W. Carleton & Company.

Piper, Jessica. 2013. "Great Railroad Strike of 1877: A Catalyst for the American Labor Movement." *The History Teacher,* November.

"Pitcairn Aircraft Company." Wikipedia. https://en.wikipedia.org/wiki/Pitcairn_Aircraft_Company.

Pitcairn, John. 1879. "Letter to Gertrude Starkey." John and Gertrude Pitcairn Papers. Glencairn Museum Archives, December 10.

"Pitcairn, Pennsylvania." Wikipedia. https://en.wikipedia.org/wiki/Pitcairn,_Pennsylvania.

Pitcairn, Robert. 1858. "Letter to John Pitcairn, Jr." Fort Wayne, IN, October.

Pitcairn, Sheila. 2004. The Pitcairn Family. February 19. http://www.pitcairnfamily.com/index.htm.

Pitcairn, Theodore. 1971. "The History of the Lord's New Church which is Nova Hierosolyma." Bryn Athyn, PA, March 25.

Pitcairn-Crabbe Foundation. https://www.pitcairn-crabbe.org/.

"Pittsburgh." Steel Cactus. https://www.steelcactus.com/OLDPGH1.html.

Pittsburgh Commercial Gazette. 1889. June 1.

Pittsburgh Daily Post. 1906. "Cassatt Here for Conference." May 3: 2.

Pittsburgh Daily Post. 1905. "Victor L. Crabbe." May 12: 2. https://www.newspapers.com/clip/24582920/victor-l-crabbe-obituary/.

Pittsburgh Post-Gazette. 1917. "Pitcairn Will Leaves Estate in Trust." July 20: 9.

Pittsburgh Post-Gazette. 1909. "'R.P.' and 'Uncle Robert'; How He Earned the Titles." July 26: 6.

Pittsburgh Press. 1905. "Denies he will retire." December 18: 8.

Pittsburgh Press. 1907. "Robert Pitcairn in Serious Condition; Run Down by Cyclist." June 21: 1. https://www.newspapers.com/image/142175277/?terms=robert%20pitcairn%20bicycle&match=1.

Pittsburgh Times. 1889. June 3.

Pitz, Marylynne. 2012. "Allegheny Arsenal Explosion: Pittsburgh's worst day during the Civil War." *Pittsburgh Post-Gazette,* September 16. https://www.post-gazette.com/life/lifestyle/2012/09/16/Allegheny-Arsenal-Explosion-Pittsburgh-s-worst-day-during-the-Civil-War/stories/201209160145.

Pitz, Marylynne. 2017. "The Next Page: The Ladies of Section 14." *Pittsburgh Post-Gazette,* July 30.

"PPG Industries." Wikipedia. https://en.wikipedia.org/wiki/PPG_Industries.

PPG Industries. *A Concern for the Future.* Pittsburgh, PA.

Progressive Labor Party. "The Pittsburgh Insurrection of 1877." Marxists.org. https://www.marxists.org/history/erol/1960-1970/insurrection.pdf.

Przybylek, Leslie. 2017. "Picturing Protest: The Great Railroad Strike of 1877." Heinz History Center. July 18. https://www.heinzhistorycenter.org/blog/western-pennsylvania-history/picturing-protest-great-railroad-strike-1877.

Railroad Age Gazette. 1909. "A Letter of the Late Robert Pitcairn." October 29: 816–817.

"Railroad Strike of 1877 Historical Marker." 1997. ExplorePAhistory. September 23. http://explorepahistory.com/hmarker.php?markerId=1-A-1C1.

Railway Age Gazette. 1911. "Railway Officers." March 24: 708.

"Raymond Pitcairn." Wikipedia. https://en.wikipedia.org/wiki/Raymond_Pitcairn.

"Red Violin." Wikipedia. https://en.wikipedia.org/wiki/The_Red_Violin.

"Relief Effort." *Johnstown Area Heritage Association.* https://www.jaha.org/attractions/johnstown-flood-museum/flood-history/the-relief-effort/.

"Renovo, Pennsylvania." Wikipedia. https://en.wikipedia.org/wiki/Renovo,_Pennsylvania.

Report of the Committee appointed to investigate the railroad riots in July, 1877. 1878. Harrisburg, PA: Lane S. Hart, State Printer. https://archive.org/details/reportcommittee03goog/page/20/mode/2up?q=Pitcairn.

Rhoads, Willard B. 1960. "The Pennsylvania Canal." *Western Pennsylvania Historical Magazine,* September: 203–238.

"Robert Logan Anderson." Find a Grave. https://www.findagrave.com/memorial/101414676/robert-logan-anderson.

"Rolling Mill Mine." Wikipedia. https://en.wikipedia.org/wiki/Rolling_Mill_Mine.

Rule Book of the American Railway Association. 1905. https://babel.hathitrust.org/cgi/pt?id=nyp.33433007752037&seq=1.

Russell, David Lee. 2013. *Eastern Air Lines: A History, 1926–1991.* Jefferson, NC: McFarland

Salvatore, Nick. 1982. *Eugene V. Debs: Citizen and Socialist.* Urbana: University of Illinois Press.

Schooley, Tim. 2020. "Cliff Forrest's firm closes on buying Pittsburgh Brewing property." *Pittsburgh Business Times,* February 3. https://www.bizjournals.com/pittsburgh/news/2020/02/03/forrests-firm-closes-on-buying-brewery.html.

Schooley, Tim. 2021. "A shot to go with Iron City Beer? Pittsburgh Brewing Company to add distillery to new brewery." *Pittsburgh Business Times,* August 31. https://www.bizjournals.com/pittsburgh/news/2021/08/27/pittsburgh-brewing-co-to-add-distillery.html.

Schotter, H.W. 1927. *The Growth and Development of the Pennsylvania Railroad Company; a Review of the Charter and Annual Reports of the Pennsylvania Railroad Company 1846 to 1926, Inclusive.* Philadelphia: Allen, Lane & Scott. https://

babel.hathitrust.org/cgi/pt?id=uc1.%24b38943&view=1up&seq=8&q1=%22public+works%22.

Seibel, Kurt. "Was George Washington Here?" Pitcairn Borough. https://pitcairnborough.us/index.php/about-us/pitcairn-history.

Serling, Robert J. 1980. *From the Captain to the Colonel: An Informal History of Eastern Airlines.* New York: Dial Press.

"Set Present Pattern." JohnstownPA. https://www.johnstownpa.com/History/hist06.html.

Shank, William H. 1965. *The Amazing Pennsylvania Canals.* York, PA: Historical Society of York County.

Shannon, B. Clay. *Still Casting Shadows: A Shared Mosaic of U.S. History, 1620–1913.* Vol. I. https://archive.org/details/StillCastingShadowsASharedMosaicOfU.s.HistoryVol.I1620-1913.

Shappee, Nathan Daniel. 1940. "A History of Johnstown and the Great Flood of 1889: A Study of Disaster and Rehabilitation." Unpublished Doctoral Dissertation, University of Pittsburgh, Pittsburgh, PA. https://digitalarchives.powerlibrary.org/papd/islandora/object/papd%3Aacacc-jtf_1036.

Sheeline, William E. 1990. "Managing a Clan Worth $1 Billion." *Fortune,* June 4.

"Shorter Catechism." Orthodox Presbyterian Church. https://www.opc.org/sc.html.

Shugerman, Jed Handelsman. 2000. "The Floodgates of Strict Liability: Bursting Reservoirs and the Adoption of *Fletcher v. Rylands* in the Gilded Age." *Yale Law Journal,* 333–377. https://openyls.law.yale.edu/bitstream/handle/20.500.13051/9337/21_110YaleLJ333_2000_2001_.pdf.

Sigstedt, Cyriel. 1952. *The Swedenborg Epic: The Life and Works of Emanuel Swedenborg.* Bookman Associates. http://swedenborgdigitallibrary.org/ES/epic43.htm.

Simonoff, Evan, and Caren Chesler. 2016. "Pitcairn Today." *Private Wealth.* September 12. https://www.fa-mag.com/news/pitcairn-today-28888.html?section=49.

Simonton, Dean Keith. 2017. "The Science of Genius." *Scientific American,* March. https://www.scientificamerican.com/article/the-science-of-genius2/.

Skrabec, Quentin, Jr. 2007. *George Westinghouse: Gentle Genius.* New York: Algora Publishing.

Smith, Frank Kingston. 1981. *Legacy of Wings: The Harold F. Pitcairn Story.* Aronson.

Smith, Kevin. 2017. "Historic Pitcairn House in Pasadena under restoration." *Pasadena Star News,* August 28.

Smithsonian American Art Museum. "How the Railroad Won the War." https://americanexperience.si.edu/wp-content/uploads/2015/02/How-the-Railroad-Won-the-War.pdf.

"Socialist Labor Party of America." Wikipedia. https://en.wikipedia.org/wiki/Socialist_Labor_Party_of_America.

Solly, Meilan. 2018. "The True Story of Robert the Bruce, Scotland's 'Outlaw King.'" *Smithsonian Magazine,* November 8. https://www.smithsonianmag.com/history/true-story-robert-bruce-scotlands-outlaw-king-180970756/.

"SS *Daniel J. Morrell.*" Wikipedia. https://en.wikipedia.org/wiki/SS_Daniel_J._Morrell.

Starkey, Gertrude. 1877. "Letter." John and Gertrude Pitcairn Papers. Glencairn Museum Archives, September.

Starkey, Gertrude. 1879. "Letter to John Pitcairn." John and Gertrude Pitcairn Papers. Philadelphia, PA: Glencairn Museum Archives, December 11.

Stashower, Daniel. 2013. "The Unsuccessful Plot to Kill Abraham Lincoln." *Smithsonian Magazine,* February. https://www.smithsonianmag.com/history/the-unsuccessful-plot-to-kill-abraham-lincoln-2013956/.

"Steel Industry Executive Summary: March 2021." 2021. US Department of Commerce: International Trade Administration. March. https://www.trade.gov/sites/default/files/2021-03/exec%20sum-March%202021.pdf.

Stephenson, Clarence D. 1961. *Pennsylvania Canal—Indiana & Westmoreland Counties.* Marion Center, PA: Stephenson.

"Sun will be requested to rise and set by railroad time." 1883. *Environment & Society Portal.* November 21. http://www.environmentandsociety.org/exhibitions/cbq-railroad/sun-will-be-requested-rise-and-set-railroad-time.

Sutor, Dave. 2021. "Historical marker OK'd for Johnstown mine disaster site." *Johnstown Tribune-Democrat,* March 11.

Swank, George Thompson. 1889. "Before the Reservoir Came." *Johnstown Weekly Tribune,* June 14.

Swank, George Thompson. 1889. *Johnstown Tribune,* October 25.

Swank, James M. 1845. "Annual Report of the Board of Canal Commissioners of Pennsylvania with accompanying documents." 253–254.

Swedenborg Foundation. https://swedenborg.com/.

Swedenborg, Emanuel. 1952. *A Brief Exposition of the Doctrine of the New Church.* London: Swedenborg Society, Inc.

"Swedenborgian Groups." Encyclopedia.com. https://www.encyclopedia.com/religion/encyclopedias-almanacs-transcripts-and-maps/swedenborgian-groups.

"Swedenborg's Life." 2021. Swedenborg Foundation. https://swedenborg.com/emanuel-swedenborg/about-life/.

Tarbell, Ida Minerva. 1904. *The History of the Standard Oil Company.* Vol. I. New York: McClure, Phillips & Company.

"Terence Powderly." Ohio History Central. https://ohiohistorycentral.org/w/Terence_Powderly.

"Theodore Pitcairn." Wikipedia. https://en.wikipedia.org/wiki/Theodore_Pitcairn.

"Thomas Alexander Scott." *Biography-Your Dictionary.* https://biography.yourdictionary.com/thomas-alexander-scott.

"Thomas Alexander Scott." Find a Grave. https://www.findagrave.com/memorial/11428591/thomas-alexander-scott.

Thomas, Scott J. "Research 2." Benshoff Hill Water. https://www.benshoffhillwater.com/research-2.

Thompson, Robert Luther. 1947. *Wiring a Continent: The History of the Telegraph Industry in the United States, 1832–1866*. Princeton: Princeton University Press.

Time. 1954. "Religion: The Great Swede." June 28. http://content.time.com/time/subscriber/article/0,33009,860897,00.html.

Toy, Vivian S. 2012. "Zeus of the Catskills." *New York Times*, June 17: 2. https://www.nytimes.com/2012/06/17/realestate/zeus-of-the-catskills.html?smid=fb-share.

Unrau, Harlan D. 1979. *Historic Structure Report; The South Fork Dam; Historical Data; Johnstown Flood National Memorial; Pennsylvania; Package No. 124*. National Park Service. https://irma.nps.gov/DataStore/DownloadFile/474407.

"US Steel To Build $3B Mill in Arkansas." 2022. CBS News Pittsburgh. January 11. https://pittsburgh.cbslocal.com/2022/01/11/us-steel-3-billion-mill-arkansas/.

"Victor Heiser." Wikipedia. https://en.wikipedia.org/wiki/Victor_Heiser.

Wall, Joseph Frazier. 1970. *Andrew Carnegie*. Pittsburgh: University of Pittsburgh Press.

Warnes, Kathy. n.d. "Another Ford—John Baptiste Ford—Builds Downriver History." Meandering Michigan History. https://meanderingmichiganhistory.weebly.com/another-ford---john-baptiste-ford-builds-downriver-history.html.

"Was Johnny Appleseed a Real Person?" *Britannica*. https://www.britannica.com/story/was-johnny-appleseed-a-real-person.

"Welcome to Big Picture Steel." USSteel. https://www.ussteel.com/.

"Welcome to Pitcairn Borough." 2021. Pitcairn Borough. https://pitcairnborough.us/.

Westinghouse, George. 1910. "History of the Air Brake." *The Electric Journal*, Jan. 1911, 227–236.

Who Was Swedenborg? Performed by Jonathan Rose. https://www.youtube.com/watch?time_continue=480&v=HEa0e8AcS78&feature=emb_title.

"Why Did Raymond Pitcairn Build Glencairn? From Cloister Studio to Castle." 2022. Glencairn Museum News. February 23. https://glencairnmuseum.org/newsletter/2022/2/22/why-did-raymond-pitcairn-build-glencairn-from-cloister-studio-to-castle.

Wiley, Samuel T., ed. 1891. *Biographical and Historical Cyclopedia of Indiana and Armstrong Counties, Pennsylvania*. Philadelphia: J.M. Gresham & Co.

"William Henry Benade, Sr." Geni.com. https://www.geni.com/people/William-Benade-Sr/6000000020572608292?through=6000000020573068673.

"William P Morris (Morrison)." Geni.com. https://www.geni.com/people/William-Morris/6000000023133489968?through=6000000030551501053.

Wilson, William Bender. 1900. *General Superintendents of the Pennsylvania Railroad Division, Pennsylvania Railroad Co*. Philadelphia: Kensington Press.

Wilson, William Bender. 1899. *History of Pennsylvania Railroad Company*. Vol. 1. Philadelphia: Henry T. Coates & Company.

Wilson, William Bender. 1913. *Robert Pitcairn 1836–1909: In Memoriam*. Holmsburg, PA. https://digital.library.pitt.edu/islandora/object/pitt%3A00c679529m/viewer#page/6/mode/2up.

Woodward, Comer Vann. 1951. *Reunion and Reaction: The Compromise of 1877 and the End of Reconstruction*. Boston: Little, Brown and Company.

"Workingmen's party of the United States." Wikipedia. https://en.wikipedia.org/wiki/Workingmen%27s_Party_of_the_United_States.

"Wormley Conference." *Britannica*. https://www.britannica.com/event/Wormley-Conference.

Young, Patrick. 2011. "1848: The Year that Created Immigrant America." Long Island Wins. March 18. https://longislandwins.com/news/national/1848-the-year-that-created-immigrant-america/.

Index

Academy Award 195
Academy Boy's School 106
Academy of the New Church 4, 34, 71–72, 73, 78, 99, 101, 104–106, 112, 171, 174, 186–187, 190
Acropolis (Athens) 76
Adirondack Mountains 181
Advent Sunday School 106
Aiken, David, Jr. 60
Aiken, Thomas 60
Aitken, Andrew (Andrew Carnegie & Thomas Carnegie uncle) 18, 20
Aitken, Anne Morrison (Andrew Carnegie & Thomas Carnegie aunt) 18, 20, 33–34
Akhenaten 74
Akron, OH 20, 114
Alabama 44
Albany, New York 12, 20
Alexandria, VA 55
Allegheny (borough) 16
Allegheny City (North Side) 1, 5, 12, 15, 16–18, 20–21, 24–25, 41, 42, 53, 67, 120, 198
Allegheny County, PA 10, 89, 126
Allegheny County Court 60, 126, 167
Allegheny Mountains 1, 12, 37, 43, 78, 118
Allegheny Portage Railroad 13–15, 37–38, 41, 43, 118–119, 120, 124–125, 144, 151
Allegheny River 7, 13–14, 16, 56, 91, 92, 109, 113, 118, 198
Allegheny River Railroad 54–55, 58–59
Allegheny Tunnel 39, 41
Allegheny U.S. Arsenal (Pittsburgh) 48, 91
Allegheny Valley 33
Alnwick Grove, PA 169–170, 172
Altoona, PA 36–39, 41, 42, 44, 64, 89, 126, 151
Altoona Division (PRR) 64

Altoona Tribune (Newspaper) 63–64
An American Doctor's Odyssey: Adventures in Forty-Five Countries (book) 143
American Federation of Labor (AFL) 97
American Iron and Steel Institute 121
American Railway Association 158
American Silica Sand Company 114
American Society of Civil Engineers (ASCE) 155
Amerique (ship) 78
Ammons, Robert 88
Amtrak 196
Amtsbezirk, Switzerland 118
Ancient Church 72
Anderson, Maggie Forbes 19
Anderson, Maj. Robert 46
Anderson, Robert Logan 19
Angel's Camp, CA 71
Annapolis, MD 48–49
Annapolis Junction, MD 48–49
Annealing 110
Anti-Vaccination League 177–178
Antwerp, Belgium 180
AO tower 138
Apocalypsis Explicata (book) (*Apocalypse Explained*) 29
Appleseed, Johnny *see* Chapman, John
Arabic 74
Arcana Coelestia (book) 31, 171; *see also* Heavenly Mysteries or Secrets of Heaven
Arkansas 46
Army Telegraph Corps 48
Arthur, Chester A. 152
Aswan Dam 74
Athens, Greece 75–76
Atlanta, GA 37, 47, 192
Atlantic City, NJ 190
Atlantic Ocean 9

Augusta, GA 37
Austria 68
Autogiro 192–194

Baggaley, Ralph 65
Ballou, Franklin "Frank" 67–71
Baltic (ship) 23–24
Baltimore, MD 22, 23, 32, 43, 45, 47, 48–50, 83–85, 192
Baltimore and Ohio Railroad (B&O) 49, 83
Bank of California 69
Bank of the United States 11
Baptistery of St. John 104
Barnes, Annie *see* Benade, Annie
Barton, Clara 152
Basutoland (Lesotho) 188
Beauregard, Pierre Gustav Toutant 46
Beaux-Arts 170
Beaver, James Addams 152
Beaver, PA 20
Becker, Max J. 155–156
Bedford, PA 32
Bedouins 74–75
Beechwood Hall (William Frew home) 163
Beethoven, Ludwig van 208
Beirut, Lebanon 75
Belgium 179–180
Bell's Auction House 32
Benade, Amelia 100
Benade, Andrew 34–35
Benade, Annie 101, 112
Benade, Kate Gibbs 172
Benade, Maria Henry 34
Benade, William Henry 34–35, 43, 53, 67–68, 71–78, 99–101, 102, 104–106, 112–113, 171–172, 182
Benade Hall 174–175, 178
Benjamin Franklin Hotel (Philadelphia) 45; *see also* Continental Hotel
Bennett, Edwin 23–24
Bennett, James 20, 23
Bennett and Brothers 20

229

Index

Berkeley Light Infantry 83
Bessemer (process, converter) 121, 123
Bethlehem (city in Israel) 75
Bethlehem, PA 34
Bible 28, 30–31, 41, 60, 72, 75, 94, 189
Big Bonanza 70
Birmingham (Pittsburgh) 20, 107
Birmingham, England 73, 104
Bishop of Skara 27
bituminous coal 16, 119
Blackstock Mill 23
Blarney (Castle, Stone) 72–73
Blue Grotto 104
Board of Directors (New Church) 172, 182
Board of Directors (Pitcairn-Crabbe Foundation) 168
Board of Directors (PPG) 110–111, 113, 117, 182
Board of Directors (PRR) 50
Board of Directors (Westinghouse Air Brake) 65, 80, 162
Bok, Edward W. 177
Bolivar, PA 145
Bolivia 180
Bonnie Brae 173
Booth, John Wilkes 50
Boston, MA 15, 32, 43, 179, 184
Boston Fire 80
Both Sides of the Vaccination Question (book) 178
Bow Ridge Tunnel 14–15
Bower, Mary 107
Braddock, PA 144
Bradley, Joseph P. 81–82
Brest, France 68
Bridal Veil Falls (Yosemite) 71
Bridge #6 139
Brienz, Switzerland 104
Brinton, Gen. Robert Morton 89, 91
British New Church 104, 106
Broad and Pine Street Station (Philadelphia, PA) 45
Brooklyn, NY 10
Brooks, David 24–26, 36
Brotherhood of Locomotive Engineers 88
Brotherhood of Locomotive Firemen 97
Brown, John 48
Brown County, OH 9
Brunelleschi (architect) 104
Brussels, Belgium 179–180
Bryn Athyn 3–4, 7, 11, 169, 173–174, 178, 180–182, 184–186, 188–191, 195, 199, 206–208
bubonic plague 176
Buffalo, New York 12, 20
Buffington, Maj. A.R. 91

Bulletin (magazine) 163
Bureau of Labor 98
Burnham, N.C. 53, 72
Burton Road Church (London) 171
Buttermilk Falls (PA) 138
Byrne, Thomas V. 84

Cairncarque 7, 60, 62, 163–164, 166–167
Cairncrest 4, 191, 194, 208
Cairnwood 4, 54, 103, 169–173, 178, 186, 190, 206–207
Cairo, Egypt 74–75
Calaveras County, CA 71
Caldwell, John, Jr. 130
California 44, 70, 71, 81167,
Calvert Street Station (Baltimore) 45
Calvin, John 2
Cambria City (Johnstown) 148
Cambria County, PA 32, 118, 126, 146, 155
Cambria Iron Works 120–121, 122, 123, 130, 136, 137, 139
Cambria Mills 147
Cambria Tribune (newspaper) 122
Camden, NJ 109
Camden and Amboy Railroad 37
Camden Station (Baltimore) 45, 84–85
Cameron, Simon 47–50
Campanile (bell tower) 104
Canaan 75
Canada 53, 181
Canal Commissioners 124
Carbon Steel Company 166
Card, W.W. 65
Carnegie, Andrew ("Andra" "Andy") 3, 5, 7, 18–21, 23–26, 34, 36, 41, 42, 44, 48–52, 64, 67, 69, 99, 101, 121, 124, 129, 130–132, 144, 148–149, 157, 162, 165, 173, 198
Carnegie, George Lauder (Thomas Carnegie son) 130
Carnegie, Lucy (Thomas Carnegie wife) 24
Carnegie, Margaret "Mag" (Andrew Carnegie & Thomas Carnegie mother) 18–20, 23, 33
Carnegie, Thomas Morrison 20–21, 52, 129, 130
Carnegie, William (Andrew Carnegie & Thomas Carnegie father) 17–20, 24, 33
Carnegie Brothers 130
Carnegie Hero Fund 2
Carnegie Institute of Pittsburgh 130, 167

Carnegie Library Commission 163
Carnegie Museum of Natural History 2
Carnegie Music Hall (Pittsburgh) 163
Carnegie Steel Company 130
Carpenter, C.A. 136
Carrère & Hastings (architects) 170
Carroll, John Lee 84–85
Carson City, NV 69–70
Cassatt, Alexander 58, 64–65, 89, 164
Cathedral Rocks (Yosemite) 71
Cather, Willa 163
Catskills 185
The Celebrated Jumping Frog of Calaveras County (book) 71
Central Park (Johnstown) 118
Century of Heroes (book) 2
Chambersburg, PA 50
Chapman, John (Johnny Appleseed) 33
Charleroi, PA 114
Charleroi Coal Company 114
Charleroi Plate Glass Company 114
Charleston, SC 46
Chattanooga, TN 156
Cherry Street Church and School (Philadelphia) 73, 101
Chesapeake and Delaware Canal 37
Chesapeake Bay 23, 48
Chester, PA 78
Chestnut Ridge, PA 144
Chicago, IL 68, 71, 94, 97, 155, 170
Chicago Board of Trade 94
Chicago Fire 80
Childs, Walter Cameron 67–68, 71, 104, 112, 169
China 56
Chinatown (San Francisco) 69
Choir Hall 184
cholera 17, 176
Christian church 30, 77
Christie's Auction House 195
Church of Scotland 33
Church of the Annunciation 75
Church of the Holy Sepulcher 75
Church of the Nativity 75
Church of the New Jerusalem 3, 172, 182–183, 185, 188–189, 194, 208
Cincinnati, OH 43, 152, 155
City of Berlin (ship) 102
Civil War 7, 44, 46–47, 50, 52, 64, 82, 91, 94, 121
Cleopatra (rail car) 163
Cleveland, Grover 97
Cleveland, OH 20, 56, 58, 83

Cleveland & Cincinnati Express 166
Cliff House 69–70
Cobh, Ireland 72
Coinage Act of 1873 80
Colchester, England 178
Coleman, Neil 126–127, 129, 139, 156–157
Colfax, Schuyler 81
Collier Trophy 193
Collyn 173
Cologne 104
Columbia, PA 13–14, 56, 124
Columbia-Philadelphia Railroad 37, 43
Columbia River 70–71
Commercial Department (PPG) 115, 180
Commercial Gazette (newspaper) 145
Commissioner of Health (PA) 176
Committee on Public Health and Sanitation (PA Legislature) 177
Committee on Public Safety (MD) 49
Committee on Train Rules 158
Commonwealth of Pennsylvania 37, 109, 168
Commonwealth vs. Hunt (U.S. Supreme Court case) 97
Comstock Lode 70
Conemaugh, PA 43, 146
Conemaugh Furnace, PA 146
Conemaugh Gap 123, 134, 145
Conemaugh Old Town 118
Conemaugh River 7, 13–14, 118, 123, 133, 136, 144–146, 151, 154
Conemaugh Viaduct 38, 139–140, 151
Confederate (Civil War) 46–48, 82
Congress, U.S. 22, 32, 81–82, 97–98
Conjugal Love (book) 76–77, 100
Connellsville, PA 103
Consolidated Rail Corporation (Conrail) 196
Consolidated Virginia Mine 70
Continental Hotel (Philadelphia) 99; *see also* Benjamin Franklin Hotel
Cooke, Sir William 22
Coopersdale, PA 123, 148
Cork, Ireland 72
Corona Chemical Company 116
Corry, PA 54–56
Coryville, PA 78, 99
Council of the Laity (New Church) 105, 172

Courcelles, Belgium 179
Court of Common Pleas (Allegheny County, PA) 60, 126, 167
Court of Quarter Sessions (Montgomery County, PA) 181
COVID-19 176
Crabbe, Elizabeth (Robert Pitcairn granddaughter) 166
Crabbe, Susan Lee (Robert Pitcairn granddaughter *see* Hunt, Susan Lee Crabbe
Crabbe, Susan Pitcairn (Robert Pitcairn daughter) *see* Pitcairn, Susan Blanche
Crabbe, Victor Lee (Robert Pitcairn son-in-law) 166
Cram, Ralph Adams 179, 184
Credit Mobilier Scandal 81
Creighton, PA 102, 107, 109–111, 114, 197–198
Cresson, PA 40, 156
Crystal City, MO 114
Crystal City Plate Glass Company 114
CSX Transportation 196
Culp, Charles 138
Cumberland, MD 84, 87
Cumberland Island, GA 24
Cumberland Valley Railroad (CVRR) 50
Curtin, Andrew 47
Curtiss Aircraft 190
Curtiss Flying School 190
Curtiss Wright 193

dahabeah 74–75
The Dalles, OR 71
Damascus 75
Damask 17–18
SS *Daniel J. Morrell* (ship) 137
Danville, KY 107
da Vinci, Leonardo 28
Davis, Amelia *see* Benade, Amelia
Davis, Clara (John Pitcairn daughter-in-law) 190–191
Davis, David 81
De Charms Hall 175
De Coelo et ejus Mirabilibus et de Inferno (book) 29
Dead Sea 75
Debs, Eugene 97
Deckert, Frank 138
Declaration of Independence (U.S.) 191
Decoration Day 137
Delaware County, PA 37
Demerara, Guiana 32
Democratic 81–82
De Pitcarne, John 9
Derry, PA 87
Dewees, Mr. 91

Diamond Plate Glass Company 114
Dickens, Charles 15
District of Columbia Volunteers 49
Ditzler Color Company 197
Divine Providence 173, 174
Divine Revelation 173, 183
Dornick Point (Johnstown) 123
double-header 87–89, 96
Downingtown, PA 45
Druses 75
Duff, Peter 107
Duff's Mercantile College (Pittsburgh) 107
Duncannon, PA 13
Duncan's Island 13
Duncansville, PA 36
Dunfermline, Scotland 17
Dunlevy, R.H. 11
Duomo (Florence) 104
Durban Society 188
Dynamics of the Soul's Domain (book) *see Oeconomia Regni Animalis*

East Birmingham (Pittsburgh) 20
East Conemaugh, PA 136, 138–139
East Liverpool, OH 20
East Pittsburgh Works 144
Eastern Airlines 193
Eastern Division Canal 13–14, 43, 124
Eastern Telegraph Line 25
Ebensburg, PA 118
Edgar Thomson Works 121, 144, 155–156
SS *Edmund Fitzgerald* (ship) 137
Edward Ford Plate Glass Company 116
Egypt 72, 74, 104, 186
Egyptian Museum 74, 77
Ehrenfeld, Emma 138
Eisenhower, Dwight D. 187
El Capitan (Yosemite) 71
El Greco 188
Elder, Cyrus 122, 137
Electoral Commission 81
Elgar, Edward 208
Elwood, IN 114
Emerson, Ralph Waldo 32
England 3, 11, 22, 27, 53, 68, 71, 73, 103, 108, 157, 208
English Channel 179
Erie, PA 52
Erie Canal 12, 20
Erie Railroad 56–58, 79, 82
Erskine Successionist Church 33
Exodus (Bible) 29
Ezekiel Tower 184

Fairmount Park (Philadelphia) 99
Falkland Islands 180
The Fallacy of Vaccination (magazine article) 177
family tree 201–205
Farman biplane 191
Farrington, Ernest 102
Faulkner, C.J. 83
The Feeding of the Five Thousand (window at Shadyside Presbyterian Church) 160–161
Fellows, W.A. 136
Felton, Samuel 45
Ferry, Thomas W. 81
Fetters Mill B&B 206
Fidelity Title & Trust 165, 167
Fife, Sheriff R.C. 89
Fifth Regiment 84
Filibuster 82
First National Bank (Johnstown) 121
Flood City 133
Florence, Italy 104
Florida 24, 44, 81–82
Forbes (magazine) 194
Ford, Edward 107, 110, 112–116, 172
Ford, Emory Low 107, 110, 112–116, 172
Ford, John Baptiste 107–111, 113–114, 199
Ford, Jonathan 107
Ford City, PA 113–114
Ford's Theatre 50
Forrest, Cliff 198
Fort Monroe 86
Fort Sumter, SC 46
Fort Wayne, IN 42–43
Fortune 500 197
Fourth U.S. Artillery 84
France 68, 76, 103, 179
Francis, James B. 155–156
Franciscus, George C. 43, 45, 50
Franklin, Benjamin 32
Franklin, PA 33
Franklin Street (Johnstown) 123
Franklin Street (Pittsburgh) 20
Fredonia, NY 68
Freeport, PA 118
French, W.H. 84
French Renaissance 170
Frew, William F. 163
Frick, Henry Clay 3, 126, 129–130, 148, 157, 163
Fteley, Alphonse 155
Fulton, John 136, 137

Gale, Leonard 22
Galicia, Poland 78
Galilei, Galileo 28
Gallitzin, PA 38–41, 43
Gallitzin Tunnels 39–41, 43
Galveston, TX 94, 150
Garden of Gethsemane 75
Garrett, David 87
Garrett, John W. 79, 83
Gaspe Peninsula 181
Gateway Union School District 160
Gatling gun 89, 91
Gautier Mill 139, 147
Gay, Edward F. 54, 56, 58
genealogy 201
General Agent (PRR) 36, 66, 158
General Assembly (Knights of Labor) 97
General Assembly (New Church) 18
General Assembly (Pennsylvania) 88
General Church 4, 178, 181, 183, 188
General Church of Pennsylvania 105–106
General Church of the Advent 171
General Church of the New Jerusalem 3, 172, 182–183, 185, 188, 189
General Convention (New Church) 71, 78, 99, 104–105, 106
General Convention of the New Jerusalem 53, 189
General Motors 193
General Time Convention 158
Genesis (Bible) 29
Geneva, Switzerland 152
Georgia 24, 44, 192
Georgia Railroad 37
Germaine (ship) 72
Germany 11, 64, 68, 179–180
Gershwin, George 208
Ghiberti's Gates of Paradise 104
giant sequoia 71
Gibbs, Kate *see* Benade, Kate Gibbs
Gillinder, William T. 23–24
Giza pyramids 74
Gladish, Richard R. 115–116
Glasgow (Scottish university) 32
Glasgow, Scotland 19, 32
Glass, Col. John P. 25
Glen, James 32, 33
Glen Eyre (railroad car) 162
Glen Tonche (Zeus of the Catskills) 185
Glenhurst (Glenn home, Bryn Athyn) 171
Glenn, Mildred (John Pitcairn daughter-in-law) 178

Glenn, Robert 102, 112, 169–170, 171, 172–173, 178
Glenn Hall 175
Gloucester Cathedral (England) 208
God 3, 8, 22, 28, 29, 30–31, 156, 178, 188–189, 199
Golden Dome 75
Gompers, Samuel 97
Gothenburg (Sweden) 29
Gothic style 179, 184
Gould, Jay 56
Gourley, H.I. 148
Government Bridge (Rock Island, IL) 68
Grandview Cemetery (Johnstown) 137, 141, 143, 150
Granger Laws 79–80
Grant, Ulysses S. 55–56, 80–81
Grant Hill (Pittsburgh) 65
Great Britain 9, 11
Great Depression 80
Great Hall (at *Glencairn*) 186, 207–208
Great Lakes 23, 43, 137
Great Western Gun Works 92
Greece 72, 75–76, 186
Greenback-Labor Party 97
Greenback Party 97
Greensburg, PA 32–33, 36, 144
Greenville, IN 107
Guthrie, George W. 16
Guyana 32

Hagerstown, MD 50
The Hague 104, 179–180
Hahnemann Medical College 63–64
Hailman Lodge (Masons) 165
Halley, Edmund 27
Hamburg, Germany 11, 64
Hanks, Henry Garber 70
Hargrove, John 32
Harmony Street (Pittsburgh) 20
Harpers Ferry 48, 128
Harper's Weekly (magazine) 92–93
Harris, Gus 87–88
Harrisburg, PA 7, 12, 32, 37, 38, 41, 43, 45, 47–48, 50–51, 52, 58, 64, 95, 162, 166
Hartranft, John Frederick 87, 89, 94–95
Haupt, Herman 38–39, 78
Hayes, Rutherford B. 81–82, 83, 85, 88, 152
Hays, W.N. 145
Heavenly Mysteries or Secrets of Heaven (book) 29; *see also* Arcana Coelestia
Heidelberg, Germany 104
Heiser, Victor 139–143
Henderson, Ailie Ferguson 19

Index

Henderson, Bruce 3–4
Herbert, James R. 84
Hero Fund 2, 165
Hice, Andrew 87
Hill of Cohesion 174
Hill of Unity 174
Hillbrook 173
History of Johnstown (dissertation) 122
History of the Pennsylvania Railroad Company 64
History of the South Fork Dam 124, 127
History of the Standard Oil Company 58
Hitchcock, E.A. 115
Hite, Ellen 155
H.L. Taylor Company 101
Hobart, Garret Augustus 163
Hogan, Catherine Kitty Morrison (Andrew Carnegie & Thomas Carnegie aunt) 20, 33, 99
Hogan, Maria (Andrew Carnegie & Thomas Carnegie cousin) 99, 173, 190
Hogan, Thomas (Andrew Carnegie & Thomas Carnegie uncle) 18, 20, 33–34, 99
Holland 104, 179, 189
Holley, Alexander Lyman 121
Hollidaysburg, PA 13–14, 38, 41, 43, 118, 120, 124, 144
Holy Ghost 30
Holy Land 3, 72, 75, 104
Holy Spirit 30
Homeopathic 43, 51, 73, 176
Homestead Strike 79
Homewood Cemetery 167–168
Homewood Station 144
Hoover, Herbert 130, 193
Horne, Durbin 130
Horseshoe Curve 38–41, 43, 78, 196
Horsham, PA 193
House of Nobles (Sweden) 28
Howard Plate Glass Company 114
Hudson River 20
Humboldt Mountains 69
Hunt, Susan Lee Crabbe (Robert Pitcairn granddaughter) 167
Huntington Valley, PA 170, 172

Illinois 10, 19, 79, 81, 152
Imperial Refining Company 56–57, 59, 67, 68
Independence Hall (Philadelphia) 45, 50
Indianapolis Sentinel (newspaper) 158
influenza 176

Inman Steamship Company 103
International Swedenborg Congress 178
Interstate Commerce Act 79
Interstate Commerce Commission 79
Iowa 79
Iron City Beer 198
Irwin, PA 144
Isabella Furnace
Isabella Street (Allegheny City) 67
Isle of Capri 104
Israel 75

Jackson, Andrew 11
Jaffa (Israel) 75
Japan 189
Jay Cooke & Company 80
J.B. Ford Company 113
Jefferson, Thomas 32
Jefferson Medical College 142
Jenner, Edward 176
Jericho 75
Jerusalem 75–76
Jesus 30–31
Jewett, Hugh J. 79
John Beck Academy 34
John the Apostle 75
Johns, Joseph 118
Johnstone, Scotland 7, 9–11
Johnstown, PA 5, 7, 13, 37, 38–39, 118–126, 130, 132
Johnstown Flood (1889) 2, 7, 43, 126–127, 133–157, 198
Johnstown Flood (book) 127
Johnstown Flood Museum 149
Johnstown Gas Company 147
Johnstown Street Railway Company 147
Johnstown Tribune (newspaper) 138
Johnstown Water Company 147
Johnstown's Flood of 1889: Power Over Truth and the Science Behind the Disaster (book) 156
Jungfrau Mountain (Switzerland) 104
Juniata Division Canal 13–14, 124
Justice family 42

Kalama, WA 71
Keller, Helen 32
Kelly Act 192
Kendall, Amos 22
Kentucky 32
Kentucky Volunteer Homespun Regiment 107
Key, David M. 82
King Alexander III (Scotland) 9

King Charles XII (Sweden) 28
King of Johnstown 121–122, 136
Kirschler, Charles F. 16
Kiskiminetas River (PA) 13
Kitchener, Canada 180
Kleinwelka, Saxony, Prussia 34
Kloman & Company 92
Knights of Labor 97
Knights Templar 165
Knox, Philander 130–132, 156, 163
Kokomo, IN 114
Kroonland (ship) 180

Labor Day 97
Ladies' Home Journal (magazine) 177
Lake Conemaugh (Western Canal Reservoir) 43, 124–126, 128, 132, 135, 137, 139
Lake Erie 12, 20, 52, 128
Lake Huron 137
Lake Titicaca (South America) 180–181
Lamon, Ward M. 45
Lancaster, PA 72, 164
Lanzone Collection 77–78
Larrabee, Mr. 95
Latrobe, PA 144
Latshaw, William 119
Lauder, Anna Maria
Lauder, George "Dod" (Andrew Carnegie & Thomas Carnegie uncle) 19
Lawrence Visscher Boyd (architects) 178
Le Havre, France 78
Le Roi Road (Point Breeze) 67
Ledger Book (South Fork Fishing & Hunting Club) 129
Lee, Robert E. 48
Lehigh and Susquehanna Railroad 63
Leishman, John G.A. 130
Leper Hospital 75
leprosy 75
Lewis, Enoch 42, 45
Libbey-Owens-Ford Glass Company (L-O-F) 116
Liberty Avenue (Pittsburgh) 65, 91–93
Library of Congress 46, 122, 134, 142, 159
limestone 109
Lincoln, Abraham 7, 44–46, 47, 50, 56, 99
Lincoln, Willie 50
Lincoln-Courier (newspaper) 163
Lincoln in the Telegraph Office (book) 49
Lindsey, Mr. 90–91
Lititz, PA 34
Little Conemaugh River

234 Index

(Johnstown) 118, 124, 126, 133, 135, 151, 154
Liverpool, England 11, 77, 102, 104, 180
Lock Haven, PA 52
Lombaert, Herman J. 36, 41–42
London (England) 30, 32, 68, 73, 101, 103–104, 113, 118, 171–172, 178, 179, 195
Long Bridge (Virginia) 50
Lookout Mountain, TN 156
Lord 3, 28, 31, 35, 42, 173, 174, 182–183, 188
Lord Byron 42
Lord's Divine Mercy 28
Lord's New Church 188, 189, 208
Los Angeles, CA 69
Louisiana 44, 81–82
Lower Union Mill 92
Loyal Hanna Coal and Coke Company 101, 103
Loyalhanna Creek (PA) 144
Lucaj, Gjilberta 207–208
Lucerne, Switzerland 112
Lusitania (ship) 180
Lycabettus, Greece 76

Macbeth 25
Macgregor, William 18
Malone, Frances 152
Mannheim, Germany 104
Mansour, Lewis 74–75
Marines, U.S. 48, 86
Market Street (Chicago) 94
Marseilles, France 76
Martin, Robert 18
Martinsburg, WV 83–84, 87, 89
Maryland 48, 49, 83, 84
Maryland Committee of Public Safety 49
Maryland National Guard 84–85
Maryland Senate 49
Massachusetts Association (New Church) 105
Matthews, Henry M. 83
Mauritshuis Museum (The Hague) 104
McCallin, Mayor (Pittsburgh) 148
McCargo, David 25
McClellan, George B. 58
McClernand, John Alexander 46
McCullough, David 122, 124, 127, 133
McDowell, N.M. 136
McEwan, Agnes (Robert Pitcairn & John Pitcairn mother) 10
McEwan, Mary 53
McEwan, Sallie 53

McGee, Christopher 163
McKean, Gov. Thomas (PA) 32
McKinley, Ida 7, 162–163
McKinley, Pres. William 7, 64, 130, 162–164
McLanahan, James 118
McLean, George A., Jr. 44
Medici Chapels 104
Mediterranean Sea 75
Melchers, Richard 179–180
Mellon, Andrew W. 130
Mellon, Richard Beatty 167
Mellon, Thomas 24
Mendelssohn, Felix 195, 208
Mesopotamia 186
Methodism 30
Metropolitan Museum of Art (New York City) 188
Mexican-American War 69
Mexico 69
Michael Tower 184
Michigan 33, 152
Middle Division (of Philadelphia and Erie Railroad) 52, 54
Middle Division (of PRR) 42, 50–52
Mifflin, PA 43
Miller Farm (Titusville, PA) 55
Milwaukee, WI 116
Mineral Point, PA 38, 138
Minneapolis, MN 152
Minnesota 79
Mississippi 44
Mississippi River 68, 141
Monaco 103
Monet, Claude 188
Monongahela River 14–15, 20, 65, 118
Monongahela Valley 144
Monroeville, PA 160
Montgomery County, PA 11, 112, 181
Moravian 34–35
Moreland Township, PA 181
Morley, R.F. 50
Morrell, Daniel Johnson 120–122, 129–130, 132, 136, 137
Morrellville Borough, PA 122, 148
Morris, Maria (Andrew Carnegie & Thomas Carnegie aunt) 20
Morris, Robert 32
Morris, William (Andrew Carnegie & Thomas Carnegie uncle) 20
Morrison, Margaret "Mag" (Andrew Carnegie & Thomas Carnegie mother) *see* Carnegie, Margaret
Morse, Samuel F.B. 22
Moses 75
Mount Tonche, NY 185

Mount Vesuvius 103
Mountain District (of PRR) 36
Mountain House, PA 41, 124
Mountain House Hotel (Cresson, PA) 156
Munn v. Illinois 79
Munro, Janet 9
Museum of Antiquities (Leiden) 104

Nashville, TN 47
Natal, South Africa 188
National Air Races 191
National Anti-Vaccination League 177
National Bank (Johnstown) 121, 122
National Grange 79
National Guard (Maryland) 84–85
National Guard (Pennsylvania) 89
National Historic District 4
National Historic Landmark 207
National Park Service 39, 128, 132, 207
National Plate Glass Association (NPGA) 115
National Refiners' Association (NRA) 59, 82
Nazareth, Israel 75
Nazareth, PA 34–35
Nazareth Hall 35
Nefertiti 74
Nevada 69, 81
New Albany, IN 107–109, 111
New Albany Glass Works 107
New Albany Rolling Mills 108
New Castle, PA 20
New Christian Religion (book) 35
New Church Educational Institute 104, 106
New Church Life (magazine) 4, 178
New England 53, 178
New Era (newspaper) 164
New Florence, PA 145
New Jerusalem Church 30, 33, 34, 53, 59, 67–69, 189, 194, 208
New Jerusalem General Convention 53
New Jerusalem Society 32
New Orleans, LA 107
New Portage Railroad (PA) 37–38, 41, 43
New Portage Tunnel (PA) 43
New York (state) 12, 20, 81, 102, 110, 115, 157, 181
New York Central Railroad 56–57, 58, 79, 82, 196
New York City 10, 19–20, 49, 51, 56–57, 58, 68, 71, 76–78, 81, 97,

Index

99, 100, 102–103, 104, 155, 162, 163, 165, 166, 170, 180, 192
New York Plate Glass Company 102, 107, 109–110
New York Stock Exchange 80
New York Sun (newspaper) 155
Newport News, VA 190
Newton, Sir Isaac 27
Niagara Falls 99, 173
Nicolay, John 44
Nile River 74–75
Nineveh, PA 134, 145, 155
Norbiton, England 101
Norfolk, VA 86
Norfolk Southern Railroad 196
North (Civil War) 47
North Berwick, ME 120
North Carolina 46, 47, 190, 192
North Oxford, MA 152
North Side (Pittsburgh) *see* Allegheny City
Northern Central Railroad 63
Nubian Desert 75

Oakland (Pittsburgh) 162, 163, 167
Oakland, CA 69
Oeconomia Regni Animalis (book) 27
Ogle, Hettie 138, 149
Ohio 33, 48, 60, 81
Ohio & Erie Canal
Ohio Falls 108
Ohio River 20, 107, 118, 152
Oil City, PA 55, 56, 58, 68
Oil Creek and Allegheny River Railroad 54–55, 58–59
Oil Creek Railroad 54–57
Oil Springs 69
Old Church 76–77
Old City Hall (Pittsburgh) 148
Oliver, Henry W. (Harry) 25
Olympia, WA 71
Omaha, NE 68
On Heaven and Its Wonders and on Hell (book) *see De Coelo et ejus Mirabilibus et de Inferno*
Opera Philosophica et Mineralia (book) 27
Oregon 44, 70, 81
O'Reilly, Henry 23
O'Reilly Telegraph 25
Osceola, IL 19

Pacific Ocean 9, 69
Packard (automobile) 207
Packsaddle (Johnstown, PA) 134
Palace Car Company 97
Palace Hotel (San Francisco) 69
Palestine 75
Panama Canal 180

Panhandle Railroad 65
Panic of 1837 11, 17–18
Panic of 1873 80–81, 97
Paris, France 68, 69, 74, 76, 78, 103–104, 112–113, 179, 188
Paris Exposition 121
Parker-Adams, Lisa 207
Parliament (England) 72
Parsons, Albert 94, 97
Parthenon 75
Pasadena, CA 167
Paterson, NJ 10
Patmos (Greece) 75
Patterson, Dr. Stuart 167
Patton Paint Company 116
Pearson, Gen. Albert 89, 91
Pelton, Col. William T. 81
Pendleton, Willard 186
Pendleton, Bishop William Frederic 171–172, 173, 176, 182
Penn Avenue (Pittsburgh) 91
Penn-Central Railroad 196
Pennsylvania 177, 207
Pennsylvania & Ohio Canal
Pennsylvania Association (New Church) 104–105
Pennsylvania Canal 43, 119
Pennsylvania Flood Relief Commission 148
Pennsylvania Legislature 45, 58, 124, 177
Pennsylvania Main Line Canal (PMLC) 12–14, 16, 20, 37, 43, 118–120, 124, 125
Pennsylvania Railroad (PRR) 3, 5, 7, 36–44, 47, 51, 52, 60, 64, 66, 68, 78, 79, 82–83, 88, 96, 112, 120, 123, 124–125, 132, 140–141, 144, 147, 162, 164–165, 196, 198
Pennypack Creek 169
Periere (ship) 68
peritonitis 173, 178
Perryville, MD 48–49
Peru 180
Peters, Col. 84
Petroleum Center, PA 56
Pharaoh Amenhotep IV 74
Pharaoh Ramses V 176
Philadelphia, PA 3–4, 5, 7, 11–15, 16, 20, 22–23, 26, 32, 35, 38, 41–43, 44–45, 48–49, 50–51, 52, 56, 63, 68, 71–72, 74, 89, 94, 99, 101, 102, 111–112, 118, 120, 124–125, 142, 147, 152, 169–171, 172, 174, 178, 190–192, 207–208
Philadelphia and Columbia Railroad 37
Philadelphia and Erie Railroad (P&E RR) 52, 54–56
Philadelphia Company 130
Philadelphia Division (of PRR) 43, 45, 50

Philadelphia, Newtown & New York Railroad 169
Philadelphia, Wilmington, and Baltimore Railroad 45
Philippine Islands 143
Philosophical and Metallurgical Works (book) *see Opera Philosophica et Mineralia*
Phipps, Henry (Harry) 101
Phipps, Henry, Jr. 130
Phoenix Hall (Pittsburgh) 88
Pickerell, W.H. 138
Pinkerton, Allan 45–46, 99
Pinkerton guards 94
Piper and Shiffler Company
Piraeus, Greece 75
Pisa, Italy 103
Pitcairn, Agnes 15
Pitcairn, Alexander (Robert Pitcairn & John Pitcairn grandfather) 9
Pitcairn, Alexander (Robert Pitcairn & John Pitcairn uncle) 34
Pitcairn, Artemas 112, 113, 116
Pitcairn, Catherine (Robert Pitcairn & John Pitcairn sister) 10
Pitcairn, Elizabeth (John Pitcairn great-granddaughter) 195, 207–208
Pitcairn, Elizabeth (Robert Pitcairn granddaughter) 166
Pitcairn, Elizabeth (Robert Pitcairn wife) 42, 60, 61, 66, 160, 163, 166–168, 198
Pitcairn, Gabriele (John Pitcairn granddaughter) 186
Pitcairn, Gertrude (John Pitcairn wife) 4, 43, 68, 100–104, 111–112, 170, 173, 182, 187, 190, 199, 203–204, 207
Pitcairn, Harold Frederick (John Pitcairn son) 4, 172, 173, 178, 181, 190–194, 206–208
Pitcairn, Helen (Robert Pitcairn & John Pitcairn half-sister) 9
Pitcairn, Hugh (Robert Pitcairn & John Pitcairn brother) 11, 21, 63–64, 102, 201
Pitcairn, Janet (Robert Pitcairn & John Pitcairn sister) 9–10
Pitcairn, Janet Currie (Robert Pitcairn & John Pitcairn grandmother) 9
Pitcairn, John, Sr. (Robert Pitcairn & John Pitcairn father) 9–11, 15, 20, 34
Pitcairn, Lillian (Robert Pitcairn daughter) 42, 60
Pitcairn, Margaret (Robert Pitcairn & John Pitcairn sister) 11, 72, 101

Index

Pitcairn, Marijke (John Pitcairn daughter-in-law) 187–189
Pitcairn, Mary (Robert Pitcairn & John Pitcairn aunt) 53
Pitcairn, Raymond (John Pitcairn son) 3, 112, 173, 176, 178–179, 184–187, 190, 194, 207
Pitcairn, Robert (Robert Pitcairn & John Pitcairn uncle) 34
Pitcairn, Robert, Jr. (Robert Pitcairn son) 66
Pitcairn, Sallie (Robert Pitcairn & John Pitcairn aunt) 53
Pitcairn, Susan Blanche (Robert Pitcairn daughter) 62, 166–167
Pitcairn, Thelemasou (John Pitcairn son) 171
Pitcairn, Theodore (John Pitcairn son) 171, 173, 178, 180–181, 187–189, 190, 194, 195, 208
Pitcairn, Vera (John Pitcairn daughter) 112, 173, 178, 190
Pitcairn, Walter Childs (John Pitcairn son) 112
Pitcairn, PA 159, 160
Pitcairn Aircraft 191–192
Pitcairn Company 194
Pitcairn-Crabbe Foundation 167–168
Pitcairn Field No. 2 191, 193
Pitcairn Flying Field 191
Pitcairn Varnish Company 116
Pitti Palace 104
Pittsburgh 120
Pittsburgh Brewing Company 198
Pittsburgh, Cincinnati, and St. Louis Railroad 63
Pittsburgh Commercial Gazette (newspaper) 145
Pittsburgh Division (PRR) 7, 44, 51, 52, 64, 79, 132, 158, 164; *see also* Western Division
Pittsburgh, Fort Wayne, and Chicago Railroad 42
Pittsburgh New Church 62, 67
Pittsburgh Opera House
Pittsburgh Plate Glass Company (see also PPG) 3, 5, 7, 110–117, 172, 179–180, 182, 185–186, 196–199
Pittsburgh Post-Gazette (newspaper) 167
Pittsburgh Press (newspaper) 164
Pittsburgh Relief Committee 148
Pittsburgh Theater 25
Pittsburgh-to-Johnstown Canal 124–125; *see also* Western Division

Plot of the Unknown (Grandview Cemetery) 150
PNC Park (Pittsburgh) 15
pneumonia 181
Point (Johnstown) 118, 123
Point Breeze (Pittsburgh) 67
Point Stadium (Johnstown) 118, 154
Poisal, Private John 83
Pool of Siloam 75
Poor Farm (Allegheny City) 91
Port Jervis, NY 178
Port Said, Egypt 75
Porter, Maj. Fitz John 48
Portland, ME 53, 104
Portland, OR 71
Postmaster General 22, 82
Potomac River 50
Powderly, Terence Vincent 97
Powell, Pastor David 34
PPG *see* Pittsburgh Plate Glass Company
Presbyterian Church 18, 33–34, 60, 165, 198
Priory Lane, Dunfermline 18
profit-sharing 116
Provincial Helpers' Conference 35
Pullman car 162–163
Pullman Palace Car Company 97

Queen Louisa Ulrika (Sweden) 29
Queen Ulrika Eleonora (Sweden) 27
Queenstown, Ireland 72

Railroad Strike (1877) 2, 7, 79, 80, 84, 87, 91–94, 96–98, 158, 198
Ralston, William Chapman 69
Rea, Samuel 132
Rebecca Street (Allegheny City) 20
Reconstruction (of the South) 82
Red Cross (American) 152–153
Red Mendelssohn 195, 208
Red Stradivarius 195
The Red Violin (movie) 195
Red Wing Linseed Oil Company 116
Redding, CA 71
Reed, Isaac G. 150
Reed, James Hay 156
Reedsdale Street (Allegheny City) 20
Reichard, William 138
Reid, James D. 36
Reilly, John 126–127
Relay, MD 49
Rembrandt 188
Renfrewshire, Scotland 7, 9–11

Rennous, Kleinle & Company 116
Renovo, PA 52–54
Republican National Convention 187
Republican Party 80–82, 121
Resident Assistant to the President 164, 198
Revelation (Bible book) 29, 75
Revolutionary War 9, 16
Richmond, Pastor John Morville 160
Richmond, VA 47–48, 192
Ridgemont 173
Rigg, Elizabeth (Robert Pitcairn wife) *see* Pitcairn, Elizabeth
Robinson's Summit, PA 37
Rock Island, IL 68
Rockefeller, John D. 52, 57, 59, 72, 78, 82–83
Rockefeller, William 72
Rockefeller Foundation 143
Rockwood, PA 152
Roebling, John 13
Rolland School (Dunfermline) 18
Rome, Italy 104, 186
Roosevelt, Theodore 64, 130
Rose, Jonathan 30
Rossford, OH 116
Rotterdam, Holland 180
Round the World tour (Andrew Carnegie) 69
Roundhouse (PRR) 83, 91, 95, 147
Rouseville, PA 56
Royal Board of Mines 28
R.P. 158–160
Ruff, Benjamin Franklin 126–127, 129, 136–137, 153, 157
Rush, Robert B. 9
Rusher, L.L. 138
Russo-Turkish War 74
Ryland's Law 157

Sacramento Valley 69
Sag Harbor, NY 19
St. Clair Street Bridge (Pittsburgh) 24
St. Gallen, Switzerland 68
St. Hubert, Quebec 192
St. Louis, MO 15, 43
St. Mary's, PA 53
St. Mary's Coal Company 53
St. Peter's Square 104
Saint-Saëns, Camille 208
Salem, NC 34, 192
Salem, OH 9
San Andreas, CA 71
San Diego, CA 69
San Francisco, CA 69–71, 94
San Jose, CA 70
sand 109, 114, 115, 184

Sandusky Street (Allegheny City) 67
Sang Hollow, PA 145–146, 148, 151
Santiago, Chile 180
Satan 30
Schamberg, Dr. Jay Frank 178
Schantz, Joseph 118
Schreck, Eugene 113
Scotland 1, 3, 5, 7, 9–11, 17, 19, 33, 63, 68, 120, 198
Scott, John (PPG) 110
Scott, Thomas A. (PRR) 36, 44, 47–50, 56–58, 79, 82–83, 87–89, 95
Scott, Sir Walter 42
Scott Plan 82
Scottish 17–18, 54, 60, 195, 196
Scottish Presbyterian Church 18
Sea of Galilee 75
Seal Rocks (CA) 69–70
Secretary of State (U.S.) 130
Secretary of Treasury (U.S.) 130
Secretary of War (U.S.) 47–50
Senator John Heinz History Center 23, 65, 164
Servia (ship) 101
Session (of church) 62
Seward, PA 145
Shade, R.W. 138
Shadyside (Pittsburgh) 60–62, 144, 160, 163, 167
Shadyside Academy 166
Shadyside Presbyterian Church 8, 60–62, 144, 160–161, 167–168, 198
Shakespeare, William 25, 42
Shappee, Nathan 122, 135
Sharp, Captain Thomas 83
Sharpsburg, PA 91
Sherman, Gen. William Tecumseh 47
Shields, James H. 102
Shinn, William P. 155–156
Shorter Catechism 18
Shugerman, Jed Handelsman 157
Shutt, Mayor A.P. 83
Sixth Regiment 84–85
Sixth Street (Pittsburgh) 53
Sixth Street Bridge (Pittsburgh) 24
Skibo 165
Slabtown (Allegheny City) 16
slag 123
smallpox 176–177
Smit, Philippe 187–188, 189
Smith, Charles S. 171
Smith, Dr. J. Kinsey 167
Smoky City 123
Socialist Labor Party 97
Socrates's Tomb 75

Solitude (George Westinghouse home) 1, 144
Somerset, PA 118
Somerset County, PA 32, 152
Sonnenberg, Switzerland 112–113
South Africa 188, 189
South America 32, 180
South Carolina 44, 81–82
South Fork, PA 43, 138–139, 151–153
South Fork Dam (PA) 124–128, 135–138, 144–145, 149, 153, 155–156
South Fork Fishing and Hunting Club 124, 126–131, 136–137, 144, 148, 156–157
South Improvement Company (SIC) 57–59
South Side (Pittsburgh) 20, 107
Special Meeting (PPG) 116
specie 11
Sphinx 74
Springfield, IL 7, 44, 50
Springfield Township, PA 37
standard gauge 47, 54
Standard Oil Company 57–59, 67, 78, 82–83, 101
Stanton, Edwin M. 50
Staple Bend Tunnel (PA) 14, 38
Starkey, Caira 101
Starkey, Cara (John Pitcairn sister-in-law) 102, 112
Starkey, Dora (John Pitcairn sister-in-law) 104
Starkey, Dr. George Rogers (John Pitcairn brother-in-law) 43, 51, 99, 101
Starkey, Gertrude (John Pitcairn wife) *see* Pitcairn, Gertrude
Starkey, Margaret (Robert Pitcairn & John Pitcairn sister) *see* Pitcairn, Margaret
Steelton tower 162
Steubenville, OH 65
Stevenson, James B. 55
Stockholm, Sweden 27, 29
Stone Arch Bridge (Johnstown) 141–143, 145, 148, 154
Stony Creek (Johnstown) 118, 123, 133, 146, 154
Stowe, Judge Edwin B. 126
Stradivari, Antonio 195
Strip District (Pittsburgh) 48, 92
Stuart, the Rev. J.P. 101
Stuart Hall (Bryn Athyn) 175
Stuttgart, Germany 68
Sudan 75
Suez Canal 75
Suffrage 81, 167

Summit Tunnel (Gallitzin, PA) 41
Supreme Court (U.S.) 16, 79, 81, 97, 194
Susquehanna Division (Northern Central Railroad) 63
Susquehanna River 13, 166
Sutro, Adolph 69–70
Swank, George Thompson 138, 146–147
Swank, James Moore 118, 122
Swartz, Judge Aaron S. 181
Swedberg 27
Swedenborg (town) 173
Swedenborg, Emanuel 2, 3, 7, 27–35, 41, 53, 67–68, 71–72, 76–77, 100, 104, 171, 177, 189
Swedenborg, Jesper 27
Swedenborg Foundation 30, 189
Swedenborgian 4, 30, 32–33, 51, 62, 67–68, 102, 113, 189, 194, 198–199
Swissvale 144
Switzerland 68, 112, 130
Sylvia (ship) 74

Tafel, Adolph L. 102
Tafel, Louis Hermann 51, 72, 102, 106
Tafel, Rudolph Leonhard 43, 51, 68, 72, 73, 104, 106
Taft, Pres. William Howard 130
Tarbell, Ida 58
Tarentum, PA 111, 113–114
Tate, Daniel 65
Taughannock Falls, NY 102
Taylor, Hascal L. 68, 70, 101
Taylor, Joseph 26, 36
Tel Aviv, Israel 75
Tell el-Amarna, Egypt 74
Temple Mount (Jerusalem) 75
Tennessee 46, 82
Tenth Pennsylvania Volunteers 164
La terrasse à Sainte-Adresse (painting) 188
Texas 44, 152
Texas and Pacific Railroad 82
Thames (river) 179
Thaw, William 130, 148, 163
Theological School (of Academy of the New Church) 73, 187
Theosophical Society 32
Thomas, Louise 207–208
Thomson, J. Edgar 37–39, 41, 43, 44, 47, 48, 78, 121, 196
Thoreau, Henry David 32
Three Rivers Stadium (Pittsburgh) 21
Tiberius 75
Tidewater Oil 99

238 Index

Tidewater Pipe Line Company 78
Tidioute, PA 58
Tilbury, England 179
Tilden, Samuel Jones 81–82
Titanic (ship) 72
Titusville, PA 54–56
Toronto, Canada 180
Trainmen's Union 88
Transcontinental Railroad 68, 82, 94
Trinity 30–31
True Christian Religion (book) 29, 32, 34, 41, 67, 104
Tunnelton, PA 14–15
Turin, Italy 78
Turtle Creek 158–159
Twain, Mark 71
Tweed Ring 81
Twenty-eighth Street (Pittsburgh) 90–91
Twenty-first Amendment 186
Twenty-sixth Street (Pittsburgh) 91
typhoid fever 50
Typhus 176

Uffizi Gallery (Florence, Italy) 104
Ulster County, NY 185
Uncle Robert 164–165, 167, 198
Unger, Col. B.J. 136
Unger, Elias J. 144
Union (Civil War) 46–48, 50
Union Army (Civil War) 7, 47, 91
Union Depot/Station (Pittsburgh) 89, 92–93, 95–96, 138, 144, 163
Union Iron Mills 92
Union Oil Company 101
Union Switch and Signal 144, 165
United Airlines 193
U.S. Ambassador 130, 179, 180
U.S. Attorney General 130
U.S. House Committee on Manufactures 121
United States Military Railroads 44
U.S. Navy 193
U.S. Secretary of State 130
U.S. Secretary of the Treasury 130
U.S. Senator 81, 130
University of Pennsylvania 190
University of Pittsburgh 131
University of Uppsala 27
Upper Union Mill 92
Urban, Marijke (John Pitcairn daughter-in-law) *see* Pitcairn, Marijke
Utah 69

Vail, Alfred 22
van Gogh, Vincent 188
Van Patten, Philip 94
Vanderbilt 194
Vanderbilt, William Henry 58, 79
Vandergriff, William 83
Vandergrift, Jacob 59, 67
Vandergrift and Forman Company 56, 59
Vatican 104
Venango County, PA 53, 58
Venice (ship) 11
Venice, Italy 68, 104
Vera Christiana Religio (book) see *True Christian Religion*
Vesuvius 103
Victoria, BC 71
Vienna, Austria 64
Village Association (Bryn Athyn) 174, 181
Virginia 32, 46, 47–48, 50
Vitro S.A.B. de C.V. 197
Vlissingen, Holland 179

Walkinshaw, J.C. 138
Wall Station, PA 159
Wall Yard (PRR) 159
Walton, PA 114
Walurba, PA 159
Washington (state) 152
Washington Capital (newspaper) 98
Washington, D.C. 7, 22, 32, 43, 44, 45, 47, 48–50, 81, 99, 115, 152, 192
Washington Street (Johnstown) 140–141
Washington Street (Pittsburgh) 20
Washington Territory 70
Watt, D.M. 103
Ways and Means Committee (U.S. House of Representatives) 162
Weekly Tribune (newspaper) 146
Welsh, Sylvester 124
Wesley, John 29–30
West Chester, PA 189
West Philadelphia, PA 45
West Virginia 46, 83
Western Canal Reservoir *see* Lake Conemaugh
Western Division (Pennsylvania Main Line Canal) 13–14, 119–120; *see also* Pittsburgh-to-Johnstown Canal
Western Division (Philadelphia and Erie RR) 52
Western Division (PRR) 36, 50, 56, 87–89, 198; *see also* Pittsburgh Division

Western Express No. 9 162
Western Penitentiary (Pennsylvania) 152
Western Theological Seminary 165
Western Union 138, 149
Western Wall (Wailing Wall) 75
Westinghouse, George 1, 5, 55, 64–65, 80, 101, 144, 148, 162, 163, 166, 167
Westinghouse, Herman 162
Westinghouse Air Brake Company 5, 55, 65, 80, 92, 144, 162, 165
Westinghouse Electric Company (WEC) 144, 162
Westinghouse Legacy 2
Westinghouse Park 2
Westminster Street (Shadyside) 60
Westmoreland County, PA 32, 155
Wheatstone, Sir Charles 22
Wheeling Light Infantry 83
Whitcomb, G.D. 65
White City (1893 Columbian Exposition) 170
White House 193
White Mountains 181
White Star Lines 72
Who Was Swedenborg (video) 30
Wiesbaden, Germany 104
Williams, Edwin H. 64–65
Williamsport, PA 78
Willow Grove Naval Air Station (PA) 191, 193
Wilmerding, PA 144
Wilson, William Bender 64, 158
Wilson, Woodrow 191
Windsor Hotel (New York City) 69, 100
Wiscasset (ship) 19
Wisconsin 79
Wood, Morrell and Company 120
Wood Street (Pittsburgh) 20, 24, 53
Woodruff sleeping car 41, 45
Woods, Charles S. 120
Woodstock, NY 185
Woodvale, PA 139, 147
Woodyard, W.H. 162
Worcester, the Rev. John 69
Words for the New Church (pamphlets) 71, 73
Workingmen's Party 94, 97
Works No. 2 (PPG) 111
World Health Assembly 176
World Health Organization 176
World War I 179, 190
World War II 153, 193, 196

World's Columbian Exposition (the "White City") 170
Wormley Hotel (Washington, D.C.) 82, 88
Worship of the Advent (Philadelphia) 102
Worthen, William E. 155

Wright, Orville 190
Wright, Wilbur 190
Wyoming 88
Wyoming Territory 69

Yellow Cross 152
YMCA (Pitcairn) 160

Yosemite Valley, CA 71
Young, Judge John 32–33
Yutzy, Sen. Enoch 90

Zurich, Switzerland 68, 104

www.ingramcontent.com/pod-product-compliance
Lightning Source LLC
Chambersburg PA
CBHW060340010526
44117CB00017B/2903